MARTIAN MANHUNTER
RINGS OF SATURN

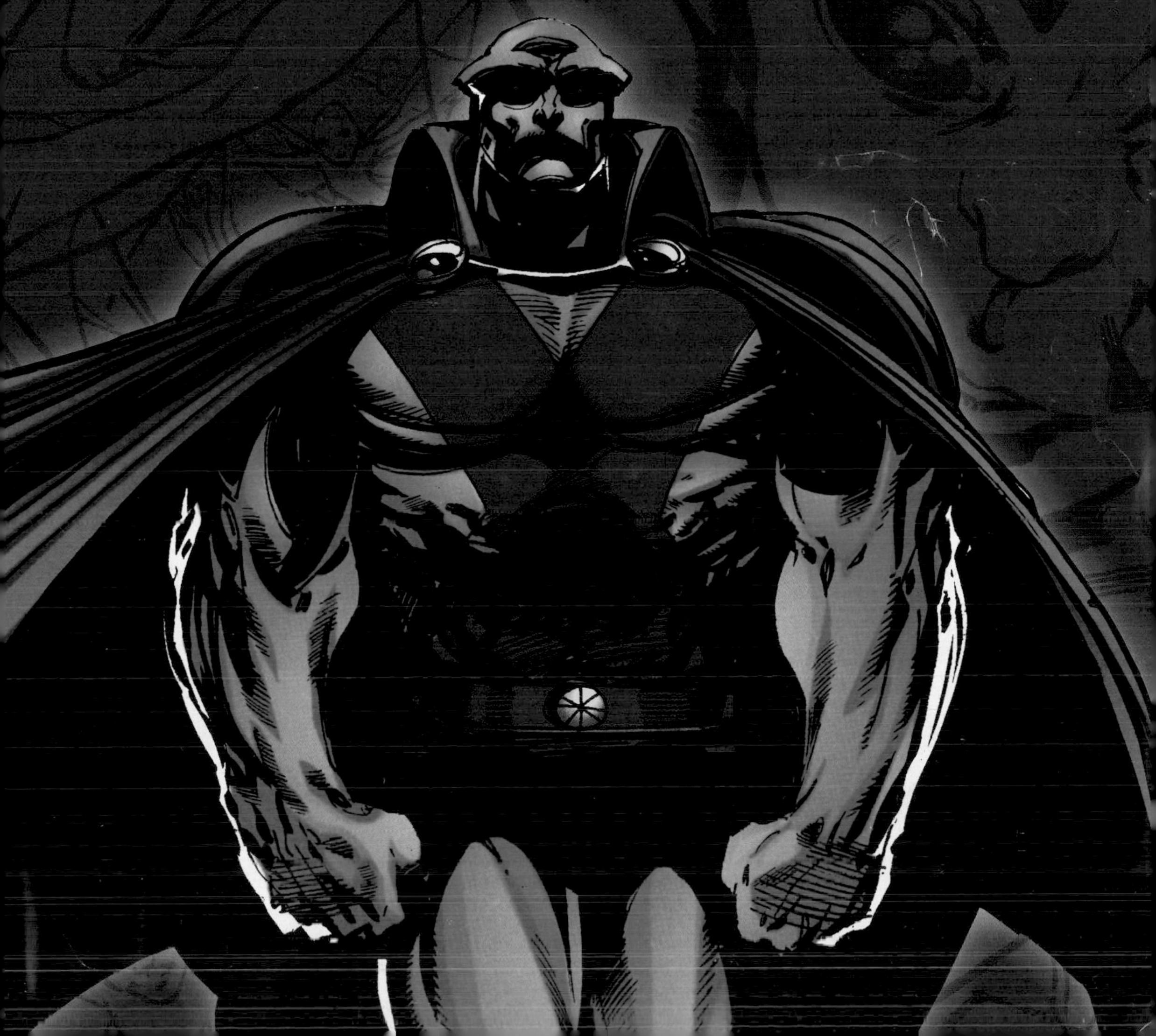

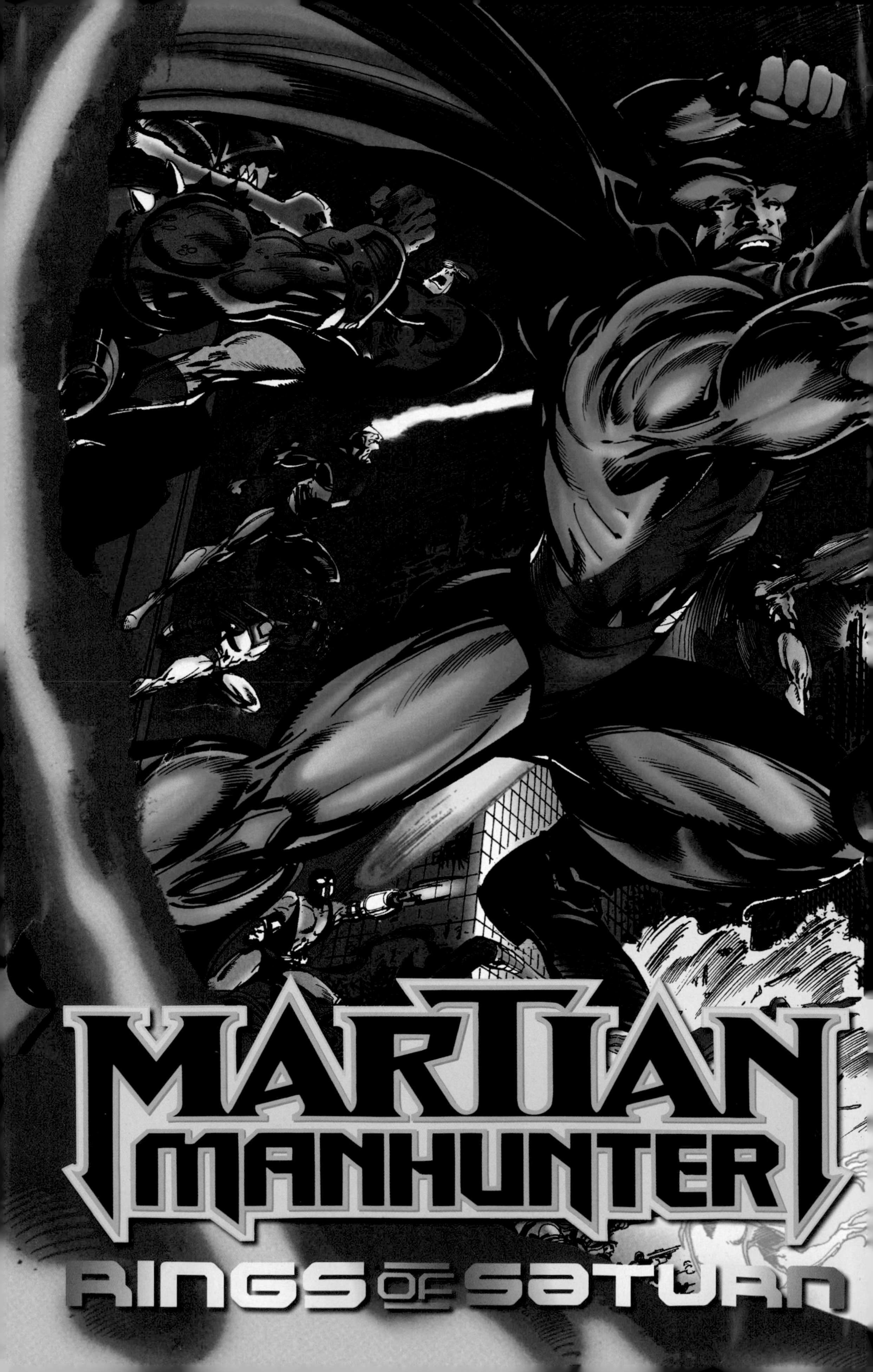
MARTIAN MANHUNTER
RINGS OF SATURN

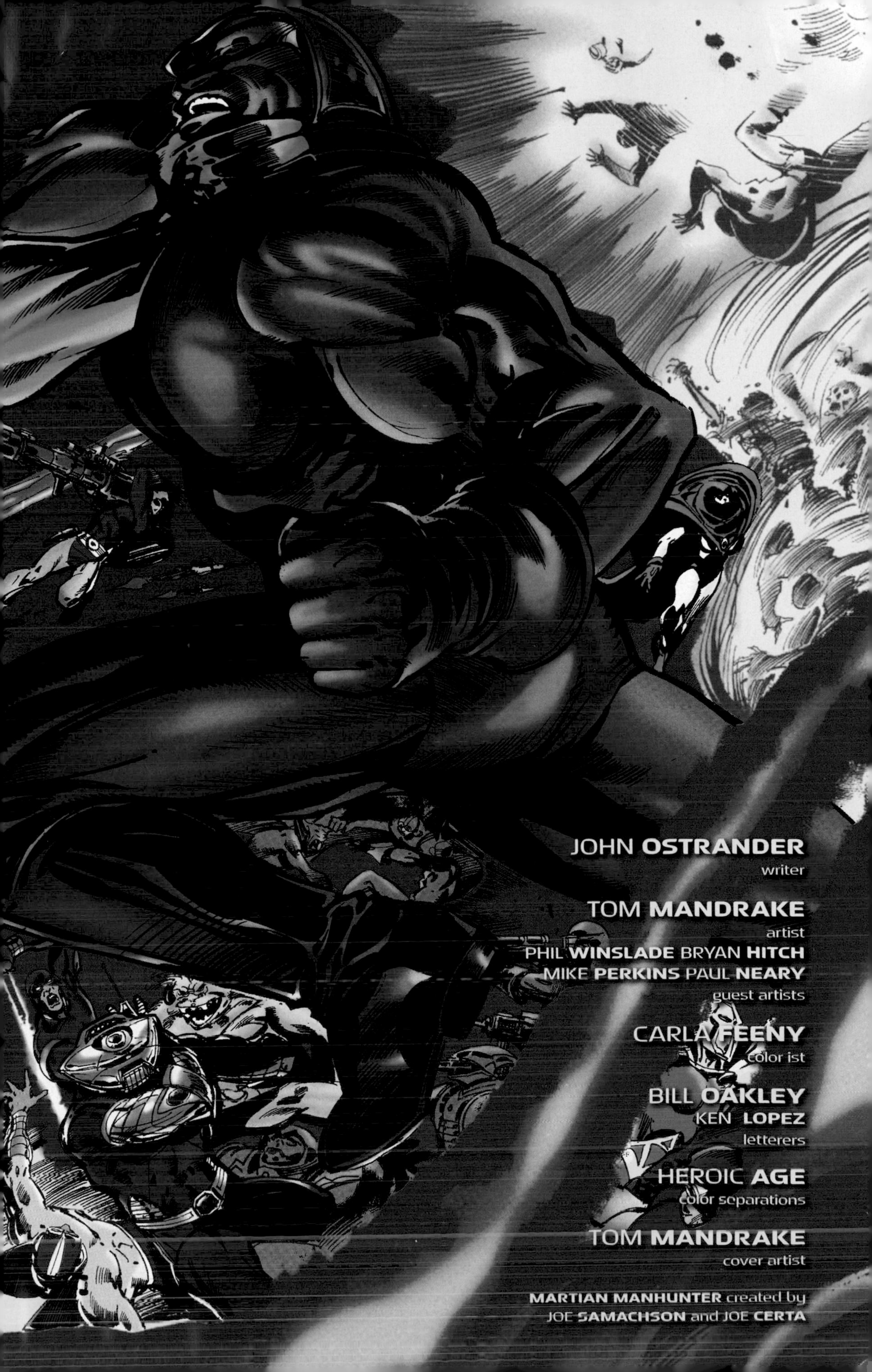

JOHN **OSTRANDER**
writer

TOM **MANDRAKE**
artist

PHIL **WINSLADE** BRYAN **HITCH**
MIKE **PERKINS** PAUL **NEARY**
guest artists

CARLA **FEENY**
colorist

BILL **OAKLEY**
KEN **LOPEZ**
letterers

HEROIC **AGE**
color separations

TOM **MANDRAKE**
cover artist

MARTIAN MANHUNTER created by
JOE **SAMACHSON** and JOE **CERTA**

PETER J. TOMASI Editor – Original Series   L.A. WILLIAMS Assistant Editor – Original Series   ROBIN WILDMAN Editor
ROBBIN BROSTERMAN Design Director – Books   CURTIS KING JR. Publication Design

BOB HARRAS Senior VP – Editor-in-Chief, DC Comics

DIANE NELSON President   DAN DIDIO and JIM LEE Co-Publishers
GEOFF JOHNS Chief Creative Officer
AMIT DESAI Senior VP – Marketing and Franchise Management
AMY GENKINS Senior VP – Business and Legal Affairs   NAIRI GARDINER Senior VP – Finance
JEFF BOISON VP – Publishing Planning   MARK CHIARELLO VP – Art Direction and Design
JOHN CUNNINGHAM VP – Marketing   TERRI CUNNINGHAM VP – Editorial Administration
LARRY GANEM VP – Talent Relations and Services ALISON GILL Senior VP – Manufacturing and Operations
HANK KANALZ Senior VP – Vertigo and Integrated Publishing   JAY KOGAN VP – Business and Legal Affairs, Publishing
JACK MAHAN VP – Business Affairs, Talent   NICK NAPOLITANO VP – Manufacturing Administration
SUE POHJA VP – Book Sales   FRED RUIZ VP – Manufacturing Operations
COURTNEY SIMMONS Senior VP – Publicity   BOB WAYNE Senior VP – Sales

MARTIAN MANHUNTER: RINGS OF SATURN
Published by DC Comics. Copyright © 2014 DC Comics. All Rights Reserved.

Originally published in single magazine form as MARTIAN MANHUNTER #10-17, MARTIAN MANHUNTER #1,000,000
Copyright © 1998, 1999, 2000 DC Comics. All Rights Reserved. All characters, their distinctive likenesses and related
elements featured in this publication are trademarks of DC Comics. The stories, characters and incidents featured in this
publication are entirely fictional. DC Comics does not read or accept unsolicited ideas, stories or artwork.

DC Comics, 1700 Broadway, New York, NY 10019
A Warner Bros. Entertainment Company
Printed by RR Donnelley, Salem, VA, USA. 8/1/14. First Printing.
ISBN: 978-1-4012-5141-3

Library of Congress Cataloging-in-Publication Data

Ostrander, John, author.
  Martian Manhunter : Rings of Saturn / John Ostrander, Tom Mandrake.
    pages cm
  ISBN 978-1-4012-5141-3 (paperback)
  1. Graphic novels. I. Mandrake, Tom, 1956- illustrator. II. Title. III. Title: Rings of Saturn.
  PN6728.M3626087 2014
  741.5'973—dc23
            2014011715

SUSTAINABLE
FORESTRY
INITIATIVE
Certified Chain of Custody
20% Certified Forest Content,
80% Certified Sourcing
www.sfiprogram.org
SFI-01042
APPLIES TO TEXT STOCK ONLY

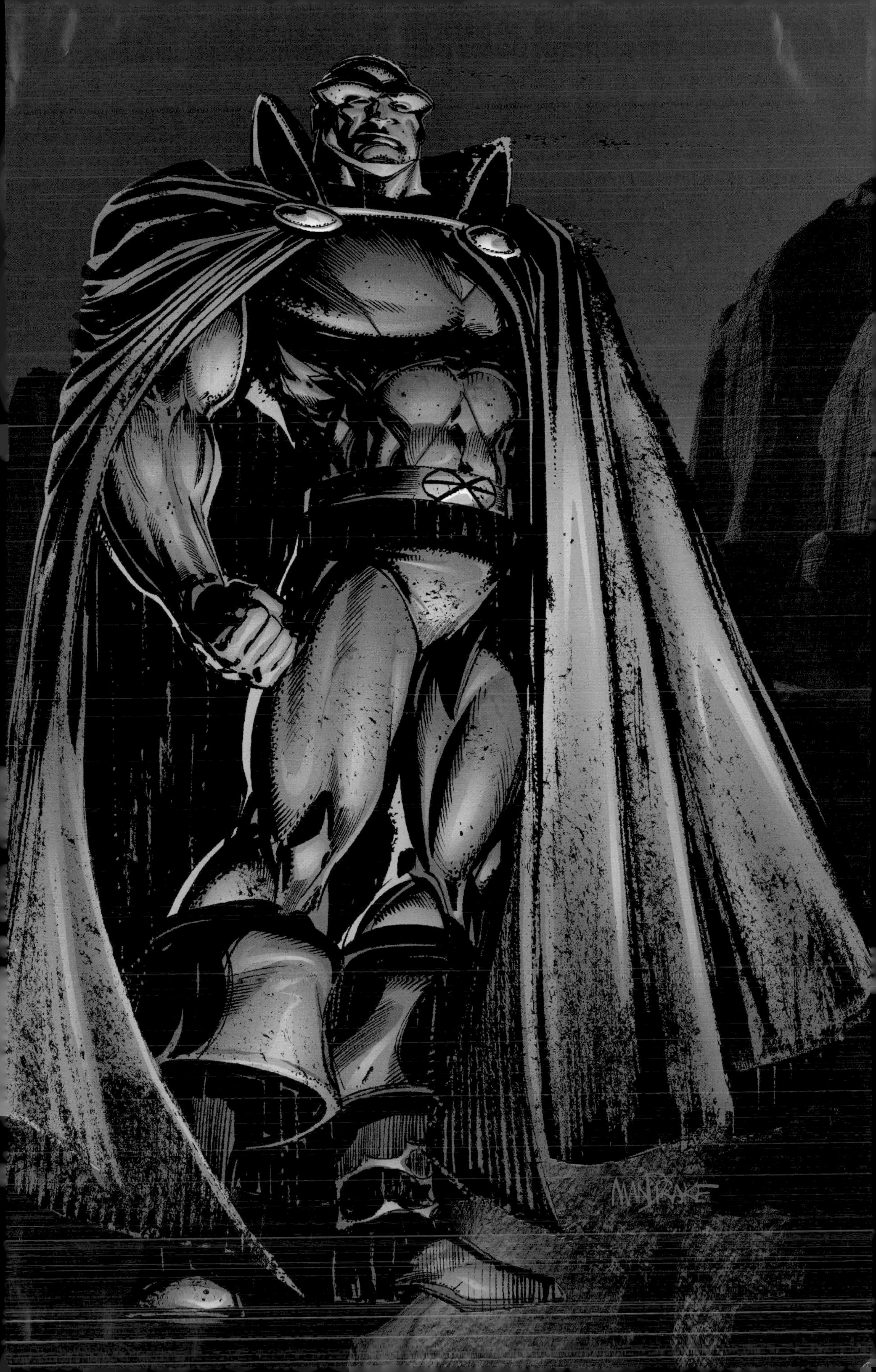
MANDRAKE

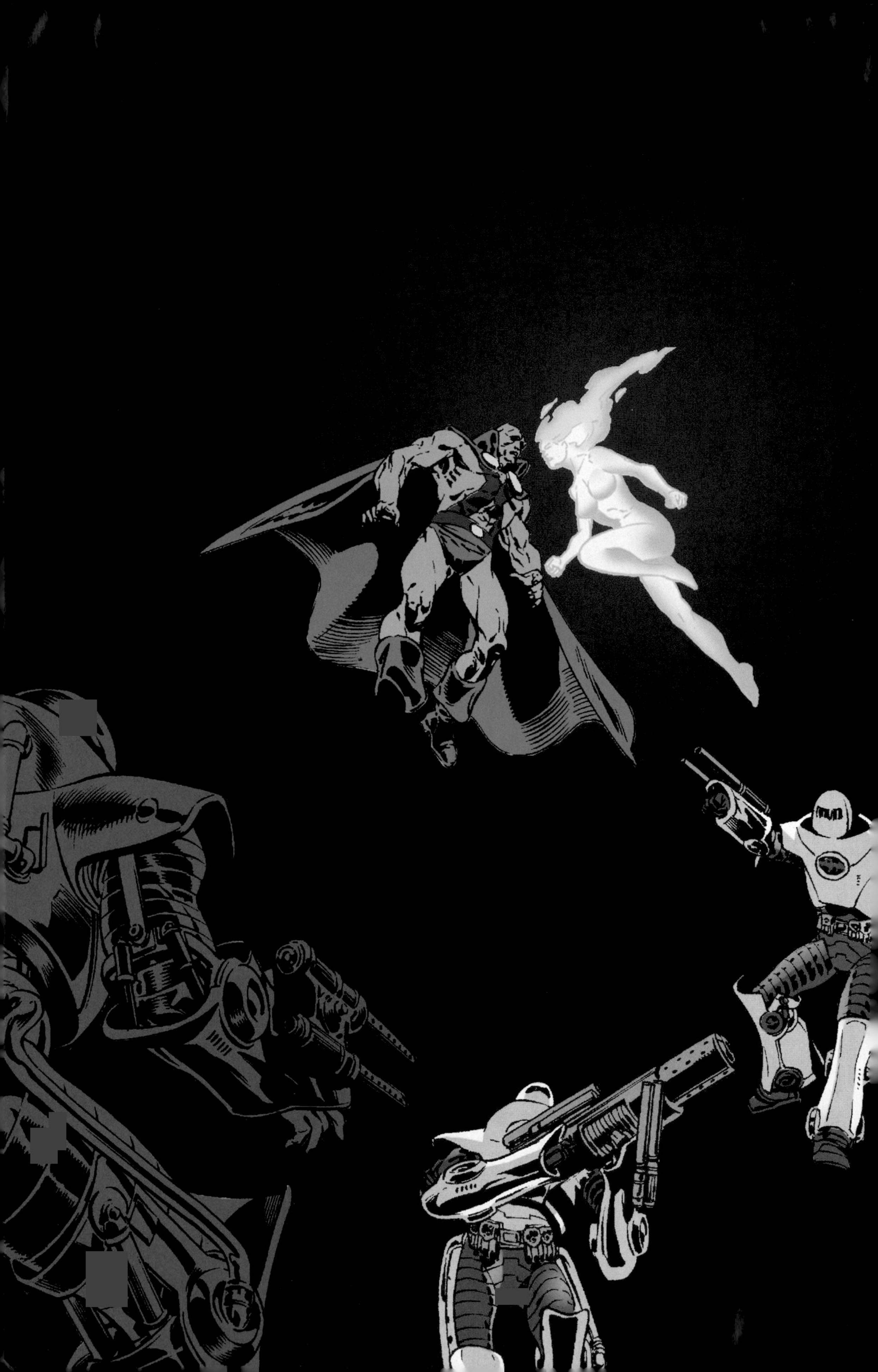

•••INPUT

DIGIPRINT

THIS IS THE SPECIAL COLLECTOR'S ITEM PRINT EDITION OF

MARTIAN MANHUNTER #1,000,000

EXACTLY REPLICATING THE WAY THIS COMIC WAS PRODUCED IN THE LATE 20TH CENTURY! ALSO AVAILABLE ON THE HEADNET AS USUAL.

DC ONE MILLION

IN THE 853RD CENTURY — EXACTLY ONE MILLION MONTHS AFTER THE DAWN OF SUPER-HEROES — HUMANITY PROSPERS IN A UTOPIAN SOCIETY BEYOND OUR IMAGINING. FROM THE DATA-FOUNDRIES OF THE PLANET MERCURY TO THE FLOATING CORAL CITIES OF NEPTUNE, THE GREAT TRADITION OF SUPER-HEROES LIVES ON. CHIEF AMONG THEM ARE THE MAGNIFICENT JUSTICE LEGION A, WHOSE MEMBERSHIP INCLUDES FUTURISTIC VERSIONS OF SUPERMAN, STARMAN, BATMAN, WONDER WOMAN, AQUAMAN, FLASH, AND HOURMAN!

JOURNEYING BACK TO THE LATE 20TH CENTURY, THESE HEROES OF THE FUTURE INVITE THEIR ANCIENT PREDECESSORS, THE JUSTICE LEAGUE OF AMERICA, TO ATTEND A WONDERFUL CELEBRATION OF THEIR HEROIC LEGACY. THE PLAN CALLS FOR EACH OF THE CORE JUSTICE LEAGUERS TO TAKE PART IN SPECTACULAR EXHIBITIONS OF PROWESS FOR THE CITIZENS OF THE 853RD CENTURY TO ENJOY, WHILE JUSTICE LEGION A IS TO REMAIN BEHIND TO SAFEGUARD 20TH-CENTURY EARTH.

BUT AS THE HEROES OF THE JLA COMMENCE THEIR CHALLENGES IN THE FUTURE, EACH OF THEIR TRIALS IS SABOTAGED BY THE UNSEEN INFLUENCE OF SOLARIS, THE TYRANT SUN. BLASTED TO WITHIN AN INCH OF HIS LIFE (IN GREEN LANTERN #1,000,000), KYLE RAYNER FALLS HELPLESSLY TOWARD THE PLANET MARS, WHOSE CHAMPION, J'ONN J'ONZZ, DISAPPEARED MYSTERIOUSLY THOUSANDS OF YEARS EARLIER...

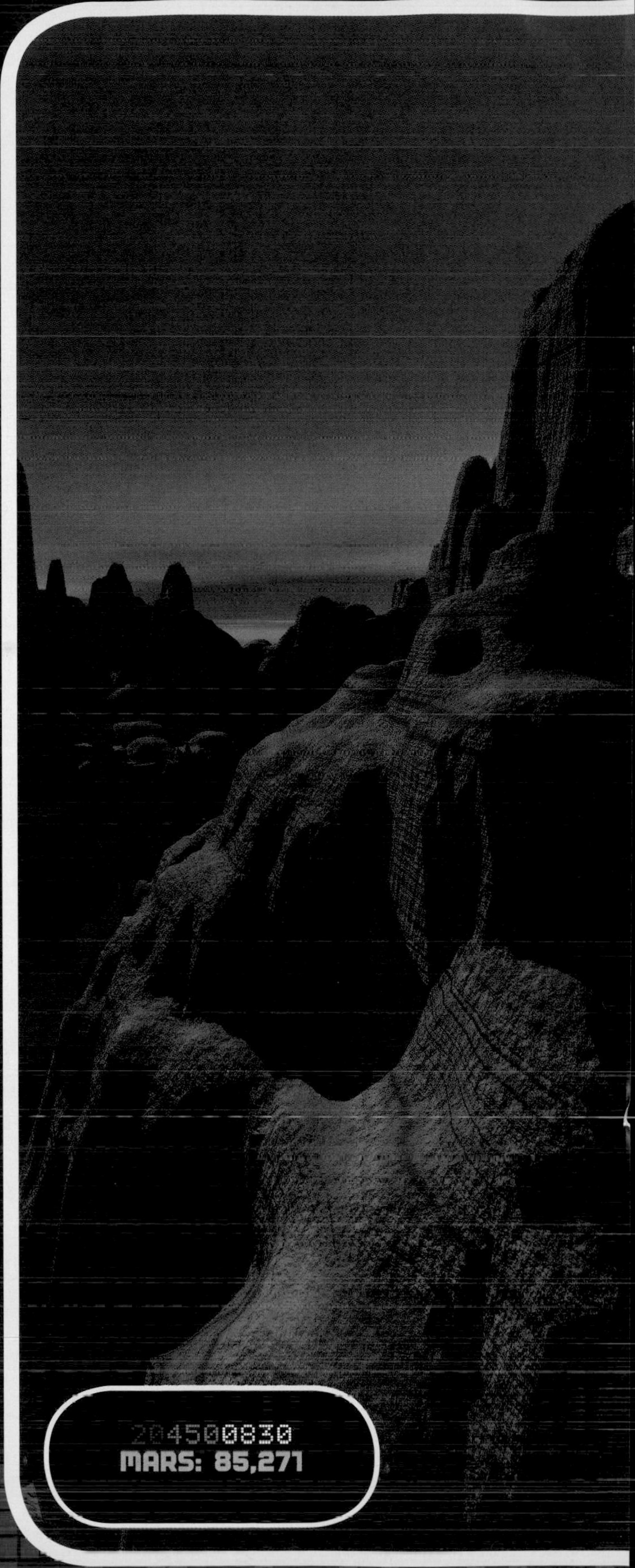
204500830
MARS: 85,271

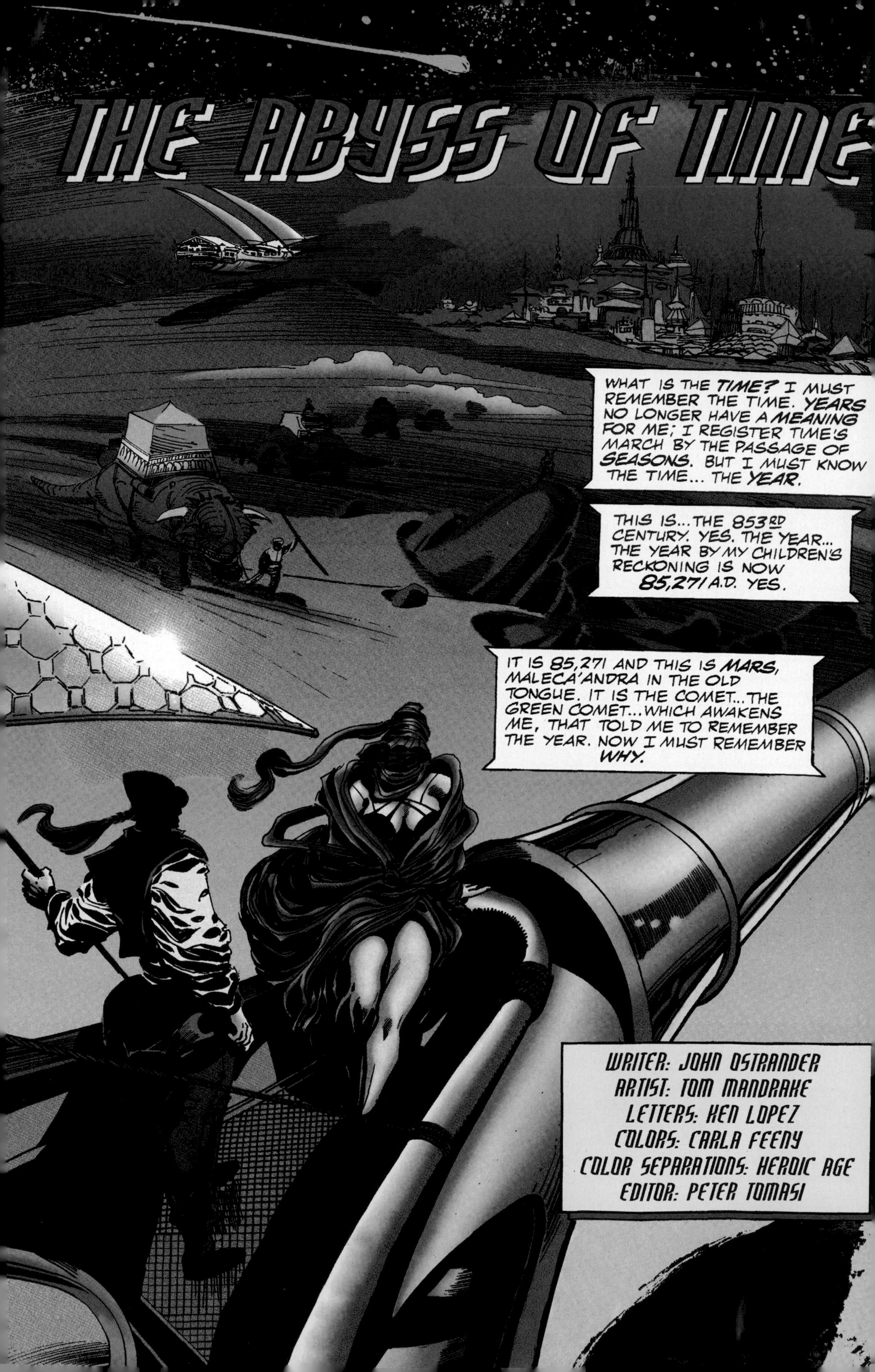
THE ABYSS OF TIME
WHAT IS THE TIME? I MUST REMEMBER THE TIME. YEARS NO LONGER HAVE A MEANING FOR ME; I REGISTER TIME'S MARCH BY THE PASSAGE OF SEASONS. BUT I MUST KNOW THE TIME... THE YEAR.
THIS IS...THE 853RD CENTURY. YES. THE YEAR... THE YEAR BY MY CHILDREN'S RECKONING IS NOW 85,271 A.D. YES.
IT IS 85,271 AND THIS IS MARS, MALECA'ANDRA IN THE OLD TONGUE. IT IS THE COMET...THE GREEN COMET...WHICH AWAKENS ME, THAT TOLD ME TO REMEMBER THE YEAR. NOW I MUST REMEMBER WHY.
WRITER: JOHN OSTRANDER
ARTIST: TOM MANDRAKE
LETTERS: KEN LOPEZ
COLORS: CARLA FEENY
COLOR SEPARATIONS: HEROIC AGE
EDITOR: PETER TOMASI

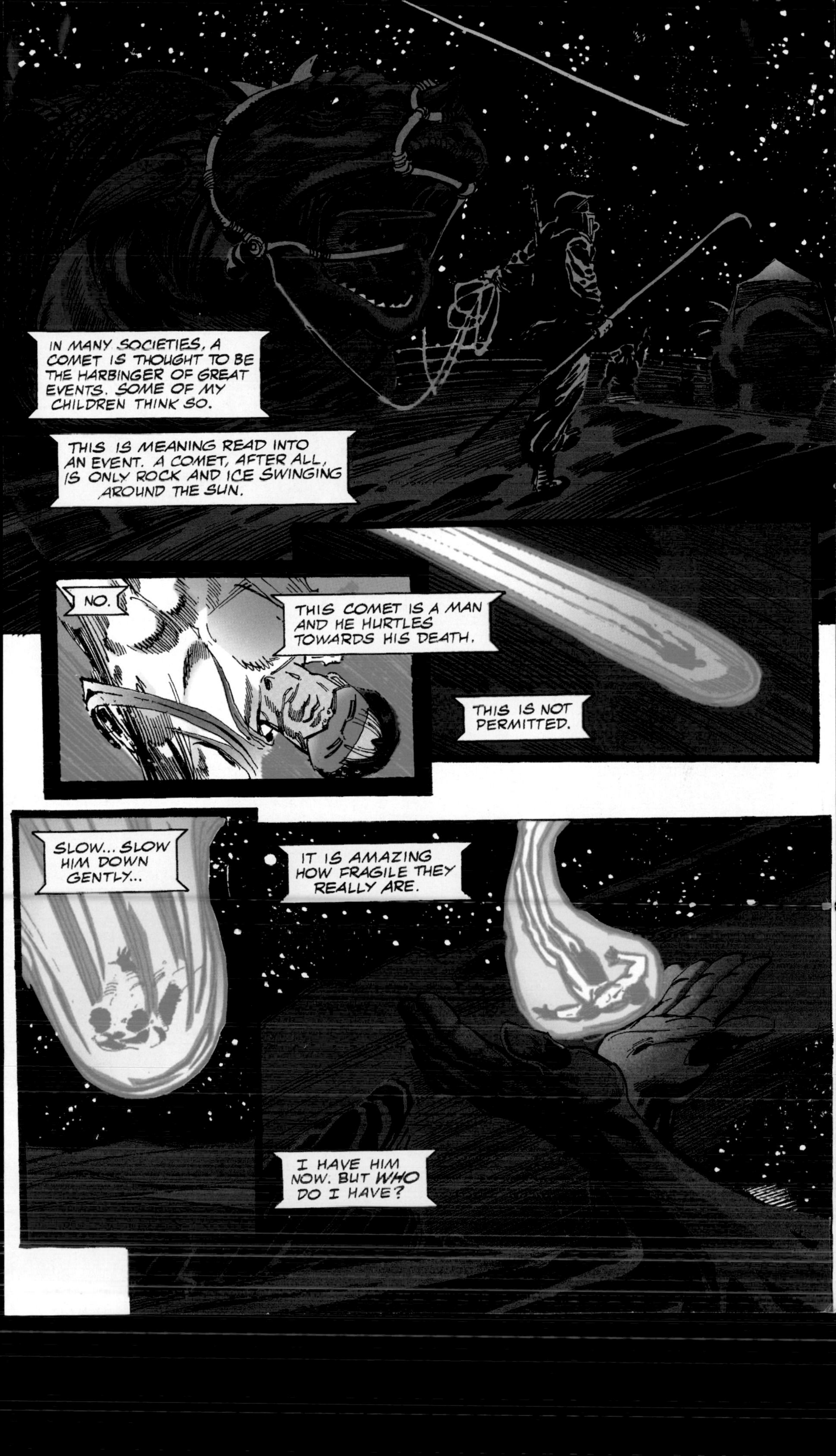
IN MANY SOCIETIES, A COMET IS THOUGHT TO BE THE HARBINGER OF GREAT EVENTS. SOME OF MY CHILDREN THINK SO.
THIS IS MEANING READ INTO AN EVENT. A COMET, AFTER ALL, IS ONLY ROCK AND ICE SWINGING AROUND THE SUN.
NO.
THIS COMET IS A MAN AND HE HURTLES TOWARDS HIS DEATH.
THIS IS NOT PERMITTED.
SLOW... SLOW HIM DOWN GENTLY...
IT IS AMAZING HOW FRAGILE THEY REALLY ARE.
I HAVE HIM NOW. BUT WHO DO I HAVE?

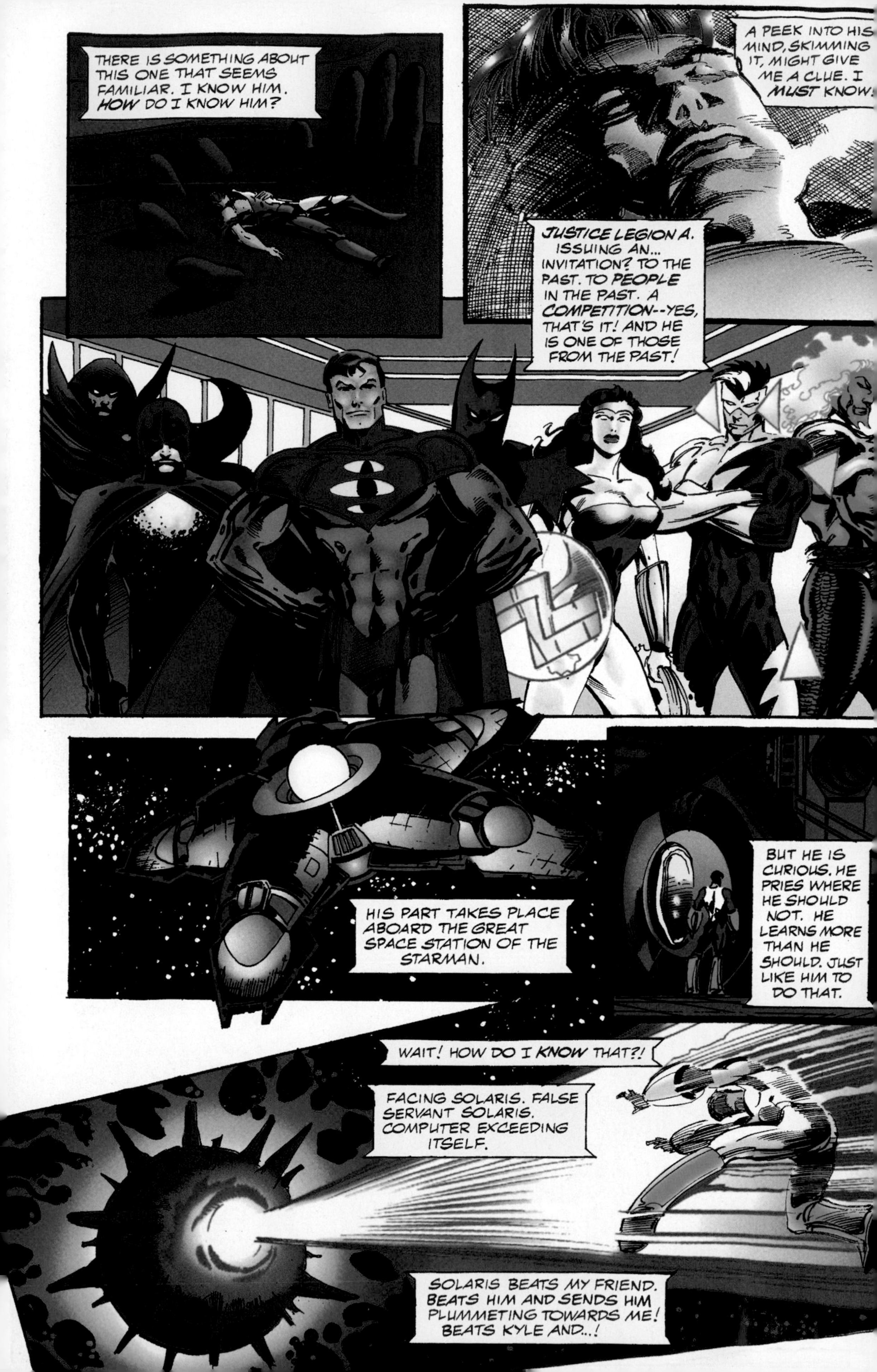
THERE IS SOMETHING ABOUT THIS ONE THAT SEEMS FAMILIAR. I KNOW HIM. HOW DO I KNOW HIM?
A PEEK INTO HIS MIND, SKIMMING IT, MIGHT GIVE ME A CLUE. I MUST KNOW!
JUSTICE LEGION A. ISSUING AN... INVITATION? TO THE PAST. TO PEOPLE IN THE PAST. A COMPETITION--YES, THAT'S IT! AND HE IS ONE OF THOSE FROM THE PAST!
HIS PART TAKES PLACE ABOARD THE GREAT SPACE STATION OF THE STARMAN.
BUT HE IS CURIOUS. HE PRIES WHERE HE SHOULD NOT. HE LEARNS MORE THAN HE SHOULD. JUST LIKE HIM TO DO THAT.
WAIT! HOW DO I KNOW THAT?!
FACING SOLARIS. FALSE SERVANT SOLARIS. COMPUTER EXCEEDING ITSELF.
SOLARIS BEATS MY FRIEND. BEATS HIM AND SENDS HIM PLUMMETING TOWARDS ME! BEATS KYLE AND...!

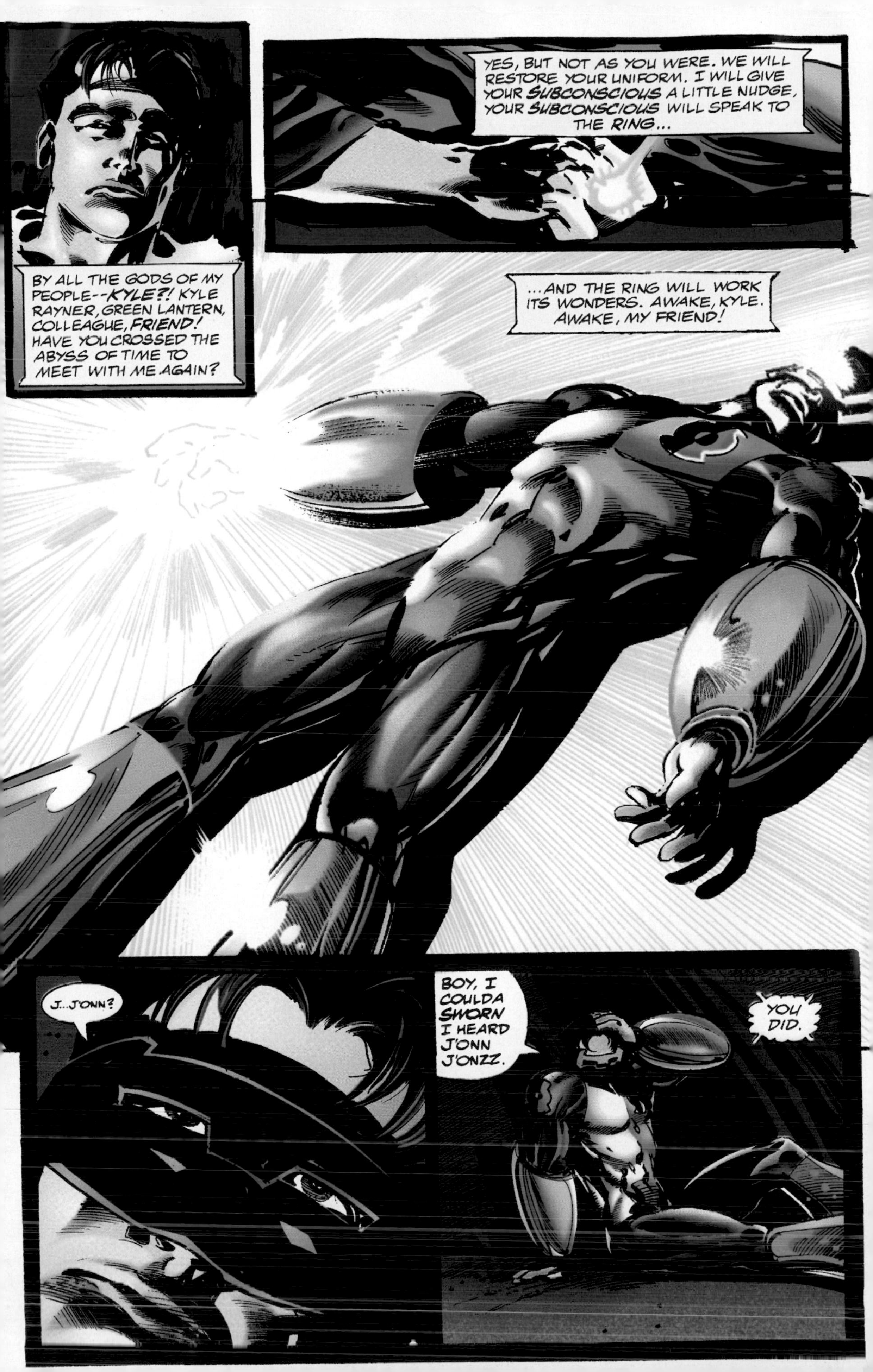
YES, BUT NOT AS YOU WERE. WE WILL RESTORE YOUR UNIFORM. I WILL GIVE YOUR SUBCONSCIOUS A LITTLE NUDGE, YOUR SUBCONSCIOUS WILL SPEAK TO THE RING...
BY ALL THE GODS OF MY PEOPLE--KYLE?! KYLE RAYNER, GREEN LANTERN, COLLEAGUE, FRIEND! HAVE YOU CROSSED THE ABYSS OF TIME TO MEET WITH ME AGAIN?
...AND THE RING WILL WORK ITS WONDERS. AWAKE, KYLE. AWAKE, MY FRIEND!
J...J'ONN?
BOY, I COULDA SWORN I HEARD J'ONN J'ONZZ.
YOU DID.

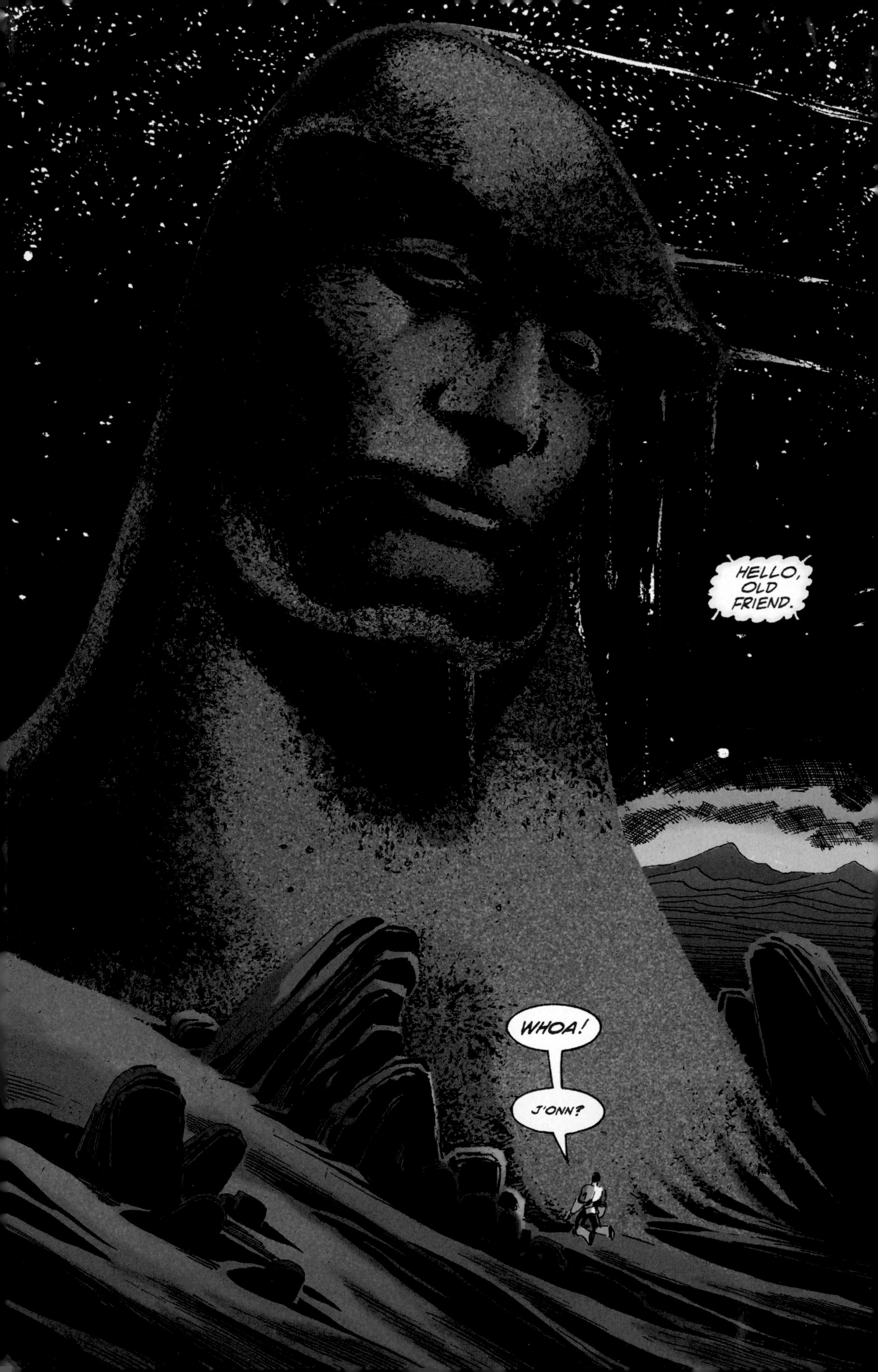
HELLO, OLD FRIEND.
WHOA!
J'ONN?

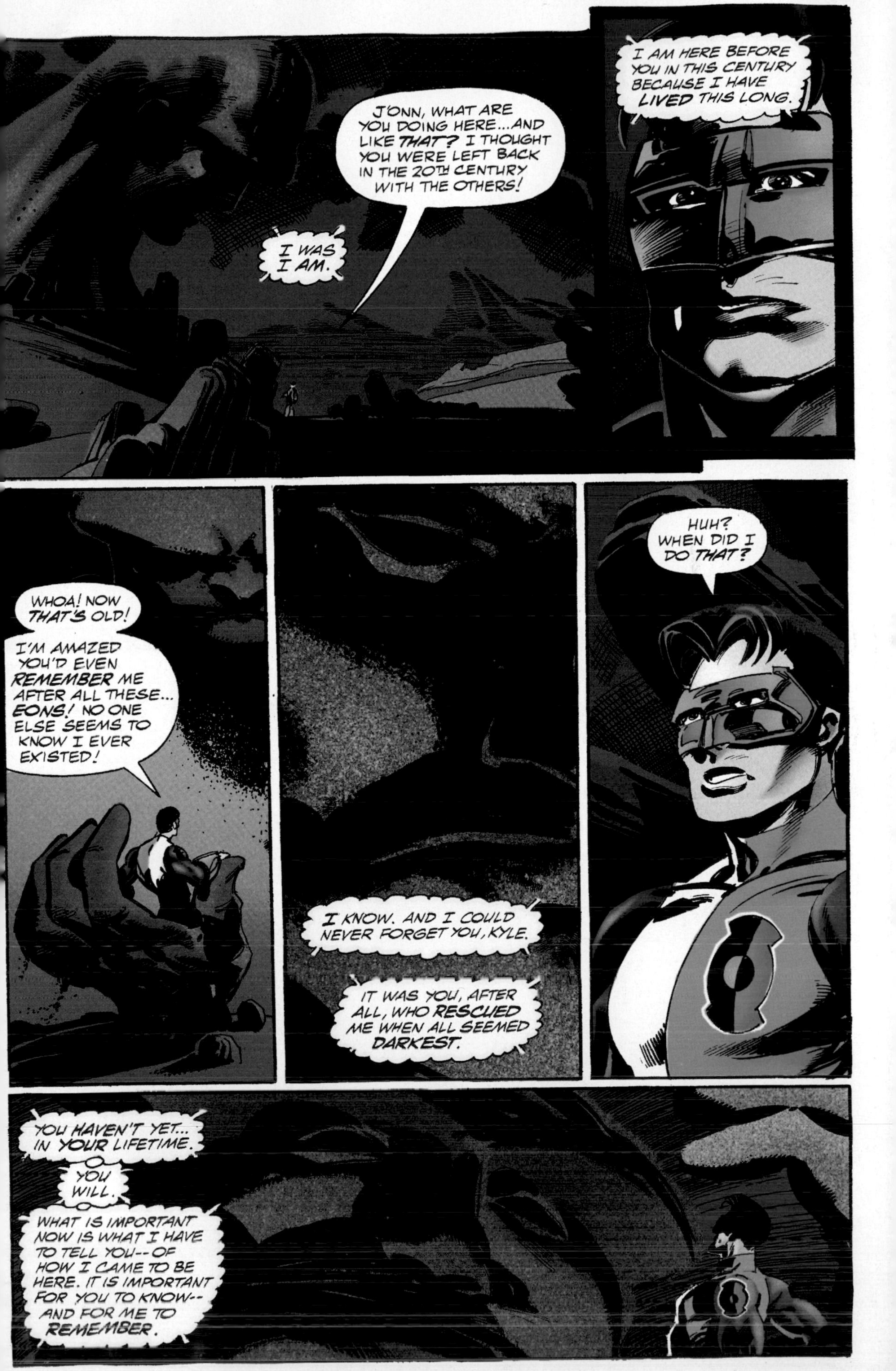
J'ONN, WHAT ARE YOU DOING HERE...AND LIKE THAT? I THOUGHT YOU WERE LEFT BACK IN THE 20TH CENTURY WITH THE OTHERS!
I WAS. I AM.
I AM HERE BEFORE YOU IN THIS CENTURY BECAUSE I HAVE LIVED THIS LONG.
WHOA! NOW THAT'S OLD!
I'M AMAZED YOU'D EVEN REMEMBER ME AFTER ALL THESE... EONS! NO ONE ELSE SEEMS TO KNOW I EVER EXISTED!
I KNOW. AND I COULD NEVER FORGET YOU, KYLE.
IT WAS YOU, AFTER ALL, WHO RESCUED ME WHEN ALL SEEMED DARKEST.
HUH? WHEN DID I DO THAT?
YOU HAVEN'T YET... IN YOUR LIFETIME.
YOU WILL.
WHAT IS IMPORTANT NOW IS WHAT I HAVE TO TELL YOU-- OF HOW I CAME TO BE HERE. IT IS IMPORTANT FOR YOU TO KNOW-- AND FOR ME TO REMEMBER.

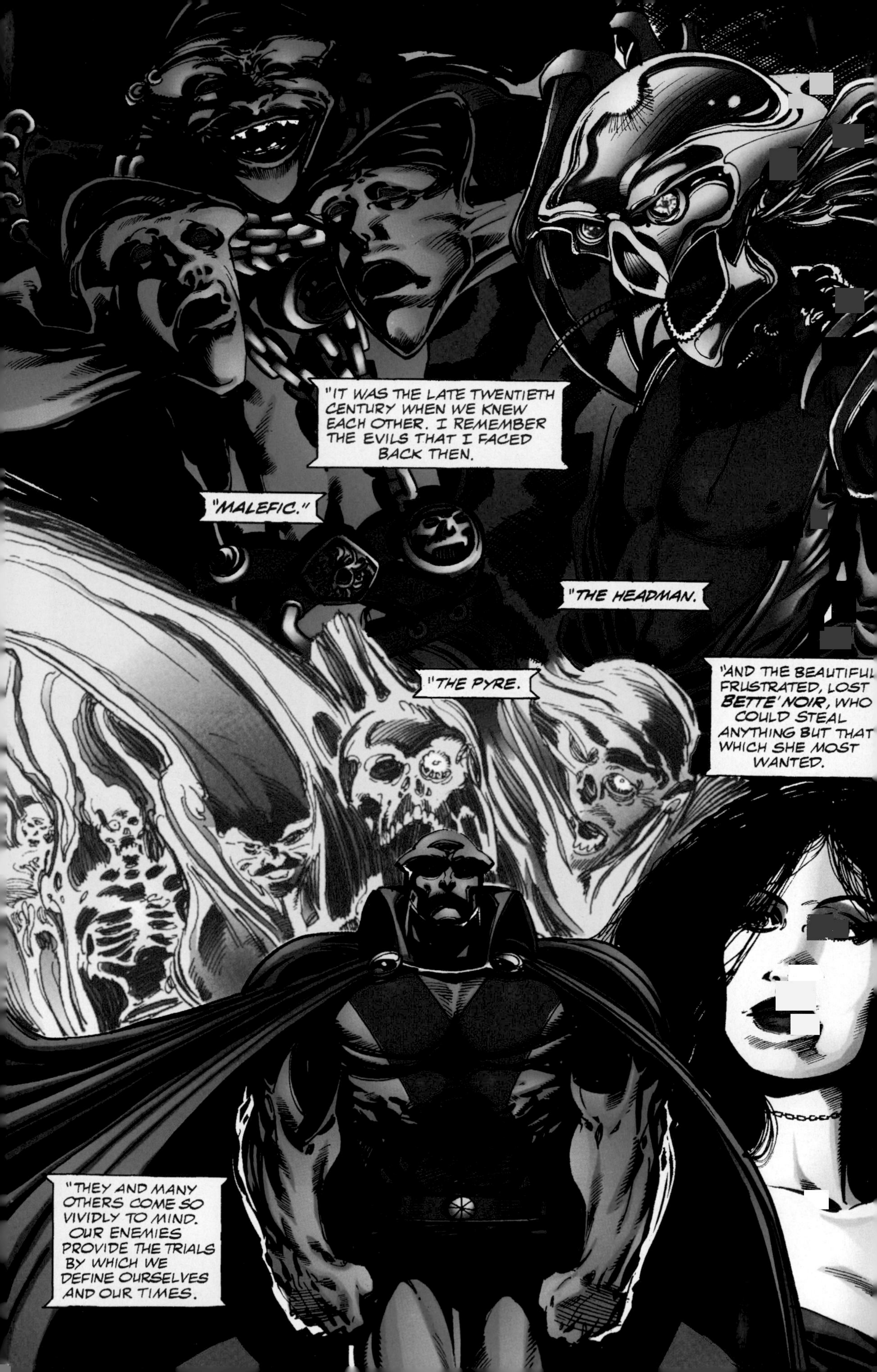
"IT WAS THE LATE TWENTIETH CENTURY WHEN WE KNEW EACH OTHER. I REMEMBER THE EVILS THAT I FACED BACK THEN.
"MALEFIC."
"THE HEADMAN.
"THE PYRE.
"AND THE BEAUTIFUL FRUSTRATED, LOST BETTE' NOIR, WHO COULD STEAL ANYTHING BUT THAT WHICH SHE MOST WANTED.
"THEY AND MANY OTHERS COME SO VIVIDLY TO MIND. OUR ENEMIES PROVIDE THE TRIALS BY WHICH WE DEFINE OURSELVES AND OUR TIMES.

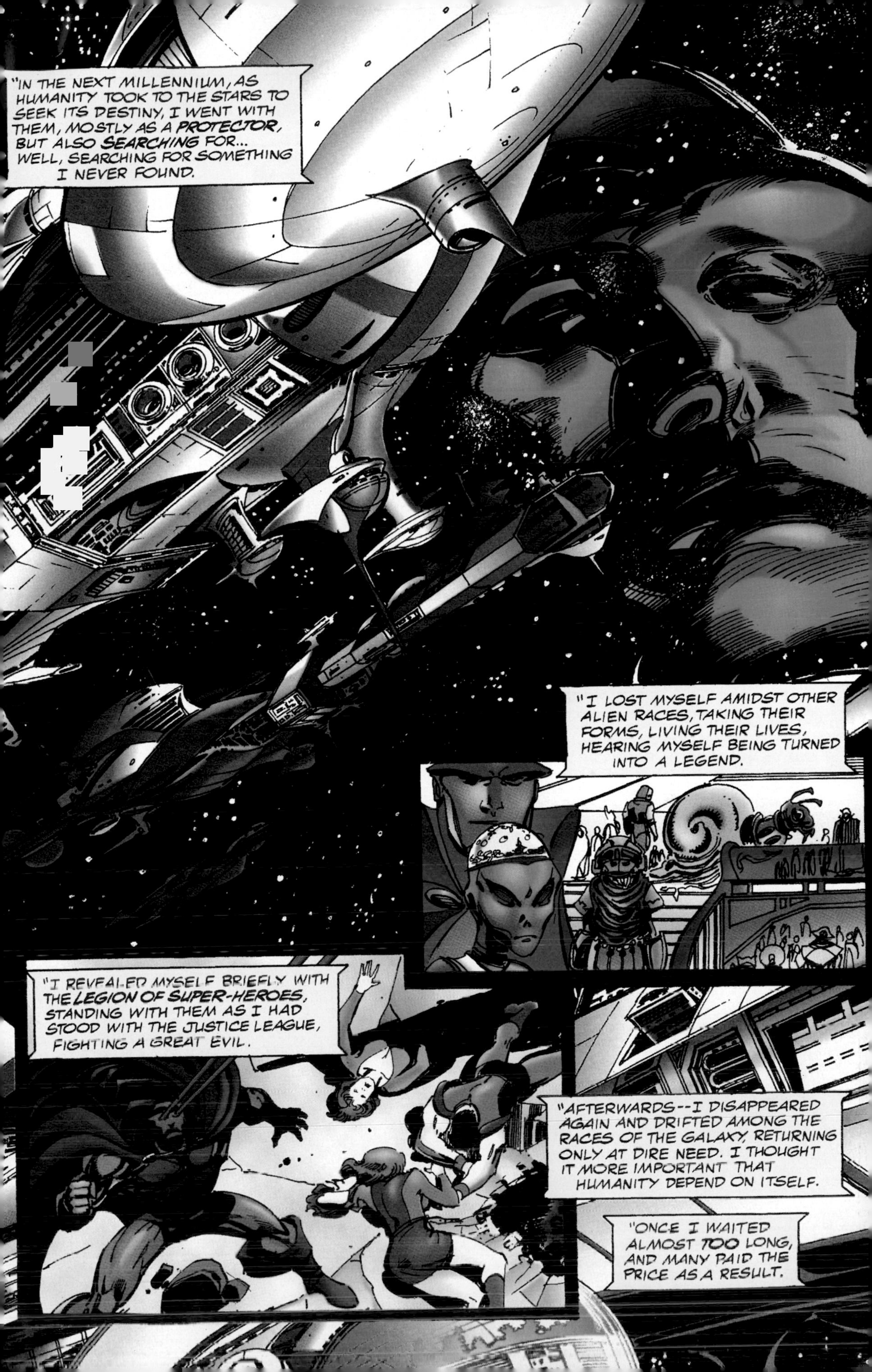
"IN THE NEXT MILLENNIUM, AS HUMANITY TOOK TO THE STARS TO SEEK ITS DESTINY, I WENT WITH THEM, MOSTLY AS A PROTECTOR, BUT ALSO SEARCHING FOR... WELL, SEARCHING FOR SOMETHING I NEVER FOUND.
"I LOST MYSELF AMIDST OTHER ALIEN RACES, TAKING THEIR FORMS, LIVING THEIR LIVES, HEARING MYSELF BEING TURNED INTO A LEGEND.
"I REVEALED MYSELF BRIEFLY WITH THE LEGION OF SUPER-HEROES, STANDING WITH THEM AS I HAD STOOD WITH THE JUSTICE LEAGUE, FIGHTING A GREAT EVIL.
"AFTERWARDS--I DISAPPEARED AGAIN AND DRIFTED AMONG THE RACES OF THE GALAXY, RETURNING ONLY AT DIRE NEED. I THOUGHT IT MORE IMPORTANT THAT HUMANITY DEPEND ON ITSELF.
"ONCE I WAITED ALMOST TOO LONG, AND MANY PAID THE PRICE AS A RESULT.

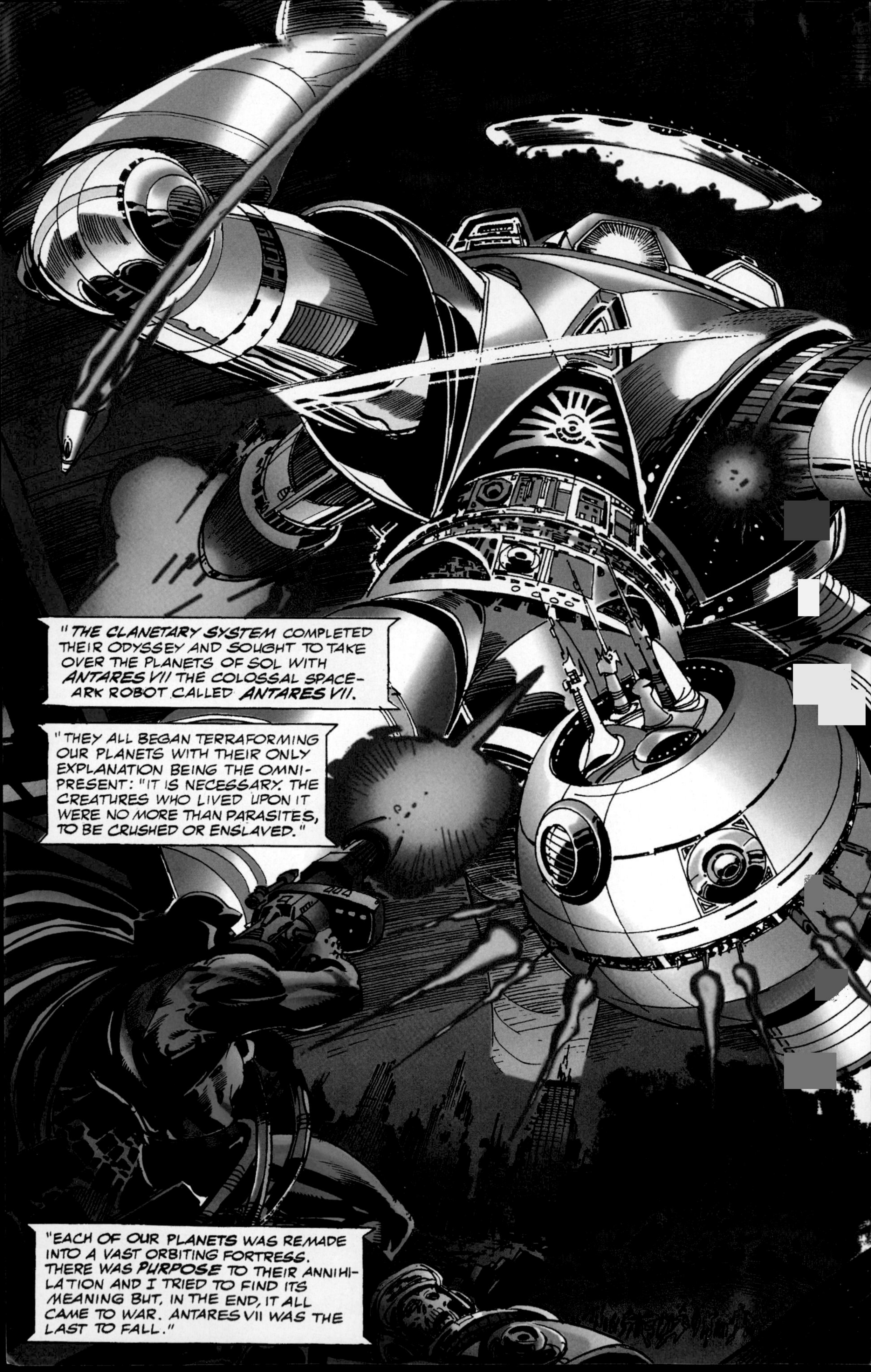
"THE CLANETARY SYSTEM COMPLETED THEIR ODYSSEY AND SOUGHT TO TAKE OVER THE PLANETS OF SOL WITH ANTARES VII THE COLOSSAL SPACE-ARK ROBOT CALLED ANTARES VII.
"THEY ALL BEGAN TERRAFORMING OUR PLANETS WITH THEIR ONLY EXPLANATION BEING THE OMNI-PRESENT: "IT IS NECESSARY. THE CREATURES WHO LIVED UPON IT WERE NO MORE THAN PARASITES, TO BE CRUSHED OR ENSLAVED."
"EACH OF OUR PLANETS WAS REMADE INTO A VAST ORBITING FORTRESS. THERE WAS PURPOSE TO THEIR ANNIHI-LATION AND I TRIED TO FIND ITS MEANING BUT, IN THE END, IT ALL CAME TO WAR. ANTARES VII WAS THE LAST TO FALL."

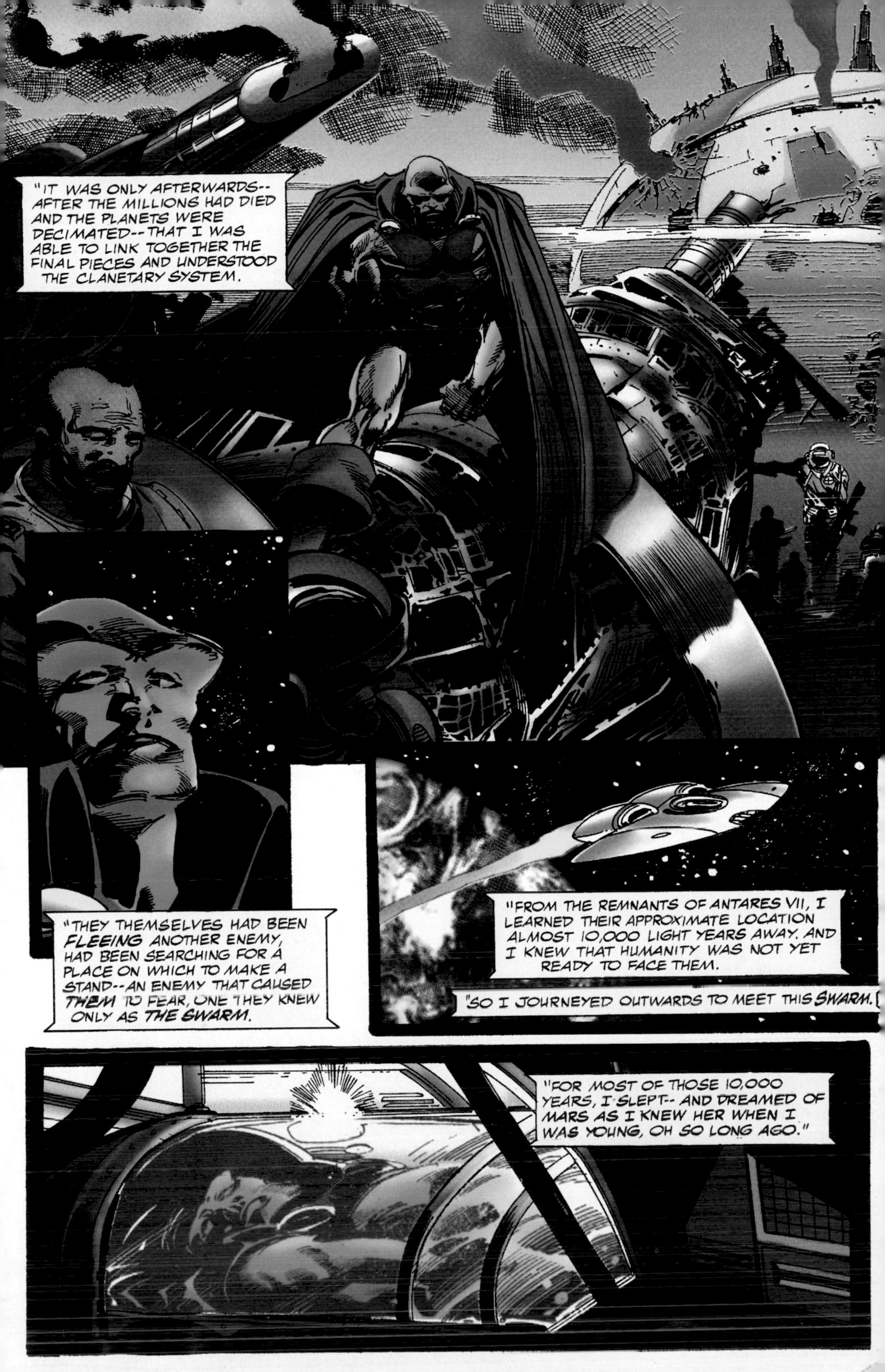
"IT WAS ONLY AFTERWARDS-- AFTER THE MILLIONS HAD DIED AND THE PLANETS WERE DECIMATED--THAT I WAS ABLE TO LINK TOGETHER THE FINAL PIECES AND UNDERSTOOD THE CLANETARY SYSTEM.
"THEY THEMSELVES HAD BEEN FLEEING ANOTHER ENEMY, HAD BEEN SEARCHING FOR A PLACE ON WHICH TO MAKE A STAND--AN ENEMY THAT CAUSED THEM TO FEAR, ONE THEY KNEW ONLY AS THE SWARM.
"FROM THE REMNANTS OF ANTARES VII, I LEARNED THEIR APPROXIMATE LOCATION ALMOST 10,000 LIGHT YEARS AWAY. AND I KNEW THAT HUMANITY WAS NOT YET READY TO FACE THEM.
"SO I JOURNEYED OUTWARDS TO MEET THIS SWARM.
"FOR MOST OF THOSE 10,000 YEARS, I SLEPT-- AND DREAMED OF MARS AS I KNEW HER WHEN I WAS YOUNG, OH SO LONG AGO."

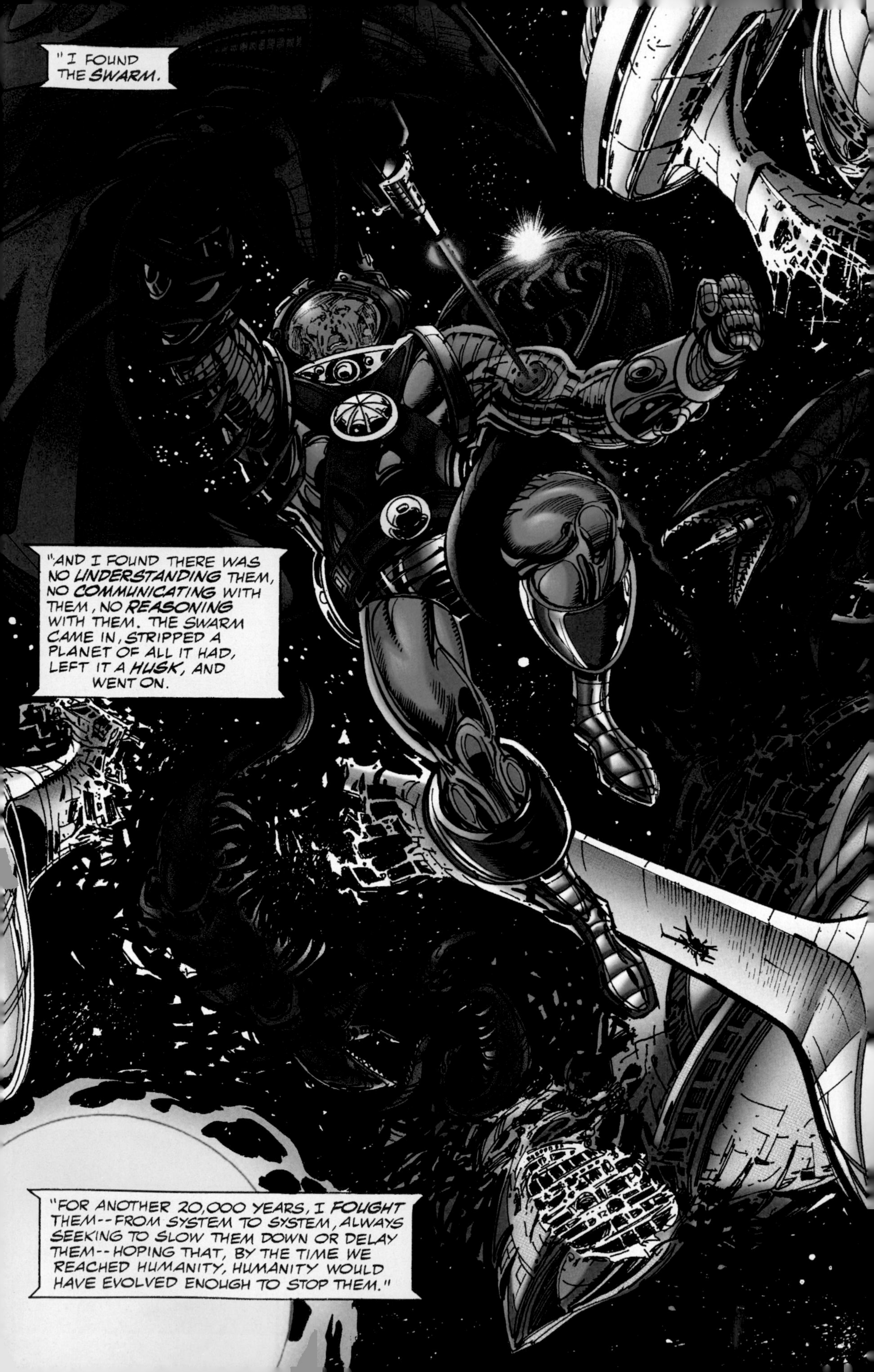
"I FOUND THE SWARM.
"AND I FOUND THERE WAS NO UNDERSTANDING THEM, NO COMMUNICATING WITH THEM, NO REASONING WITH THEM. THE SWARM CAME IN, STRIPPED A PLANET OF ALL IT HAD, LEFT IT A HUSK, AND WENT ON.
"FOR ANOTHER 20,000 YEARS, I FOUGHT THEM--FROM SYSTEM TO SYSTEM, ALWAYS SEEKING TO SLOW THEM DOWN OR DELAY THEM--HOPING THAT, BY THE TIME WE REACHED HUMANITY, HUMANITY WOULD HAVE EVOLVED ENOUGH TO STOP THEM."

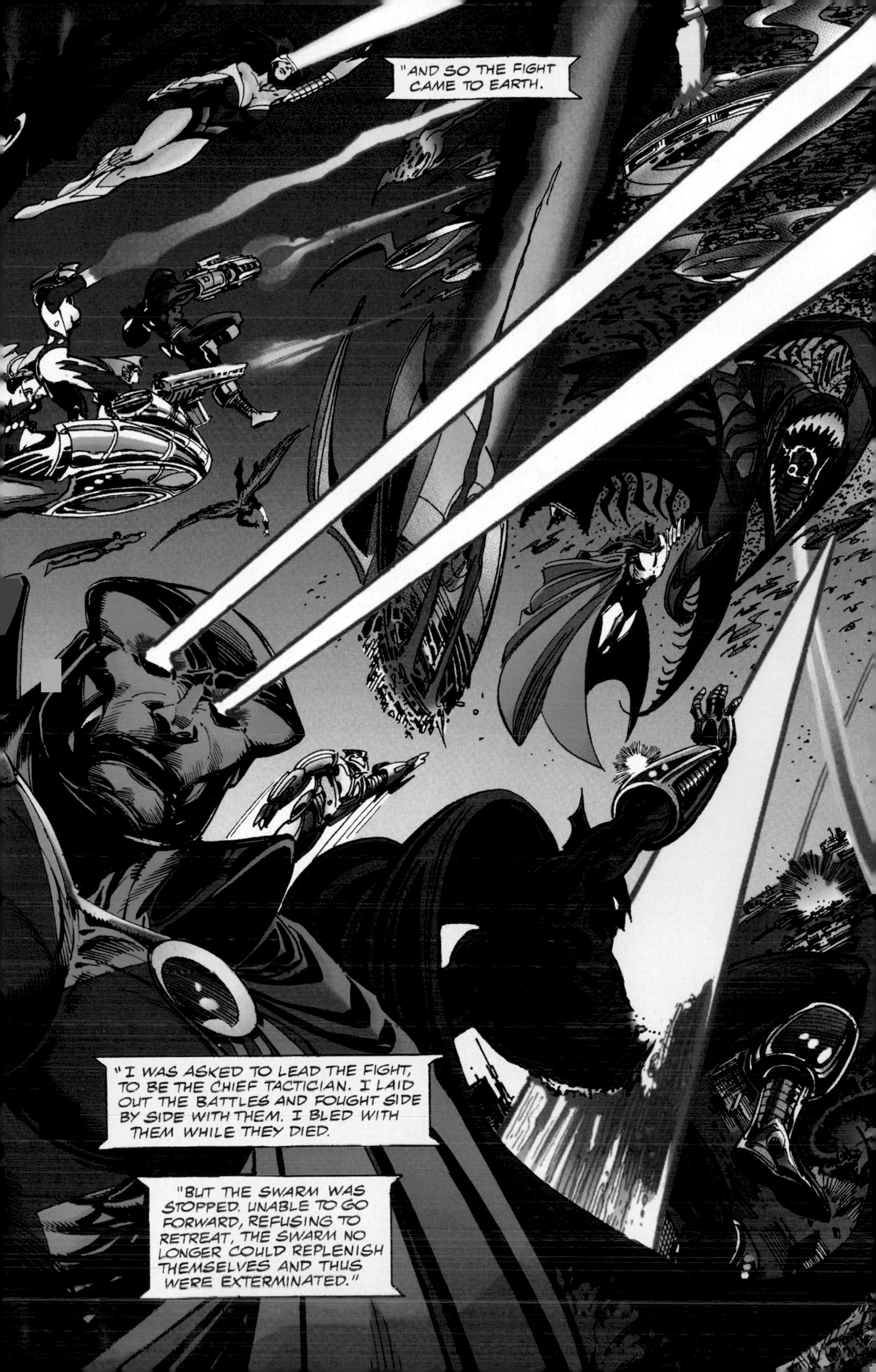
"AND SO THE FIGHT CAME TO EARTH.
"I WAS ASKED TO LEAD THE FIGHT, TO BE THE CHIEF TACTICIAN. I LAID OUT THE BATTLES AND FOUGHT SIDE BY SIDE WITH THEM. I BLED WITH THEM WHILE THEY DIED.
"BUT THE SWARM WAS STOPPED. UNABLE TO GO FORWARD, REFUSING TO RETREAT, THE SWARM NO LONGER COULD REPLENISH THEMSELVES AND THUS WERE EXTERMINATED."

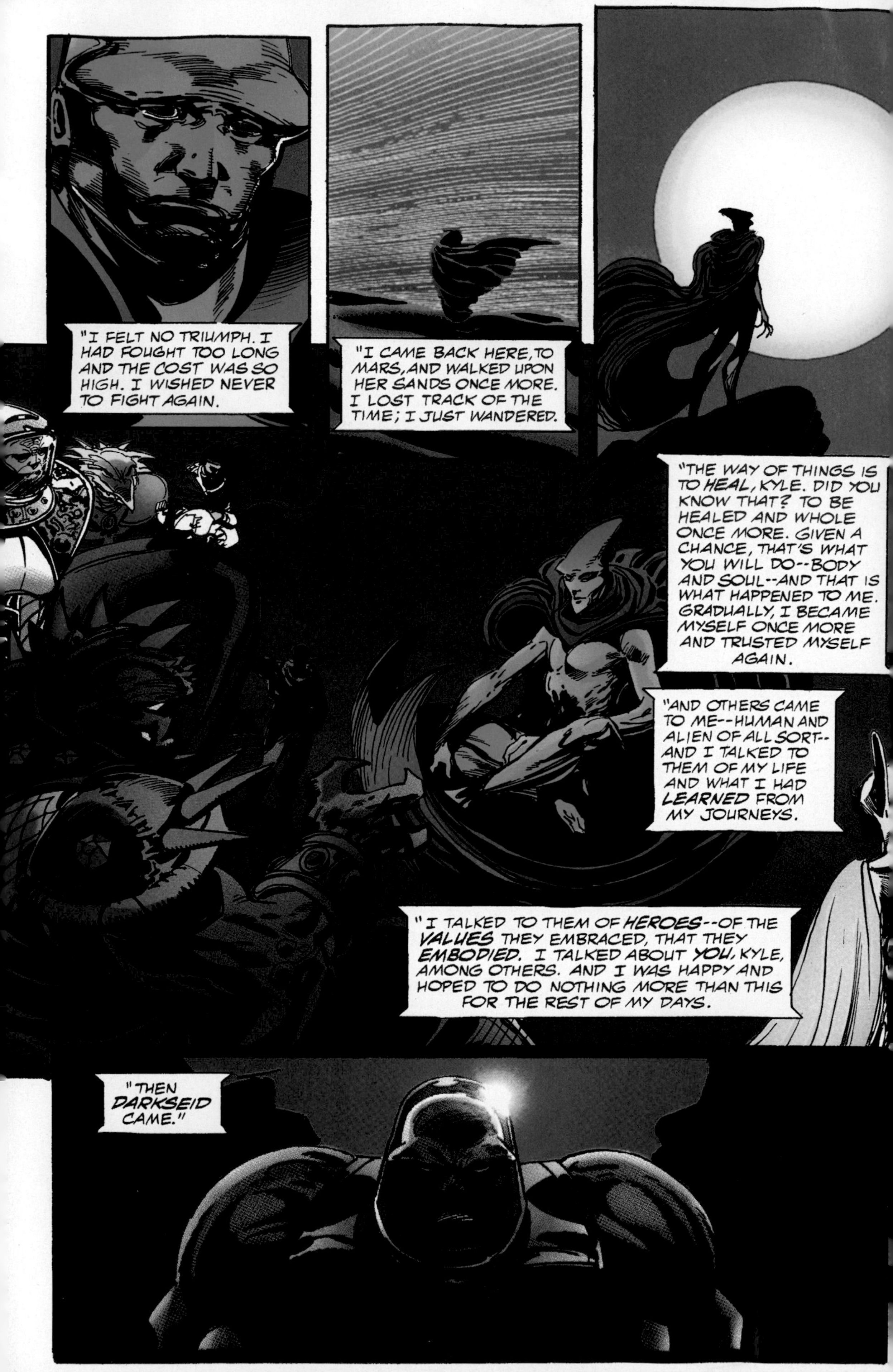
"I FELT NO TRIUMPH. I HAD FOUGHT TOO LONG AND THE COST WAS SO HIGH. I WISHED NEVER TO FIGHT AGAIN.
"I CAME BACK HERE, TO MARS, AND WALKED UPON HER SANDS ONCE MORE. I LOST TRACK OF THE TIME; I JUST WANDERED.
"THE WAY OF THINGS IS TO HEAL, KYLE. DID YOU KNOW THAT? TO BE HEALED AND WHOLE ONCE MORE. GIVEN A CHANCE, THAT'S WHAT YOU WILL DO--BODY AND SOUL--AND THAT IS WHAT HAPPENED TO ME. GRADUALLY, I BECAME MYSELF ONCE MORE AND TRUSTED MYSELF AGAIN.
"AND OTHERS CAME TO ME--HUMAN AND ALIEN OF ALL SORT--AND I TALKED TO THEM OF MY LIFE AND WHAT I HAD LEARNED FROM MY JOURNEYS.
"I TALKED TO THEM OF HEROES--OF THE VALUES THEY EMBRACED, THAT THEY EMBODIED. I TALKED ABOUT YOU, KYLE, AMONG OTHERS. AND I WAS HAPPY AND HOPED TO DO NOTHING MORE THAN THIS FOR THE REST OF MY DAYS.
"THEN DARKSEID CAME."

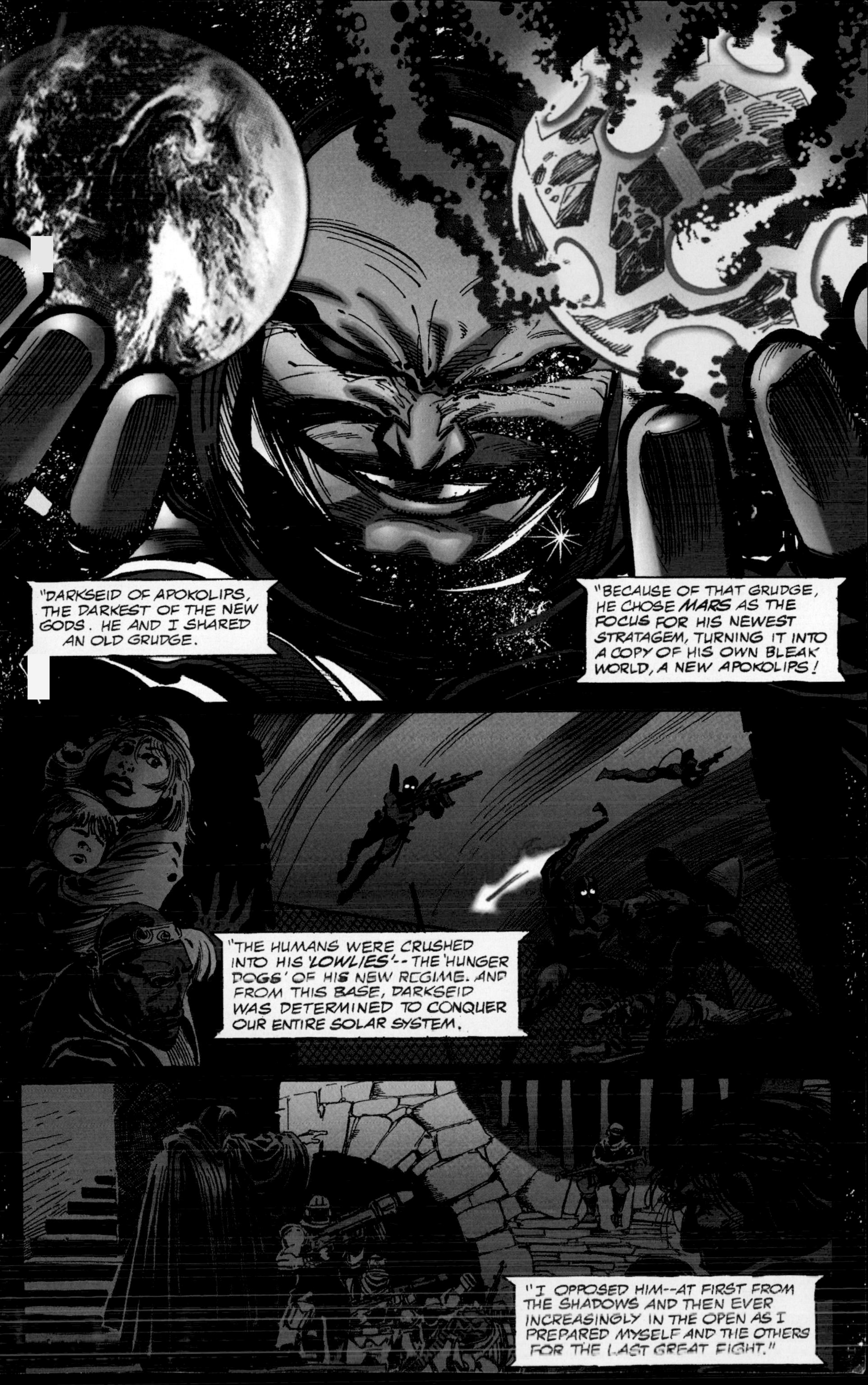
"DARKSEID OF APOKOLIPS, THE DARKEST OF THE NEW GODS. HE AND I SHARED AN OLD GRUDGE.
"BECAUSE OF THAT GRUDGE, HE CHOSE MARS AS THE FOCUS FOR HIS NEWEST STRATAGEM, TURNING IT INTO A COPY OF HIS OWN BLEAK WORLD, A NEW APOKOLIPS!
"THE HUMANS WERE CRUSHED INTO HIS 'LOWLIES'-- THE 'HUNGER DOGS' OF HIS NEW REGIME. AND FROM THIS BASE, DARKSEID WAS DETERMINED TO CONQUER OUR ENTIRE SOLAR SYSTEM.
"I OPPOSED HIM--AT FIRST FROM THE SHADOWS AND THEN EVER INCREASINGLY IN THE OPEN AS I PREPARED MYSELF AND THE OTHERS FOR THE LAST GREAT FIGHT."

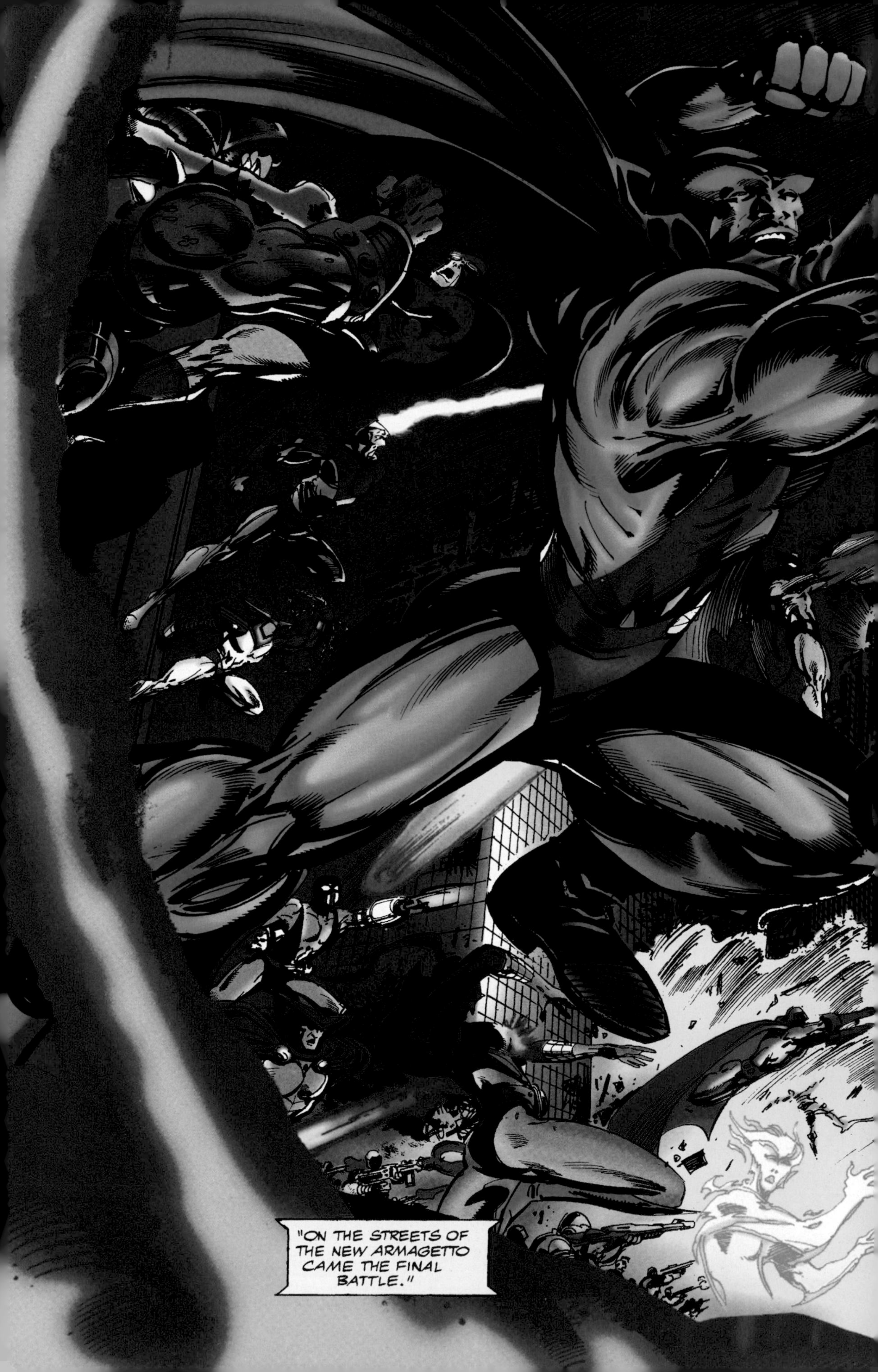
"ON THE STREETS OF THE NEW ARMAGETTO CAME THE FINAL BATTLE."

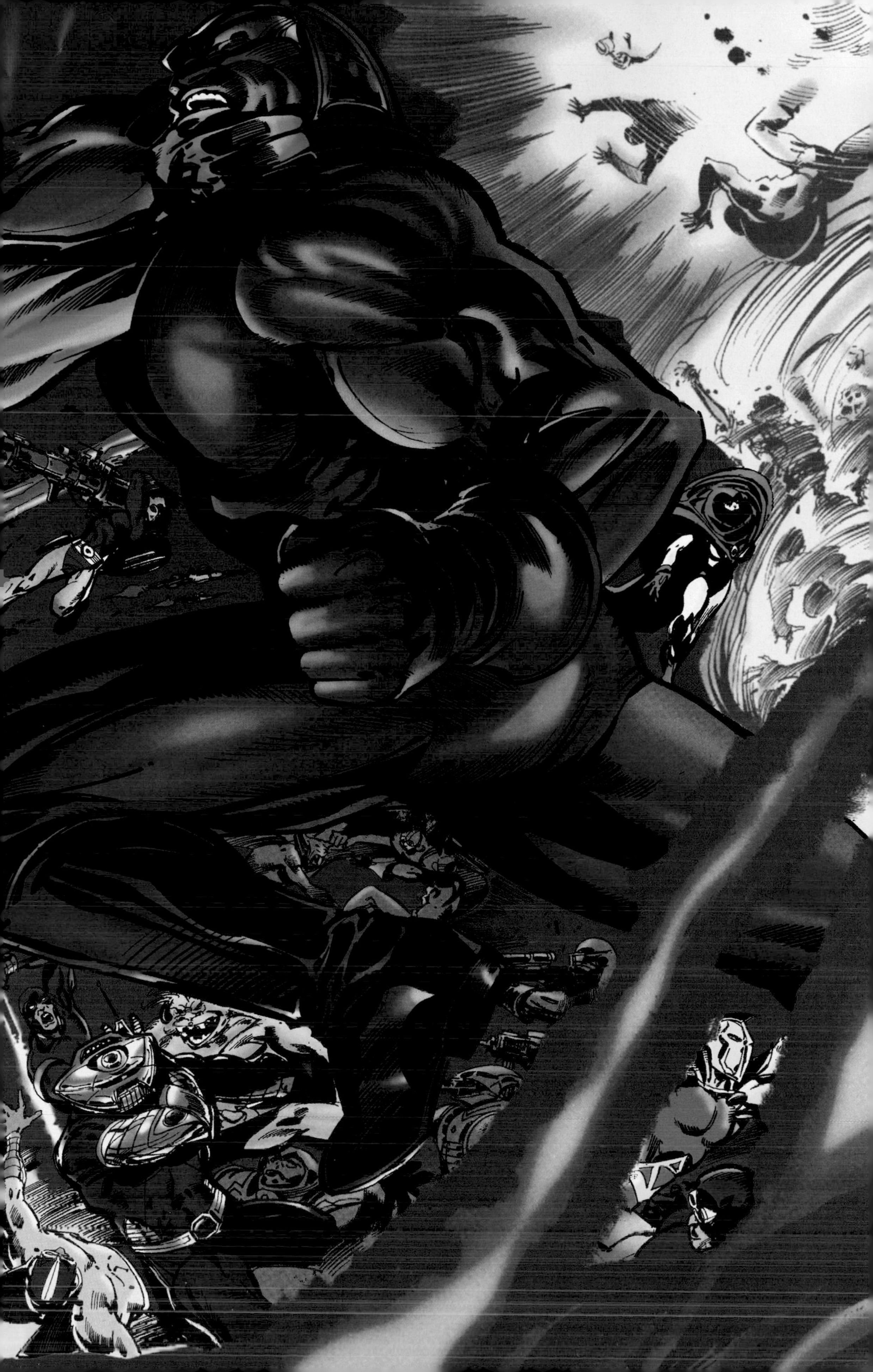

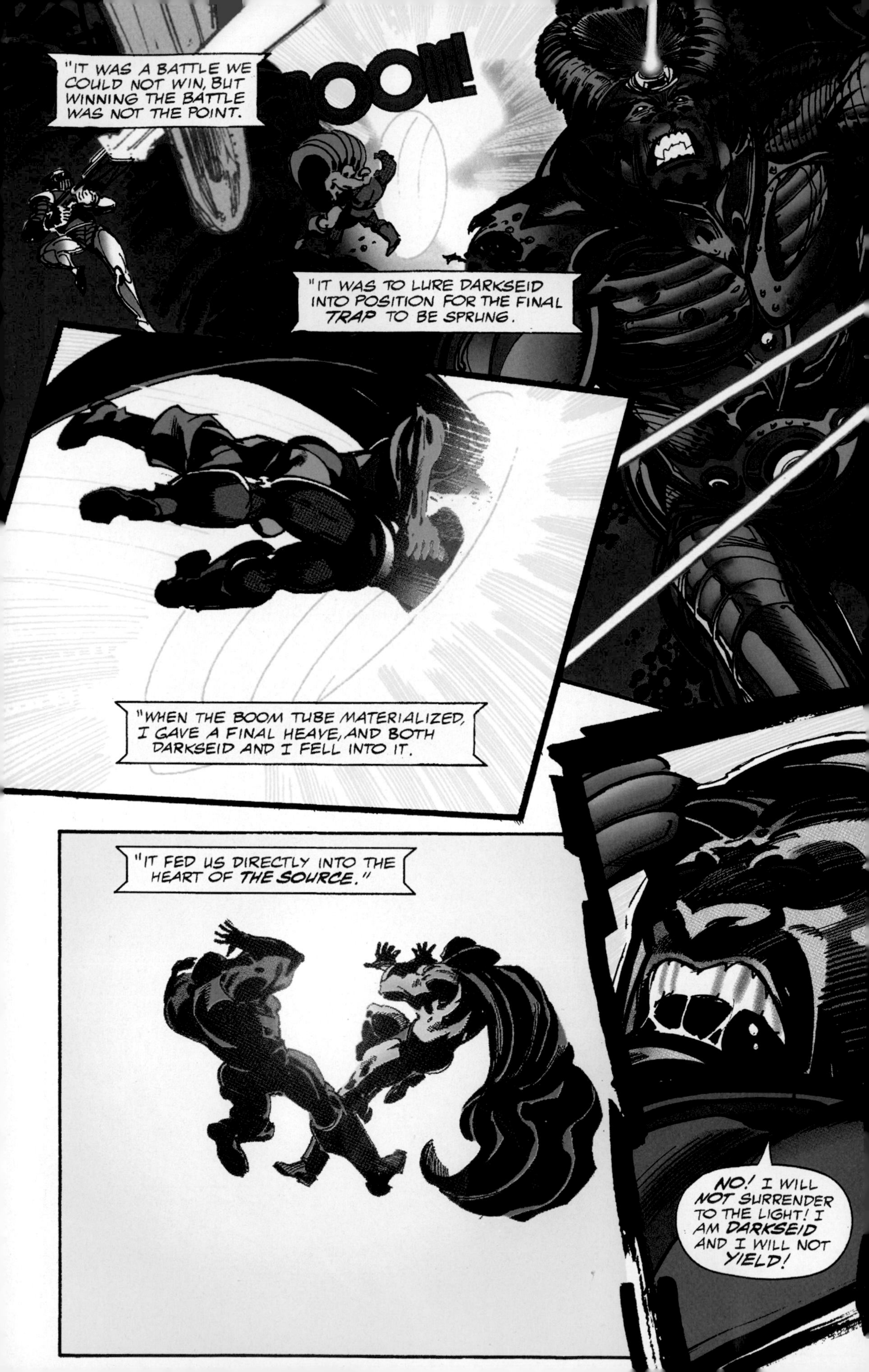
"IT WAS A BATTLE WE COULD NOT WIN, BUT WINNING THE BATTLE WAS NOT THE POINT.
BOOM!
"IT WAS TO LURE DARKSEID INTO POSITION FOR THE FINAL TRAP TO BE SPRUNG.
"WHEN THE BOOM TUBE MATERIALIZED, I GAVE A FINAL HEAVE, AND BOTH DARKSEID AND I FELL INTO IT.
"IT FED US DIRECTLY INTO THE HEART OF THE SOURCE."
NO! I WILL NOT SURRENDER TO THE LIGHT! I AM DARKSEID AND I WILL NOT YIELD!

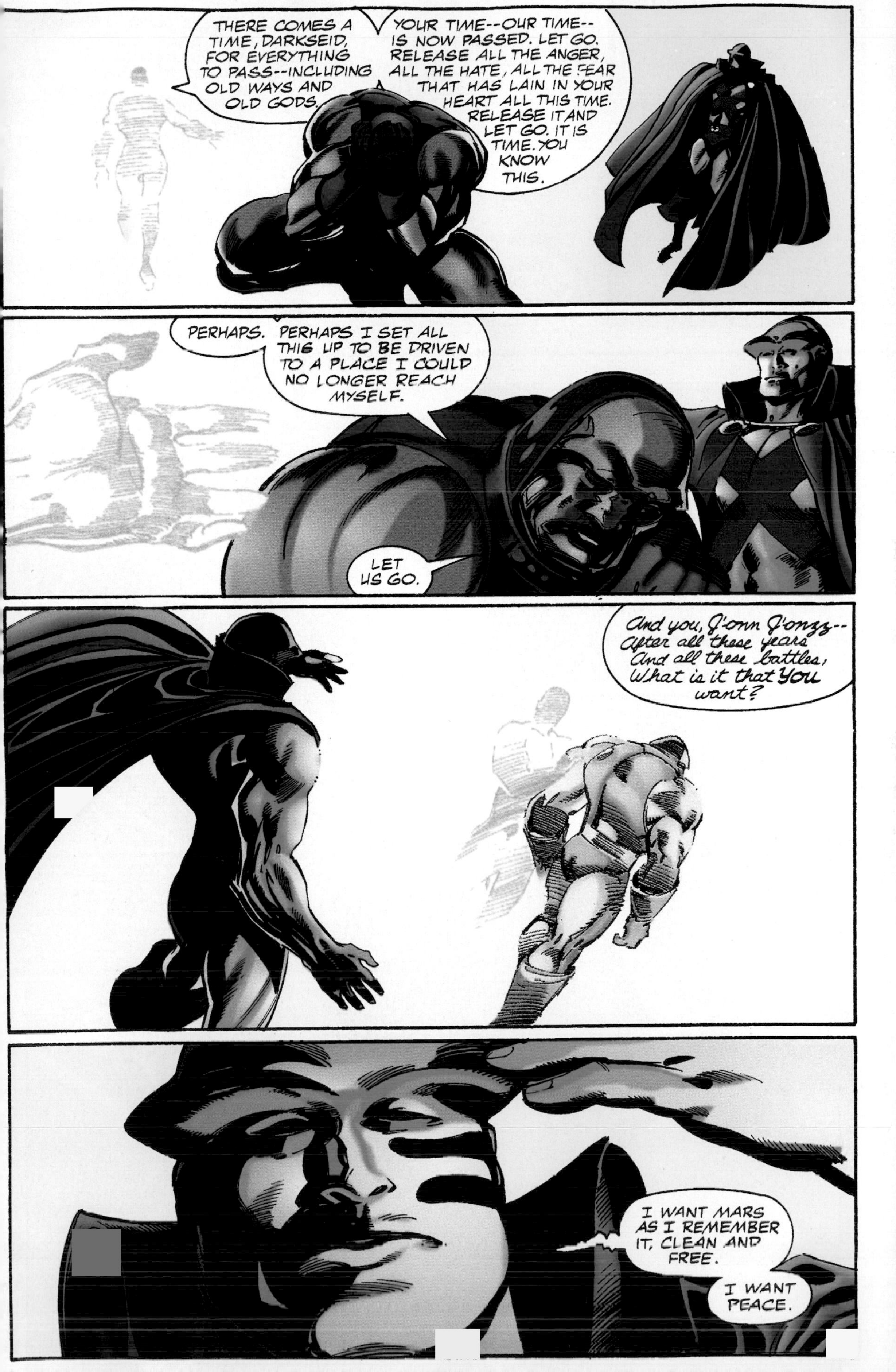
THERE COMES A TIME, DARKSEID, FOR EVERYTHING TO PASS--INCLUDING OLD WAYS AND OLD GODS.
YOUR TIME--OUR TIME--IS NOW PASSED. LET GO. RELEASE ALL THE ANGER, ALL THE HATE, ALL THE FEAR THAT HAS LAIN IN YOUR HEART ALL THIS TIME. RELEASE IT AND LET GO. IT IS TIME. YOU KNOW THIS.
PERHAPS. PERHAPS I SET ALL THIS UP TO BE DRIVEN TO A PLACE I COULD NO LONGER REACH MYSELF.
LET US GO.
And you, J'onn J'onzz--After all these years And all these battles, What is it that YOU want?
I WANT MARS AS I REMEMBER IT, CLEAN AND FREE.
I WANT PEACE.

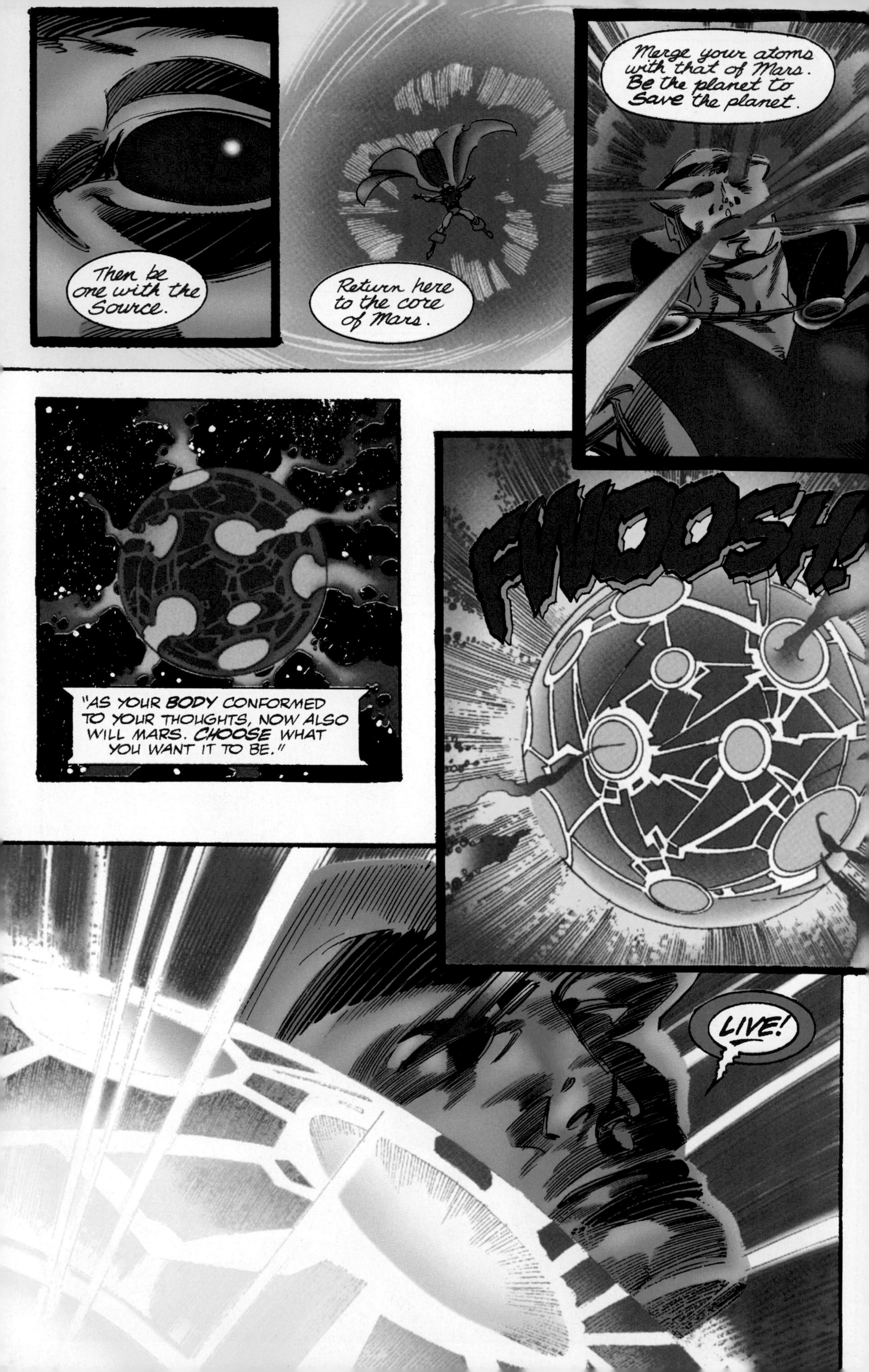
Then be one with the Source.
Return here to the core of Mars.
Merge your atoms with that of Mars. Be the planet to Save the planet.
"AS YOUR BODY CONFORMED TO YOUR THOUGHTS, NOW ALSO WILL MARS. CHOOSE WHAT YOU WANT IT TO BE."
FWOOSH!
LIVE!

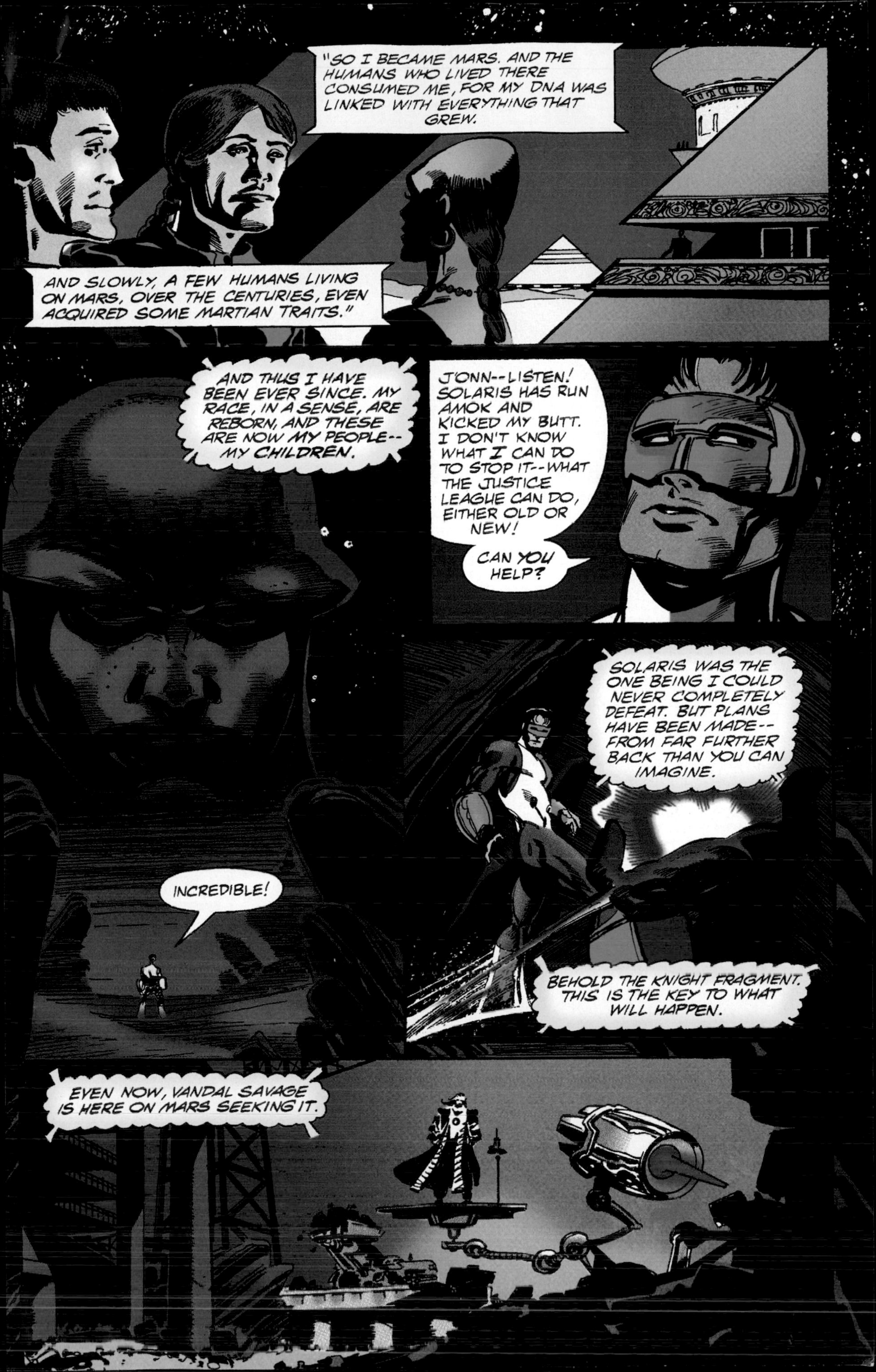
"SO I BECAME MARS. AND THE HUMANS WHO LIVED THERE CONSUMED ME, FOR MY DNA WAS LINKED WITH EVERYTHING THAT GREW.
AND SLOWLY, A FEW HUMANS LIVING ON MARS, OVER THE CENTURIES, EVEN ACQUIRED SOME MARTIAN TRAITS."
AND THUS I HAVE BEEN EVER SINCE. MY RACE, IN A SENSE, ARE REBORN, AND THESE ARE NOW MY PEOPLE-- MY CHILDREN.
J'ONN--LISTEN! SOLARIS HAS RUN AMOK AND KICKED MY BUTT. I DON'T KNOW WHAT I CAN DO TO STOP IT--WHAT THE JUSTICE LEAGUE CAN DO, EITHER OLD OR NEW!
CAN YOU HELP?
INCREDIBLE!
SOLARIS WAS THE ONE BEING I COULD NEVER COMPLETELY DEFEAT. BUT PLANS HAVE BEEN MADE-- FROM FAR FURTHER BACK THAN YOU CAN IMAGINE.
BEHOLD THE KNIGHT FRAGMENT. THIS IS THE KEY TO WHAT WILL HAPPEN.
EVEN NOW, VANDAL SAVAGE IS HERE ON MARS SEEKING IT.

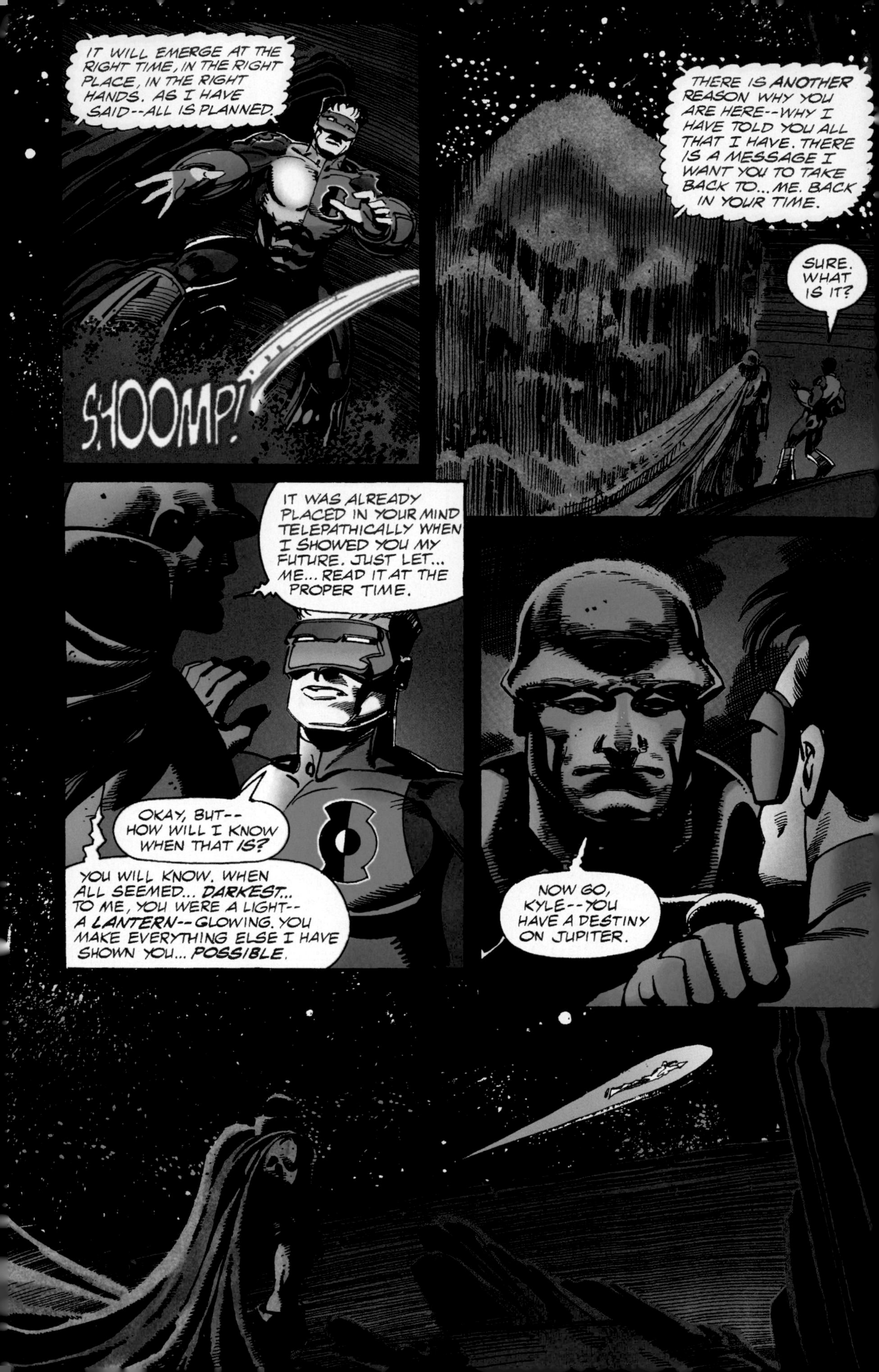
IT WILL EMERGE AT THE RIGHT TIME, IN THE RIGHT PLACE, IN THE RIGHT HANDS. AS I HAVE SAID--ALL IS PLANNED.
SHOOMP!
THERE IS ANOTHER REASON WHY YOU ARE HERE--WHY I HAVE TOLD YOU ALL THAT I HAVE. THERE IS A MESSAGE I WANT YOU TO TAKE BACK TO... ME. BACK IN YOUR TIME.
SURE. WHAT IS IT?
IT WAS ALREADY PLACED IN YOUR MIND TELEPATHICALLY WHEN I SHOWED YOU MY FUTURE. JUST LET... ME... READ IT AT THE PROPER TIME.
OKAY, BUT-- HOW WILL I KNOW WHEN THAT IS?
YOU WILL KNOW. WHEN ALL SEEMED... DARKEST... TO ME, YOU WERE A LIGHT-- A LANTERN--GLOWING. YOU MAKE EVERYTHING ELSE I HAVE SHOWN YOU... POSSIBLE.
NOW GO, KYLE--YOU HAVE A DESTINY ON JUPITER.

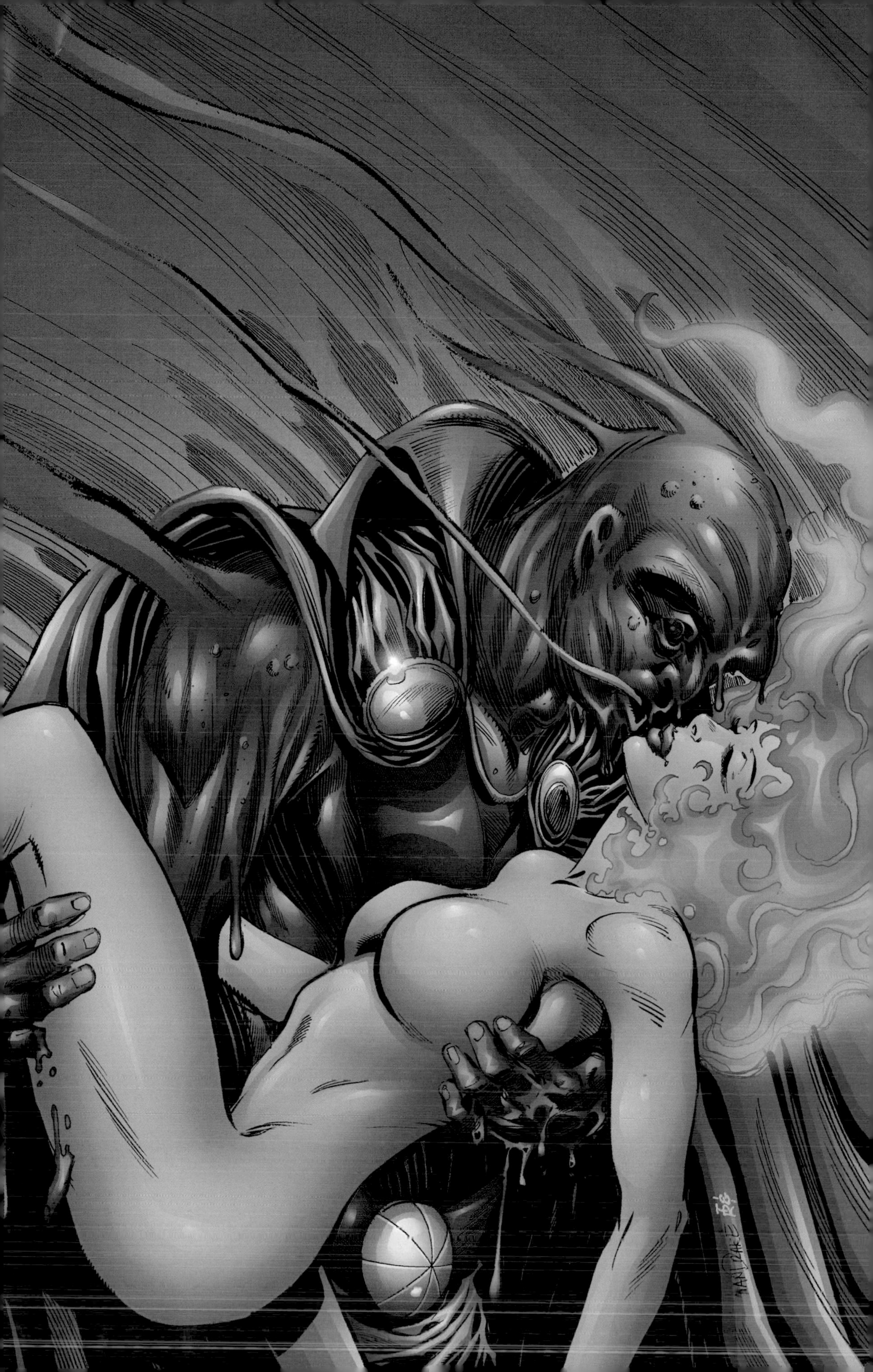

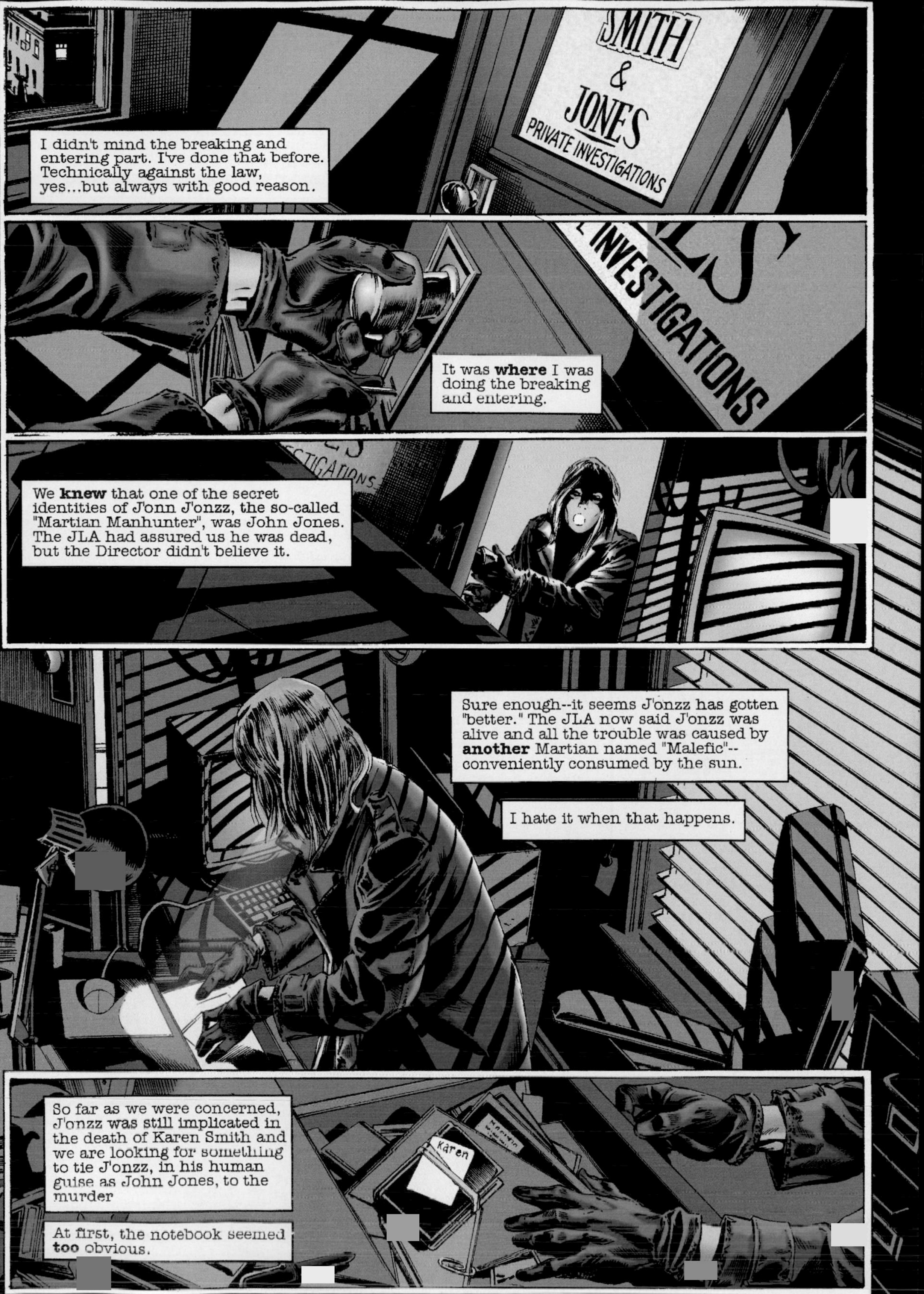
SMITH & JONES PRIVATE INVESTIGATIONS
I didn't mind the breaking and entering part. I've done that before. Technically against the law, yes...but always with good reason.
INVESTIGATIONS
It was **where** I was doing the breaking and entering.
We **knew** that one of the secret identities of J'onn J'onzz, the so-called "Martian Manhunter", was John Jones. The JLA had assured us he was dead, but the Director didn't believe it.
Sure enough--it seems J'onzz has gotten "better." The JLA now said J'onzz was alive and all the trouble was caused by **another** Martian named "Malefic"--conveniently consumed by the sun.
I hate it when that happens.
So far as we were concerned, J'onzz was still implicated in the death of Karen Smith and we are looking for something to tie J'onzz, in his human guise as John Jones, to the murder
Karen
At first, the notebook seemed **too** obvious.

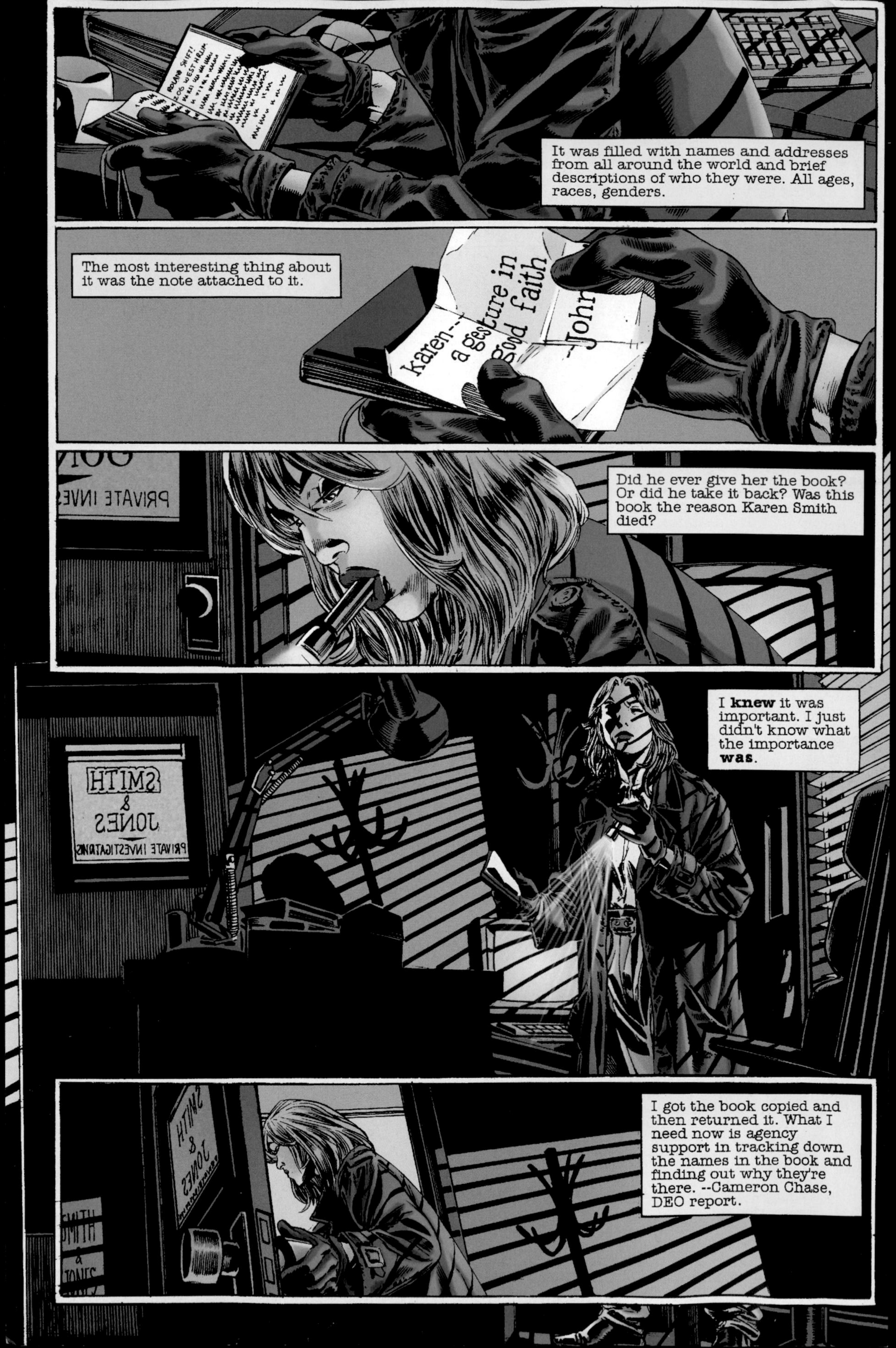
It was filled with names and addresses from all around the world and brief descriptions of who they were. All ages, races, genders.
The most interesting thing about it was the note attached to it.
Karen-- a gesture in good faith --John
Did he ever give her the book? Or did he take it back? Was this book the reason Karen Smith died?
I **knew** it was important. I just didn't know what the importance **was**.
I got the book copied and then returned it. What I need now is agency support in tracking down the names in the book and finding out why they're there. --Cameron Chase, DEO report.

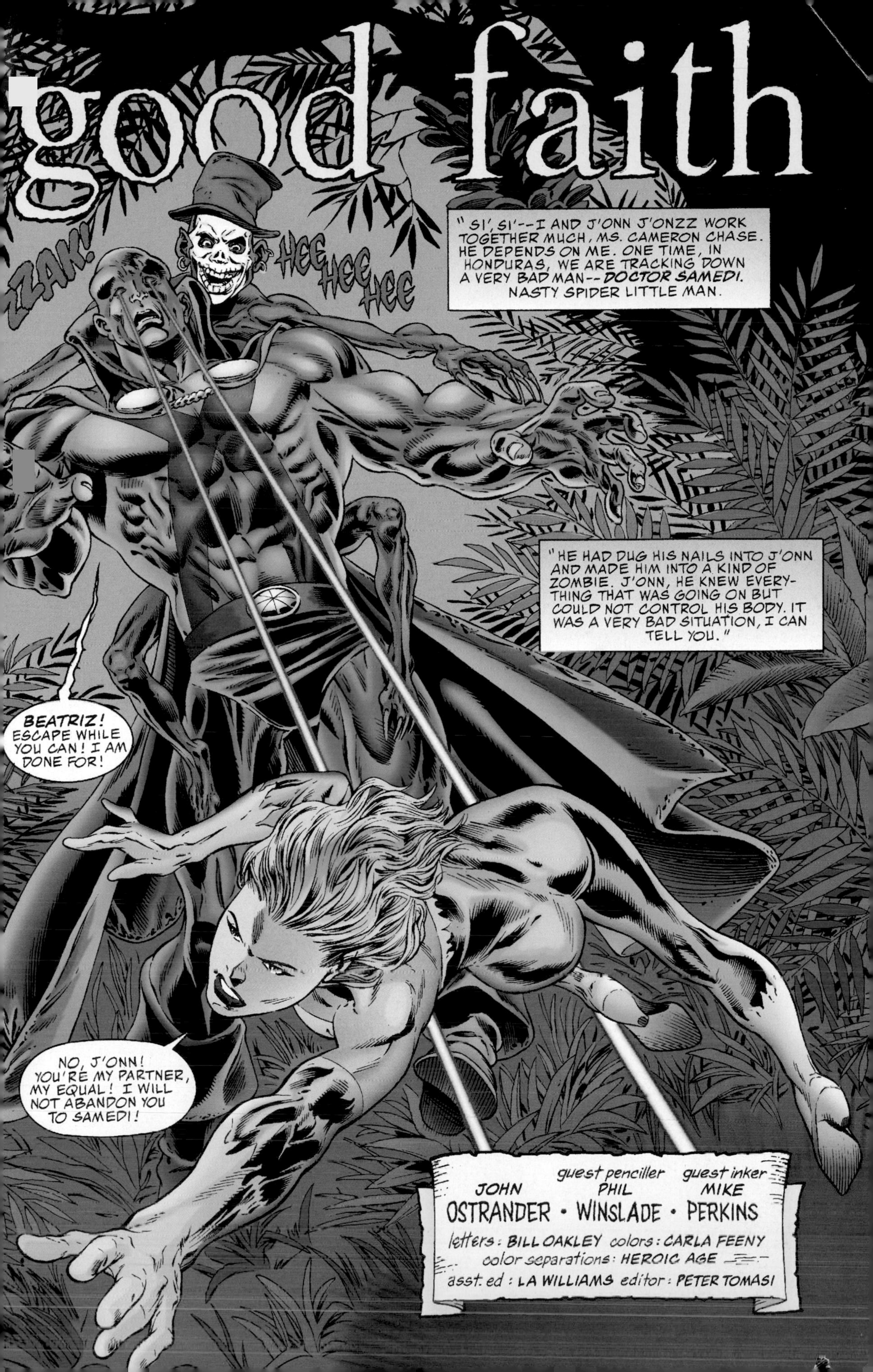
good faith
"SI', SI'--I AND J'ONN J'ONZZ WORK TOGETHER MUCH, MS. CAMERON CHASE. HE DEPENDS ON ME. ONE TIME, IN HONDURAS, WE ARE TRACKING DOWN A VERY BAD MAN--DOCTOR SAMEDI. NASTY SPIDER LITTLE MAN.
ZZAK!
HEE HEE HEE
"HE HAD DUG HIS NAILS INTO J'ONN AND MADE HIM INTO A KIND OF ZOMBIE. J'ONN, HE KNEW EVERYTHING THAT WAS GOING ON BUT COULD NOT CONTROL HIS BODY. IT WAS A VERY BAD SITUATION, I CAN TELL YOU."
BEATRIZ! ESCAPE WHILE YOU CAN! I AM DONE FOR!
NO, J'ONN! YOU'RE MY PARTNER, MY EQUAL! I WILL NOT ABANDON YOU TO SAMEDI!
JOHN OSTRANDER • guest penciller PHIL WINSLADE • guest inker MIKE PERKINS
letters: BILL OAKLEY colors: CARLA FEENY
color separations: HEROIC AGE
asst. ed: LA WILLIAMS editor: PETER TOMASI

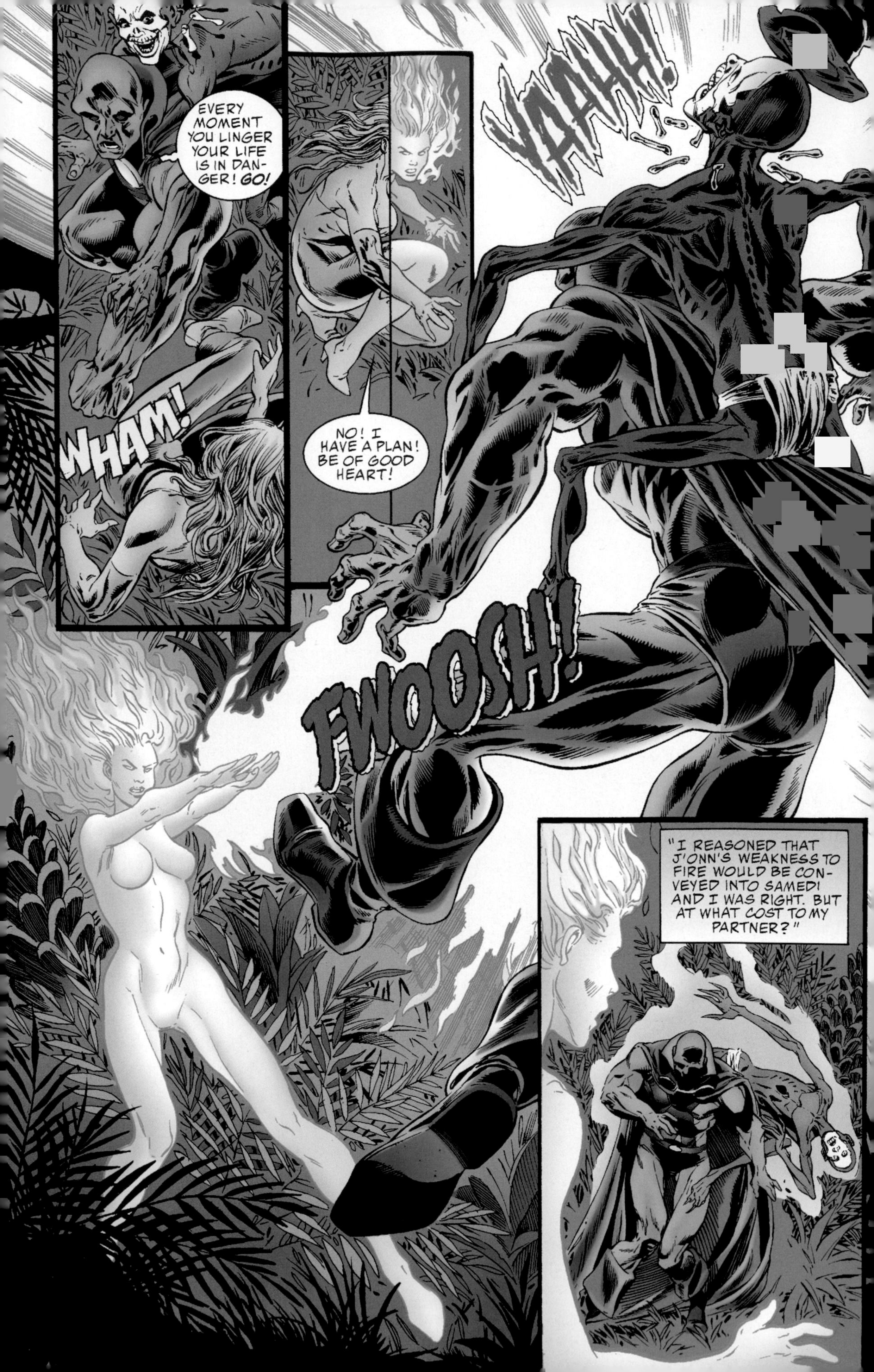
EVERY MOMENT YOU LINGER YOUR LIFE IS IN DANGER! GO!
WHAM!
NO! I HAVE A PLAN! BE OF GOOD HEART!
YAAHH!
FWOOSH!
"I REASONED THAT J'ONN'S WEAKNESS TO FIRE WOULD BE CONVEYED INTO SAMEDI AND I WAS RIGHT. BUT AT WHAT COST TO MY PARTNER?"

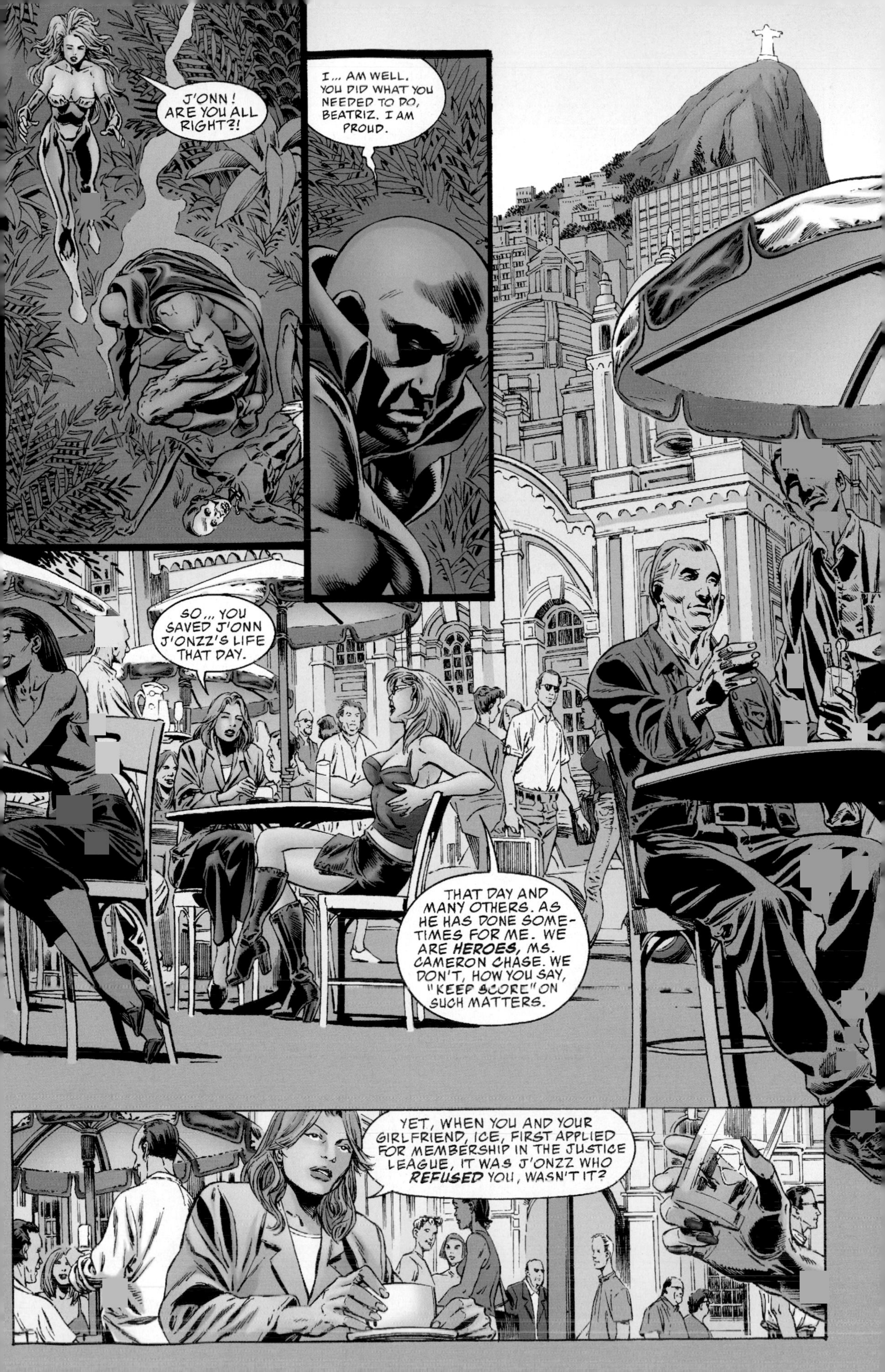
J'ONN! ARE YOU ALL RIGHT?!
I... AM WELL. YOU DID WHAT YOU NEEDED TO DO, BEATRIZ. I AM PROUD.
SO... YOU SAVED J'ONN J'ONZZ'S LIFE THAT DAY.
THAT DAY AND MANY OTHERS. AS HE HAS DONE SOMETIMES FOR ME. WE ARE HEROES, MS. CAMERON CHASE. WE DON'T, HOW YOU SAY, "KEEP SCORE" ON SUCH MATTERS.
YET, WHEN YOU AND YOUR GIRLFRIEND, ICE, FIRST APPLIED FOR MEMBERSHIP IN THE JUSTICE LEAGUE, IT WAS J'ONZZ WHO REFUSED YOU, WASN'T IT?

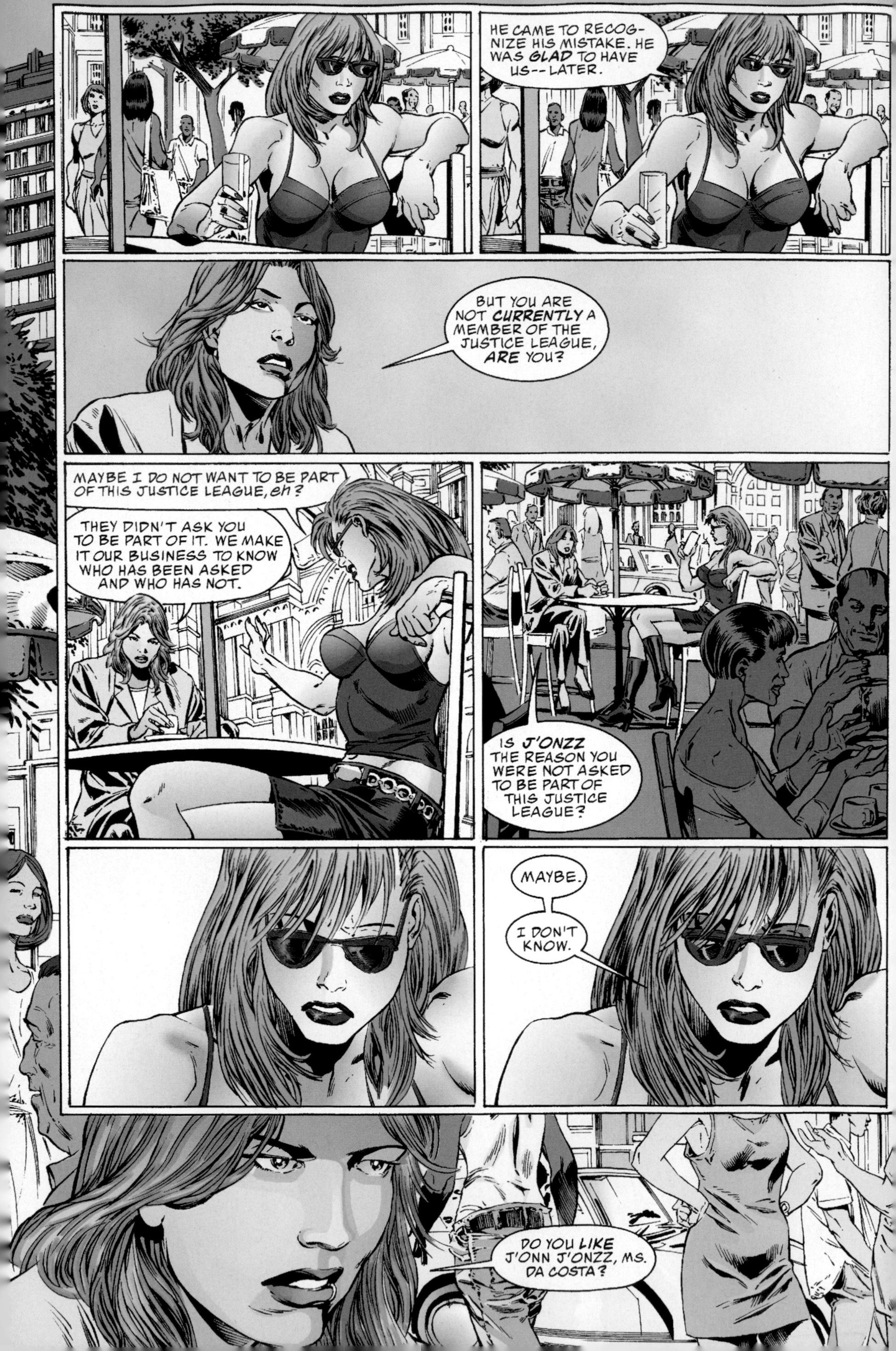
HE CAME TO RECOGNIZE HIS MISTAKE. HE WAS GLAD TO HAVE US--LATER.
BUT YOU ARE NOT CURRENTLY A MEMBER OF THE JUSTICE LEAGUE, ARE YOU?
MAYBE I DO NOT WANT TO BE PART OF THIS JUSTICE LEAGUE, eh?
THEY DIDN'T ASK YOU TO BE PART OF IT. WE MAKE IT OUR BUSINESS TO KNOW WHO HAS BEEN ASKED AND WHO HAS NOT.
IS J'ONZZ THE REASON YOU WERE NOT ASKED TO BE PART OF THIS JUSTICE LEAGUE?
MAYBE.
I DON'T KNOW.
DO YOU LIKE J'ONN J'ONZZ, MS. DA COSTA?

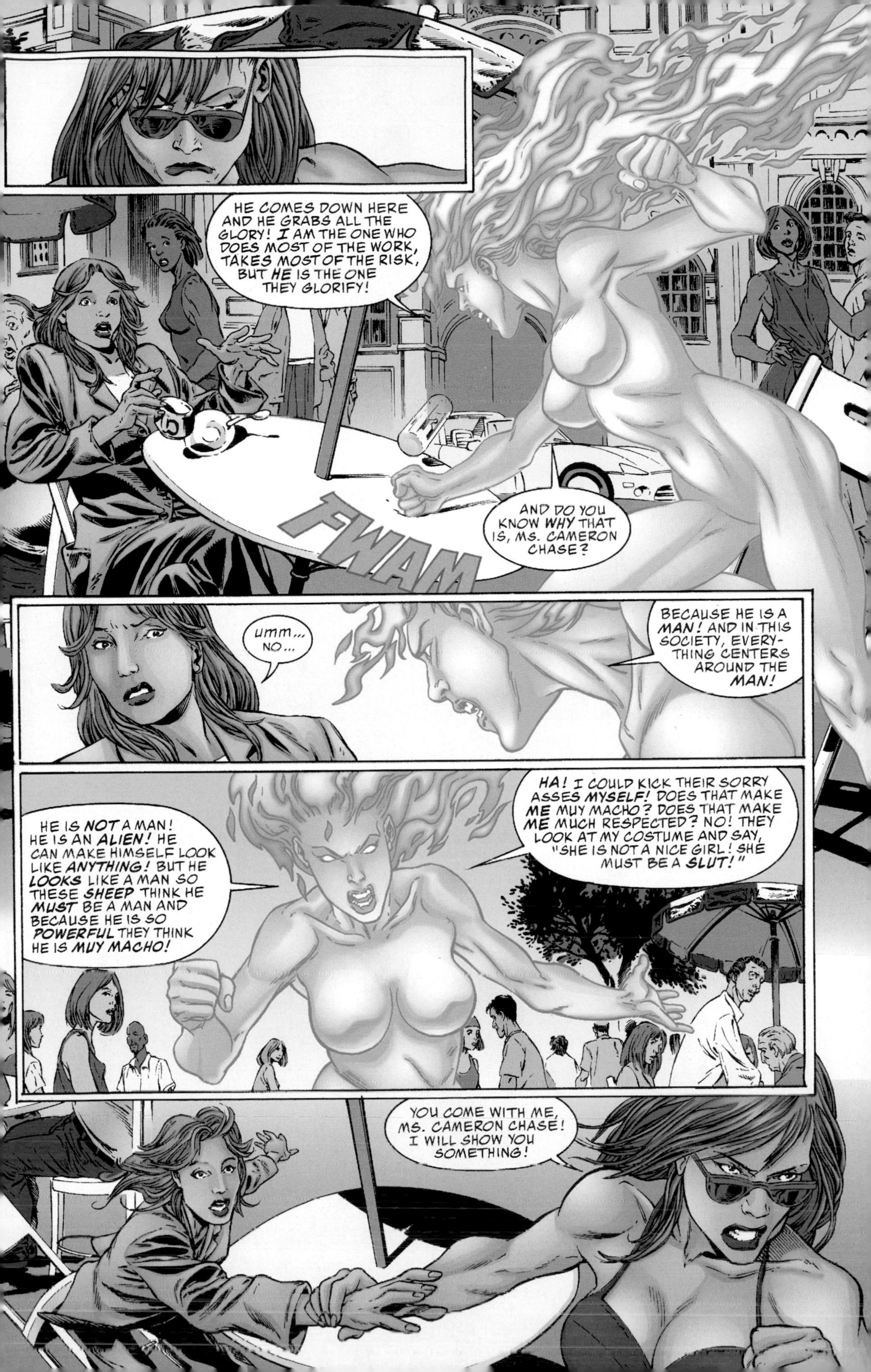
HE COMES DOWN HERE AND HE GRABS ALL THE GLORY! I AM THE ONE WHO DOES MOST OF THE WORK, TAKES MOST OF THE RISK, BUT HE IS THE ONE THEY GLORIFY!
FWAM
AND DO YOU KNOW WHY THAT IS, MS. CAMERON CHASE?
umm... NO...
BECAUSE HE IS A MAN! AND IN THIS SOCIETY, EVERY-THING CENTERS AROUND THE MAN!
HE IS NOT A MAN! HE IS AN ALIEN! HE CAN MAKE HIMSELF LOOK LIKE ANYTHING! BUT HE LOOKS LIKE A MAN SO THESE SHEEP THINK HE MUST BE A MAN AND BECAUSE HE IS SO POWERFUL THEY THINK HE IS MUY MACHO!
HA! I COULD KICK THEIR SORRY ASSES MYSELF! DOES THAT MAKE ME MUY MACHO? DOES THAT MAKE ME MUCH RESPECTED? NO! THEY LOOK AT MY COSTUME AND SAY, "SHE IS NOT A NICE GIRL! SHE MUST BE A SLUT!"
YOU COME WITH ME, MS. CAMERON CHASE! I WILL SHOW YOU SOMETHING!

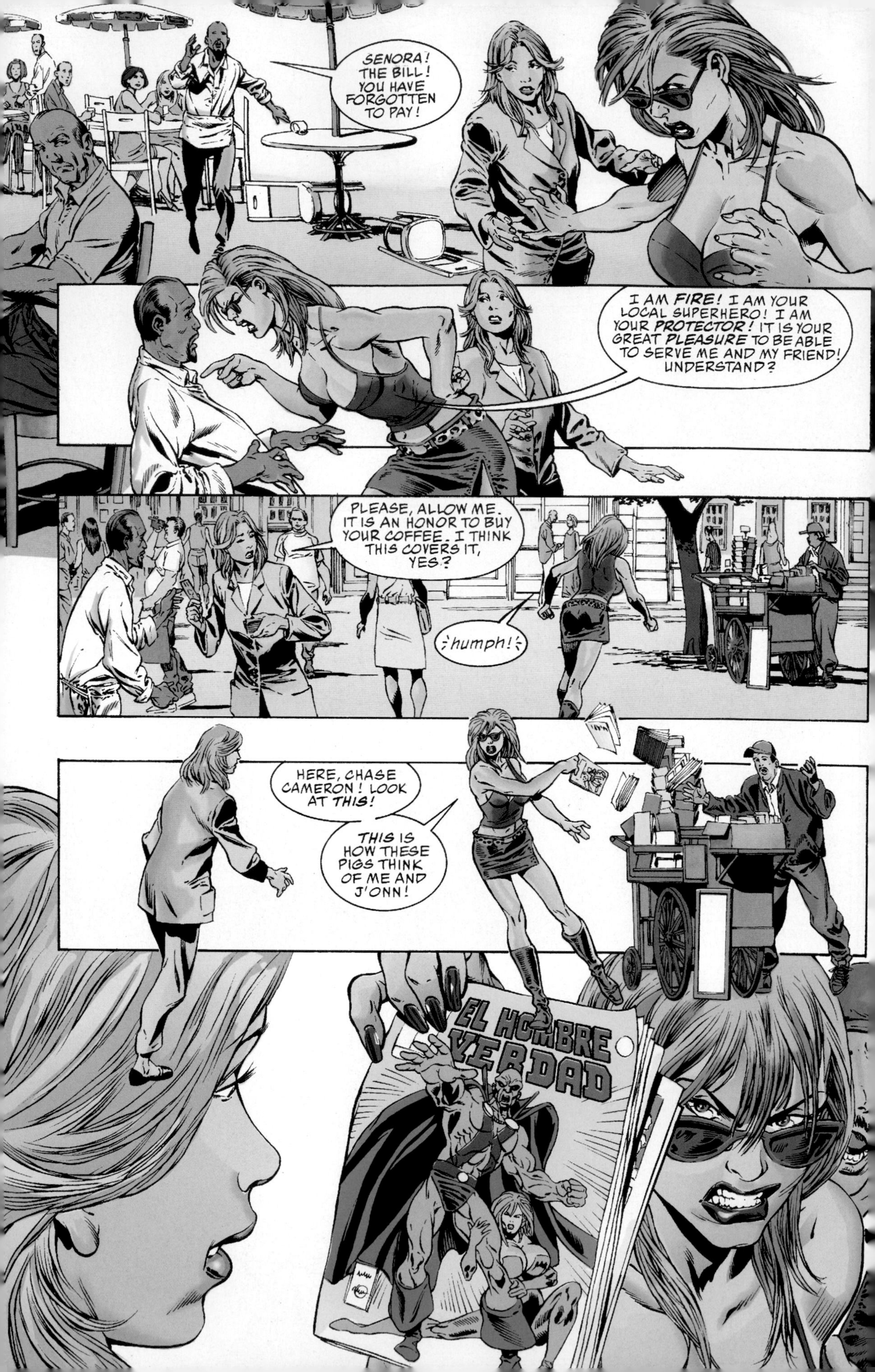
SENORA! THE BILL! YOU HAVE FORGOTTEN TO PAY!
I AM FIRE! I AM YOUR LOCAL SUPERHERO! I AM YOUR PROTECTOR! IT IS YOUR GREAT PLEASURE TO BE ABLE TO SERVE ME AND MY FRIEND! UNDERSTAND?
PLEASE, ALLOW ME. IT IS AN HONOR TO BUY YOUR COFFEE. I THINK THIS COVERS IT, YES?
humph!
HERE, CHASE CAMERON! LOOK AT THIS!
THIS IS HOW THESE PIGS THINK OF ME AND J'ONN!
EL HOMBRE VERDAD

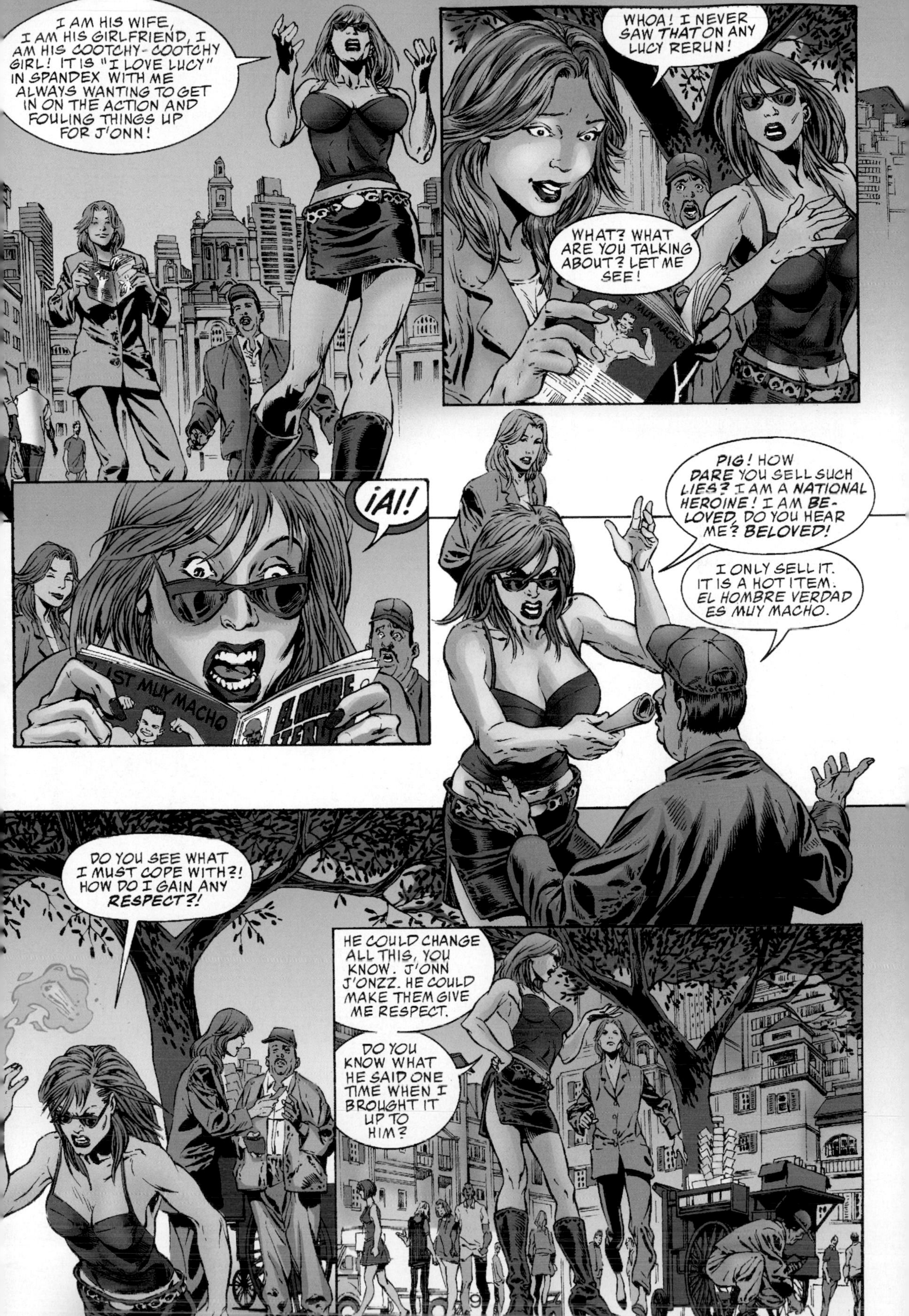
I AM HIS WIFE, I AM HIS GIRLFRIEND, I AM HIS COOTCHY-COOTCHY GIRL! IT IS "I LOVE LUCY" IN SPANDEX WITH ME ALWAYS WANTING TO GET IN ON THE ACTION AND FOULING THINGS UP FOR J'ONN!
WHOA! I NEVER SAW THAT ON ANY LUCY RERUN!
WHAT? WHAT ARE YOU TALKING ABOUT? LET ME SEE!
ST MUY MACHO
¡AI!
ST MUY MACHO
PIG! HOW DARE YOU SELL SUCH LIES? I AM A NATIONAL HEROINE! I AM BE-LOVED, DO YOU HEAR ME? BELOVED!
I ONLY SELL IT. IT IS A HOT ITEM. EL HOMBRE VERDAD ES MUY MACHO.
DO YOU SEE WHAT I MUST COPE WITH?! HOW DO I GAIN ANY RESPECT?!
HE COULD CHANGE ALL THIS, YOU KNOW. J'ONN J'ONZZ. HE COULD MAKE THEM GIVE ME RESPECT.
DO YOU KNOW WHAT HE SAID ONE TIME WHEN I BROUGHT IT UP TO HIM?

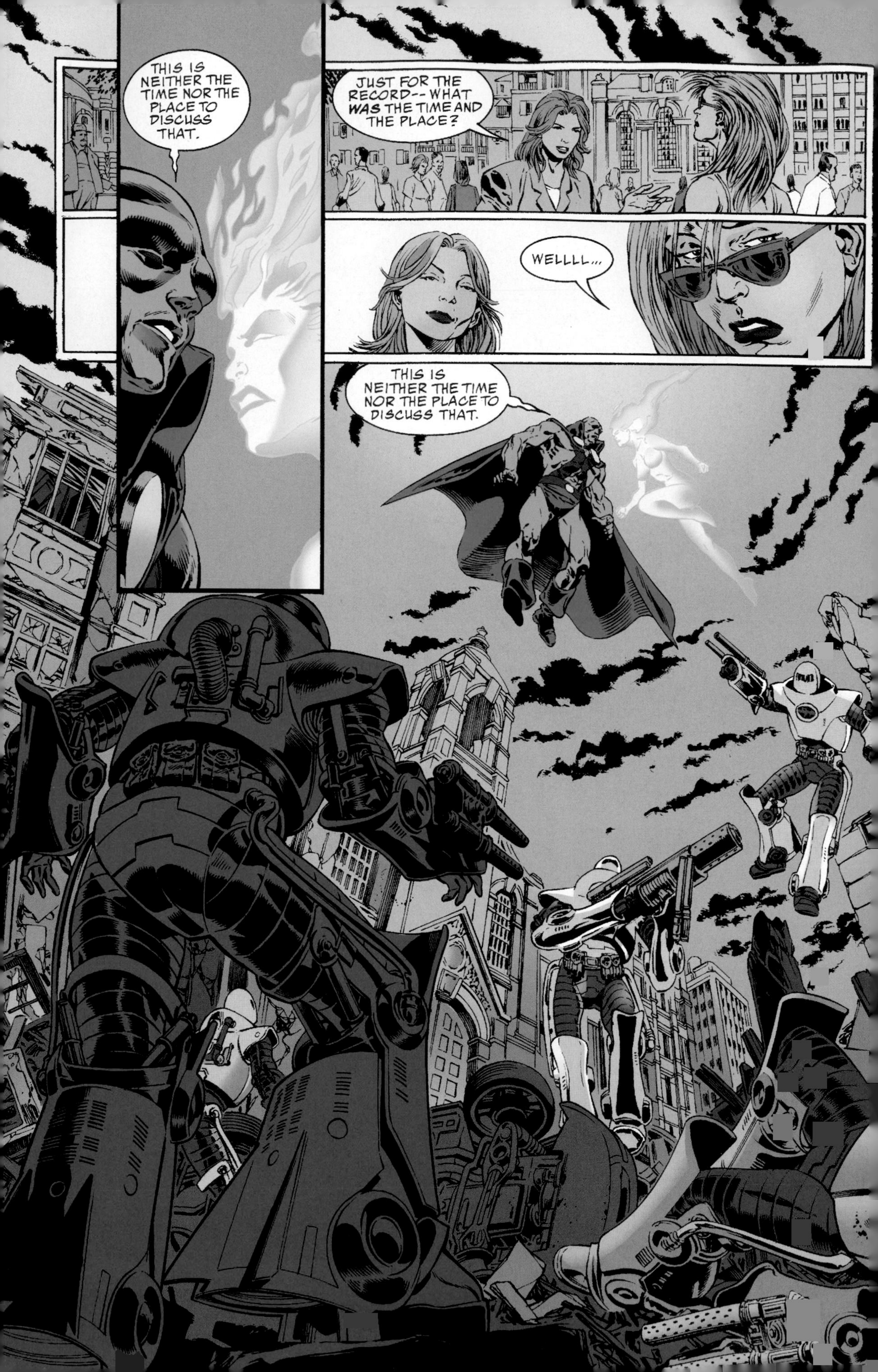
THIS IS NEITHER THE TIME NOR THE PLACE TO DISCUSS THAT.
JUST FOR THE RECORD-- WHAT WAS THE TIME AND THE PLACE?
WELLLL...
THIS IS NEITHER THE TIME NOR THE PLACE TO DISCUSS THAT.

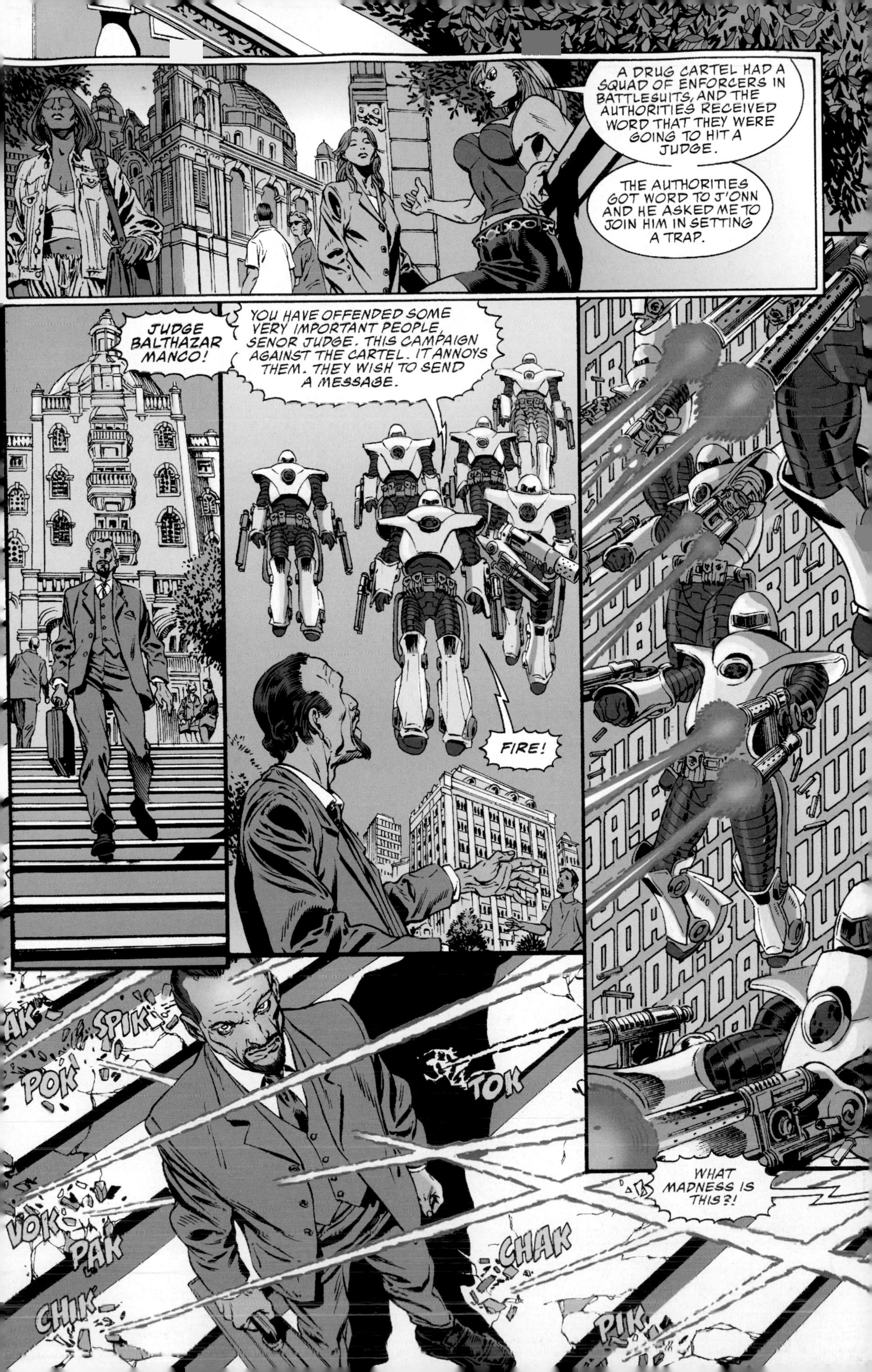
A DRUG CARTEL HAD A SQUAD OF ENFORCERS IN BATTLESUITS, AND THE AUTHORITIES RECEIVED WORD THAT THEY WERE GOING TO HIT A JUDGE.
THE AUTHORITIES GOT WORD TO J'ONN AND HE ASKED ME TO JOIN HIM IN SETTING A TRAP.
JUDGE BALTHAZAR MANCO!
YOU HAVE OFFENDED SOME VERY IMPORTANT PEOPLE, SENOR JUDGE. THIS CAMPAIGN AGAINST THE CARTEL. IT ANNOYS THEM. THEY WISH TO SEND A MESSAGE.
FIRE!
AK
SPIK
POK
TOK
VOK
PAK
CHAK
CHIK
PIK
WHAT MADNESS IS THIS?!

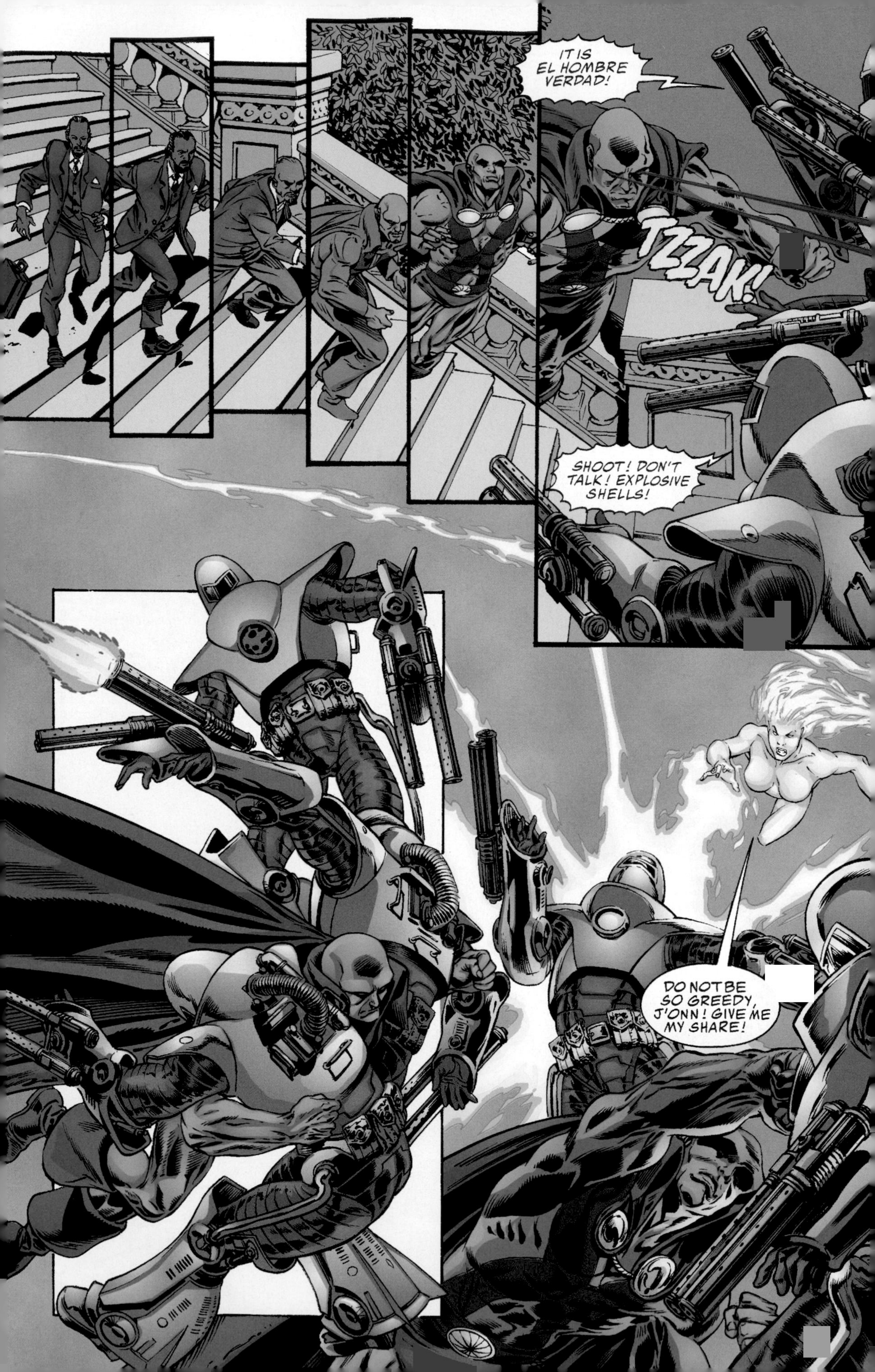
IT IS EL HOMBRE VERDAD!
TZZAK!
SHOOT! DON'T TALK! EXPLOSIVE SHELLS!
DO NOT BE SO GREEDY, J'ONN! GIVE ME MY SHARE!

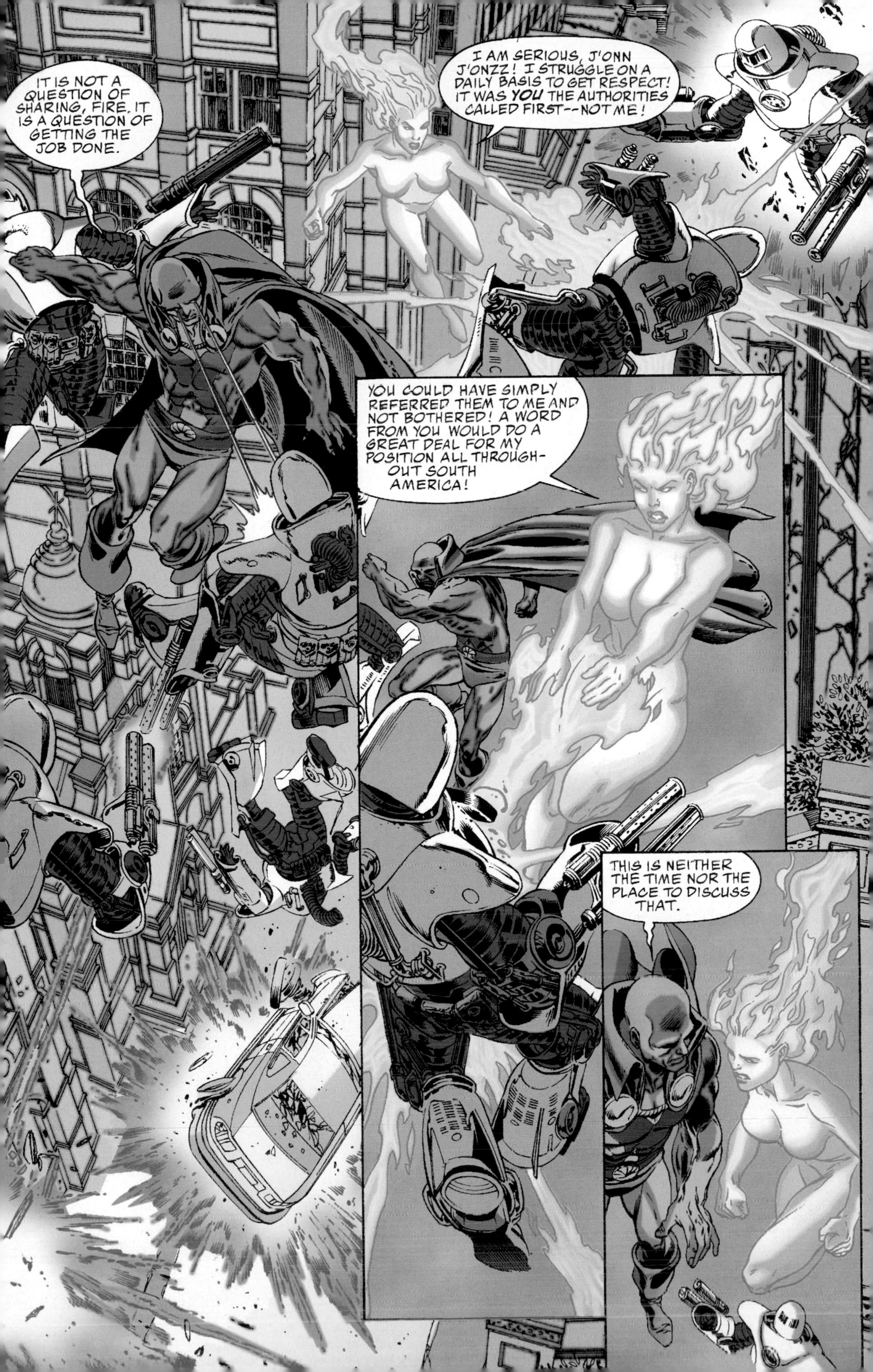
IT IS NOT A QUESTION OF SHARING, FIRE. IT IS A QUESTION OF GETTING THE JOB DONE.
I AM SERIOUS, J'ONN J'ONZZ! I STRUGGLE ON A DAILY BASIS TO GET RESPECT! IT WAS *YOU* THE AUTHORITIES CALLED FIRST--NOT ME!
YOU COULD HAVE SIMPLY REFERRED THEM TO ME AND NOT BOTHERED! A WORD FROM YOU WOULD DO A GREAT DEAL FOR MY POSITION ALL THROUGH-OUT SOUTH AMERICA!
THIS IS NEITHER THE TIME NOR THE PLACE TO DISCUSS THAT.

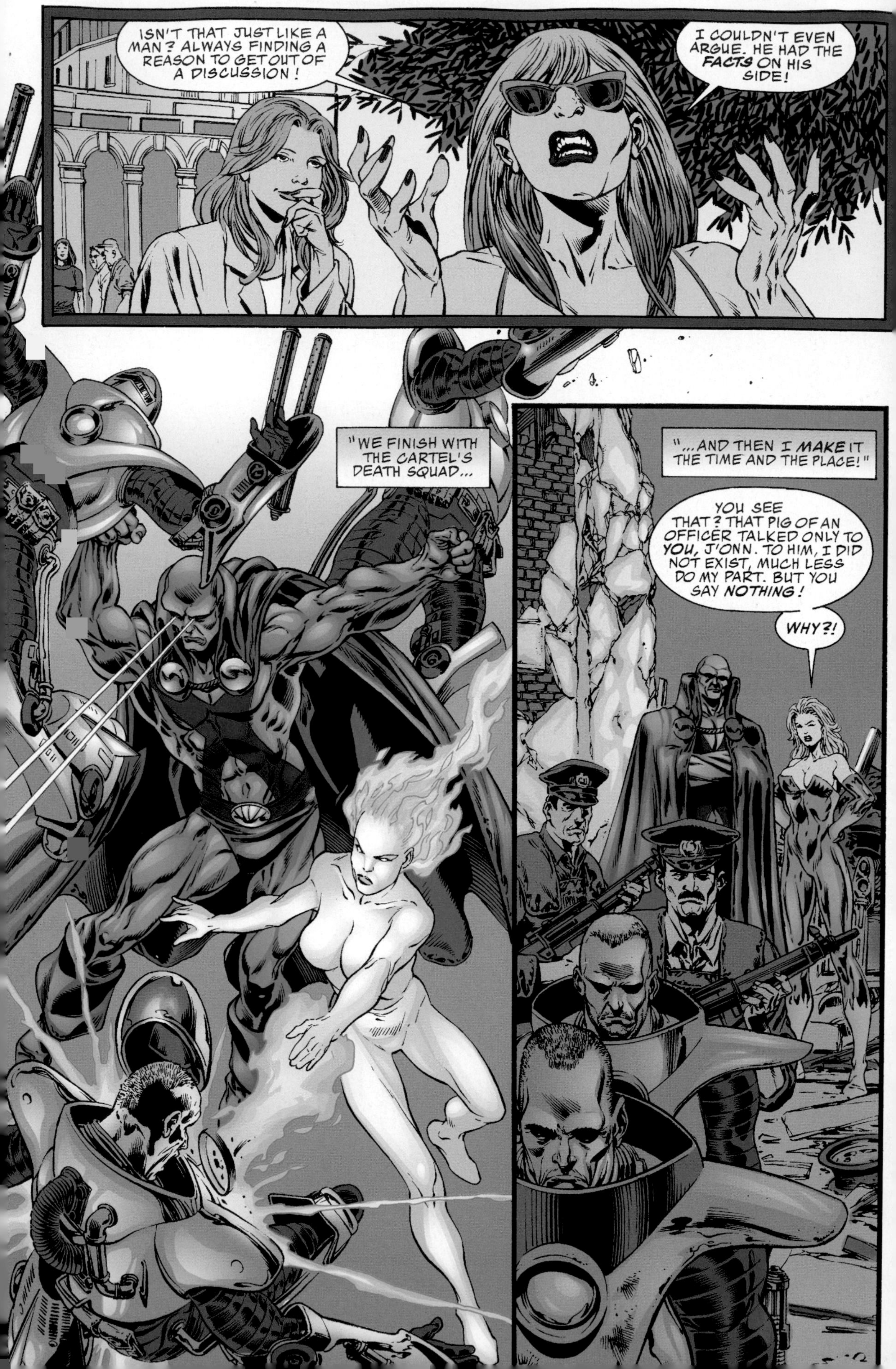
ISN'T THAT JUST LIKE A MAN? ALWAYS FINDING A REASON TO GET OUT OF A DISCUSSION!
I COULDN'T EVEN ARGUE. HE HAD THE FACTS ON HIS SIDE!
"WE FINISH WITH THE CARTEL'S DEATH SQUAD...
"...AND THEN I MAKE IT THE TIME AND THE PLACE!"
YOU SEE THAT? THAT PIG OF AN OFFICER TALKED ONLY TO YOU, J'ONN. TO HIM, I DID NOT EXIST, MUCH LESS DO MY PART. BUT YOU SAY NOTHING!
WHY?!

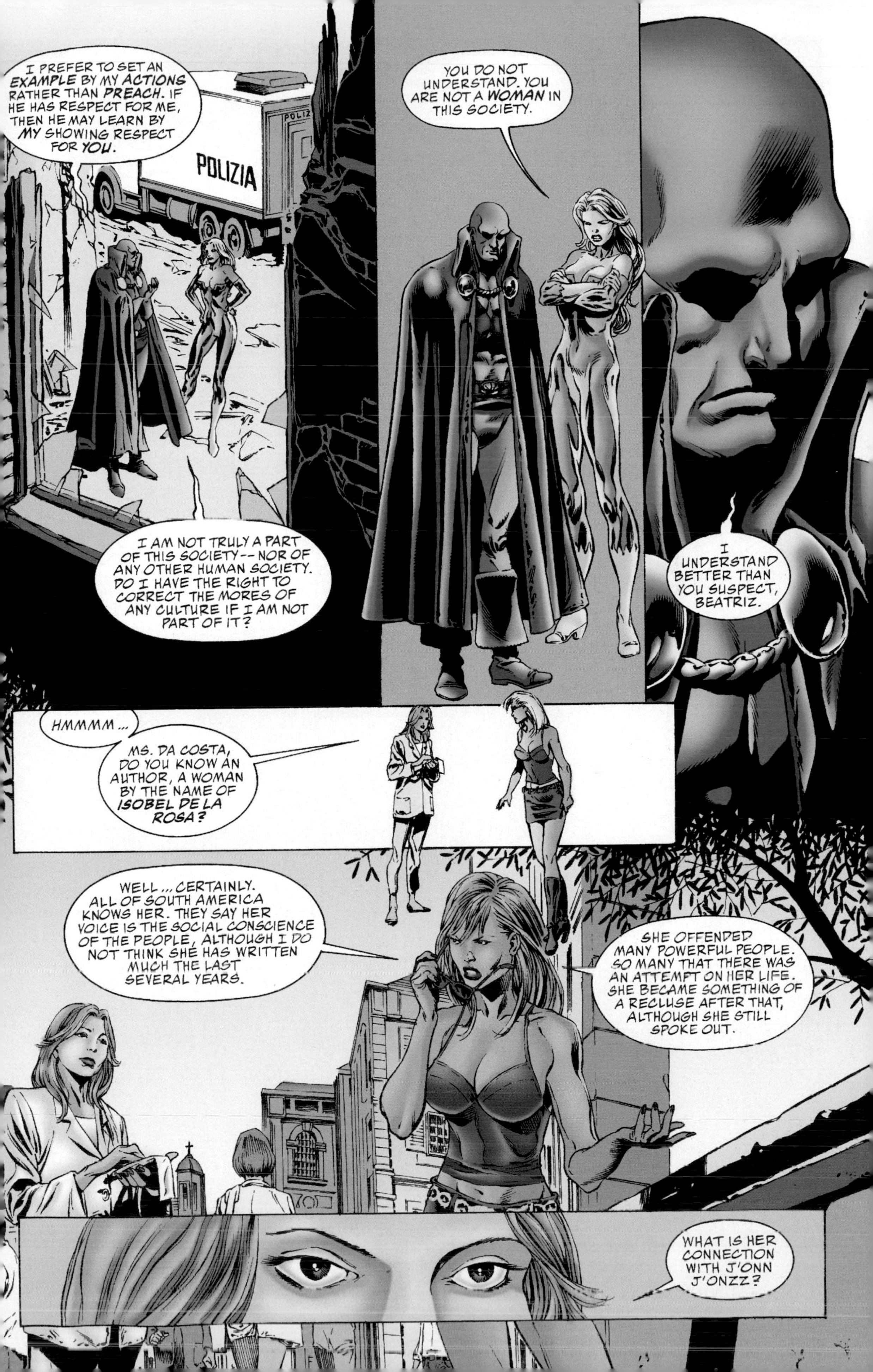

I PREFER TO SET AN EXAMPLE BY MY ACTIONS RATHER THAN PREACH. IF HE HAS RESPECT FOR ME, THEN HE MAY LEARN BY MY SHOWING RESPECT FOR YOU.
POLIZIA
POLIZIA
I AM NOT TRULY A PART OF THIS SOCIETY-- NOR OF ANY OTHER HUMAN SOCIETY. DO I HAVE THE RIGHT TO CORRECT THE MORES OF ANY CULTURE IF I AM NOT PART OF IT?
YOU DO NOT UNDERSTAND. YOU ARE NOT A WOMAN IN THIS SOCIETY.
I UNDERSTAND BETTER THAN YOU SUSPECT, BEATRIZ.
HMMMM...
MS. DA COSTA, DO YOU KNOW AN AUTHOR, A WOMAN BY THE NAME OF ISOBEL DE LA ROSA?
WELL ... CERTAINLY. ALL OF SOUTH AMERICA KNOWS HER. THEY SAY HER VOICE IS THE SOCIAL CONSCIENCE OF THE PEOPLE, ALTHOUGH I DO NOT THINK SHE HAS WRITTEN MUCH THE LAST SEVERAL YEARS.
SHE OFFENDED MANY POWERFUL PEOPLE. SO MANY THAT THERE WAS AN ATTEMPT ON HER LIFE. SHE BECAME SOMETHING OF A RECLUSE AFTER THAT, ALTHOUGH SHE STILL SPOKE OUT.
WHAT IS HER CONNECTION WITH J'ONN J'ONZZ?

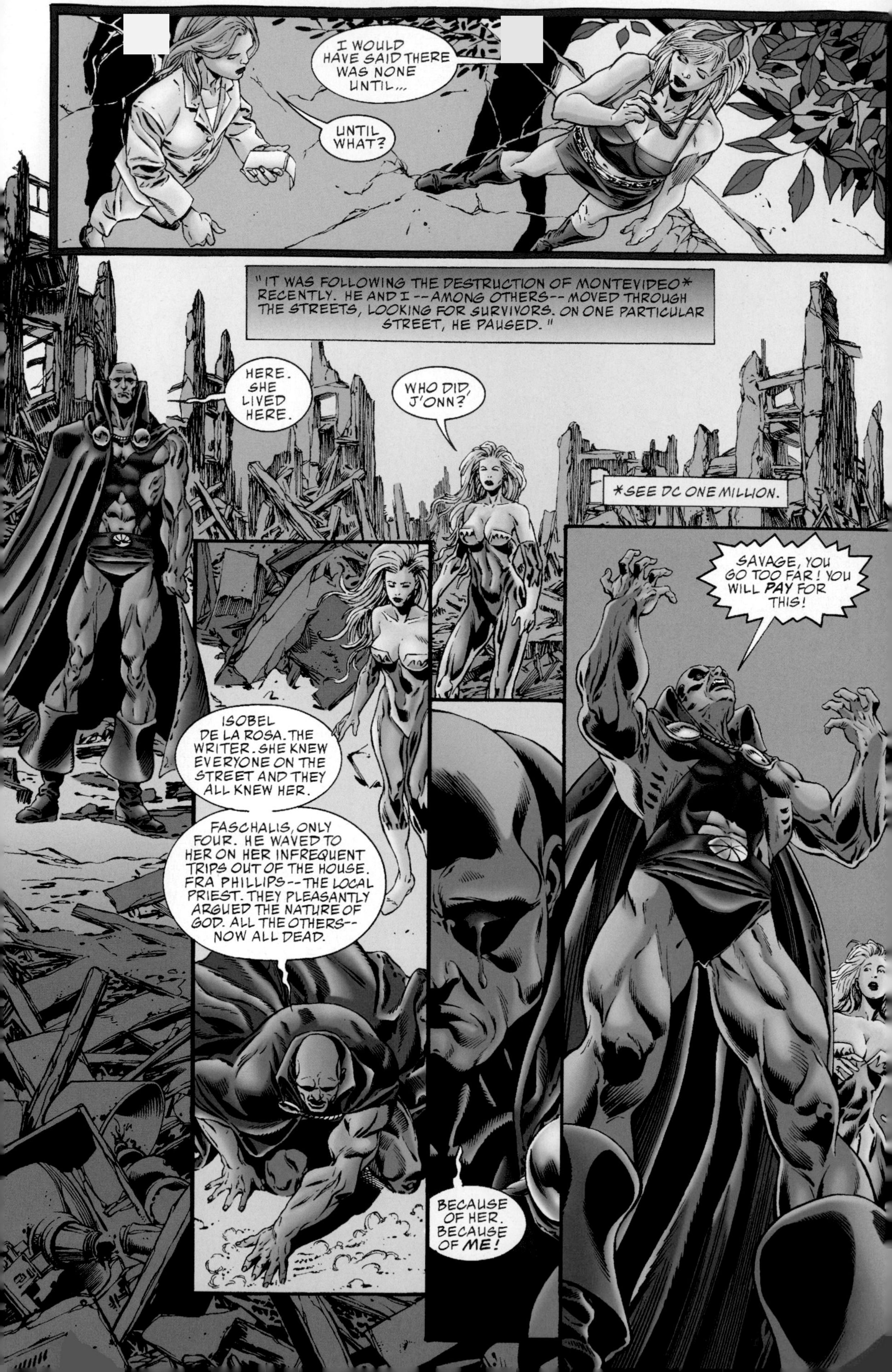
I WOULD HAVE SAID THERE WAS NONE UNTIL...
UNTIL WHAT?
"IT WAS FOLLOWING THE DESTRUCTION OF MONTEVIDEO* RECENTLY. HE AND I --AMONG OTHERS-- MOVED THROUGH THE STREETS, LOOKING FOR SURVIVORS. ON ONE PARTICULAR STREET, HE PAUSED."
HERE. SHE LIVED HERE.
WHO DID, J'ONN?
*SEE DC ONE MILLION.
ISOBEL DE LA ROSA. THE WRITER. SHE KNEW EVERYONE ON THE STREET AND THEY ALL KNEW HER.
FASCHALIS, ONLY FOUR. HE WAVED TO HER ON HER INFREQUENT TRIPS OUT OF THE HOUSE. FRA PHILLIPS--THE LOCAL PRIEST. THEY PLEASANTLY ARGUED THE NATURE OF GOD. ALL THE OTHERS-- NOW ALL DEAD.
BECAUSE OF HER. BECAUSE OF ME!
SAVAGE, YOU GO TOO FAR! YOU WILL PAY FOR THIS!

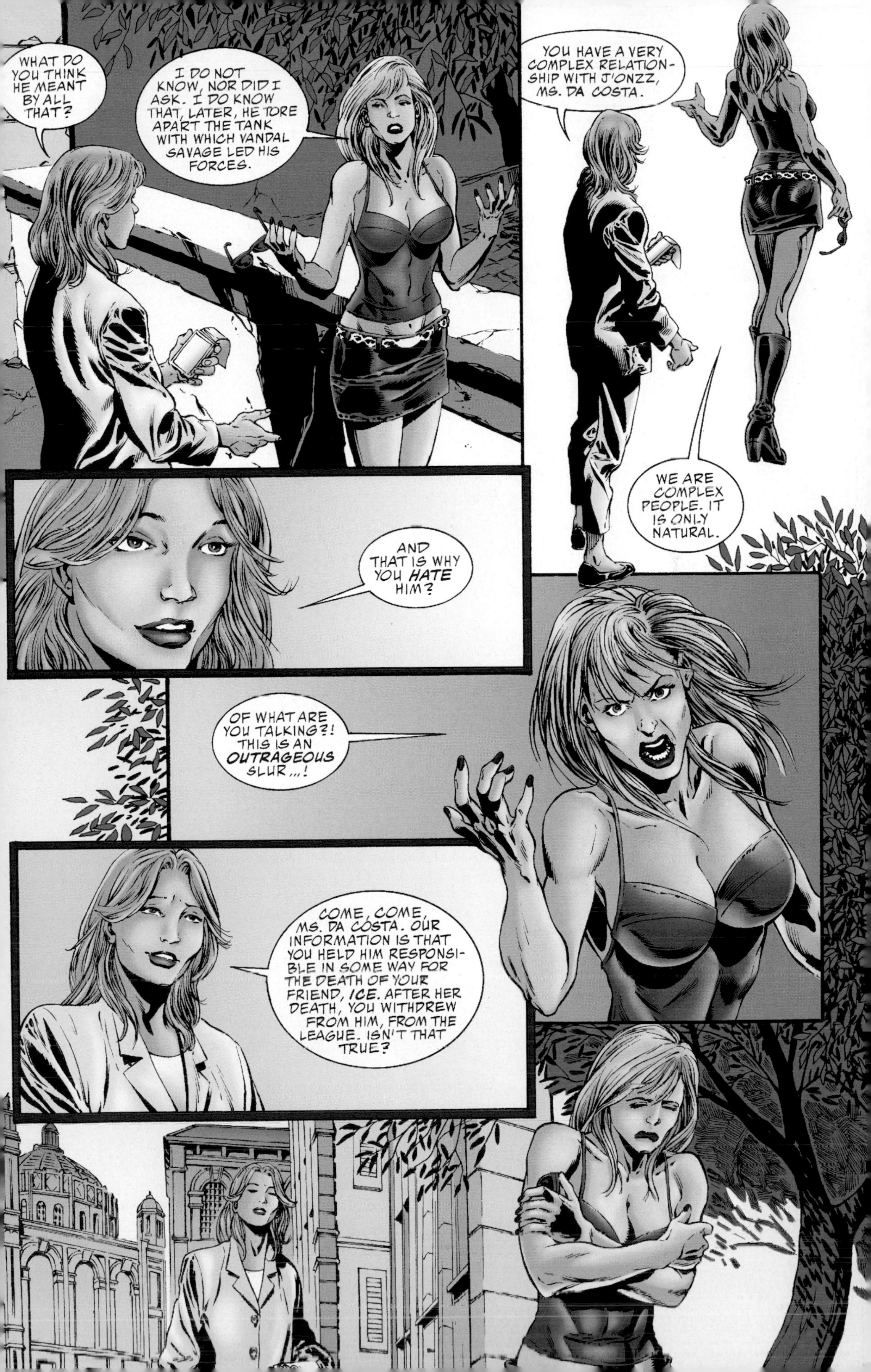
WHAT DO YOU THINK HE MEANT BY ALL THAT?
I DO NOT KNOW, NOR DID I ASK. I DO KNOW THAT, LATER, HE TORE APART THE TANK WITH WHICH VANDAL SAVAGE LED HIS FORCES.
YOU HAVE A VERY COMPLEX RELATIONSHIP WITH J'ONZZ, MS. DA COSTA.
WE ARE COMPLEX PEOPLE. IT IS ONLY NATURAL.
AND THAT IS WHY YOU HATE HIM?
OF WHAT ARE YOU TALKING?! THIS IS AN OUTRAGEOUS SLUR...!
COME, COME, MS. DA COSTA. OUR INFORMATION IS THAT YOU HELD HIM RESPONSIBLE IN SOME WAY FOR THE DEATH OF YOUR FRIEND, ICE. AFTER HER DEATH, YOU WITHDREW FROM HIM, FROM THE LEAGUE. ISN'T THAT TRUE?

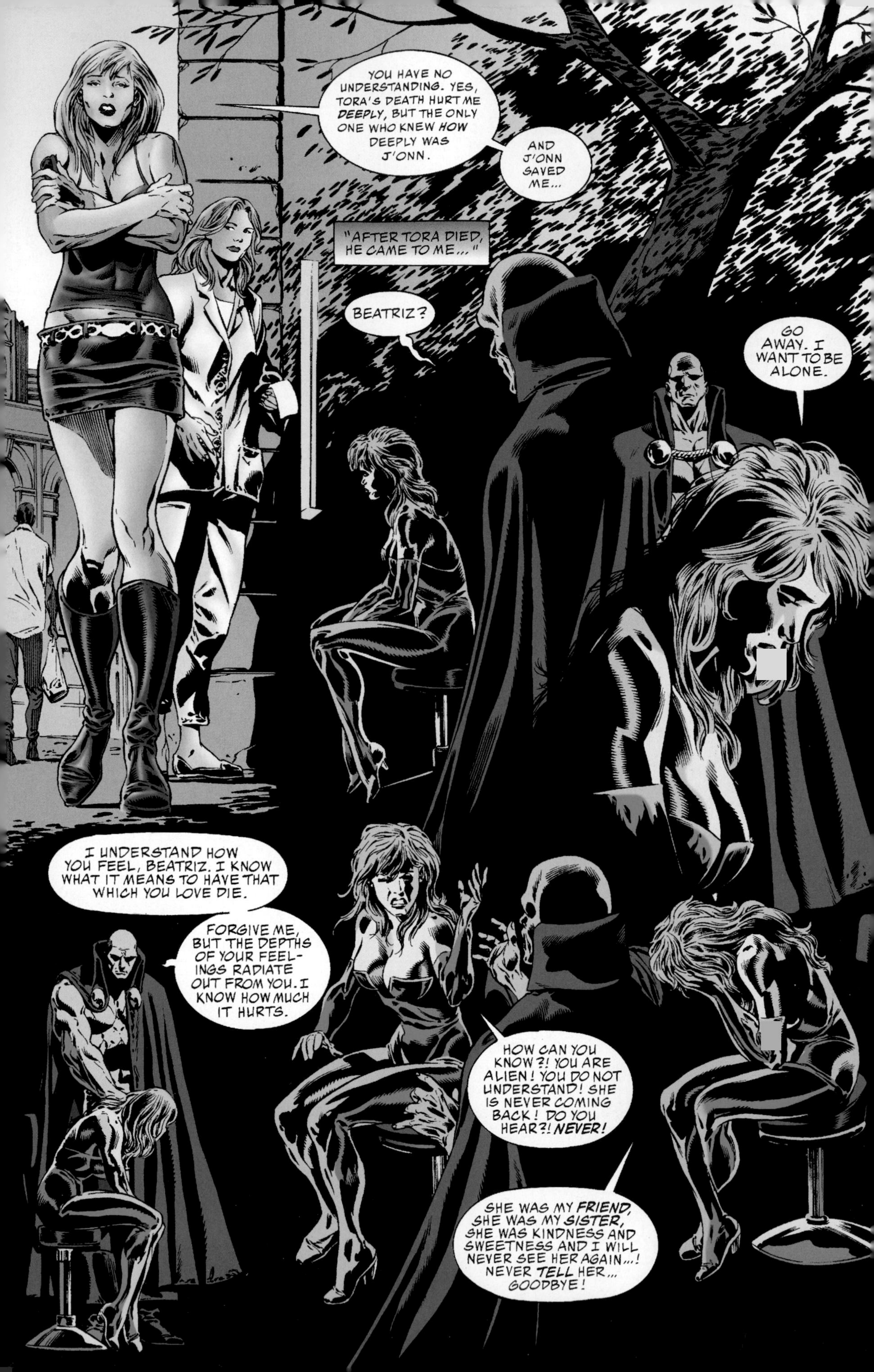
YOU HAVE NO UNDERSTANDING. YES, TORA'S DEATH HURT ME DEEPLY, BUT THE ONLY ONE WHO KNEW HOW DEEPLY WAS J'ONN.
AND J'ONN SAVED ME...
"AFTER TORA DIED, HE CAME TO ME..."
BEATRIZ?
GO AWAY. I WANT TO BE ALONE.
I UNDERSTAND HOW YOU FEEL, BEATRIZ. I KNOW WHAT IT MEANS TO HAVE THAT WHICH YOU LOVE DIE.
FORGIVE ME, BUT THE DEPTHS OF YOUR FEEL-INGS RADIATE OUT FROM YOU. I KNOW HOW MUCH IT HURTS.
HOW CAN YOU KNOW?! YOU ARE ALIEN! YOU DO NOT UNDERSTAND! SHE IS NEVER COMING BACK! DO YOU HEAR?! NEVER!
SHE WAS MY FRIEND, SHE WAS MY SISTER, SHE WAS KINDNESS AND SWEETNESS AND I WILL NEVER SEE HER AGAIN...! NEVER TELL HER... GOODBYE!

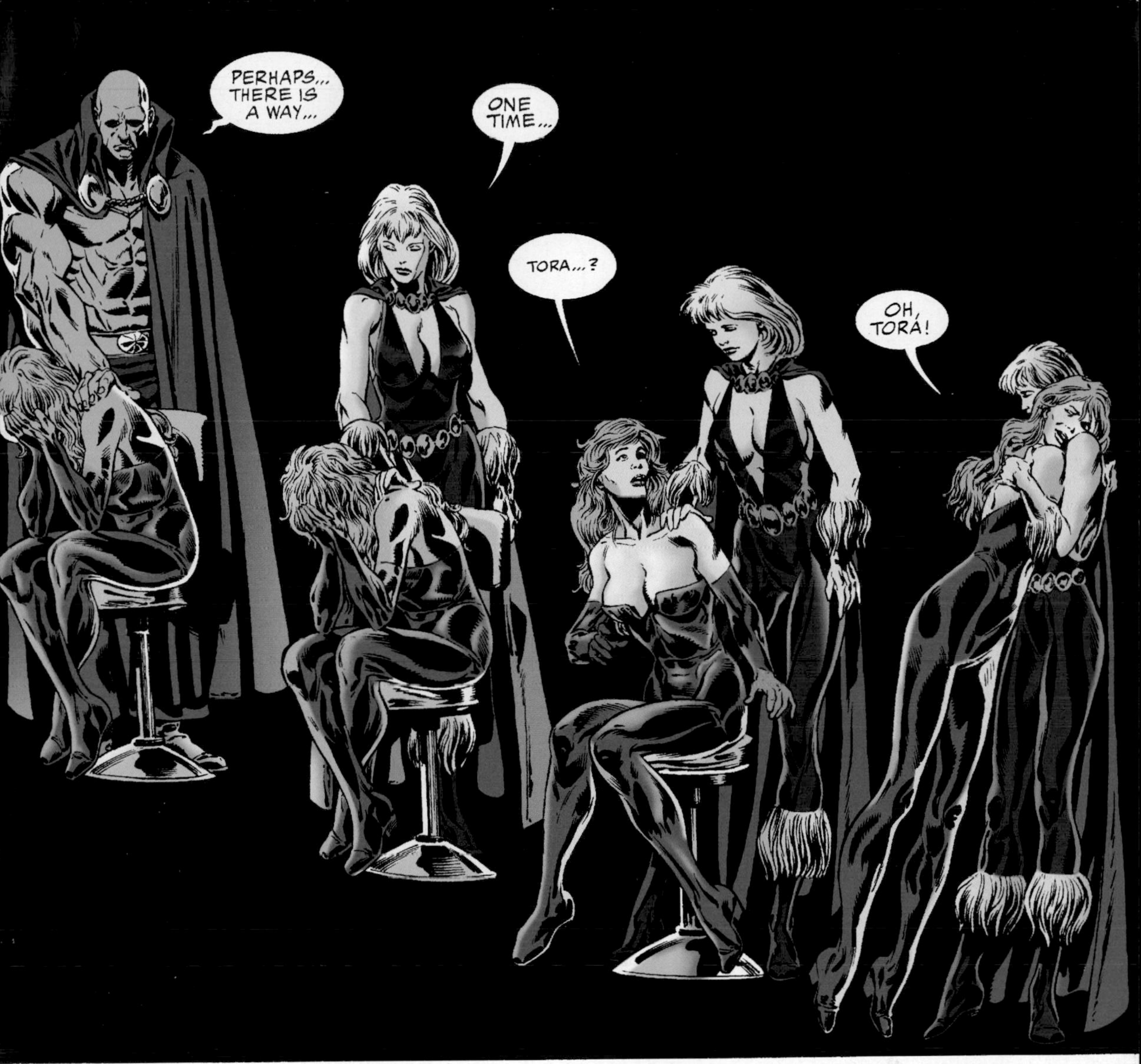
PERHAPS... THERE IS A WAY...
ONE TIME...
TORA...?
OH, TORA!

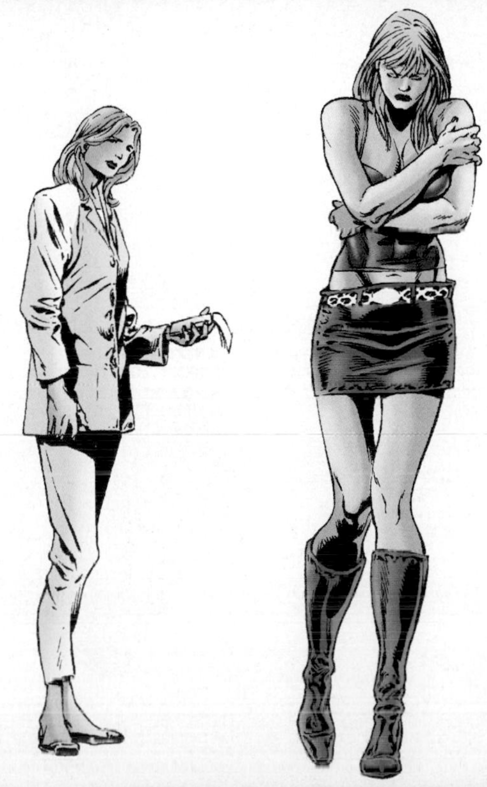

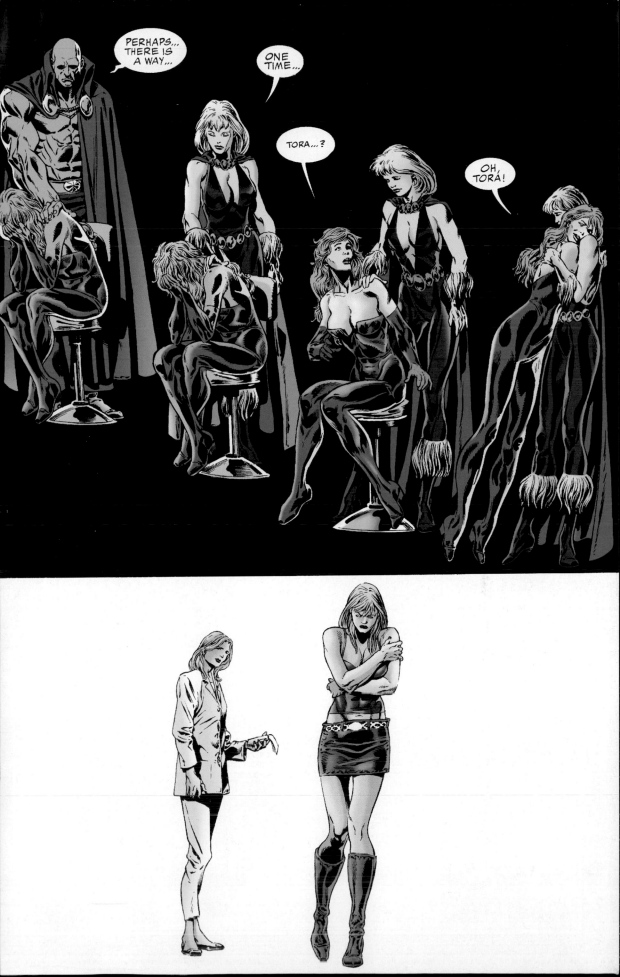

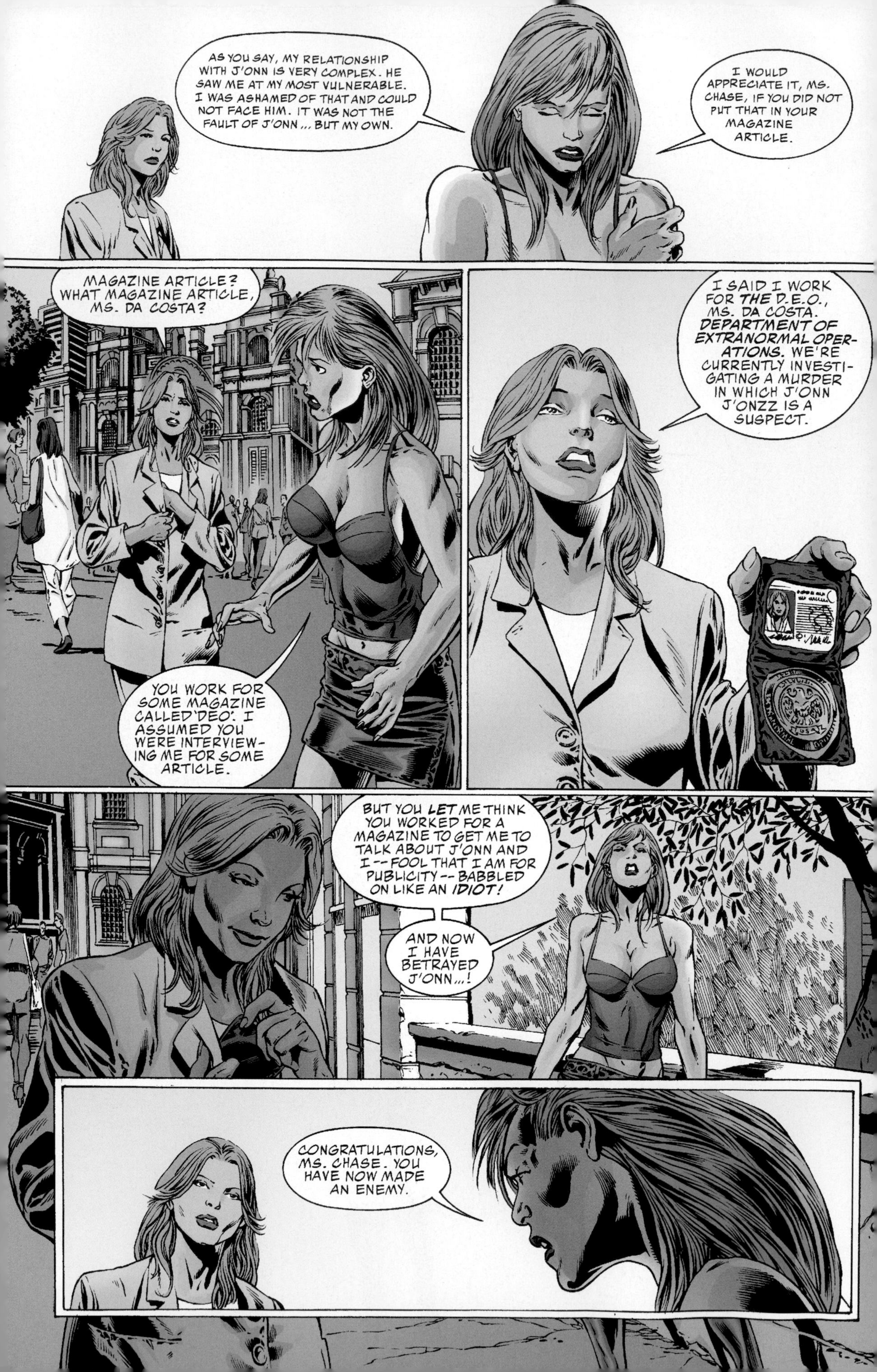
AS YOU SAY, MY RELATIONSHIP WITH J'ONN IS VERY COMPLEX. HE SAW ME AT MY MOST VULNERABLE. I WAS ASHAMED OF THAT AND COULD NOT FACE HIM. IT WAS NOT THE FAULT OF J'ONN ... BUT MY OWN.
I WOULD APPRECIATE IT, MS. CHASE, IF YOU DID NOT PUT THAT IN YOUR MAGAZINE ARTICLE.
MAGAZINE ARTICLE? WHAT MAGAZINE ARTICLE, MS. DA COSTA?
YOU WORK FOR SOME MAGAZINE CALLED 'DEO'. I ASSUMED YOU WERE INTERVIEWING ME FOR SOME ARTICLE.
I SAID I WORK FOR THE D.E.O., MS. DA COSTA. DEPARTMENT OF EXTRANORMAL OPERATIONS. WE'RE CURRENTLY INVESTIGATING A MURDER IN WHICH J'ONN J'ONZZ IS A SUSPECT.
BUT YOU LET ME THINK YOU WORKED FOR A MAGAZINE TO GET ME TO TALK ABOUT J'ONN AND I -- FOOL THAT I AM FOR PUBLICITY -- BABBLED ON LIKE AN IDIOT!
AND NOW I HAVE BETRAYED J'ONN...!
CONGRATULATIONS, MS. CHASE. YOU HAVE NOW MADE AN ENEMY.

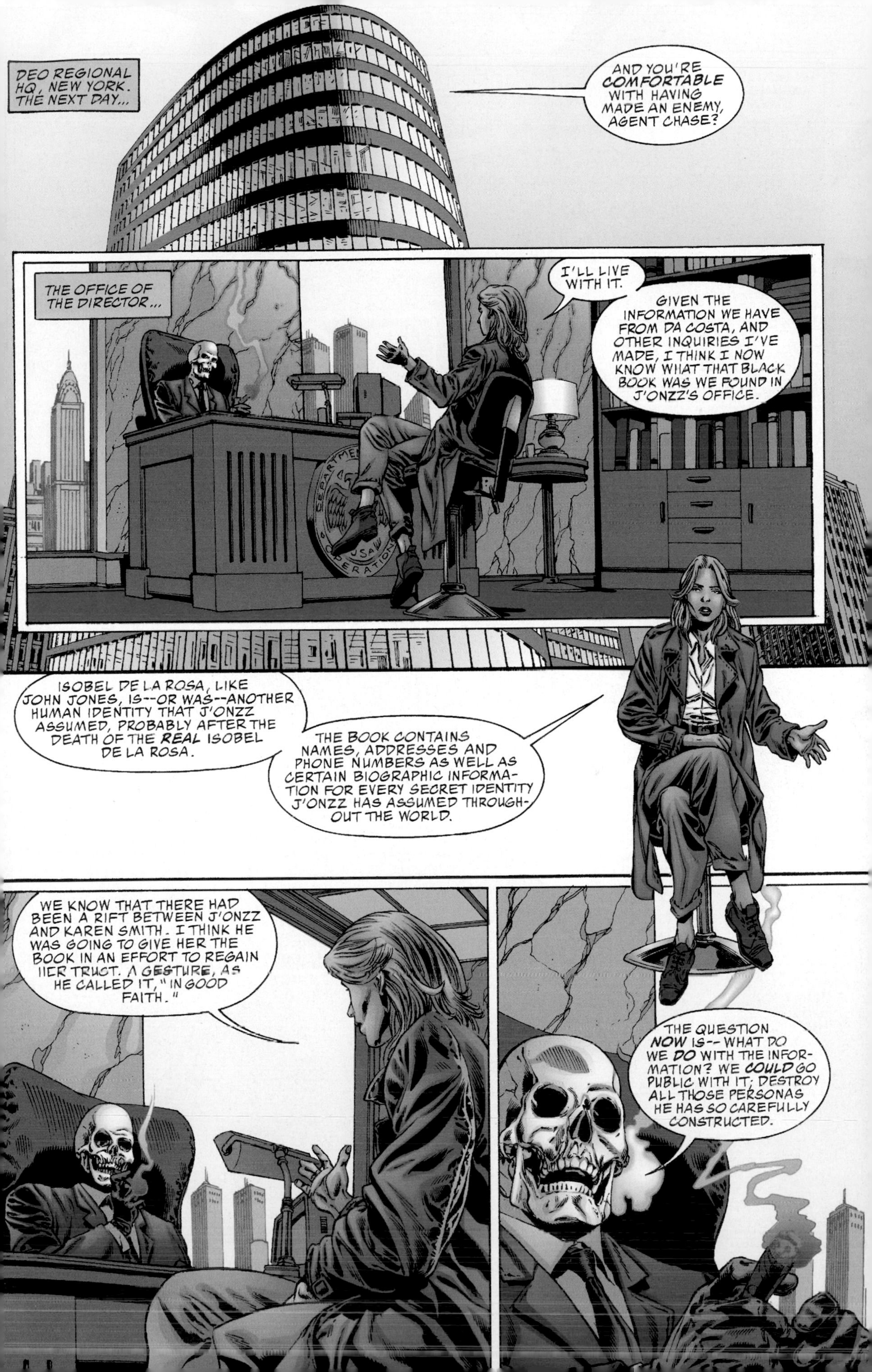
DEO REGIONAL HQ, NEW YORK. THE NEXT DAY...
AND YOU'RE COMFORTABLE WITH HAVING MADE AN ENEMY, AGENT CHASE?
THE OFFICE OF THE DIRECTOR...
I'LL LIVE WITH IT.
GIVEN THE INFORMATION WE HAVE FROM DA COSTA, AND OTHER INQUIRIES I'VE MADE, I THINK I NOW KNOW WHAT THAT BLACK BOOK WAS WE FOUND IN J'ONZZ'S OFFICE.
DEPARTMENT OF EXTRANORMAL OPERATIONS USA
ISOBEL DE LA ROSA, LIKE JOHN JONES, IS--OR WAS--ANOTHER HUMAN IDENTITY THAT J'ONZZ ASSUMED, PROBABLY AFTER THE DEATH OF THE REAL ISOBEL DE LA ROSA.
THE BOOK CONTAINS NAMES, ADDRESSES AND PHONE NUMBERS AS WELL AS CERTAIN BIOGRAPHIC INFORMATION FOR EVERY SECRET IDENTITY J'ONZZ HAS ASSUMED THROUGHOUT THE WORLD.
WE KNOW THAT THERE HAD BEEN A RIFT BETWEEN J'ONZZ AND KAREN SMITH. I THINK HE WAS GOING TO GIVE HER THE BOOK IN AN EFFORT TO REGAIN HER TRUST. A GESTURE, AS HE CALLED IT, "IN GOOD FAITH."
THE QUESTION NOW IS-- WHAT DO WE DO WITH THE INFORMATION? WE COULD GO PUBLIC WITH IT; DESTROY ALL THOSE PERSONAS HE HAS SO CAREFULLY CONSTRUCTED.

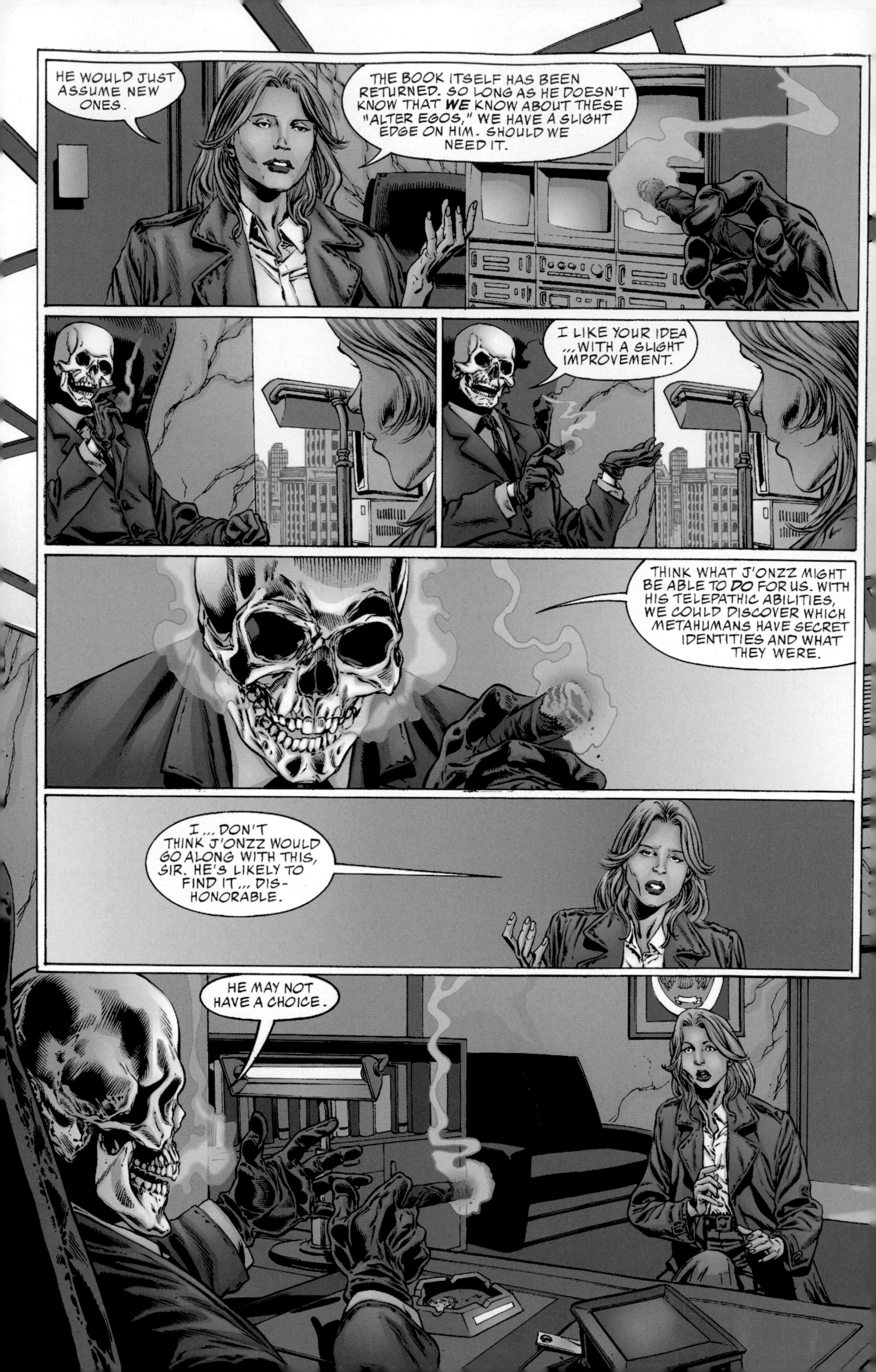
HE WOULD JUST ASSUME NEW ONES.
THE BOOK ITSELF HAS BEEN RETURNED. SO LONG AS HE DOESN'T KNOW THAT WE KNOW ABOUT THESE "ALTER EGOS," WE HAVE A SLIGHT EDGE ON HIM. SHOULD WE NEED IT.
I LIKE YOUR IDEA ...WITH A SLIGHT IMPROVEMENT.
THINK WHAT J'ONZZ MIGHT BE ABLE TO DO FOR US. WITH HIS TELEPATHIC ABILITIES, WE COULD DISCOVER WHICH METAHUMANS HAVE SECRET IDENTITIES AND WHAT THEY WERE.
I... DON'T THINK J'ONZZ WOULD GO ALONG WITH THIS, SIR. HE'S LIKELY TO FIND IT... DIS-HONORABLE.
HE MAY NOT HAVE A CHOICE.

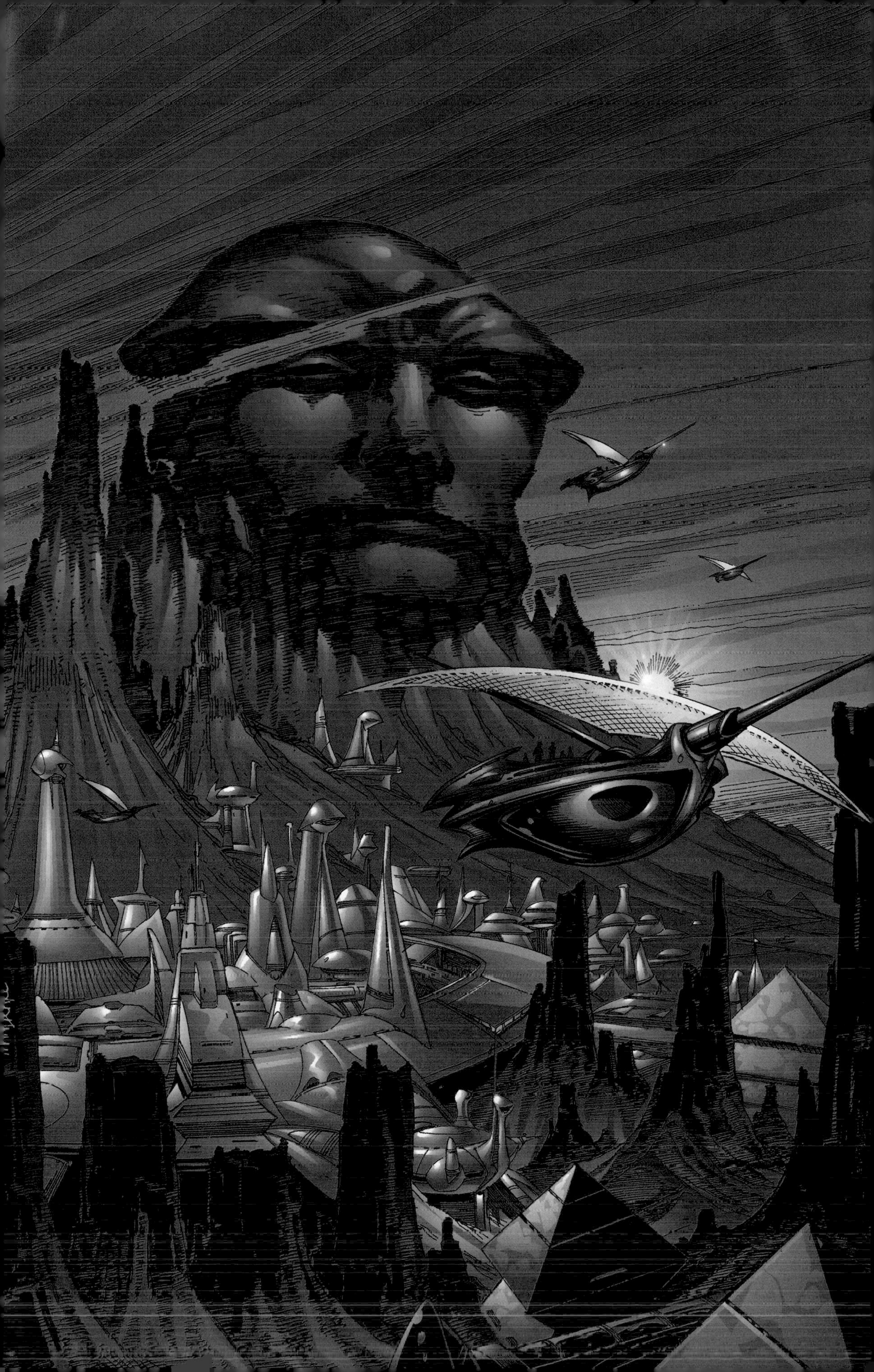

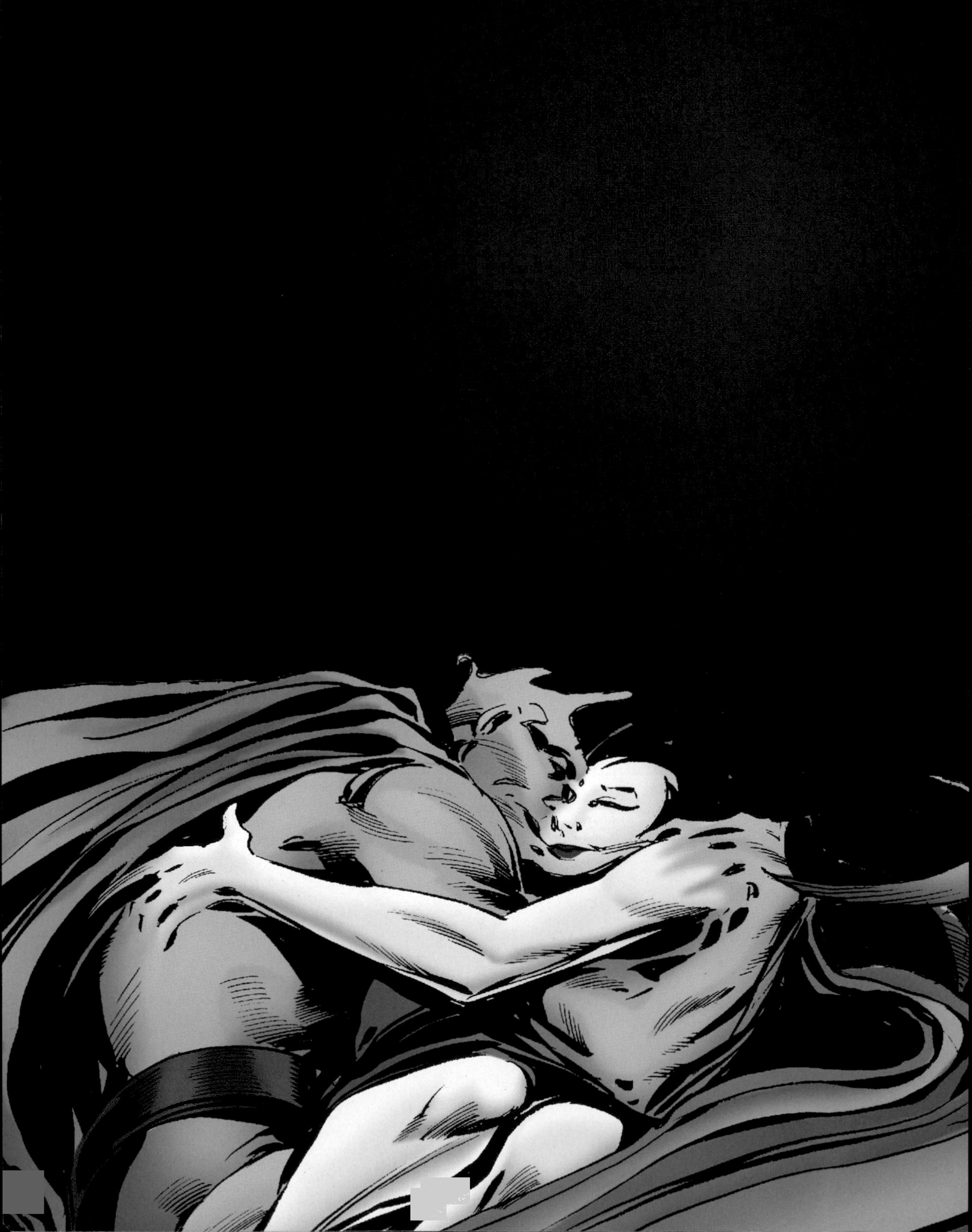

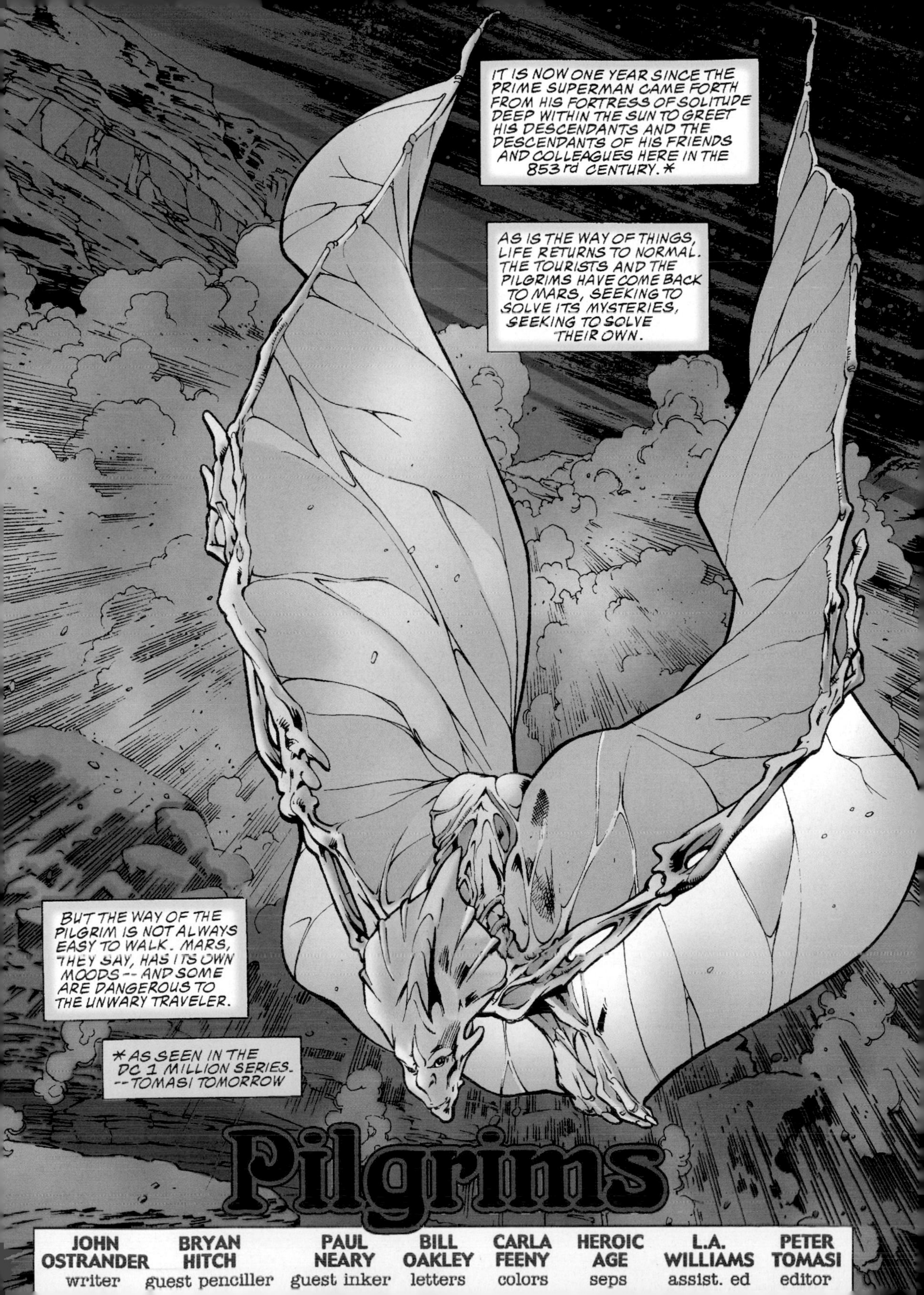
IT IS NOW ONE YEAR SINCE THE PRIME SUPERMAN CAME FORTH FROM HIS FORTRESS OF SOLITUDE DEEP WITHIN THE SUN TO GREET HIS DESCENDANTS AND THE DESCENDANTS OF HIS FRIENDS AND COLLEAGUES HERE IN THE 853rd CENTURY.*
AS IS THE WAY OF THINGS, LIFE RETURNS TO NORMAL. THE TOURISTS AND THE PILGRIMS HAVE COME BACK TO MARS, SEEKING TO SOLVE ITS MYSTERIES, SEEKING TO SOLVE THEIR OWN.
BUT THE WAY OF THE PILGRIM IS NOT ALWAYS EASY TO WALK. MARS, THEY SAY, HAS ITS OWN MOODS -- AND SOME ARE DANGEROUS TO THE UNWARY TRAVELER.
*AS SEEN IN THE DC 1 MILLION SERIES. --TOMASI TOMORROW
Pilgrims
JOHN OSTRANDER writer
BRYAN HITCH guest penciller
PAUL NEARY guest inker
BILL OAKLEY letters
CARLA FEENY colors
HEROIC AGE seps
L.A. WILLIAMS assist. ed
PETER TOMASI editor

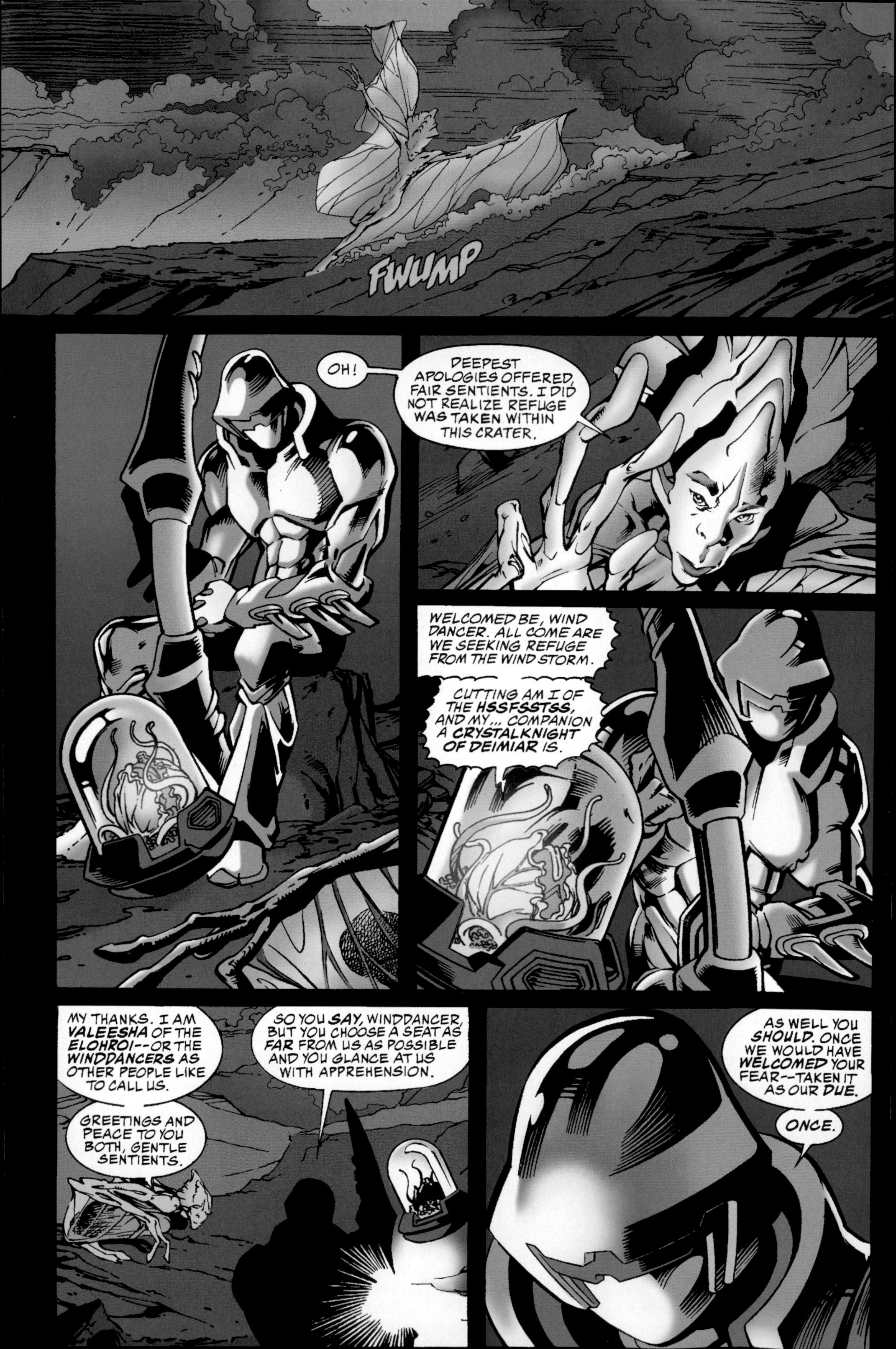
FWUMP
OH!
DEEPEST APOLOGIES OFFERED, FAIR SENTIENTS. I DID NOT REALIZE REFUGE WAS TAKEN WITHIN THIS CRATER.
WELCOMED BE, WIND DANCER. ALL COME ARE WE SEEKING REFUGE FROM THE WIND STORM.
CUTTING AM I OF THE HSSFSSTSS, AND MY... COMPANION A CRYSTALKNIGHT OF DEIMIAR IS.
MY THANKS. I AM VALEESHA OF THE ELOHROI--OR THE WINDDANCERS AS OTHER PEOPLE LIKE TO CALL US.
GREETINGS AND PEACE TO YOU BOTH, GENTLE SENTIENTS.
SO YOU SAY, WINDDANCER, BUT YOU CHOOSE A SEAT AS FAR FROM US AS POSSIBLE AND YOU GLANCE AT US WITH APPREHENSION.
AS WELL YOU SHOULD. ONCE WE WOULD HAVE WELCOMED YOUR FEAR--TAKEN IT AS OUR DUE.
ONCE.

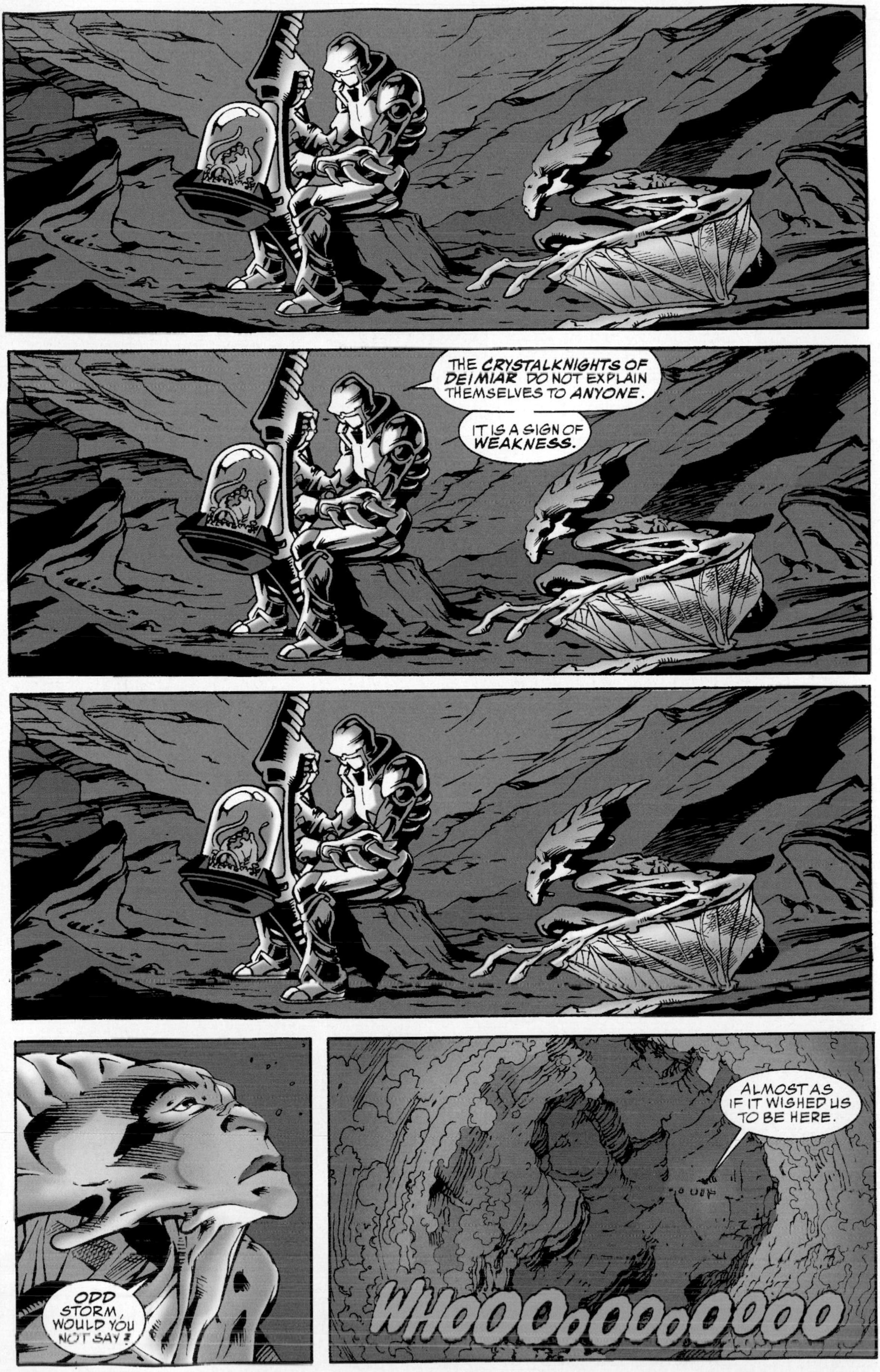
THE CRYSTALKNIGHTS OF DEIMIAR DO NOT EXPLAIN THEMSELVES TO ANYONE.
IT IS A SIGN OF WEAKNESS.
ODD STORM, WOULD YOU NOT SAY?
ALMOST AS IF IT WISHED US TO BE HERE.
WHOOOOoOOOoOOOO

THE STORIES THEY TELL OF THIS PLANET ARE SO STRANGE. THE LEGENDS SAY THAT THE GREAT GREEN MAN—THE J'ONN J'ONZZ—THE MANHUNTER OF MARS—THEY SAY HIS SPIRIT STILL IS HERE.

THIS IS SO, MAYBE? DO YOU *KNOW* OF THE J'ONN J'ONZZ?

KNOW OF HIM DO WE. ANCIENT ALSO OUR TALES. DEEP THE ROOTS OF MEMORY. TALES WE TELL OF *TWO* GREEN MEN—ONE OF OUR CREATION, ONE OF OUR SALVATION.

"TALE BEGINS BEFORE DO WE. SOIL WE CALLED HOME ISOLATED WAS AND OF GREAT PROMISE BUT YOUNG AND, IN PARTS, HOSTILE."

"BEFORE WE KNEW OURSELVES OR THE PLANET OR ANYTHING BEYOND THE CYCLES OF SUN AND RAIN AND NIGHT AND COLD THIS WAS."

"THEN SOMETHING OUR-SELF INVADED AND STARTED TO GROW!"

SNAP KROM POP

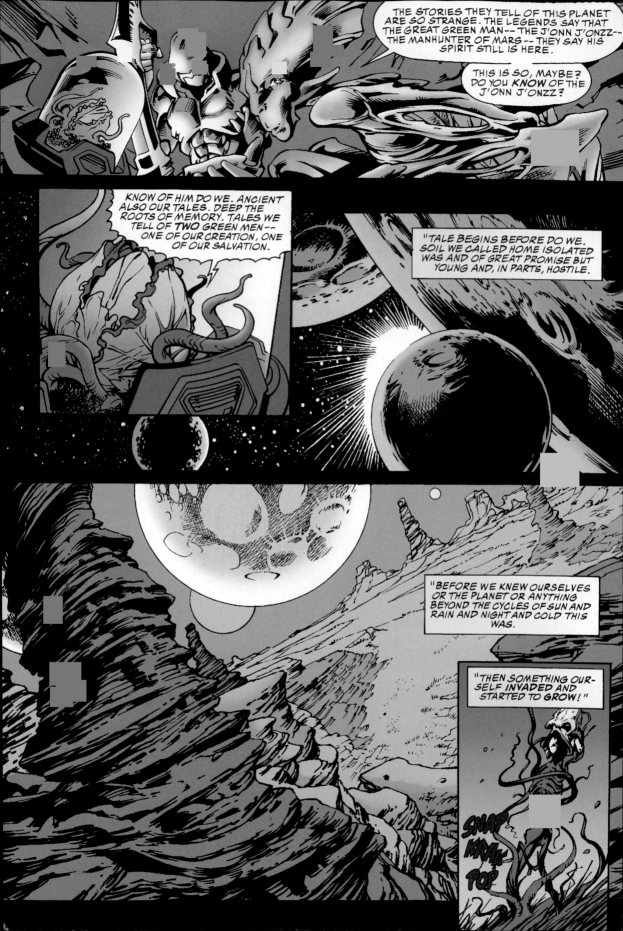

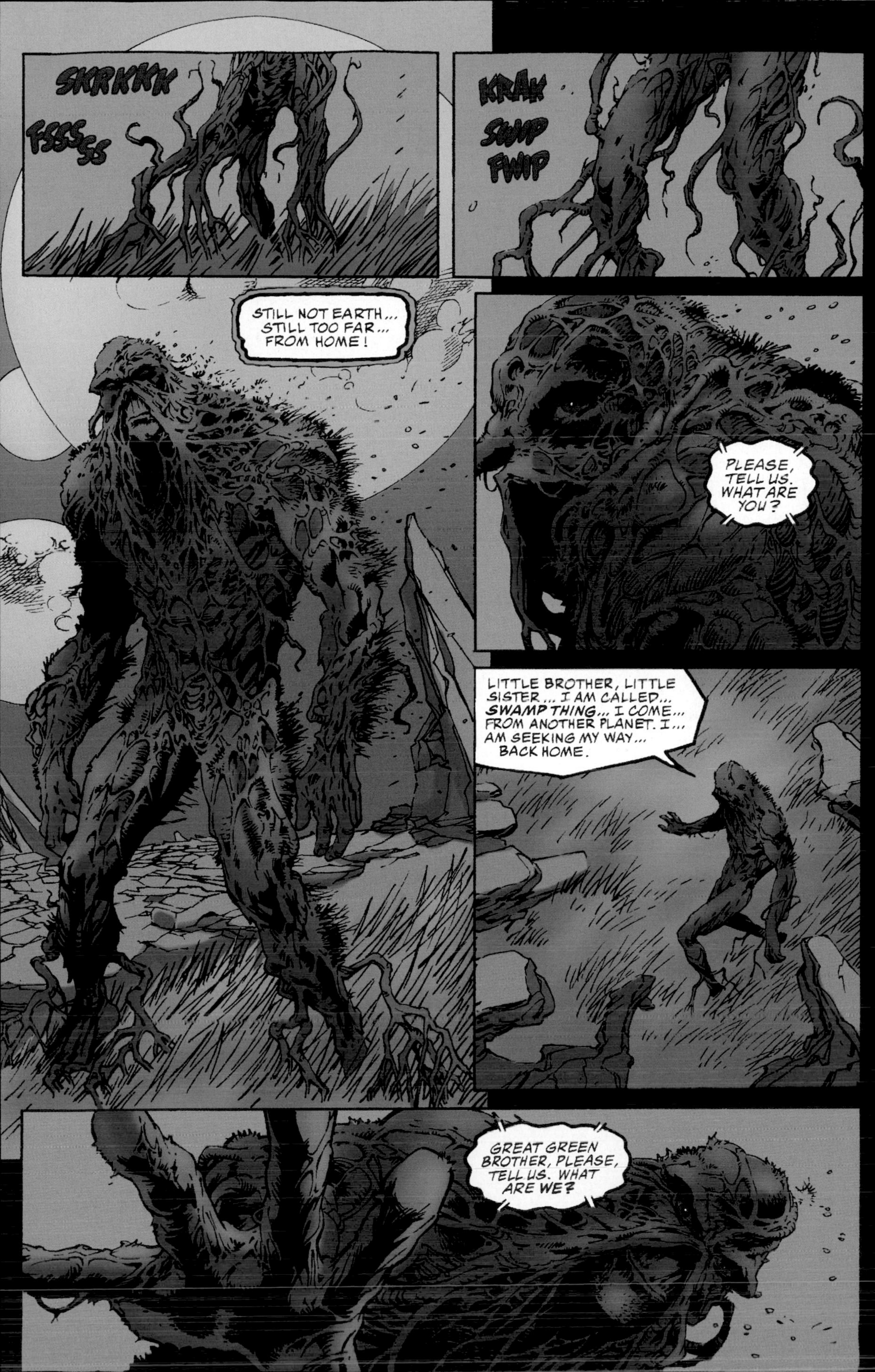
SKRKKK
FSSSSSS
KRAK
SWAP
FWIP
STILL NOT EARTH... STILL TOO FAR... FROM HOME!
PLEASE, TELL US. WHAT ARE YOU?
LITTLE BROTHER, LITTLE SISTER... I AM CALLED... SWAMP THING... I COME... FROM ANOTHER PLANET. I... AM SEEKING MY WAY... BACK HOME.
GREAT GREEN BROTHER, PLEASE, TELL US. WHAT ARE WE?

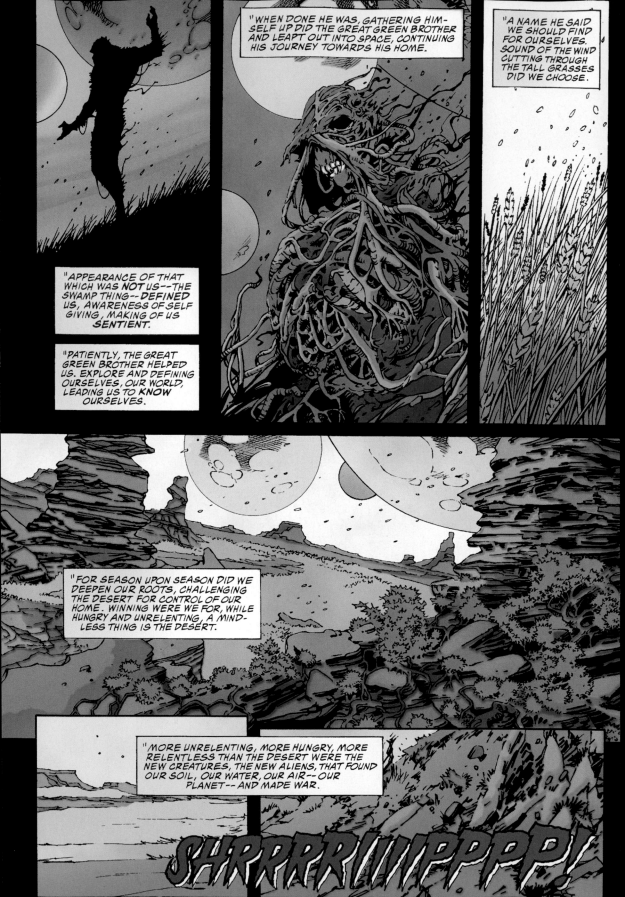

"WHEN DONE HE WAS, GATHERING HIMSELF UP DID THE GREAT GREEN BROTHER AND LEAPT OUT INTO SPACE, CONTINUING HIS JOURNEY TOWARDS HIS HOME.

"A NAME HE SAID WE SHOULD FIND FOR OURSELVES. SOUND OF THE WIND CUTTING THROUGH THE TALL GRASSES DID WE CHOOSE.

"APPEARANCE OF THAT WHICH WAS NOT US--THE SWAMP THING--DEFINED US, AWARENESS OF SELF GIVING, MAKING OF US SENTIENT.

"PATIENTLY, THE GREAT GREEN BROTHER HELPED US. EXPLORE AND DEFINING OURSELVES, OUR WORLD, LEADING US TO KNOW OURSELVES.

"FOR SEASON UPON SEASON DID WE DEEPEN OUR ROOTS, CHALLENGING THE DESERT FOR CONTROL OF OUR HOME. WINNING WERE WE FOR, WHILE HUNGRY AND UNRELENTING, A MINDLESS THING IS THE DESERT.

"MORE UNRELENTING, MORE HUNGRY, MORE RELENTLESS THAN THE DESERT WERE THE NEW CREATURES, THE NEW ALIENS, THAT FOUND OUR SOIL, OUR WATER, OUR AIR-- OUR PLANET-- AND MADE WAR.

SHRRRRIIIIPPPP!

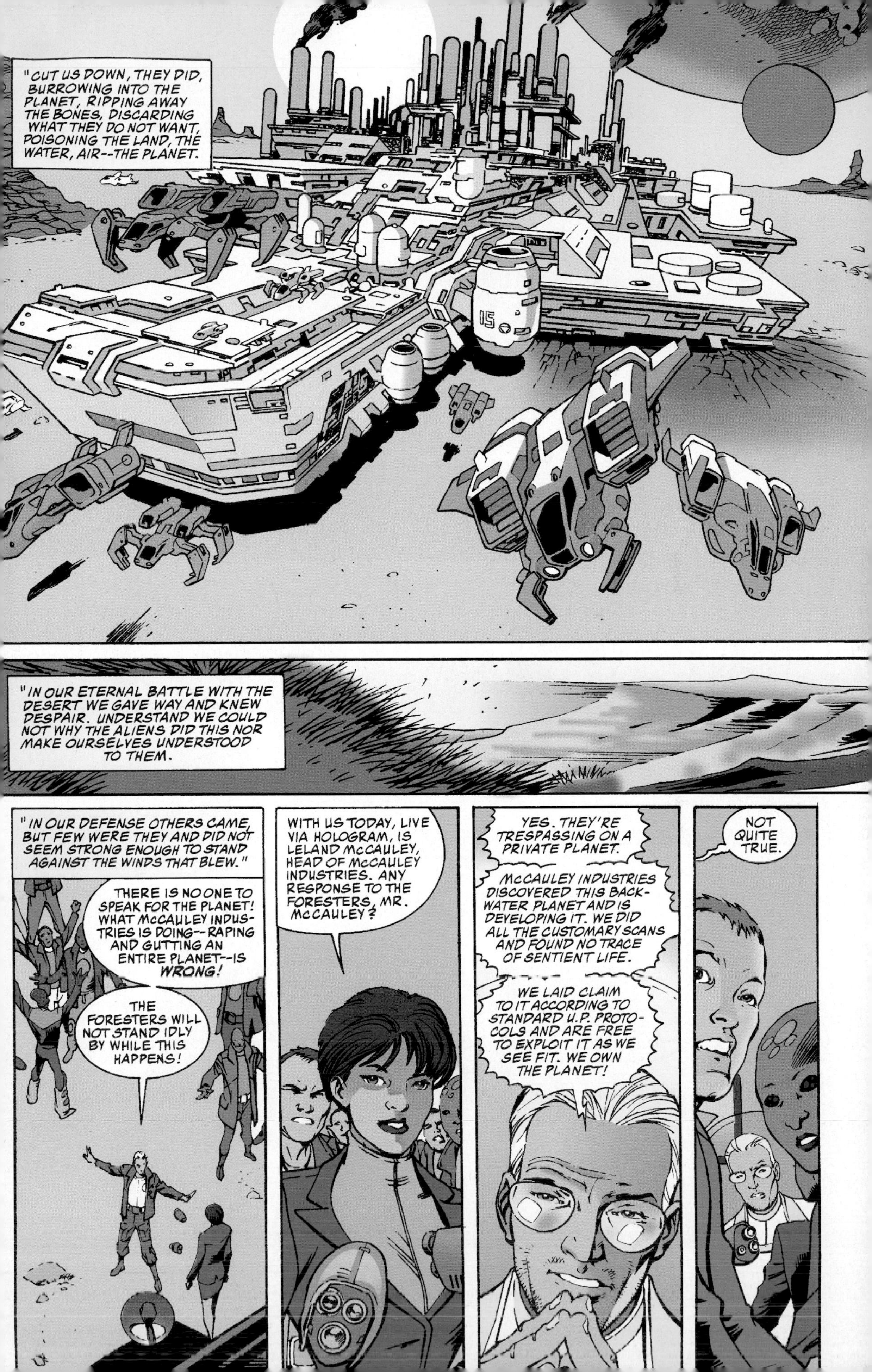
"CUT US DOWN, THEY DID, BURROWING INTO THE PLANET, RIPPING AWAY THE BONES, DISCARDING WHAT THEY DO NOT WANT, POISONING THE LAND, THE WATER, AIR--THE PLANET.
15
"IN OUR ETERNAL BATTLE WITH THE DESERT WE GAVE WAY AND KNEW DESPAIR. UNDERSTAND WE COULD NOT WHY THE ALIENS DID THIS NOR MAKE OURSELVES UNDERSTOOD TO THEM.
"IN OUR DEFENSE OTHERS CAME, BUT FEW WERE THEY AND DID NOT SEEM STRONG ENOUGH TO STAND AGAINST THE WINDS THAT BLEW."
THERE IS NO ONE TO SPEAK FOR THE PLANET! WHAT McCAULEY INDUSTRIES IS DOING-- RAPING AND GUTTING AN ENTIRE PLANET--IS WRONG!
THE FORESTERS WILL NOT STAND IDLY BY WHILE THIS HAPPENS!
WITH US TODAY, LIVE VIA HOLOGRAM, IS LELAND McCAULEY, HEAD OF McCAULEY INDUSTRIES. ANY RESPONSE TO THE FORESTERS, MR. McCAULEY?
YES. THEY'RE TRESPASSING ON A PRIVATE PLANET.
McCAULEY INDUSTRIES DISCOVERED THIS BACKWATER PLANET AND IS DEVELOPING IT. WE DID ALL THE CUSTOMARY SCANS AND FOUND NO TRACE OF SENTIENT LIFE.
WE LAID CLAIM TO IT ACCORDING TO STANDARD U.P. PROTOCOLS AND ARE FREE TO EXPLOIT IT AS WE SEE FIT. WE OWN THE PLANET!
NOT QUITE TRUE.

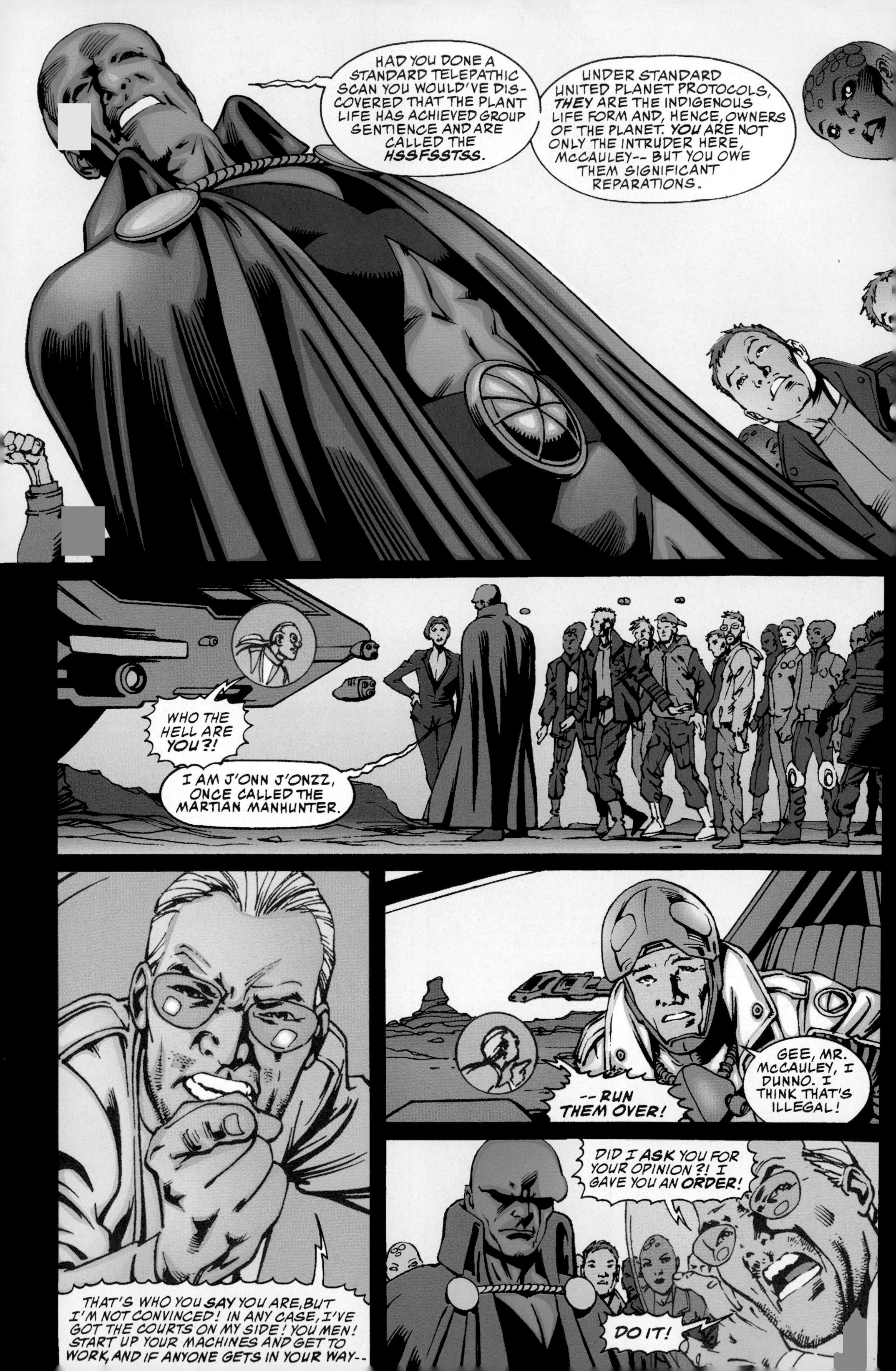

HAD YOU DONE A STANDARD TELEPATHIC SCAN YOU WOULD'VE DISCOVERED THAT THE PLANT LIFE HAS ACHIEVED GROUP SENTIENCE AND ARE CALLED THE HSSFSSTSS.
UNDER STANDARD UNITED PLANET PROTOCOLS, THEY ARE THE INDIGENOUS LIFE FORM AND, HENCE, OWNERS OF THE PLANET. YOU ARE NOT ONLY THE INTRUDER HERE, McCAULEY-- BUT YOU OWE THEM SIGNIFICANT REPARATIONS.
WHO THE HELL ARE YOU?!
I AM J'ONN J'ONZZ, ONCE CALLED THE MARTIAN MANHUNTER.
THAT'S WHO YOU SAY YOU ARE, BUT I'M NOT CONVINCED! IN ANY CASE, I'VE GOT THE COURTS ON MY SIDE! YOU MEN! START UP YOUR MACHINES AND GET TO WORK, AND IF ANYONE GETS IN YOUR WAY--
--RUN THEM OVER!
GEE, MR. McCAULEY, I DUNNO. I THINK THAT'S ILLEGAL!
DID I ASK YOU FOR YOUR OPINION?! I GAVE YOU AN ORDER!
DO IT!

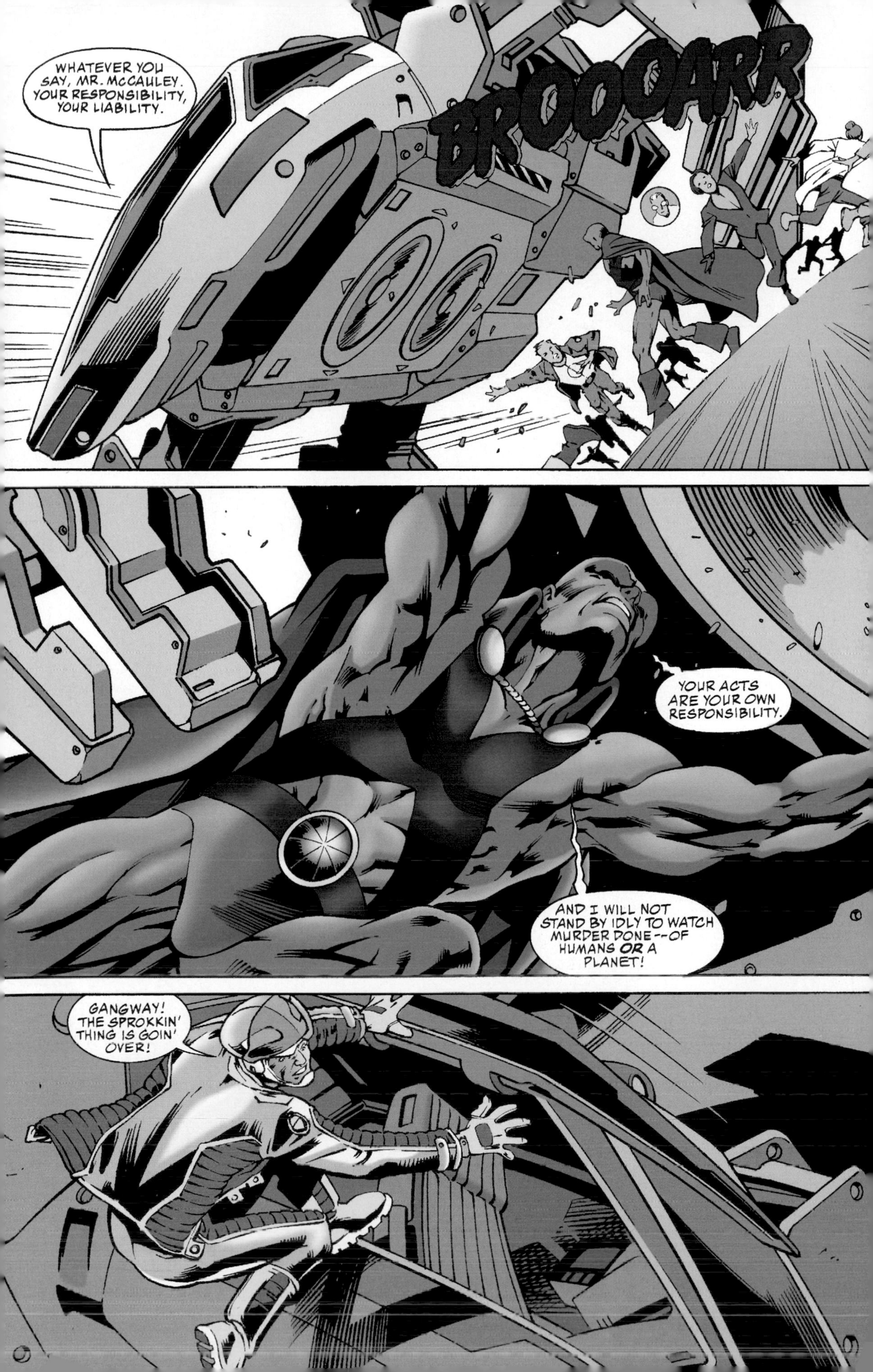
WHATEVER YOU SAY, MR. McCAULEY. YOUR RESPONSIBILITY, YOUR LIABILITY.
BROOOARR
YOUR ACTS ARE YOUR OWN RESPONSIBILITY.
AND I WILL NOT STAND BY IDLY TO WATCH MURDER DONE--OF HUMANS OR A PLANET!
GANGWAY! THE SPROKKIN' THING IS GOIN' OVER!

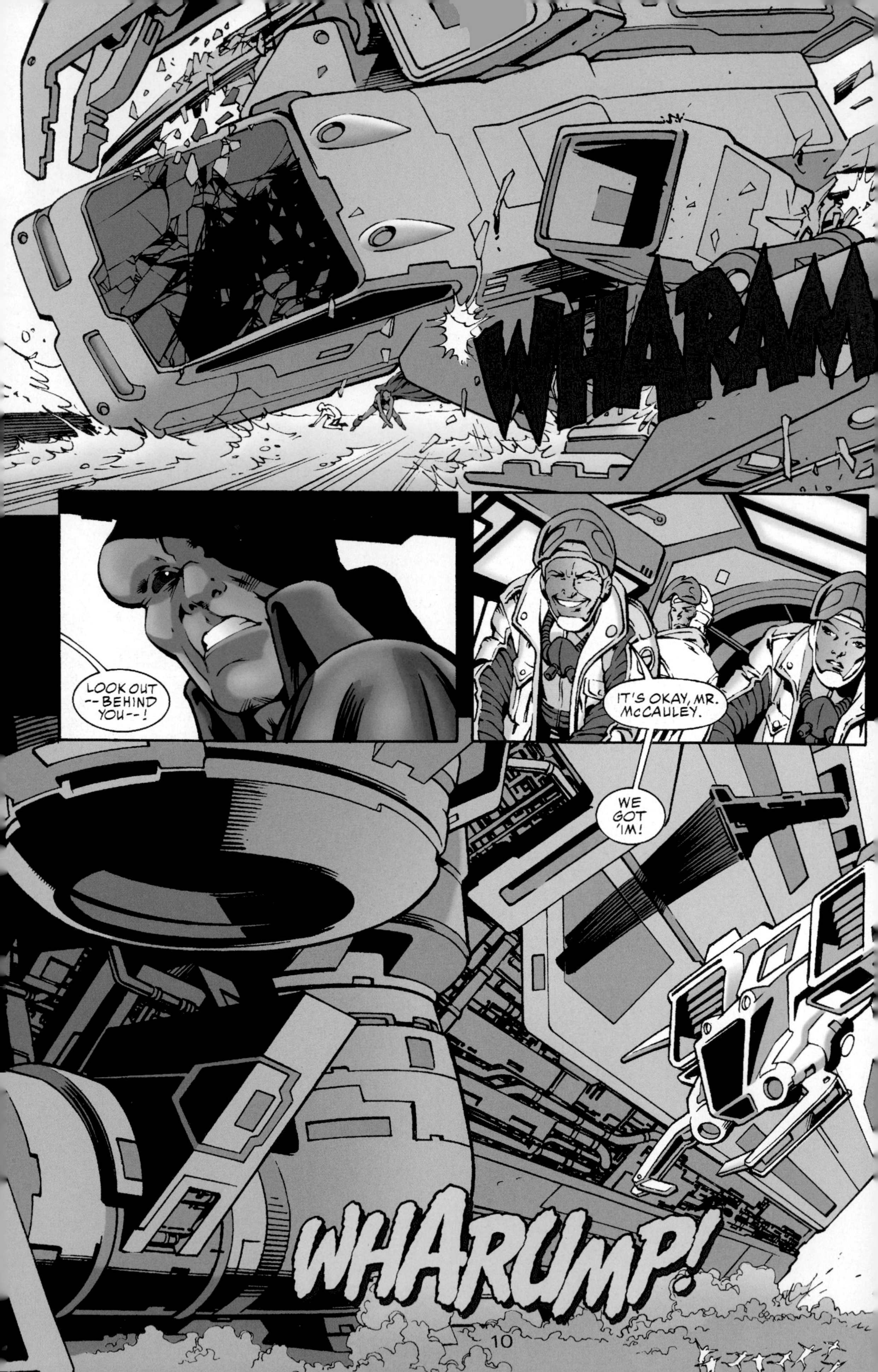
WHARAM
LOOK OUT --BEHIND YOU--!
IT'S OKAY, MR. McCAULEY.
WE GOT 'IM!
WHARUMP!

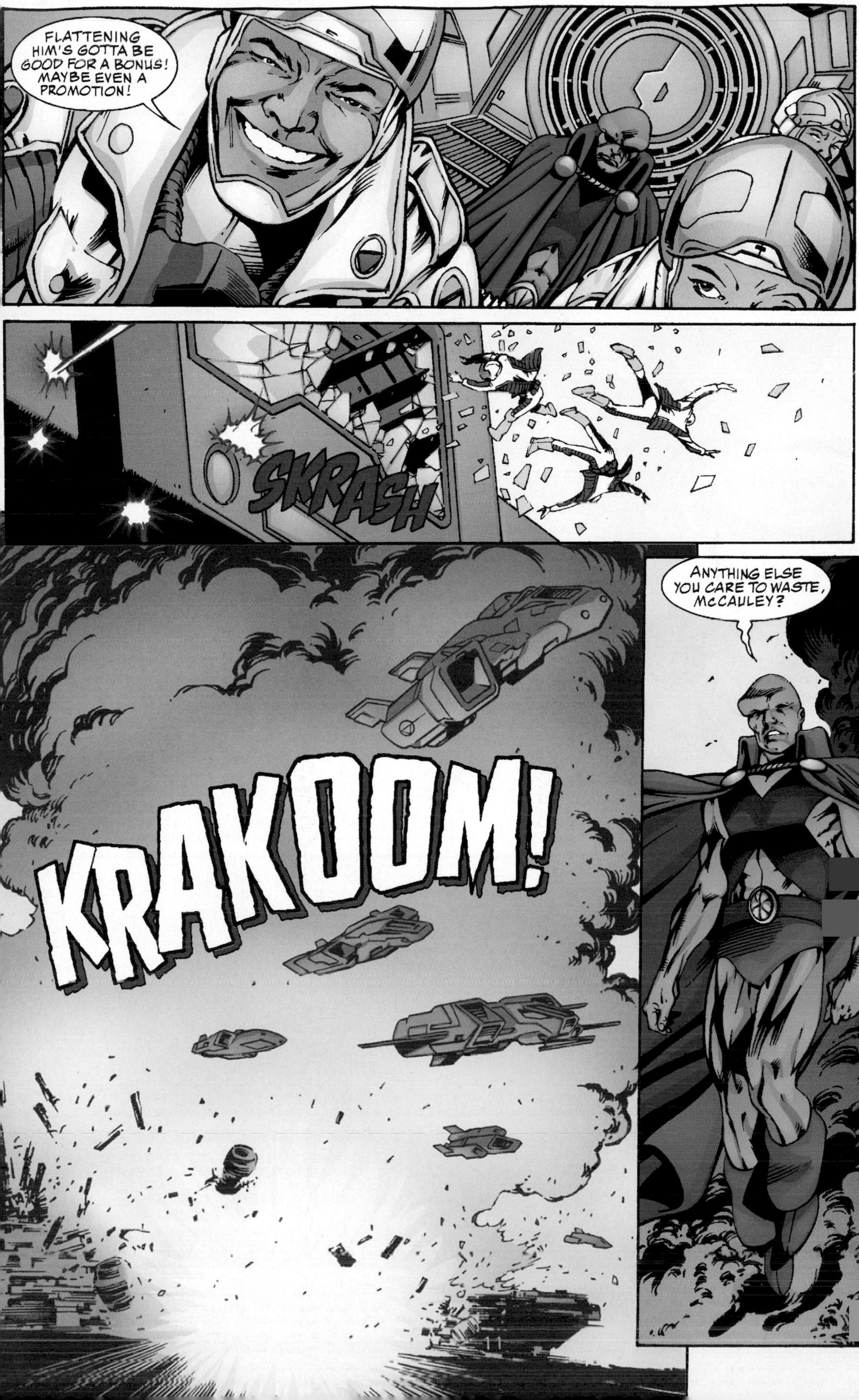
FLATTENING HIM'S GOTTA BE GOOD FOR A BONUS! MAYBE EVEN A PROMOTION!
SKRASH
KRAKOOM!
ANYTHING ELSE YOU CARE TO WASTE, McCAULEY?

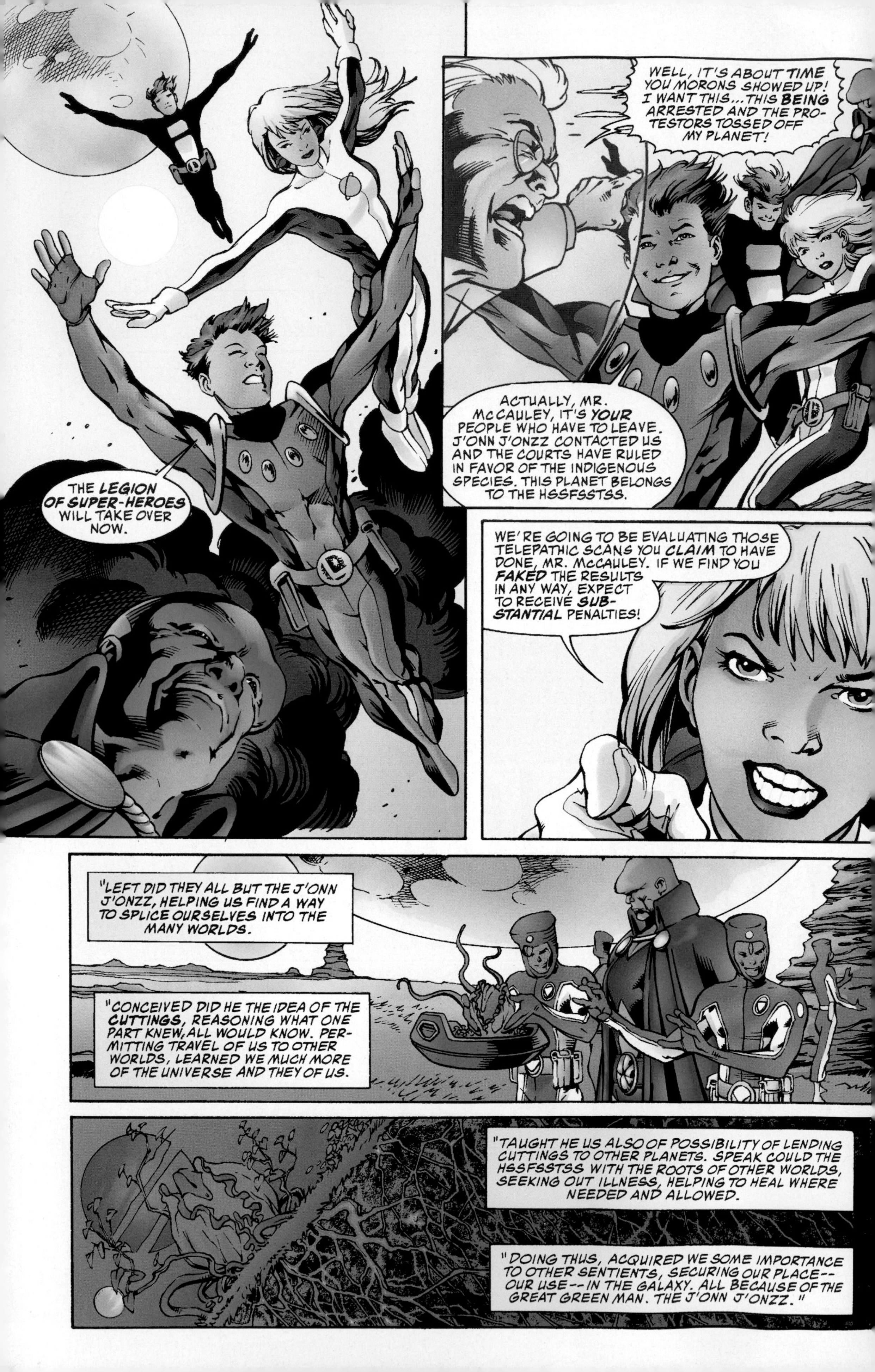
WELL, IT'S ABOUT TIME YOU MORONS SHOWED UP! I WANT THIS...THIS BEING ARRESTED AND THE PROTESTORS TOSSED OFF MY PLANET!
THE LEGION OF SUPER-HEROES WILL TAKE OVER NOW.
ACTUALLY, MR. McCAULEY, IT'S YOUR PEOPLE WHO HAVE TO LEAVE. J'ONN J'ONZZ CONTACTED US AND THE COURTS HAVE RULED IN FAVOR OF THE INDIGENOUS SPECIES. THIS PLANET BELONGS TO THE HSSFSSTSS.
WE'RE GOING TO BE EVALUATING THOSE TELEPATHIC SCANS YOU CLAIM TO HAVE DONE, MR. McCAULEY. IF WE FIND YOU FAKED THE RESULTS IN ANY WAY, EXPECT TO RECEIVE SUBSTANTIAL PENALTIES!
"LEFT DID THEY ALL BUT THE J'ONN J'ONZZ, HELPING US FIND A WAY TO SPLICE OURSELVES INTO THE MANY WORLDS.
"CONCEIVED DID HE THE IDEA OF THE CUTTINGS, REASONING WHAT ONE PART KNEW, ALL WOULD KNOW. PERMITTING TRAVEL OF US TO OTHER WORLDS, LEARNED WE MUCH MORE OF THE UNIVERSE AND THEY OF US.
"TAUGHT HE US ALSO OF POSSIBILITY OF LENDING CUTTINGS TO OTHER PLANETS. SPEAK COULD THE HSSFSSTSS WITH THE ROOTS OF OTHER WORLDS, SEEKING OUT ILLNESS, HELPING TO HEAL WHERE NEEDED AND ALLOWED.
"DOING THUS, ACQUIRED WE SOME IMPORTANCE TO OTHER SENTIENTS, SECURING OUR PLACE-- OUR USE-- IN THE GALAXY. ALL BECAUSE OF THE GREAT GREEN MAN. THE J'ONN J'ONZZ."

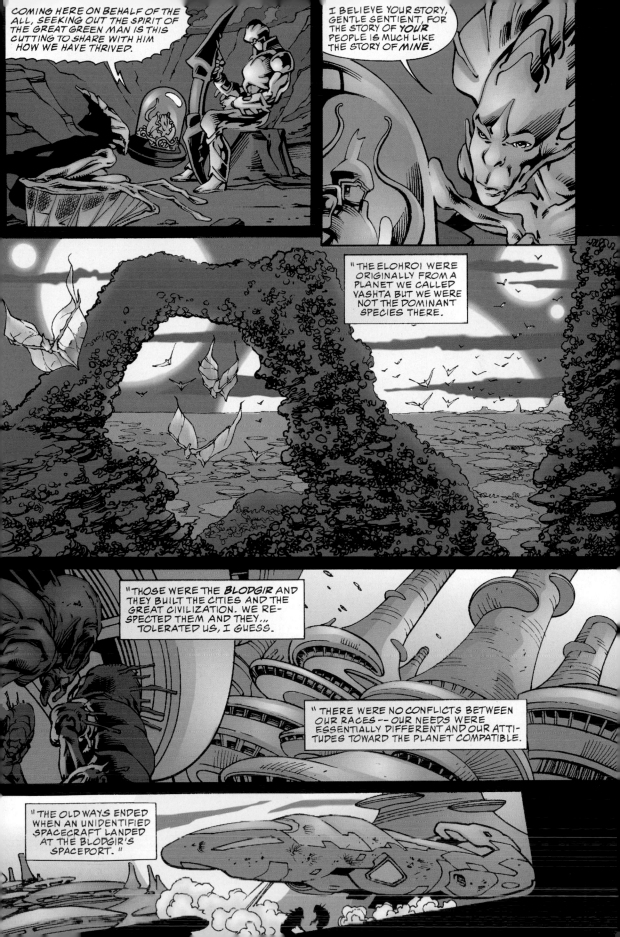

COMING HERE ON BEHALF OF THE ALL, SEEKING OUT THE SPIRIT OF THE GREAT GREEN MAN IS THIS CUTTING TO SHARE WITH HIM HOW WE HAVE THRIVED.

I BELIEVE YOUR STORY, GENTLE SENTIENT, FOR THE STORY OF *YOUR* PEOPLE IS MUCH LIKE THE STORY OF *MINE*.

"THE ELOHROI WERE ORIGINALLY FROM A PLANET WE CALLED VASHTA BUT WE WERE NOT THE DOMINANT SPECIES THERE.

"THOSE WERE THE *BLODGIR* AND THEY BUILT THE CITIES AND THE GREAT CIVILIZATION. WE RESPECTED THEM AND THEY... TOLERATED US, I GUESS.

"THERE WERE NO CONFLICTS BETWEEN OUR RACES -- OUR NEEDS WERE ESSENTIALLY DIFFERENT AND OUR ATTITUDES TOWARD THE PLANET COMPATIBLE.

"THE OLD WAYS ENDED WHEN AN UNIDENTIFIED SPACECRAFT LANDED AT THE BLODGIR'S SPACEPORT."

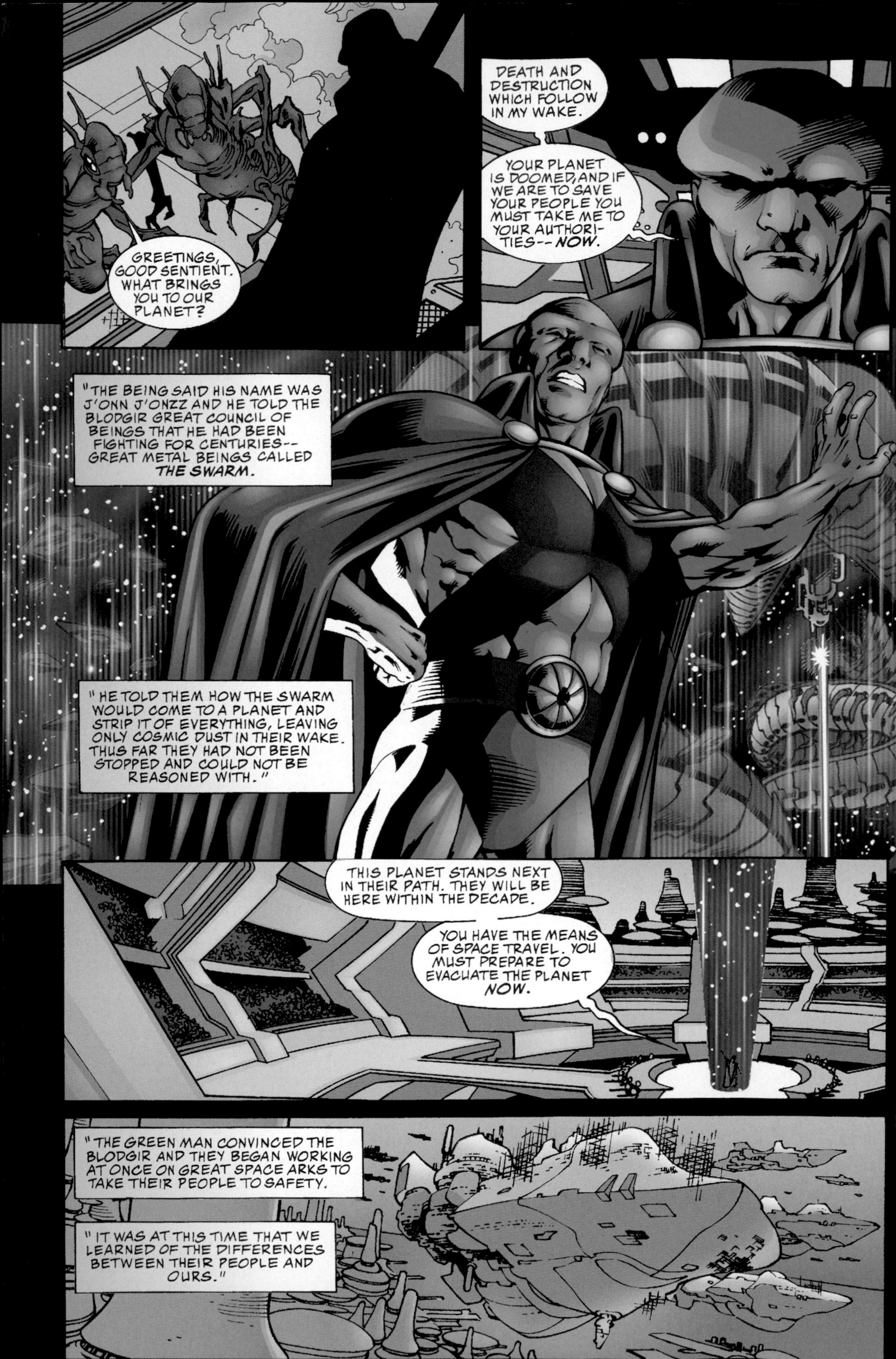
GREETINGS, GOOD SENTIENT. WHAT BRINGS YOU TO OUR PLANET?
DEATH AND DESTRUCTION WHICH FOLLOW IN MY WAKE.
YOUR PLANET IS DOOMED, AND IF WE ARE TO SAVE YOUR PEOPLE YOU MUST TAKE ME TO YOUR AUTHORITIES-- NOW.
"THE BEING SAID HIS NAME WAS J'ONN J'ONZZ AND HE TOLD THE BLODGIR GREAT COUNCIL OF BEINGS THAT HE HAD BEEN FIGHTING FOR CENTURIES-- GREAT METAL BEINGS CALLED THE SWARM.
"HE TOLD THEM HOW THE SWARM WOULD COME TO A PLANET AND STRIP IT OF EVERYTHING, LEAVING ONLY COSMIC DUST IN THEIR WAKE. THUS FAR THEY HAD NOT BEEN STOPPED AND COULD NOT BE REASONED WITH."
THIS PLANET STANDS NEXT IN THEIR PATH. THEY WILL BE HERE WITHIN THE DECADE.
YOU HAVE THE MEANS OF SPACE TRAVEL. YOU MUST PREPARE TO EVACUATE THE PLANET NOW.
"THE GREEN MAN CONVINCED THE BLODGIR AND THEY BEGAN WORKING AT ONCE ON GREAT SPACE ARKS TO TAKE THEIR PEOPLE TO SAFETY.
"IT WAS AT THIS TIME THAT WE LEARNED OF THE DIFFERENCES BETWEEN THEIR PEOPLE AND OURS."

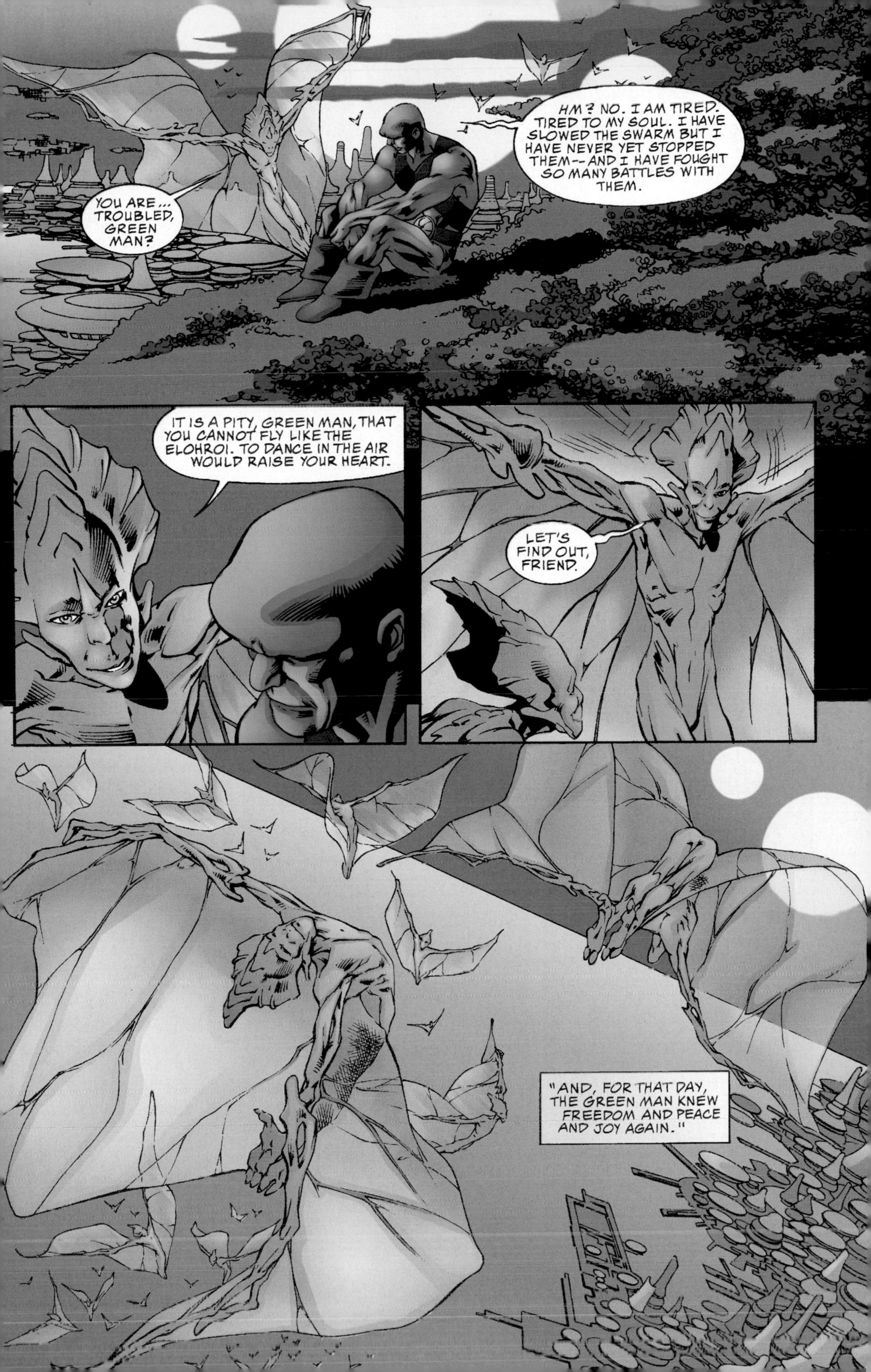
YOU ARE... TROUBLED, GREEN MAN?
HM? NO. I AM TIRED. TIRED TO MY SOUL. I HAVE SLOWED THE SWARM BUT I HAVE NEVER YET STOPPED THEM--AND I HAVE FOUGHT SO MANY BATTLES WITH THEM.
IT IS A PITY, GREEN MAN, THAT YOU CANNOT FLY LIKE THE ELOHROI. TO DANCE IN THE AIR WOULD RAISE YOUR HEART.
LET'S FIND OUT, FRIEND.
"AND, FOR THAT DAY, THE GREEN MAN KNEW FREEDOM AND PEACE AND JOY AGAIN."

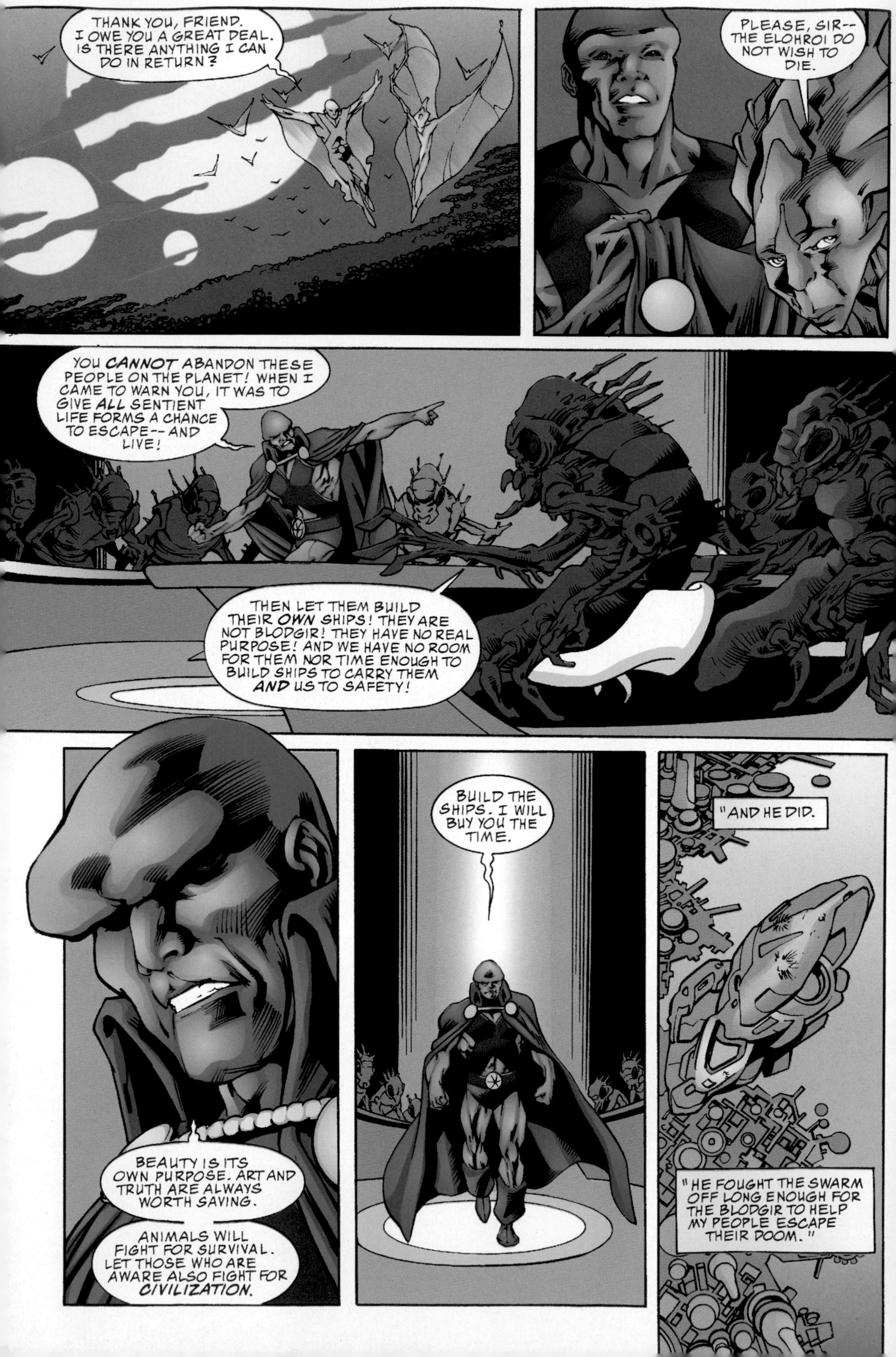
THANK YOU, FRIEND. I OWE YOU A GREAT DEAL. IS THERE ANYTHING I CAN DO IN RETURN?
PLEASE, SIR-- THE ELOHROI DO NOT WISH TO DIE.
YOU CANNOT ABANDON THESE PEOPLE ON THE PLANET! WHEN I CAME TO WARN YOU, IT WAS TO GIVE ALL SENTIENT LIFE FORMS A CHANCE TO ESCAPE-- AND LIVE!
THEN LET THEM BUILD THEIR OWN SHIPS! THEY ARE NOT BLODGIR! THEY HAVE NO REAL PURPOSE! AND WE HAVE NO ROOM FOR THEM NOR TIME ENOUGH TO BUILD SHIPS TO CARRY THEM AND US TO SAFETY!
BEAUTY IS ITS OWN PURPOSE. ART AND TRUTH ARE ALWAYS WORTH SAVING.
ANIMALS WILL FIGHT FOR SURVIVAL. LET THOSE WHO ARE AWARE ALSO FIGHT FOR CIVILIZATION.
BUILD THE SHIPS. I WILL BUY YOU THE TIME.
"AND HE DID.
"HE FOUGHT THE SWARM OFF LONG ENOUGH FOR THE BLODGIR TO HELP MY PEOPLE ESCAPE THEIR DOOM."

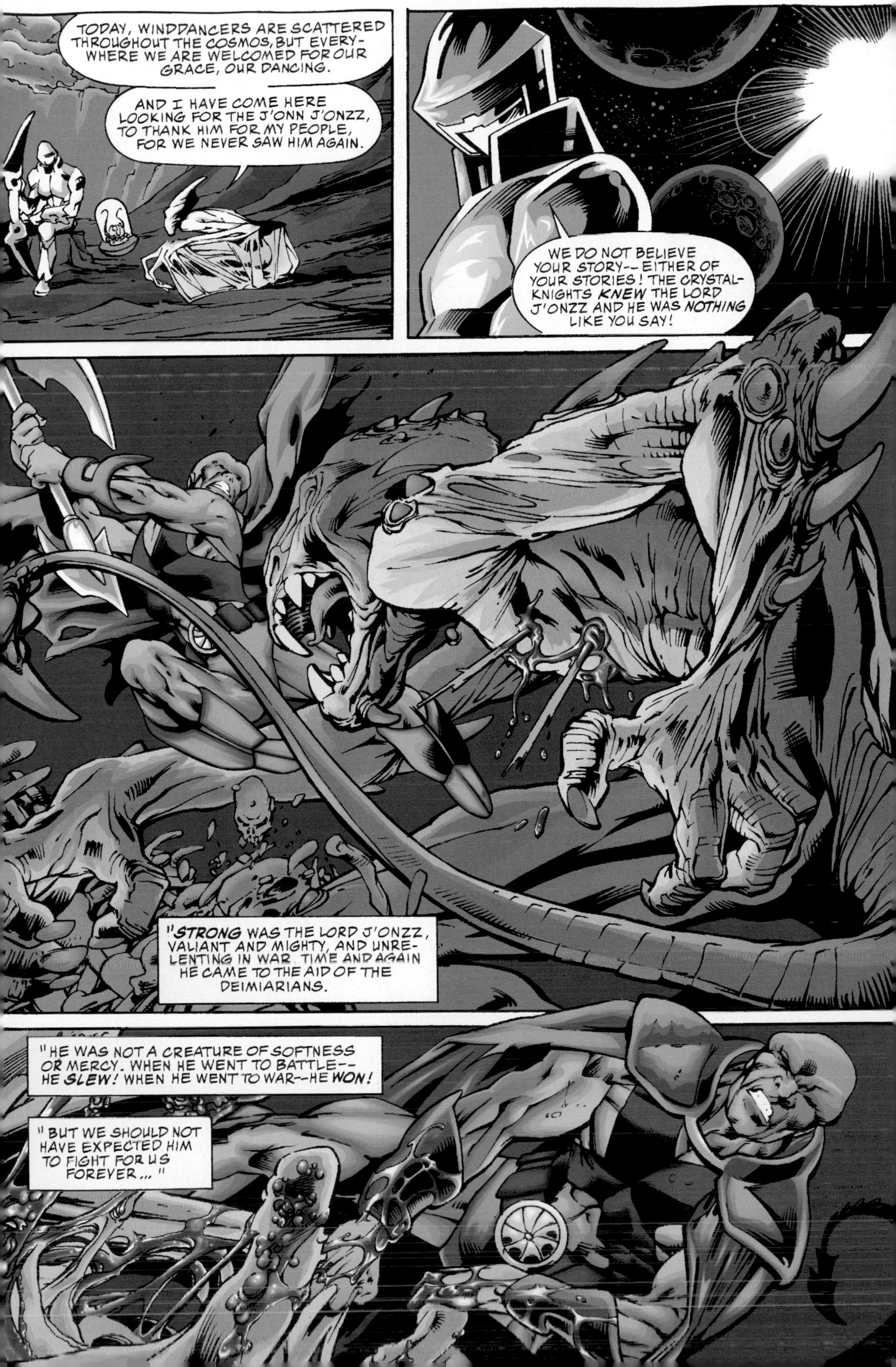
TODAY, WINDDANCERS ARE SCATTERED THROUGHOUT THE COSMOS, BUT EVERY-WHERE WE ARE WELCOMED FOR OUR GRACE, OUR DANCING.
AND I HAVE COME HERE LOOKING FOR THE J'ONN J'ONZZ, TO THANK HIM FOR MY PEOPLE, FOR WE NEVER SAW HIM AGAIN.
WE DO NOT BELIEVE YOUR STORY-- EITHER OF YOUR STORIES! THE CRYSTAL-KNIGHTS KNEW THE LORD J'ONZZ AND HE WAS NOTHING LIKE YOU SAY!
"STRONG WAS THE LORD J'ONZZ, VALIANT AND MIGHTY, AND UNRE-LENTING IN WAR. TIME AND AGAIN HE CAME TO THE AID OF THE DEIMIARIANS.
"HE WAS NOT A CREATURE OF SOFTNESS OR MERCY. WHEN HE WENT TO BATTLE-- HE SLEW! WHEN HE WENT TO WAR--HE WON!
"BUT WE SHOULD NOT HAVE EXPECTED HIM TO FIGHT FOR US FOREVER..."

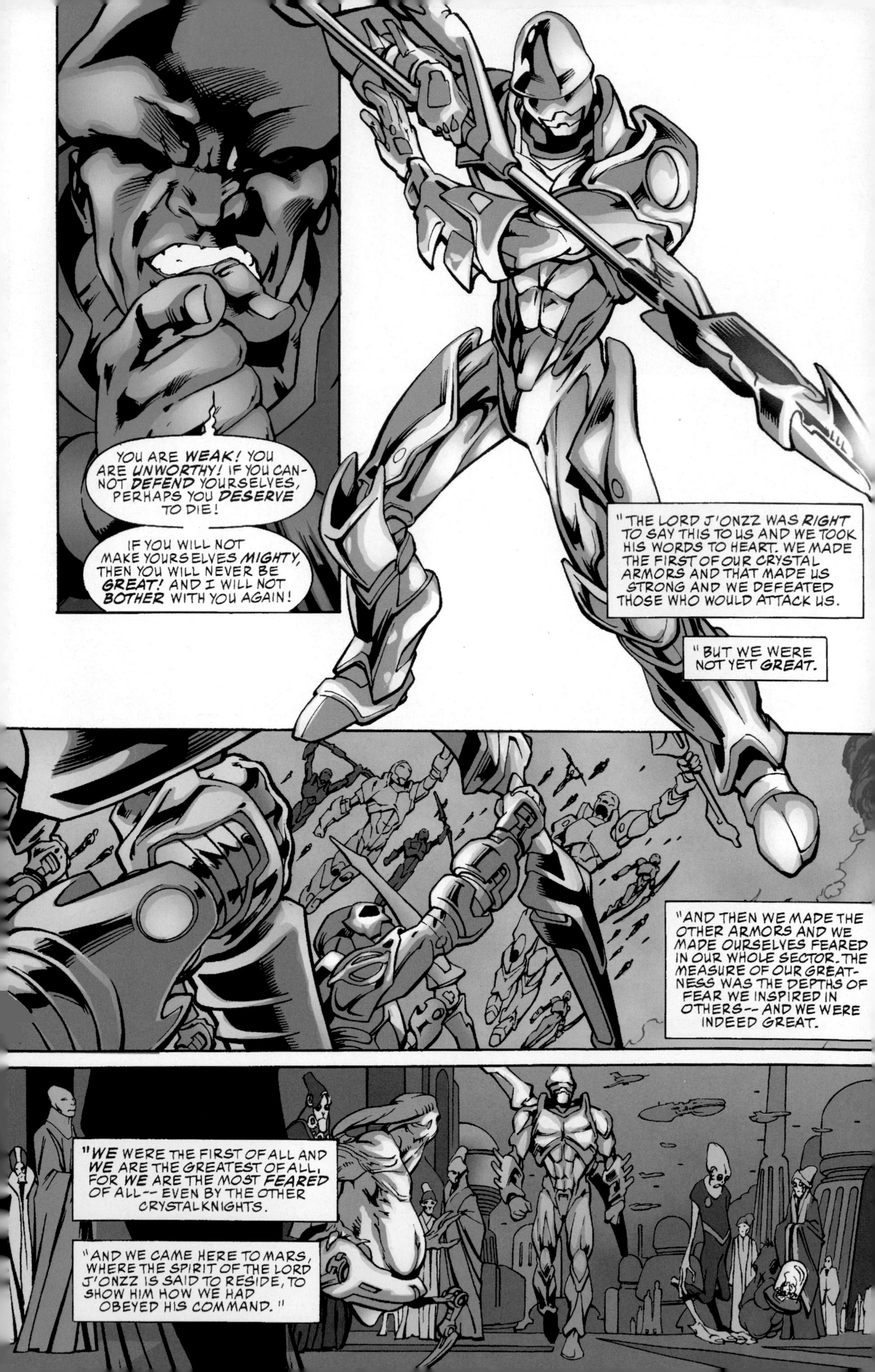
YOU ARE WEAK! YOU ARE UNWORTHY! IF YOU CANNOT DEFEND YOURSELVES, PERHAPS YOU DESERVE TO DIE!
IF YOU WILL NOT MAKE YOURSELVES MIGHTY, THEN YOU WILL NEVER BE GREAT! AND I WILL NOT BOTHER WITH YOU AGAIN!
"THE LORD J'ONZZ WAS RIGHT TO SAY THIS TO US AND WE TOOK HIS WORDS TO HEART. WE MADE THE FIRST OF OUR CRYSTAL ARMORS AND THAT MADE US STRONG AND WE DEFEATED THOSE WHO WOULD ATTACK US.
"BUT WE WERE NOT YET GREAT.
"AND THEN WE MADE THE OTHER ARMORS AND WE MADE OURSELVES FEARED IN OUR WHOLE SECTOR. THE MEASURE OF OUR GREATNESS WAS THE DEPTHS OF FEAR WE INSPIRED IN OTHERS-- AND WE WERE INDEED GREAT.
"WE WERE THE FIRST OF ALL AND WE ARE THE GREATEST OF ALL, FOR WE ARE THE MOST FEARED OF ALL-- EVEN BY THE OTHER CRYSTALKNIGHTS.
"AND WE CAME HERE TO MARS, WHERE THE SPIRIT OF THE LORD J'ONZZ IS SAID TO RESIDE, TO SHOW HIM HOW WE HAD OBEYED HIS COMMAND."

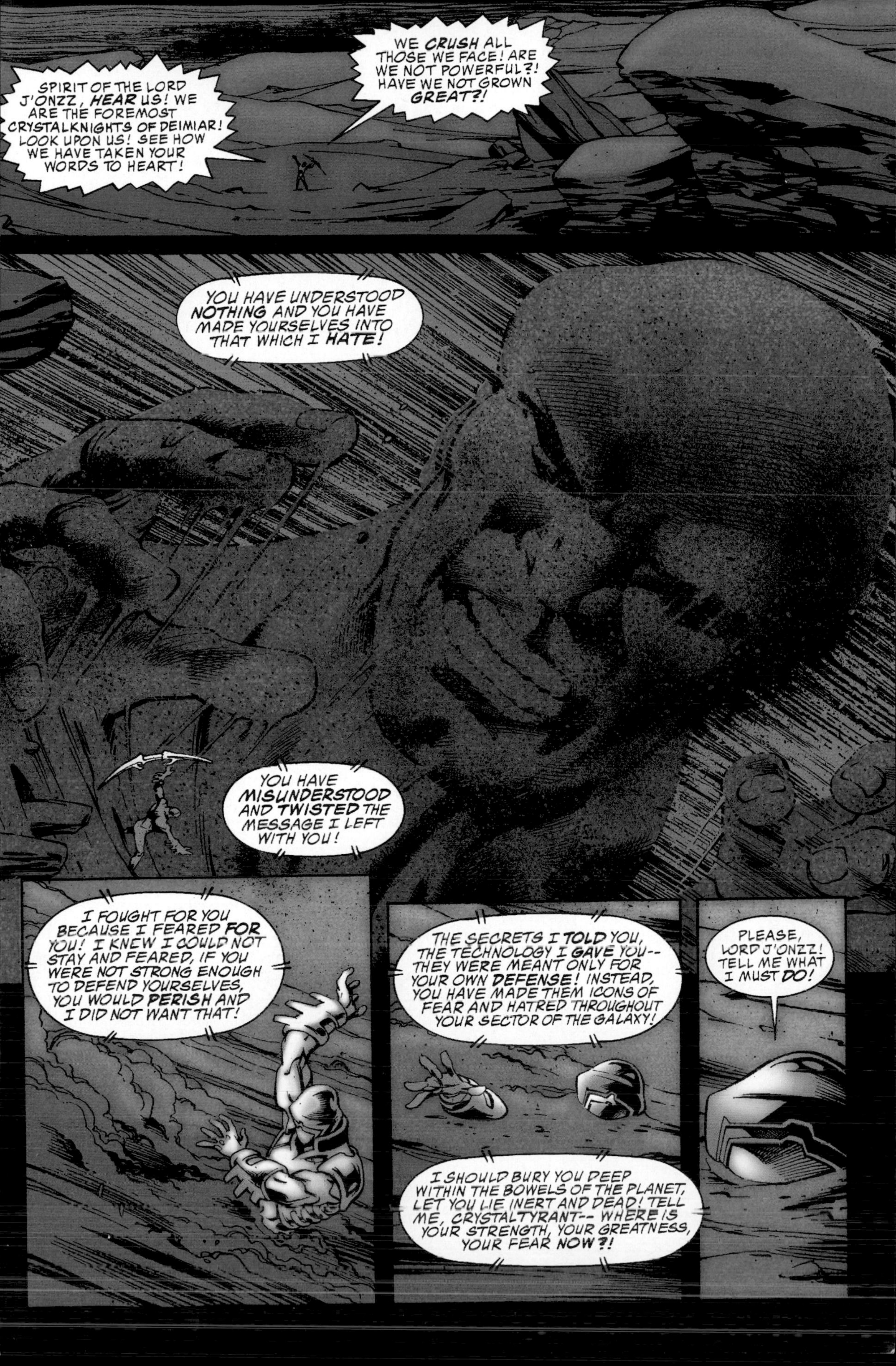
SPIRIT OF THE LORD J'ONZZ, HEAR US! WE ARE THE FOREMOST CRYSTALKNIGHTS OF DEIMIAR! LOOK UPON US! SEE HOW WE HAVE TAKEN YOUR WORDS TO HEART!
WE CRUSH ALL THOSE WE FACE! ARE WE NOT POWERFUL?! HAVE WE NOT GROWN GREAT?!
YOU HAVE UNDERSTOOD NOTHING AND YOU HAVE MADE YOURSELVES INTO THAT WHICH I HATE!
YOU HAVE MISUNDERSTOOD AND TWISTED THE MESSAGE I LEFT WITH YOU!
I FOUGHT FOR YOU BECAUSE I FEARED FOR YOU! I KNEW I COULD NOT STAY AND FEARED, IF YOU WERE NOT STRONG ENOUGH TO DEFEND YOURSELVES, YOU WOULD PERISH AND I DID NOT WANT THAT!
THE SECRETS I TOLD YOU, THE TECHNOLOGY I GAVE YOU-- THEY WERE MEANT ONLY FOR YOUR OWN DEFENSE! INSTEAD, YOU HAVE MADE THEM ICONS OF FEAR AND HATRED THROUGHOUT YOUR SECTOR OF THE GALAXY!
PLEASE, LORD J'ONZZ! TELL ME WHAT I MUST DO!
I SHOULD BURY YOU DEEP WITHIN THE BOWELS OF THE PLANET, LET YOU LIE INERT AND DEAD! TELL ME, CRYSTALTYRANT-- WHERE IS YOUR STRENGTH, YOUR GREATNESS, YOUR FEAR NOW?!

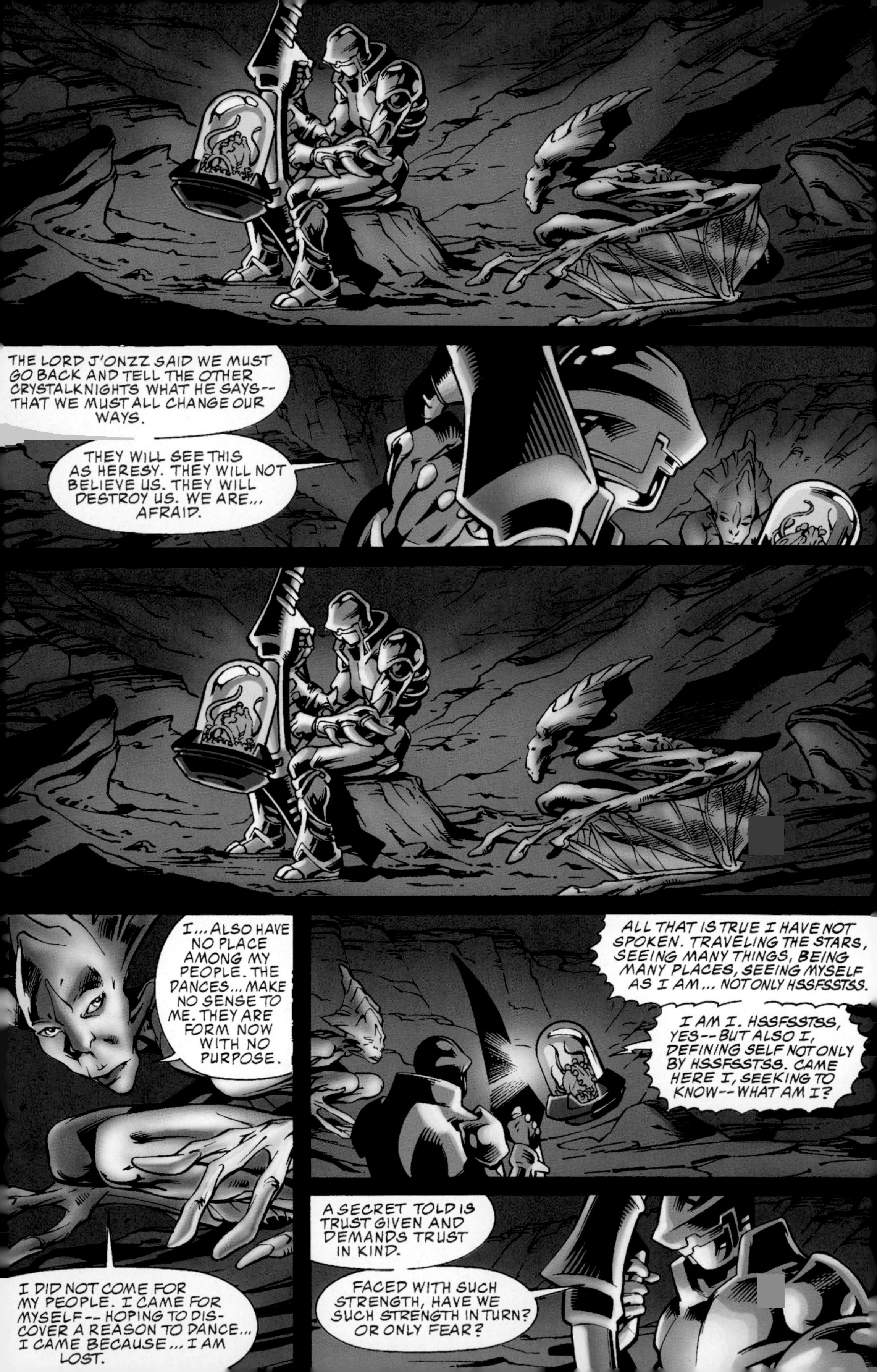
THE LORD J'ONZZ SAID WE MUST GO BACK AND TELL THE OTHER CRYSTALKNIGHTS WHAT HE SAYS-- THAT WE MUST ALL CHANGE OUR WAYS.
THEY WILL SEE THIS AS HERESY. THEY WILL NOT BELIEVE US. THEY WILL DESTROY US. WE ARE... AFRAID.
I... ALSO HAVE NO PLACE AMONG MY PEOPLE. THE DANCES... MAKE NO SENSE TO ME. THEY ARE FORM NOW WITH NO PURPOSE.
I DID NOT COME FOR MY PEOPLE. I CAME FOR MYSELF-- HOPING TO DISCOVER A REASON TO DANCE... I CAME BECAUSE... I AM LOST.
ALL THAT IS TRUE I HAVE NOT SPOKEN. TRAVELING THE STARS, SEEING MANY THINGS, BEING MANY PLACES, SEEING MYSELF AS I AM... NOT ONLY HSSFSSTSS.
I AM I. HSSFSSTSS, YES--BUT ALSO I, DEFINING SELF NOT ONLY BY HSSFSSTSS. CAME HERE I, SEEKING TO KNOW--WHAT AM I?
A SECRET TOLD IS TRUST GIVEN AND DEMANDS TRUST IN KIND.
FACED WITH SUCH STRENGTH, HAVE WE SUCH STRENGTH IN TURN? OR ONLY FEAR?

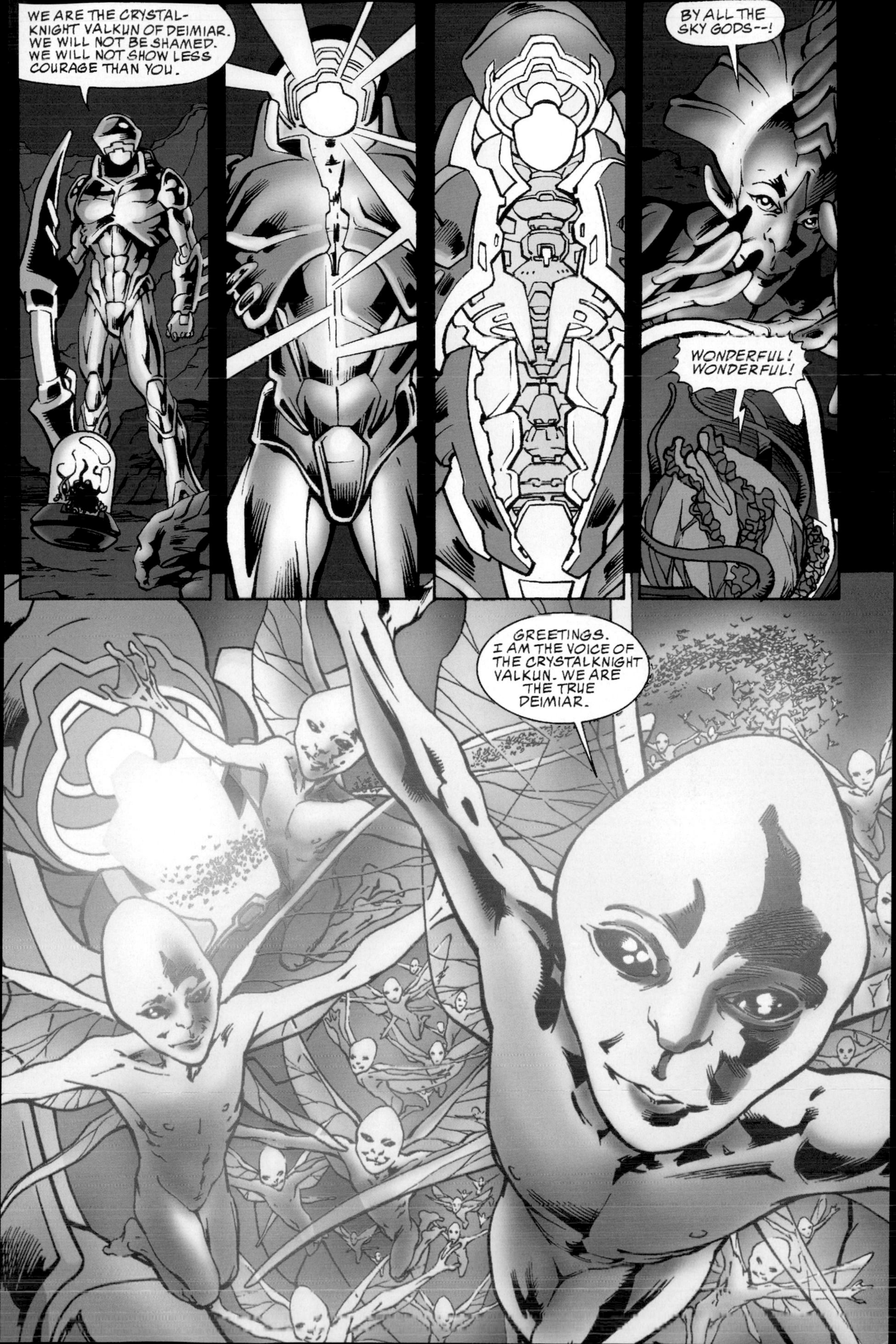
WE ARE THE CRYSTAL-KNIGHT VALKUN OF DEIMIAR. WE WILL NOT BE SHAMED. WE WILL NOT SHOW LESS COURAGE THAN YOU.
BY ALL THE SKY GODS--!
WONDERFUL! WONDERFUL!
GREETINGS. I AM THE VOICE OF THE CRYSTALKNIGHT VALKUN. WE ARE THE TRUE DEIMIAR.

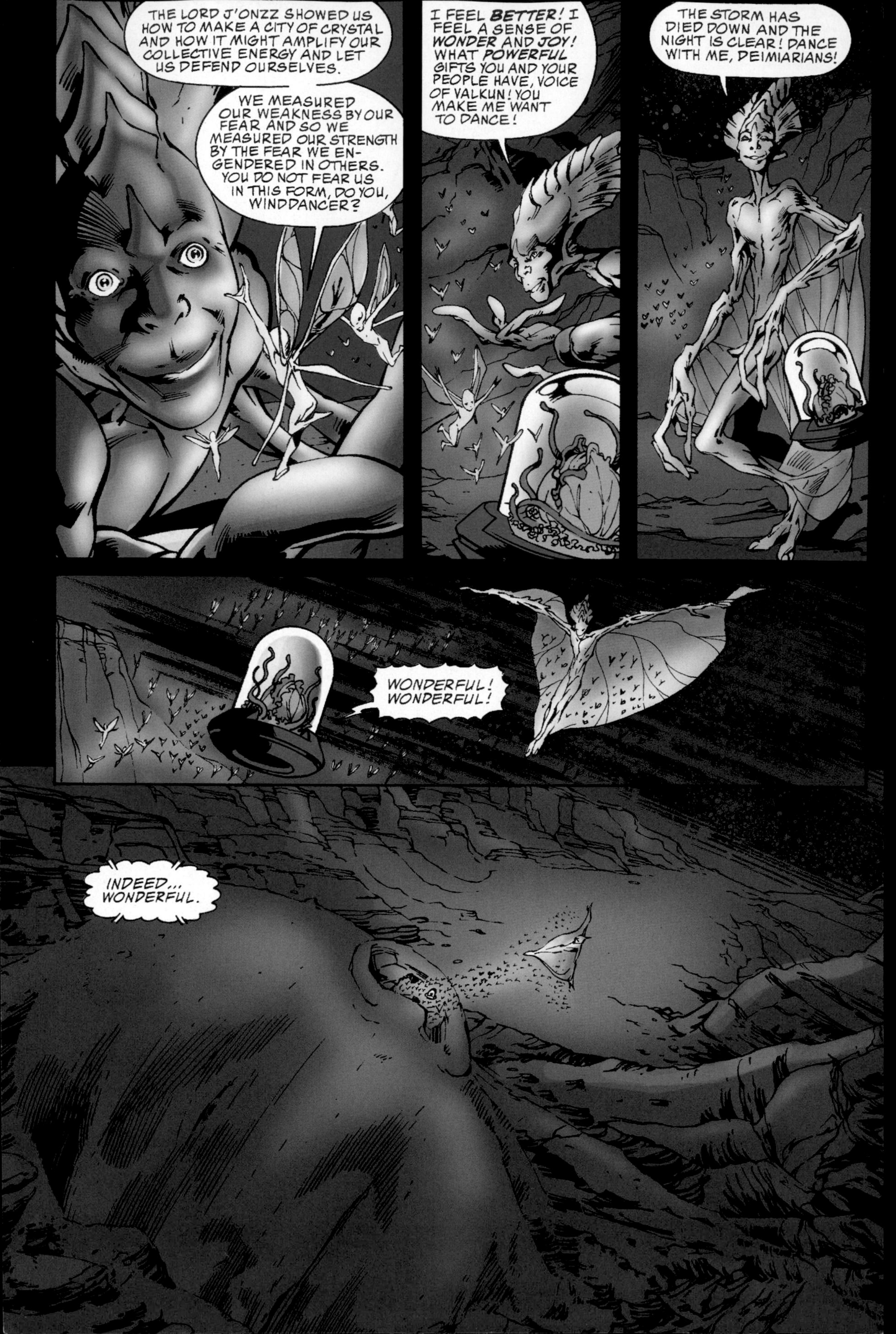
THE LORD J'ONZZ SHOWED US HOW TO MAKE A CITY OF CRYSTAL AND HOW IT MIGHT AMPLIFY OUR COLLECTIVE ENERGY AND LET US DEFEND OURSELVES.
WE MEASURED OUR WEAKNESS BY OUR FEAR AND SO WE MEASURED OUR STRENGTH BY THE FEAR WE ENGENDERED IN OTHERS. YOU DO NOT FEAR US IN THIS FORM, DO YOU, WINDDANCER?
I FEEL **BETTER**! I FEEL A SENSE OF **WONDER** AND **JOY**! WHAT **POWERFUL** GIFTS YOU AND YOUR PEOPLE HAVE, VOICE OF VALKUN! YOU MAKE ME WANT TO DANCE!
THE STORM HAS DIED DOWN AND THE NIGHT IS CLEAR! DANCE WITH ME, DEIMIARIANS!
WONDERFUL! WONDERFUL!
INDEED... WONDERFUL.

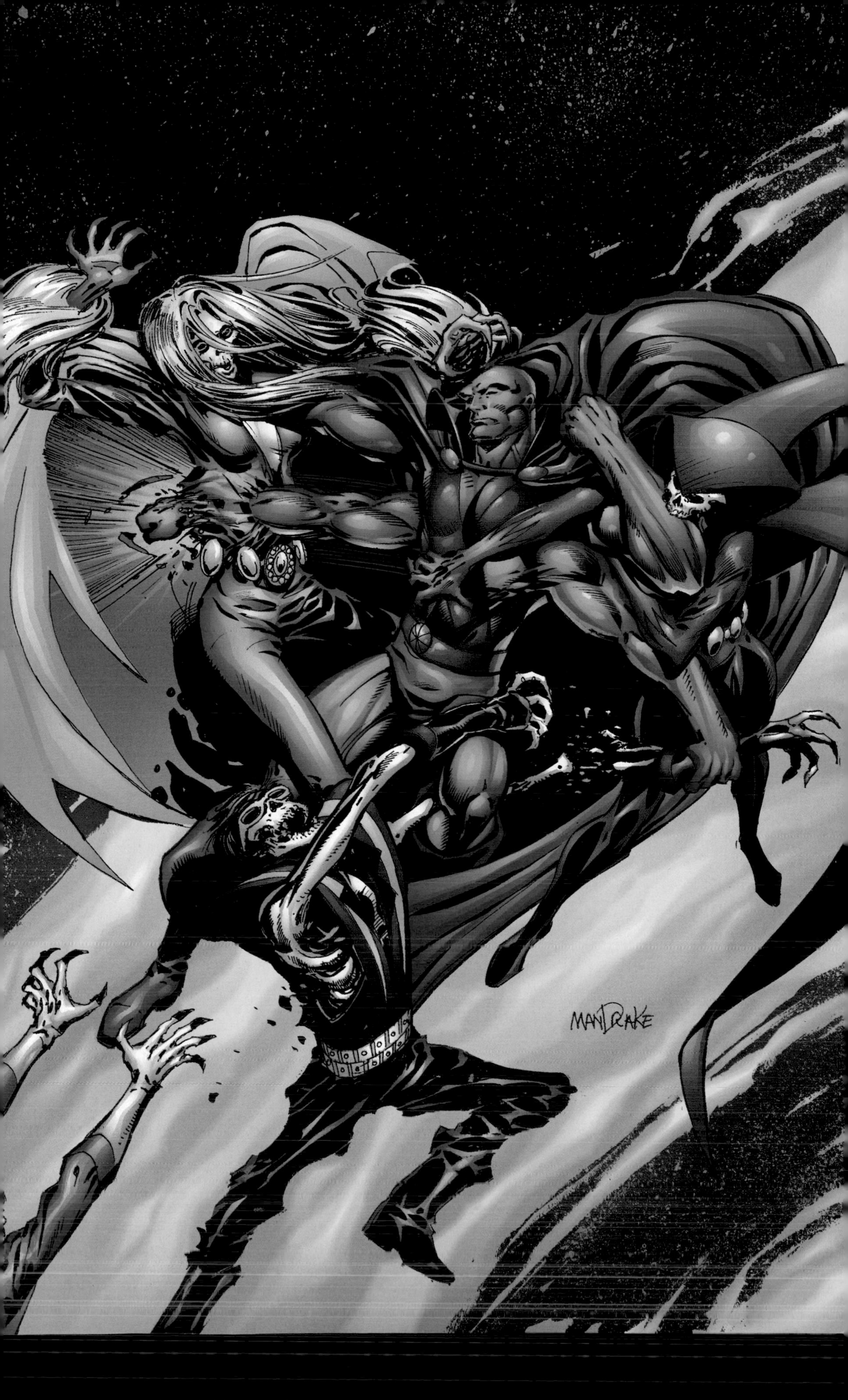
MANDRAKE

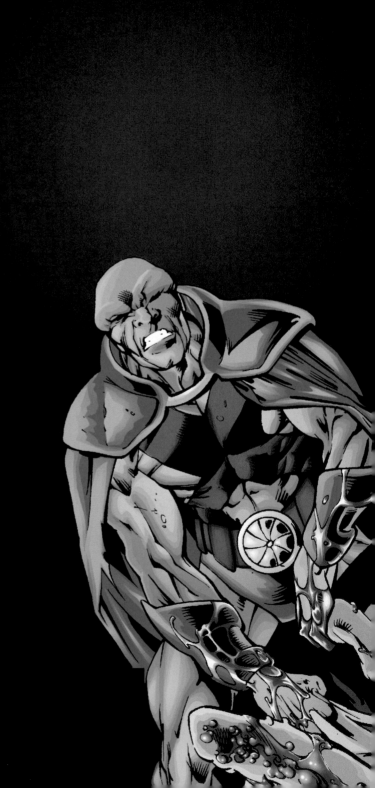

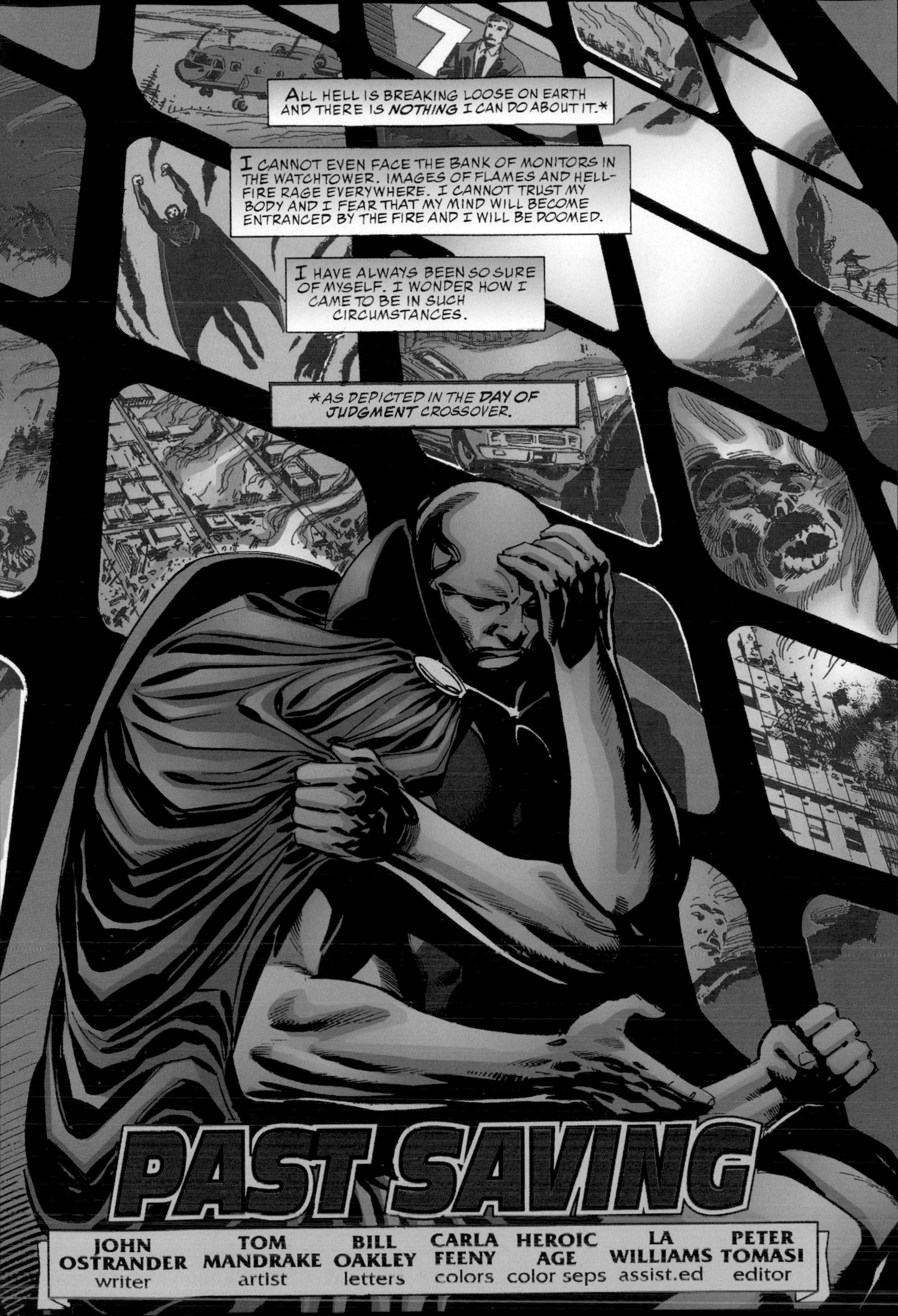

ALL HELL IS BREAKING LOOSE ON EARTH AND THERE IS NOTHING I CAN DO ABOUT IT.*
I CANNOT EVEN FACE THE BANK OF MONITORS IN THE WATCHTOWER. IMAGES OF FLAMES AND HELL-FIRE RAGE EVERYWHERE. I CANNOT TRUST MY BODY AND I FEAR THAT MY MIND WILL BECOME ENTRANCED BY THE FIRE AND I WILL BE DOOMED.
I HAVE ALWAYS BEEN SO SURE OF MYSELF. I WONDER HOW I CAME TO BE IN SUCH CIRCUMSTANCES.
*AS DEPICTED IN THE DAY OF JUDGMENT CROSSOVER.
PAST SAVING
JOHN OSTRANDER writer
TOM MANDRAKE artist
BILL OAKLEY letters
CARLA FEENY colors
HEROIC AGE color seps
LA WILLIAMS assist.ed
PETER TOMASI editor

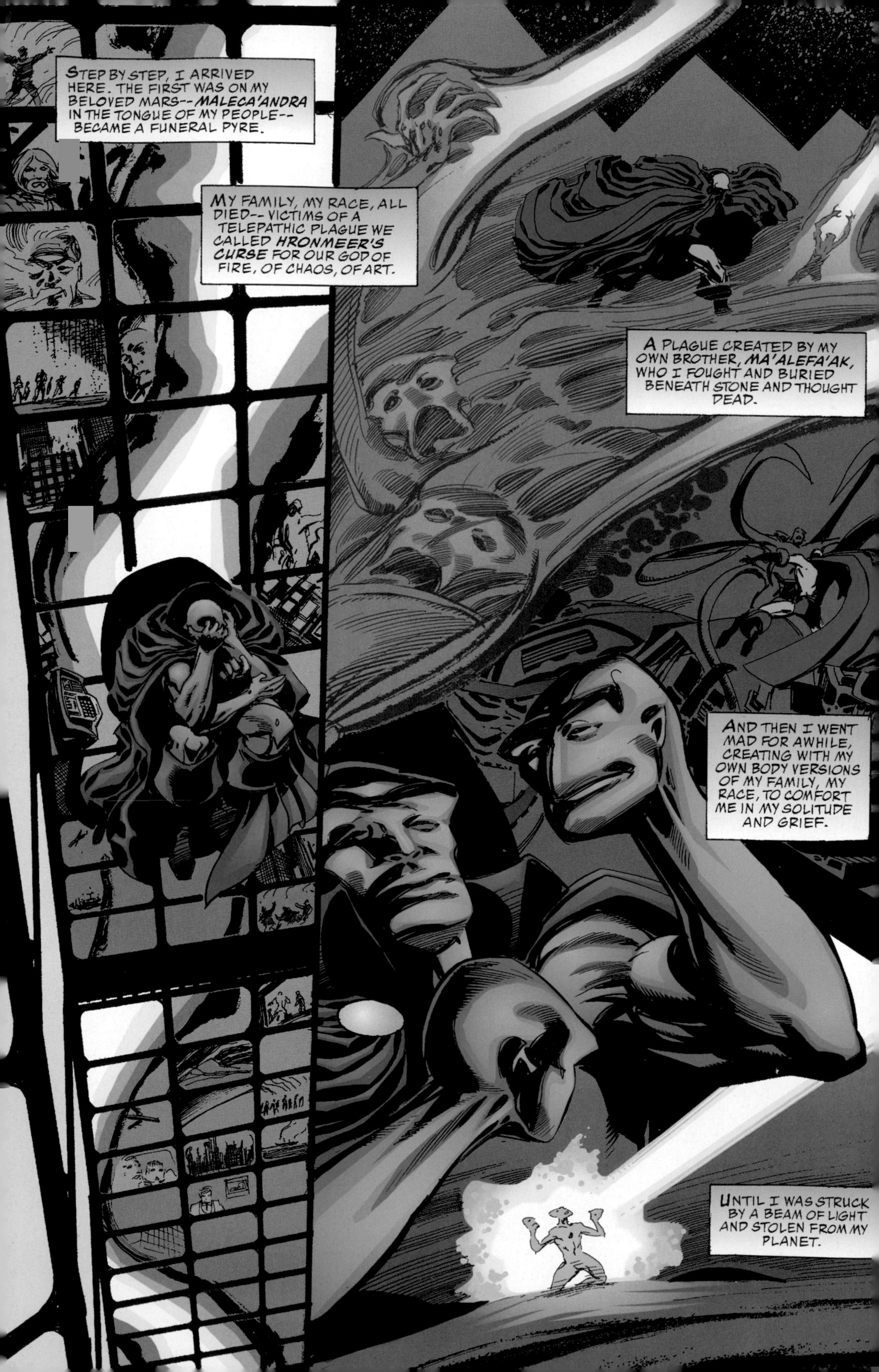
STEP BY STEP, I ARRIVED HERE. THE FIRST WAS ON MY BELOVED MARS--MALECA'ANDRA IN THE TONGUE OF MY PEOPLE--BECAME A FUNERAL PYRE.
MY FAMILY, MY RACE, ALL DIED-- VICTIMS OF A TELEPATHIC PLAGUE WE CALLED HRONMEER'S CURSE FOR OUR GOD OF FIRE, OF CHAOS, OF ART.
A PLAGUE CREATED BY MY OWN BROTHER, MA'ALEFA'AK, WHO I FOUGHT AND BURIED BENEATH STONE AND THOUGHT DEAD.
AND THEN I WENT MAD FOR AWHILE, CREATING WITH MY OWN BODY VERSIONS OF MY FAMILY, MY RACE, TO COMFORT ME IN MY SOLITUDE AND GRIEF.
UNTIL I WAS STRUCK BY A BEAM OF LIGHT AND STOLEN FROM MY PLANET.

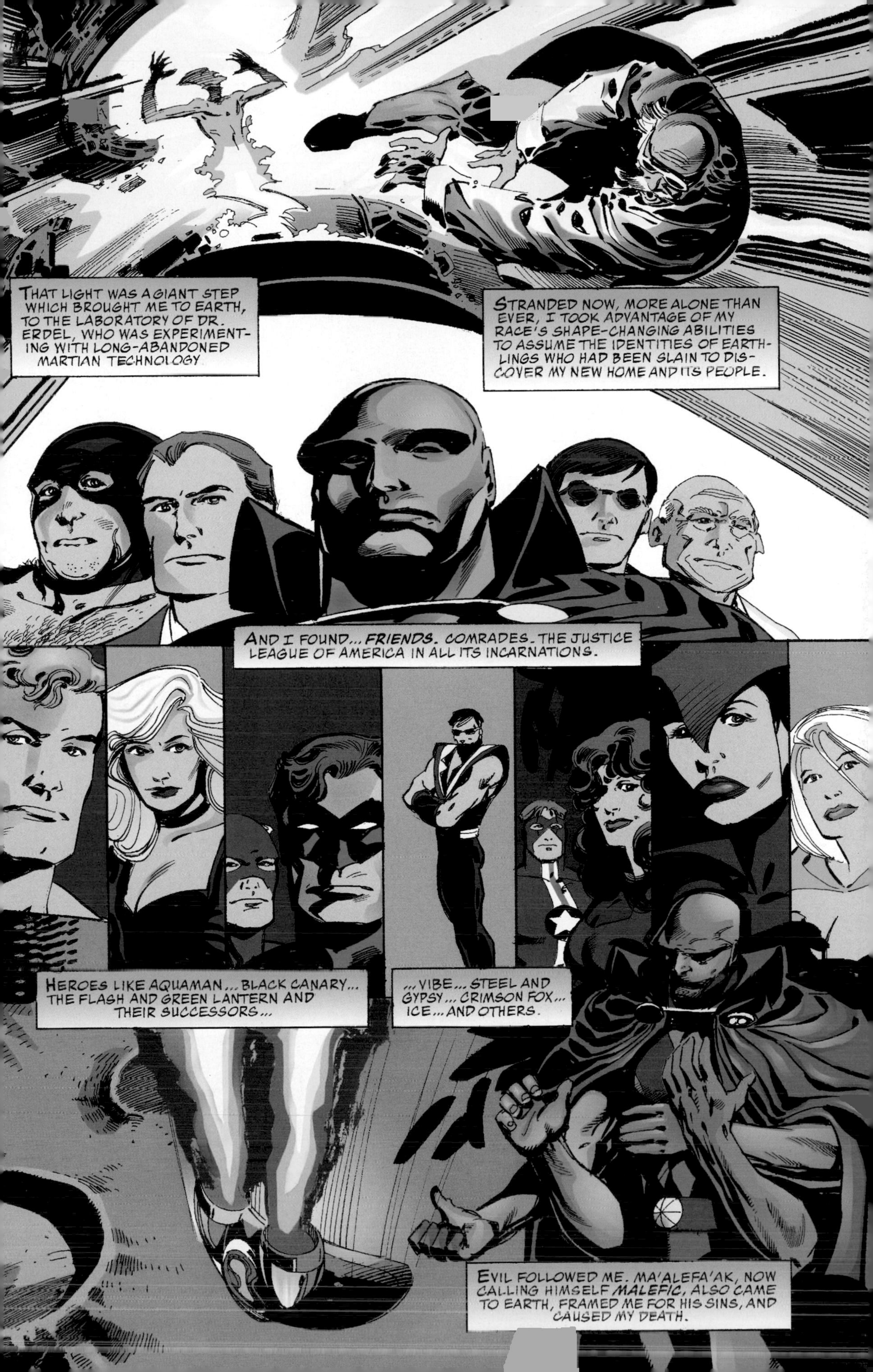
THAT LIGHT WAS A GIANT STEP WHICH BROUGHT ME TO EARTH, TO THE LABORATORY OF DR. ERDEL, WHO WAS EXPERIMENTING WITH LONG-ABANDONED MARTIAN TECHNOLOGY.
STRANDED NOW, MORE ALONE THAN EVER, I TOOK ADVANTAGE OF MY RACE'S SHAPE-CHANGING ABILITIES TO ASSUME THE IDENTITIES OF EARTHLINGS WHO HAD BEEN SLAIN TO DISCOVER MY NEW HOME AND ITS PEOPLE.
AND I FOUND... FRIENDS. COMRADES. THE JUSTICE LEAGUE OF AMERICA IN ALL ITS INCARNATIONS.
HEROES LIKE AQUAMAN... BLACK CANARY... THE FLASH AND GREEN LANTERN AND THEIR SUCCESSORS...
...VIBE... STEEL AND GYPSY... CRIMSON FOX... ICE... AND OTHERS.
EVIL FOLLOWED ME. MA'ALEFA'AK, NOW CALLING HIMSELF MALEFIC, ALSO CAME TO EARTH, FRAMED ME FOR HIS SINS, AND CAUSED MY DEATH.

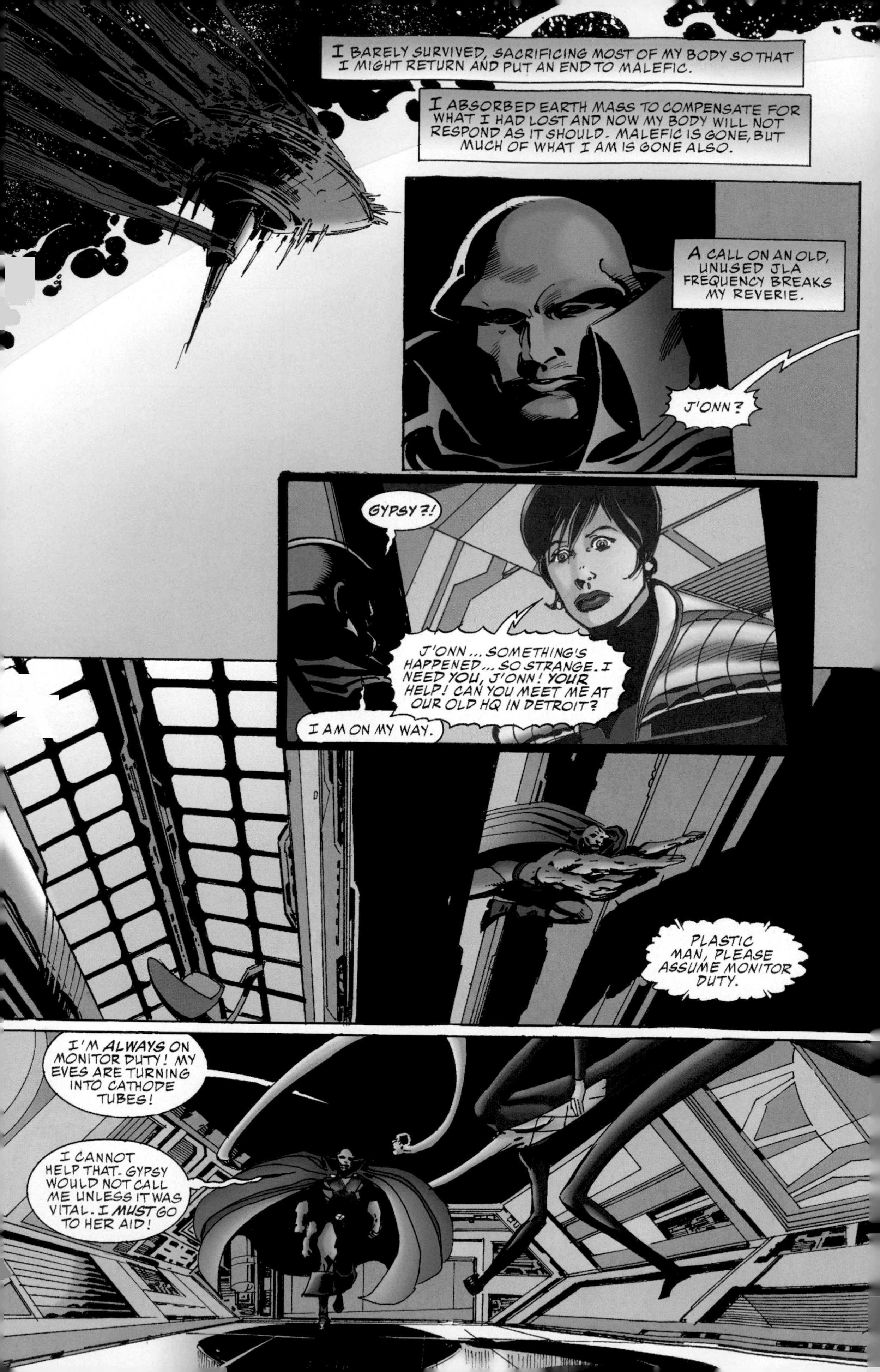
I BARELY SURVIVED, SACRIFICING MOST OF MY BODY SO THAT I MIGHT RETURN AND PUT AN END TO MALEFIC.
I ABSORBED EARTH MASS TO COMPENSATE FOR WHAT I HAD LOST AND NOW MY BODY WILL NOT RESPOND AS IT SHOULD. MALEFIC IS GONE, BUT MUCH OF WHAT I AM IS GONE ALSO.
A CALL ON AN OLD, UNUSED JLA FREQUENCY BREAKS MY REVERIE.
J'ONN?
GYPSY?!
J'ONN... SOMETHING'S HAPPENED... SO STRANGE. I NEED YOU, J'ONN! YOUR HELP! CAN YOU MEET ME AT OUR OLD HQ IN DETROIT?
I AM ON MY WAY.
PLASTIC MAN, PLEASE ASSUME MONITOR DUTY.
I'M ALWAYS ON MONITOR DUTY! MY EYES ARE TURNING INTO CATHODE TUBES!
I CANNOT HELP THAT. GYPSY WOULD NOT CALL ME UNLESS IT WAS VITAL. I MUST GO TO HER AID!

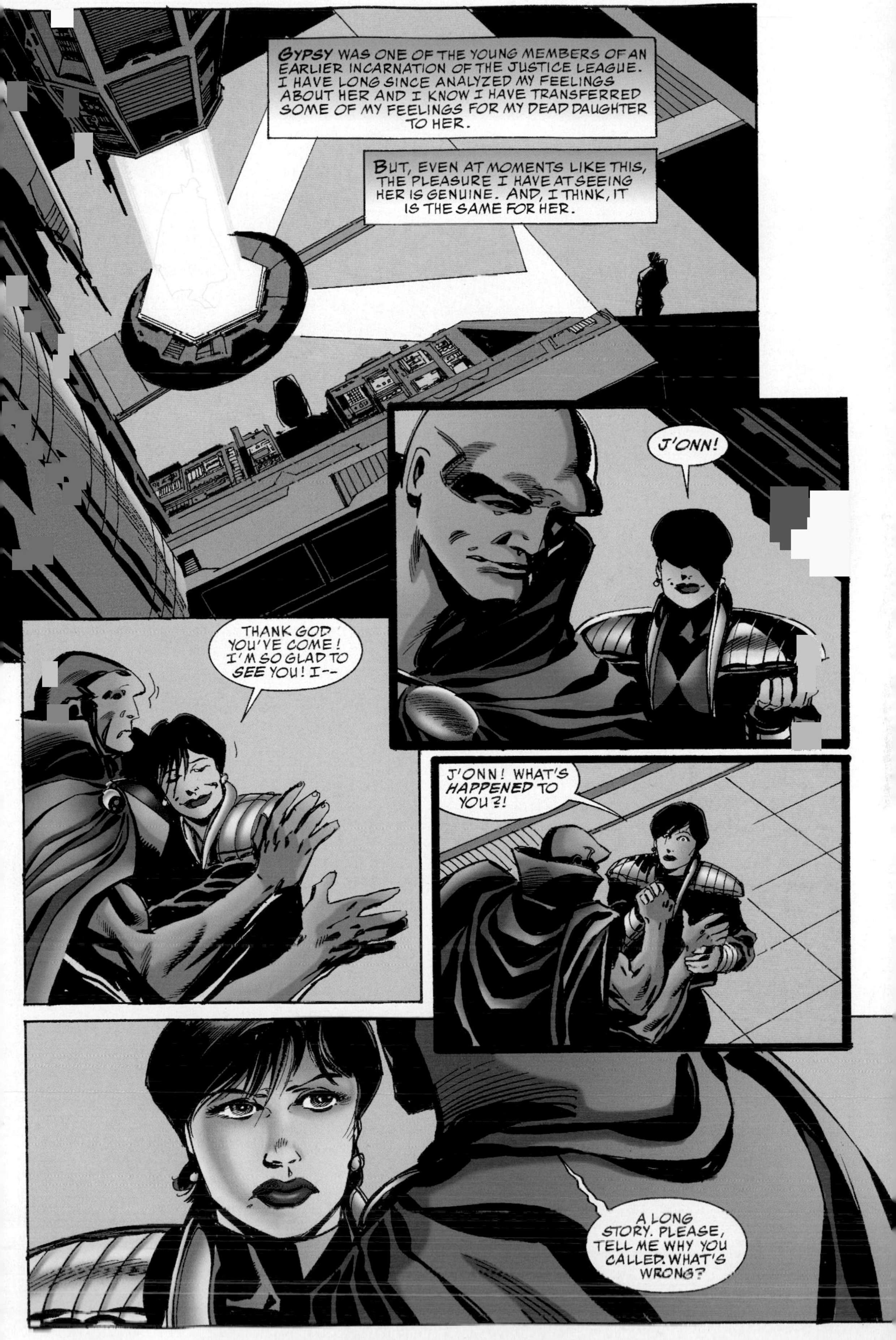
GYPSY WAS ONE OF THE YOUNG MEMBERS OF AN EARLIER INCARNATION OF THE JUSTICE LEAGUE. I HAVE LONG SINCE ANALYZED MY FEELINGS ABOUT HER AND I KNOW I HAVE TRANSFERRED SOME OF MY FEELINGS FOR MY DEAD DAUGHTER TO HER.
BUT, EVEN AT MOMENTS LIKE THIS, THE PLEASURE I HAVE AT SEEING HER IS GENUINE. AND, I THINK, IT IS THE SAME FOR HER.
J'ONN!
THANK GOD YOU'VE COME! I'M SO GLAD TO SEE YOU! I--
J'ONN! WHAT'S HAPPENED TO YOU?!
A LONG STORY. PLEASE, TELL ME WHY YOU CALLED. WHAT'S WRONG?

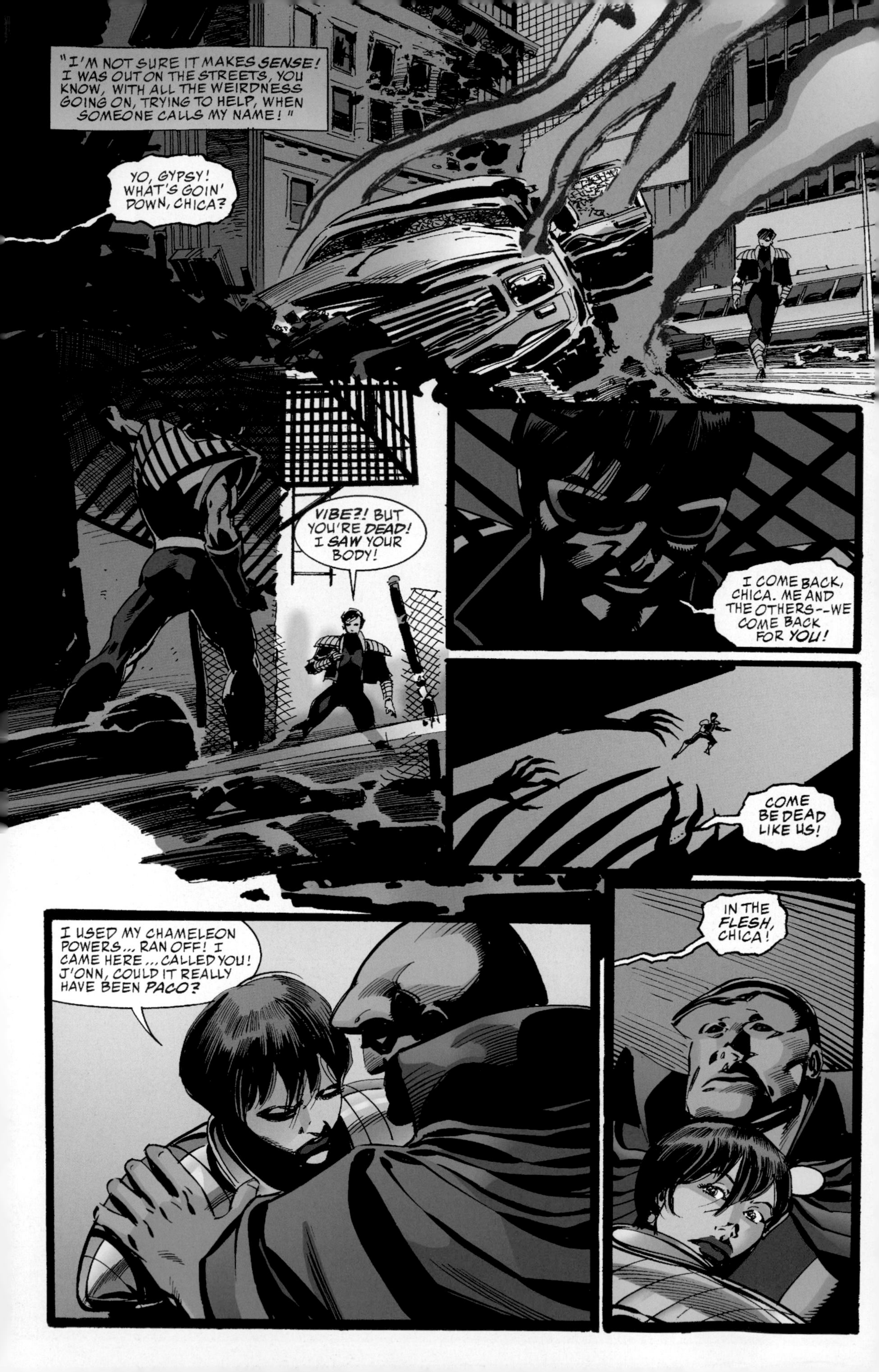
"I'M NOT SURE IT MAKES SENSE! I WAS OUT ON THE STREETS, YOU KNOW, WITH ALL THE WEIRDNESS GOING ON, TRYING TO HELP, WHEN SOMEONE CALLS MY NAME!"
YO, GYPSY! WHAT'S GOIN' DOWN, CHICA?
VIBE?! BUT YOU'RE DEAD! I SAW YOUR BODY!
I COME BACK, CHICA. ME AND THE OTHERS--WE COME BACK FOR YOU!
COME BE DEAD LIKE US!
I USED MY CHAMELEON POWERS... RAN OFF! I CAME HERE... CALLED YOU! J'ONN, COULD IT REALLY HAVE BEEN PACO?
IN THE FLESH, CHICA!

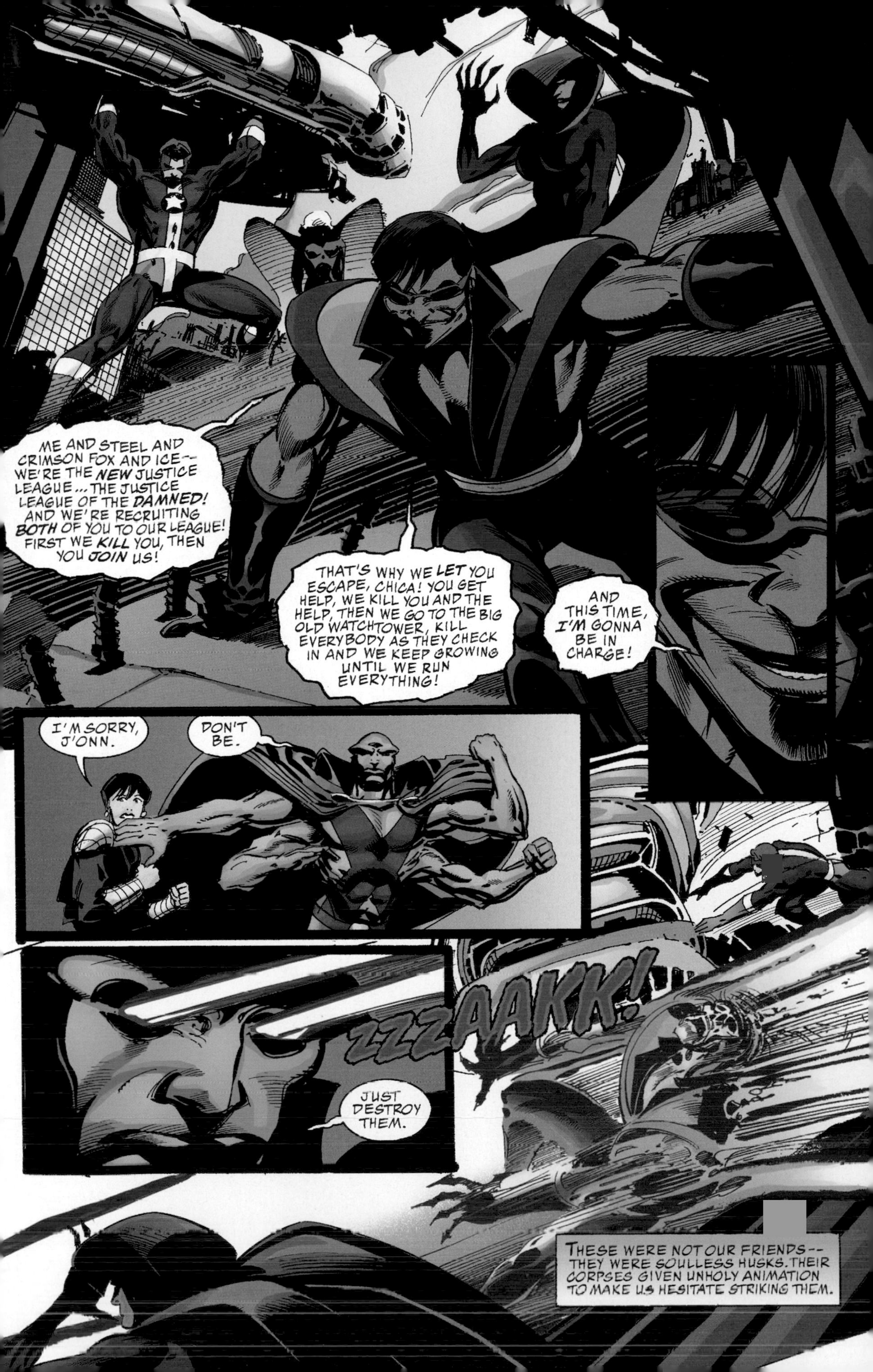
ME AND STEEL AND CRIMSON FOX AND ICE-- WE'RE THE NEW JUSTICE LEAGUE... THE JUSTICE LEAGUE OF THE DAMNED! AND WE'RE RECRUITING BOTH OF YOU TO OUR LEAGUE! FIRST WE KILL YOU, THEN YOU JOIN US!
THAT'S WHY WE LET YOU ESCAPE, CHICA! YOU GET HELP, WE KILL YOU AND THE HELP, THEN WE GO TO THE BIG OLD WATCHTOWER, KILL EVERYBODY AS THEY CHECK IN AND WE KEEP GROWING UNTIL WE RUN EVERYTHING!
AND THIS TIME, I'M GONNA BE IN CHARGE!
I'M SORRY, J'ONN.
DON'T BE.
JUST DESTROY THEM.
ZZZAAKK!
THESE WERE NOT OUR FRIENDS-- THEY WERE SOULLESS HUSKS. THEIR CORPSES GIVEN UNHOLY ANIMATION TO MAKE US HESITATE STRIKING THEM.

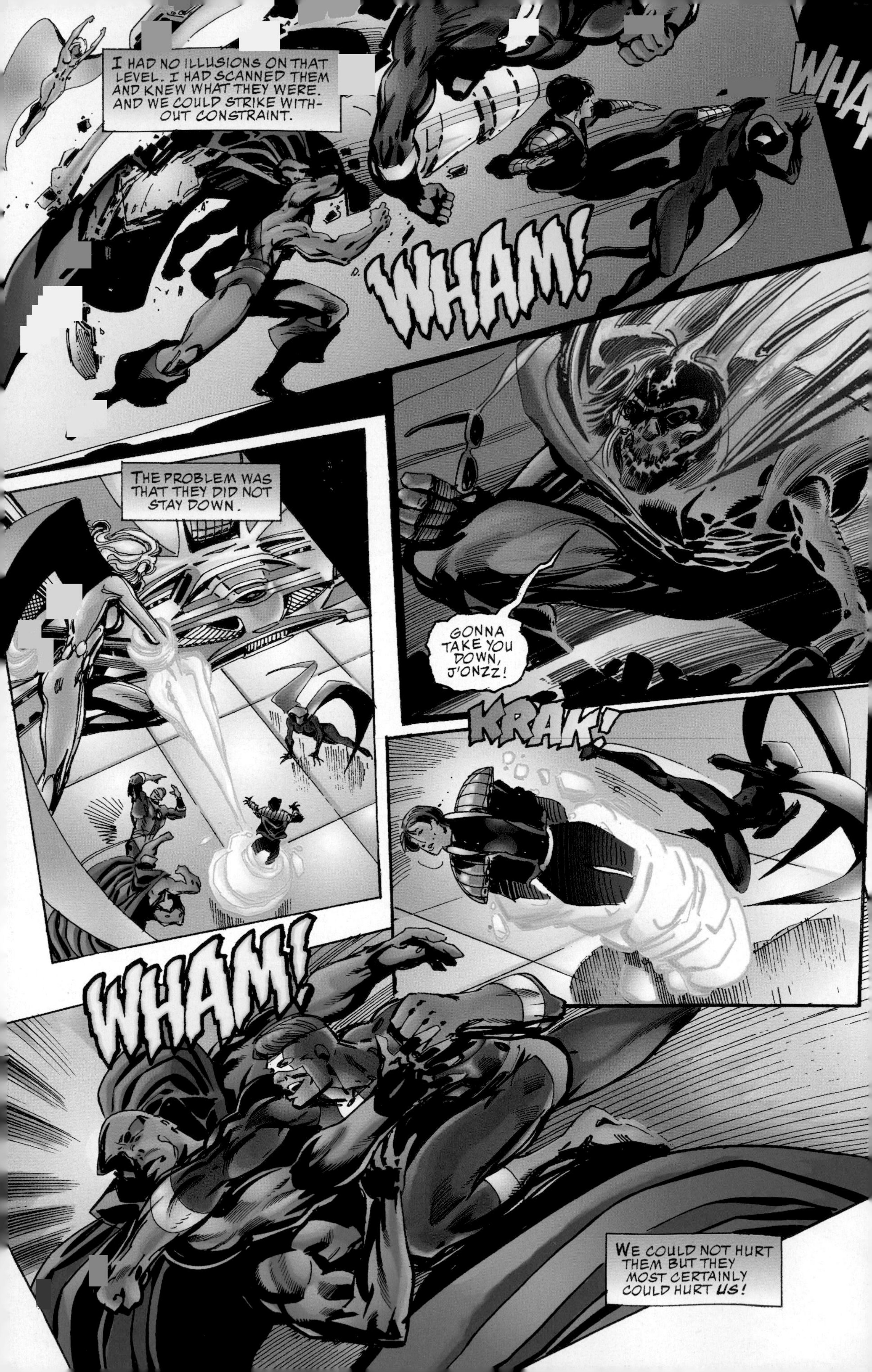

I HAD NO ILLUSIONS ON THAT LEVEL. I HAD SCANNED THEM AND KNEW WHAT THEY WERE. AND WE COULD STRIKE WITHOUT CONSTRAINT.
WHAM!
WHAM!
THE PROBLEM WAS THAT THEY DID NOT STAY DOWN.
GONNA TAKE YOU DOWN, J'ONZZ!
KRAK!
WHAM!
WE COULD NOT HURT THEM BUT THEY MOST CERTAINLY COULD HURT US!

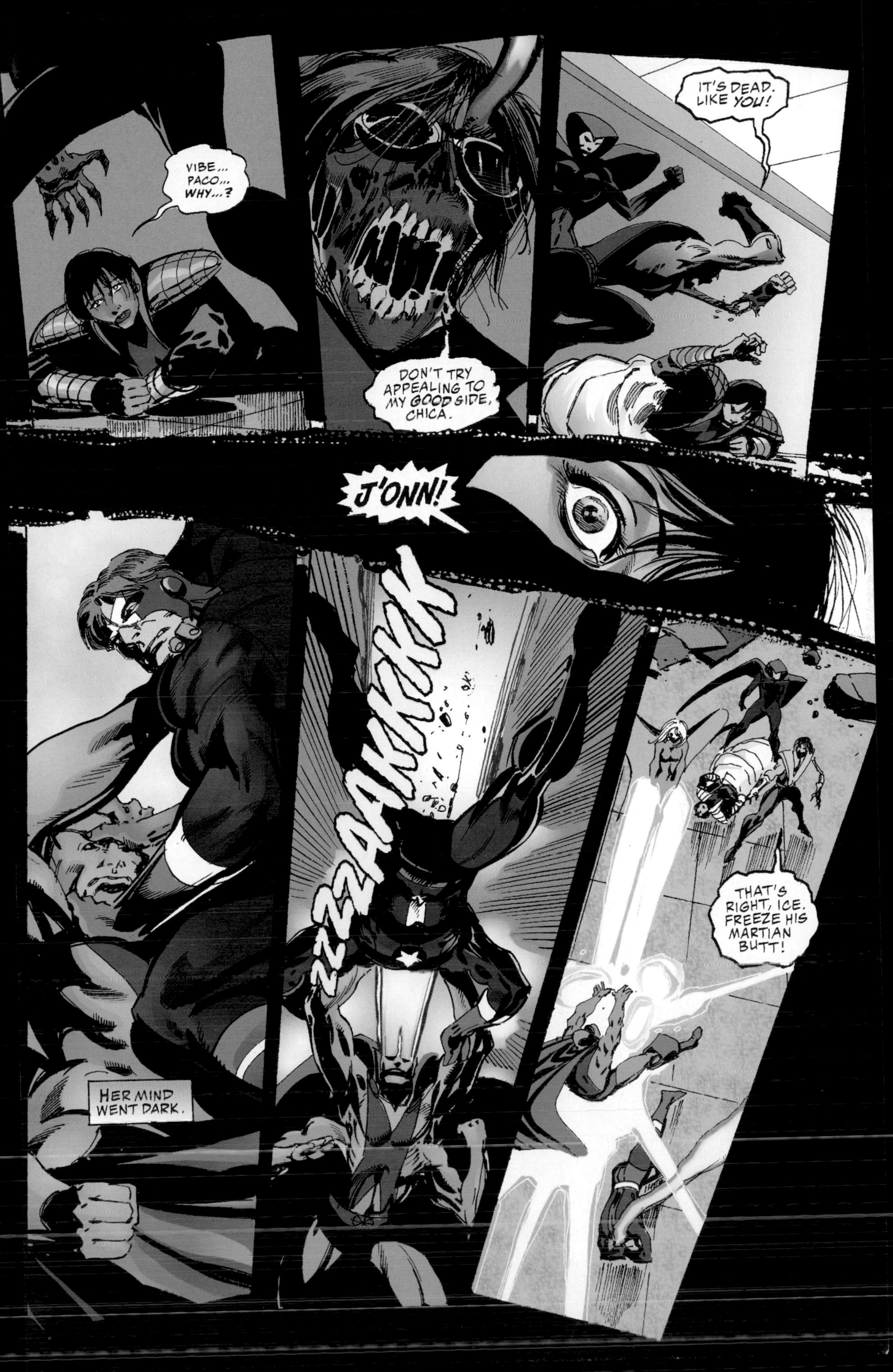
VIBE... PACO... WHY...?
DON'T TRY APPEALING TO MY GOOD SIDE, CHICA.
IT'S DEAD. LIKE YOU!
J'ONN!
HER MIND WENT DARK.
ZZZZZAAKKKK
THAT'S RIGHT, ICE. FREEZE HIS MARTIAN BUTT!

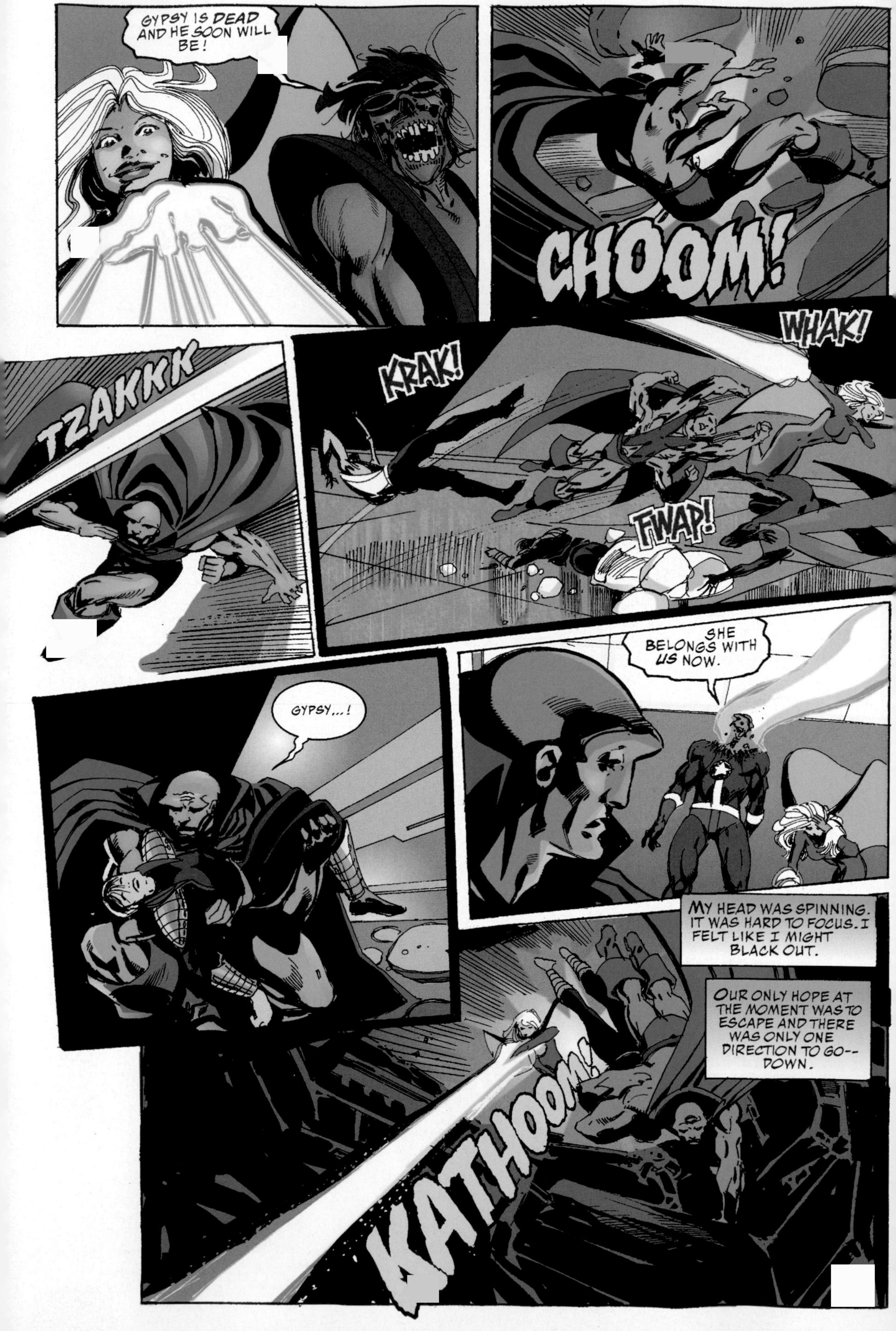

GYPSY IS DEAD AND HE SOON WILL BE!
CHOOM!
TZAKKK
KRAK!
WHAK!
FWAP!
GYPSY...!
SHE BELONGS WITH US NOW.
MY HEAD WAS SPINNING. IT WAS HARD TO FOCUS. I FELT LIKE I MIGHT BLACK OUT.
OUR ONLY HOPE AT THE MOMENT WAS TO ESCAPE AND THERE WAS ONLY ONE DIRECTION TO GO-- DOWN.
KATHOOM!

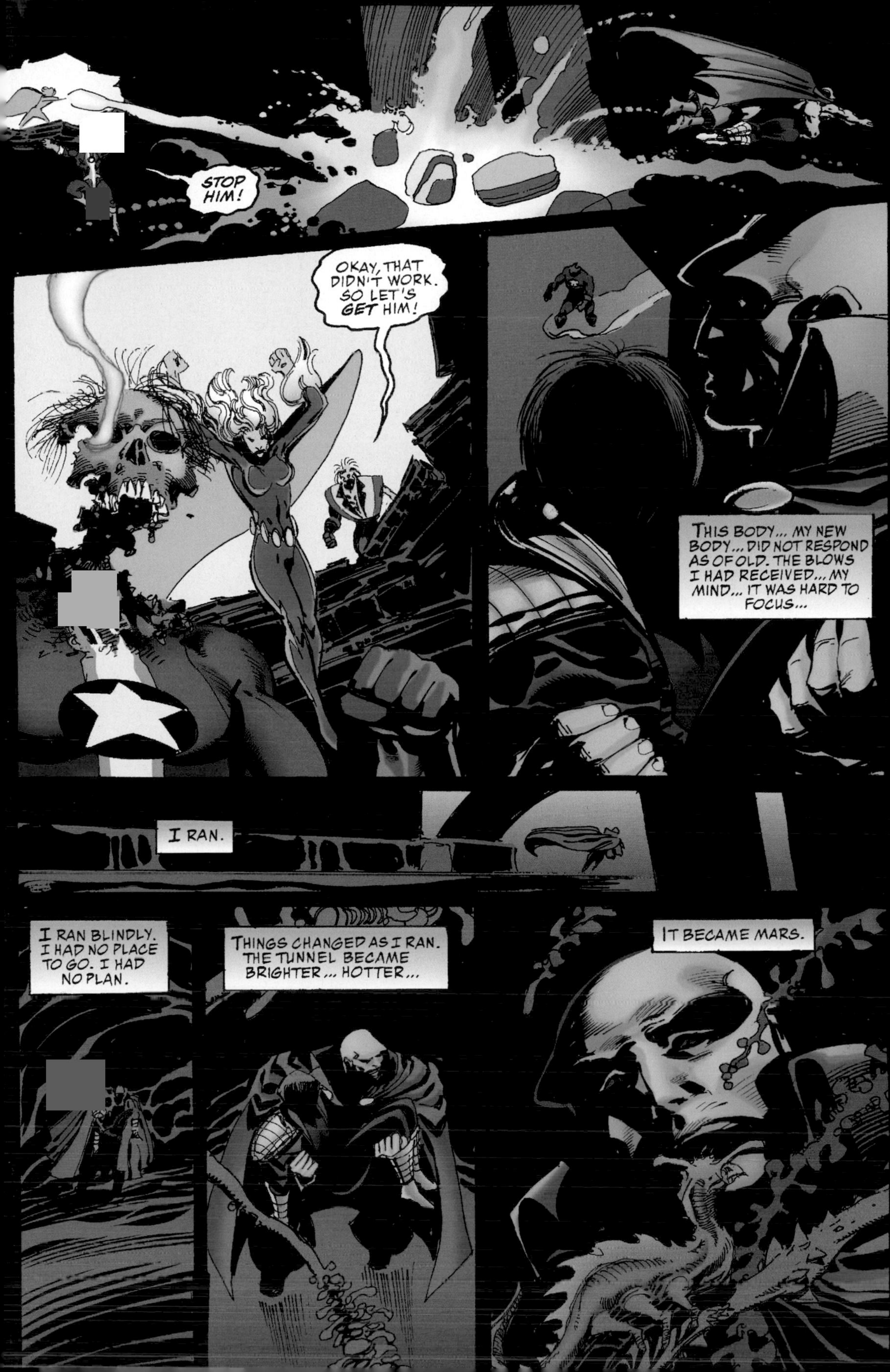
STOP HIM!
OKAY, THAT DIDN'T WORK. SO LET'S GET HIM!
THIS BODY... MY NEW BODY... DID NOT RESPOND AS OF OLD. THE BLOWS I HAD RECEIVED... MY MIND... IT WAS HARD TO FOCUS...
I RAN.
I RAN BLINDLY. I HAD NO PLACE TO GO. I HAD NO PLAN.
THINGS CHANGED AS I RAN. THE TUNNEL BECAME BRIGHTER... HOTTER...
IT BECAME MARS.

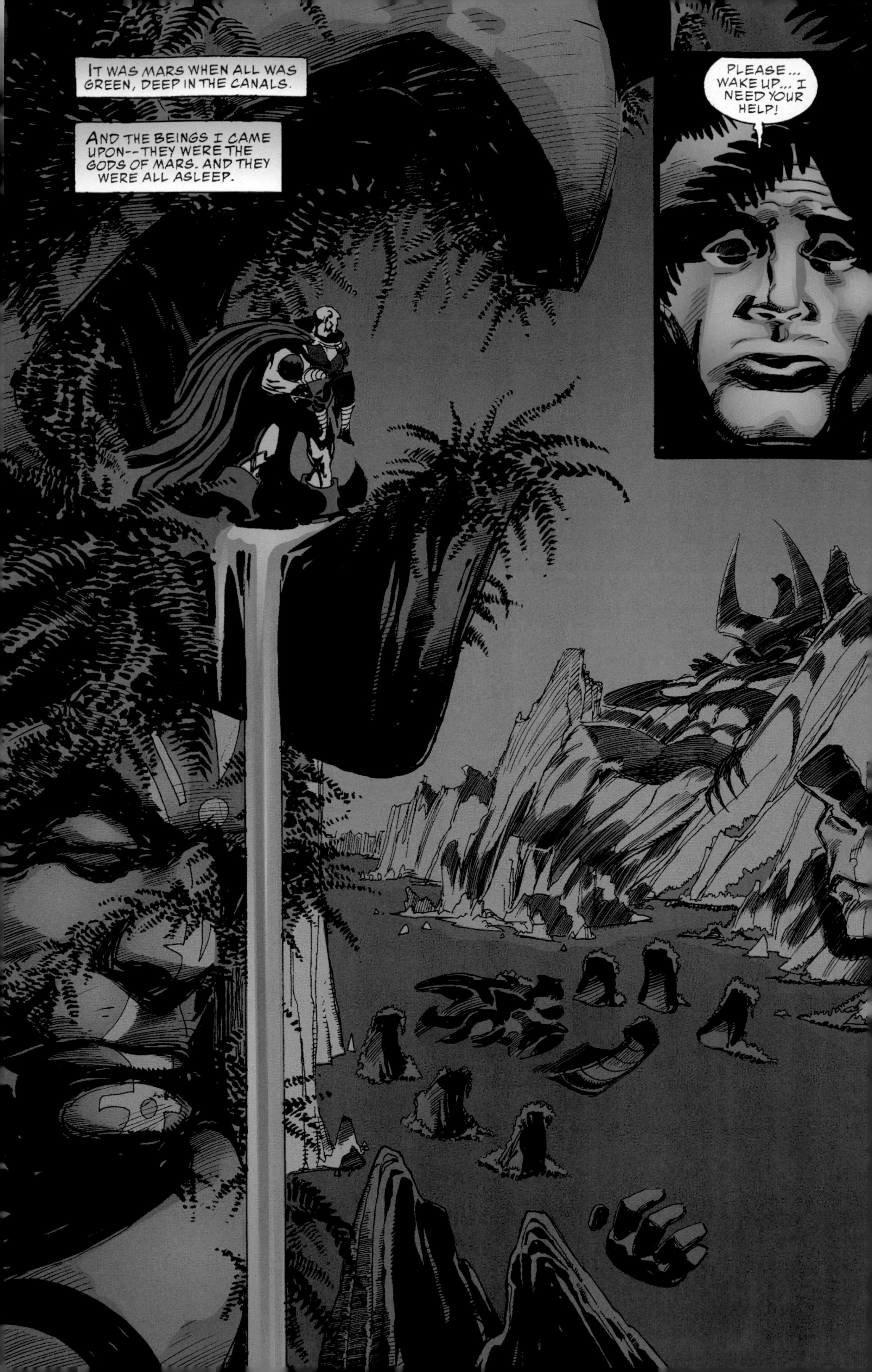
IT WAS MARS WHEN ALL WAS GREEN, DEEP IN THE CANALS.
AND THE BEINGS I CAME UPON--THEY WERE THE GODS OF MARS. AND THEY WERE ALL ASLEEP.
PLEASE... WAKE UP... I NEED YOUR HELP!

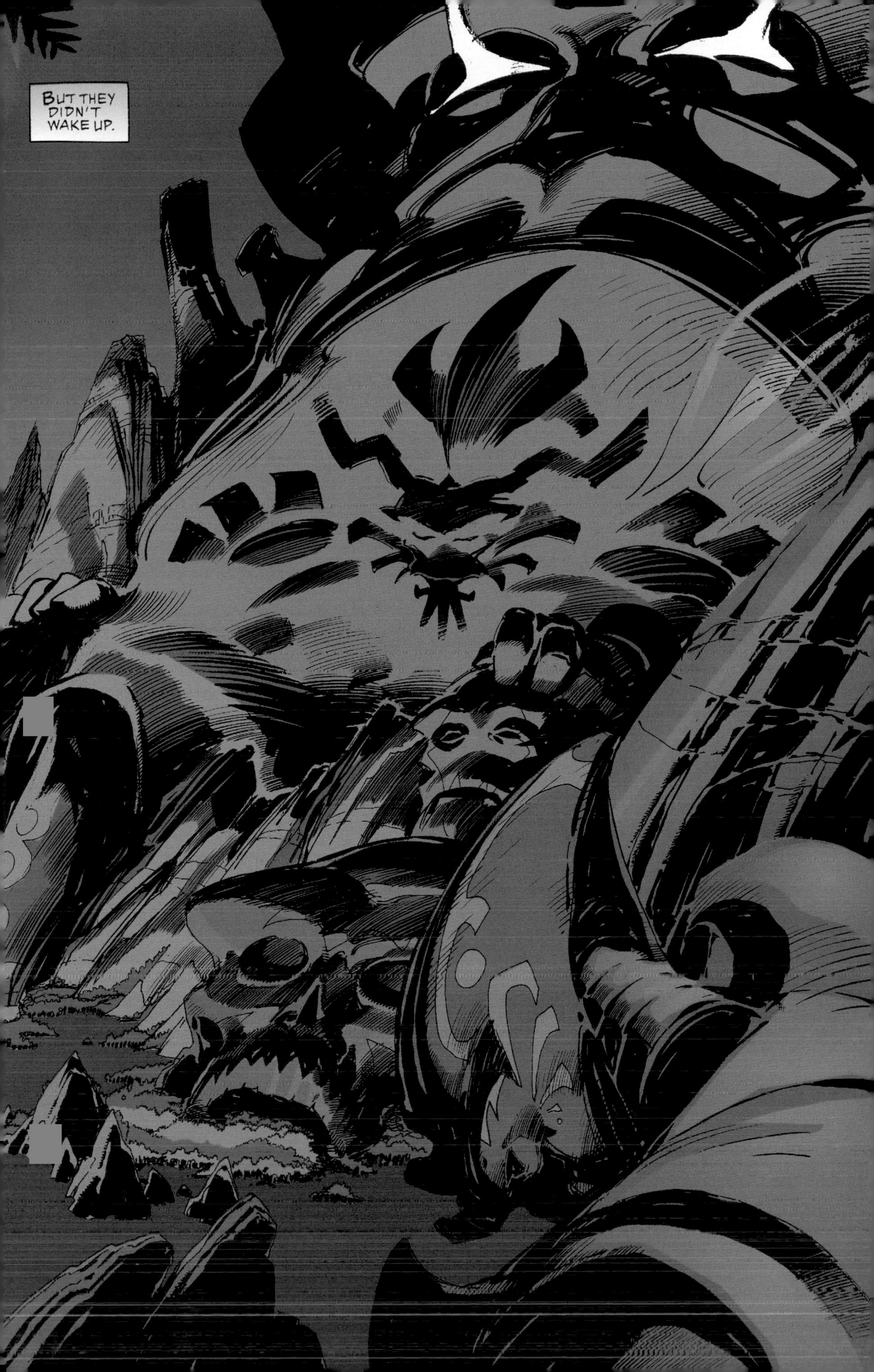
BUT THEY DIDN'T WAKE UP.

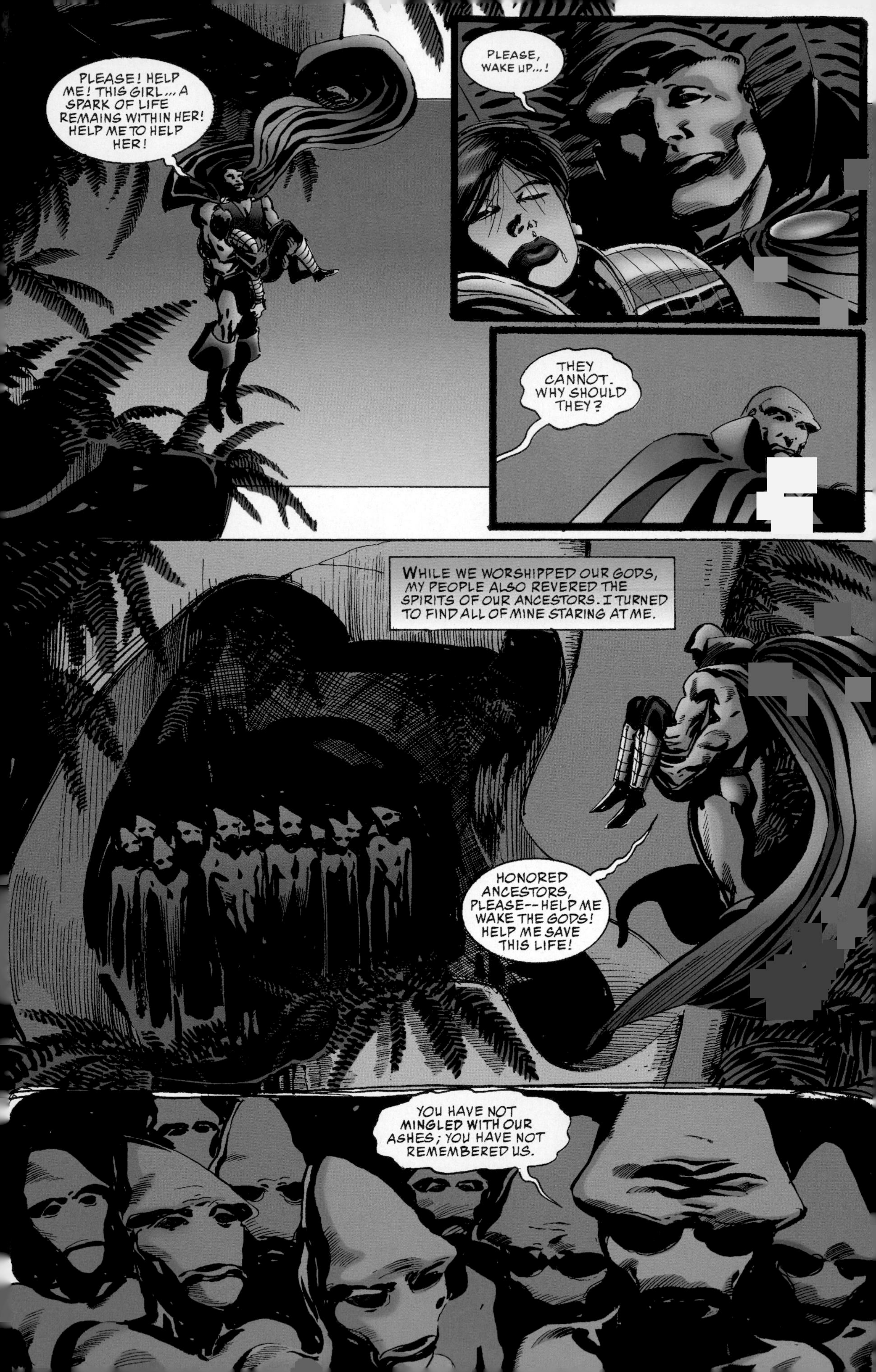
PLEASE! HELP ME! THIS GIRL... A SPARK OF LIFE REMAINS WITHIN HER! HELP ME TO HELP HER!
PLEASE, WAKE UP...!
THEY CANNOT. WHY SHOULD THEY?
WHILE WE WORSHIPPED OUR GODS, MY PEOPLE ALSO REVERED THE SPIRITS OF OUR ANCESTORS. I TURNED TO FIND ALL OF MINE STARING AT ME.
HONORED ANCESTORS, PLEASE--HELP ME WAKE THE GODS! HELP ME SAVE THIS LIFE!
YOU HAVE NOT MINGLED WITH OUR ASHES; YOU HAVE NOT REMEMBERED US.

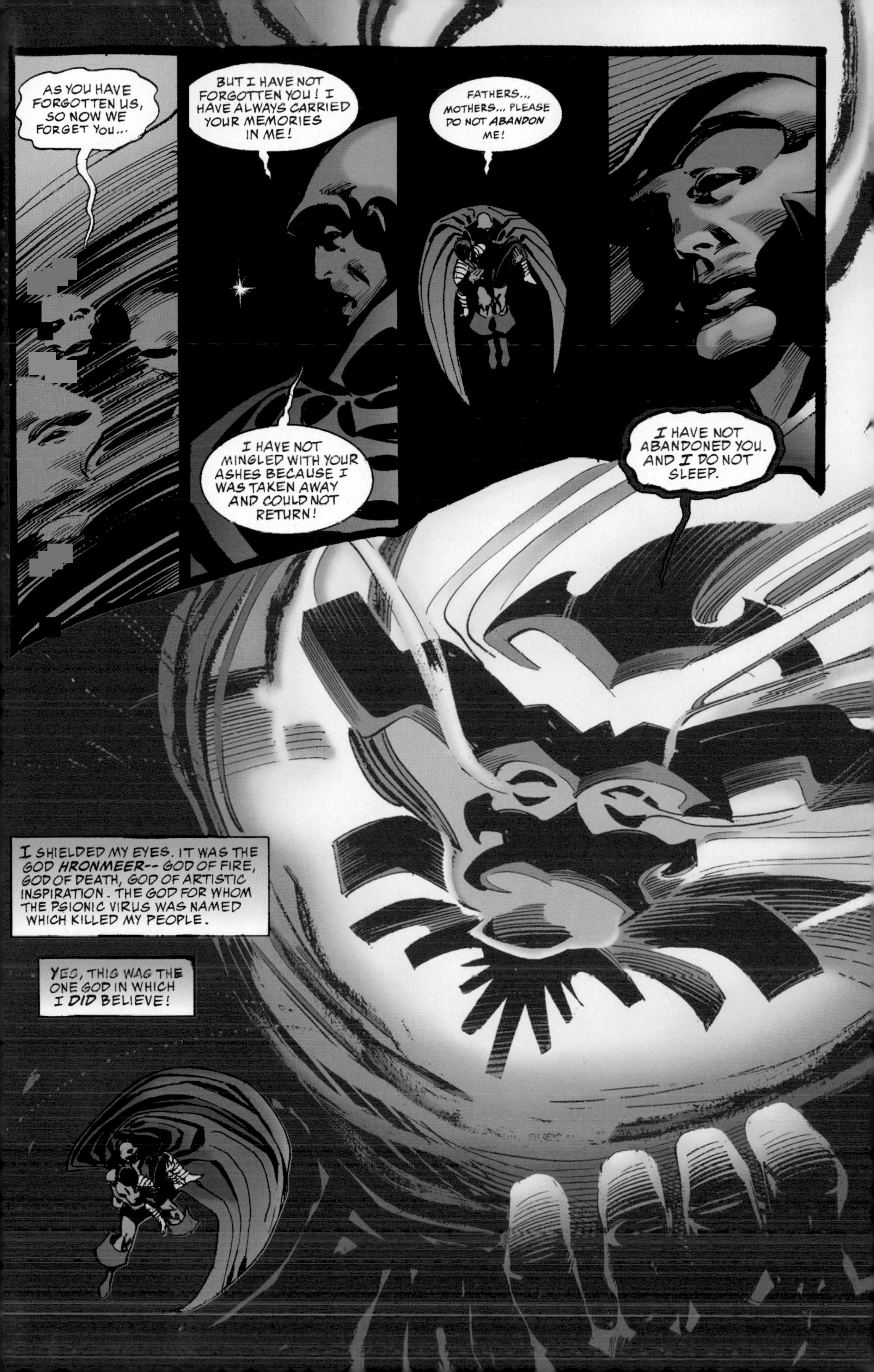
AS YOU HAVE FORGOTTEN US, SO NOW WE FORGET YOU...
BUT I HAVE NOT FORGOTTEN YOU! I HAVE ALWAYS CARRIED YOUR MEMORIES IN ME!
I HAVE NOT MINGLED WITH YOUR ASHES BECAUSE I WAS TAKEN AWAY AND COULD NOT RETURN!
FATHERS... MOTHERS... PLEASE DO NOT *ABANDON* ME!
I HAVE NOT ABANDONED YOU. AND *I* DO NOT SLEEP.
I SHIELDED MY EYES. IT WAS THE GOD *HRONMEER*-- GOD OF FIRE, GOD OF DEATH, GOD OF ARTISTIC INSPIRATION. THE GOD FOR WHOM THE PSIONIC VIRUS WAS NAMED WHICH KILLED MY PEOPLE.
YES, THIS WAS THE ONE GOD IN WHICH I *DID* BELIEVE!

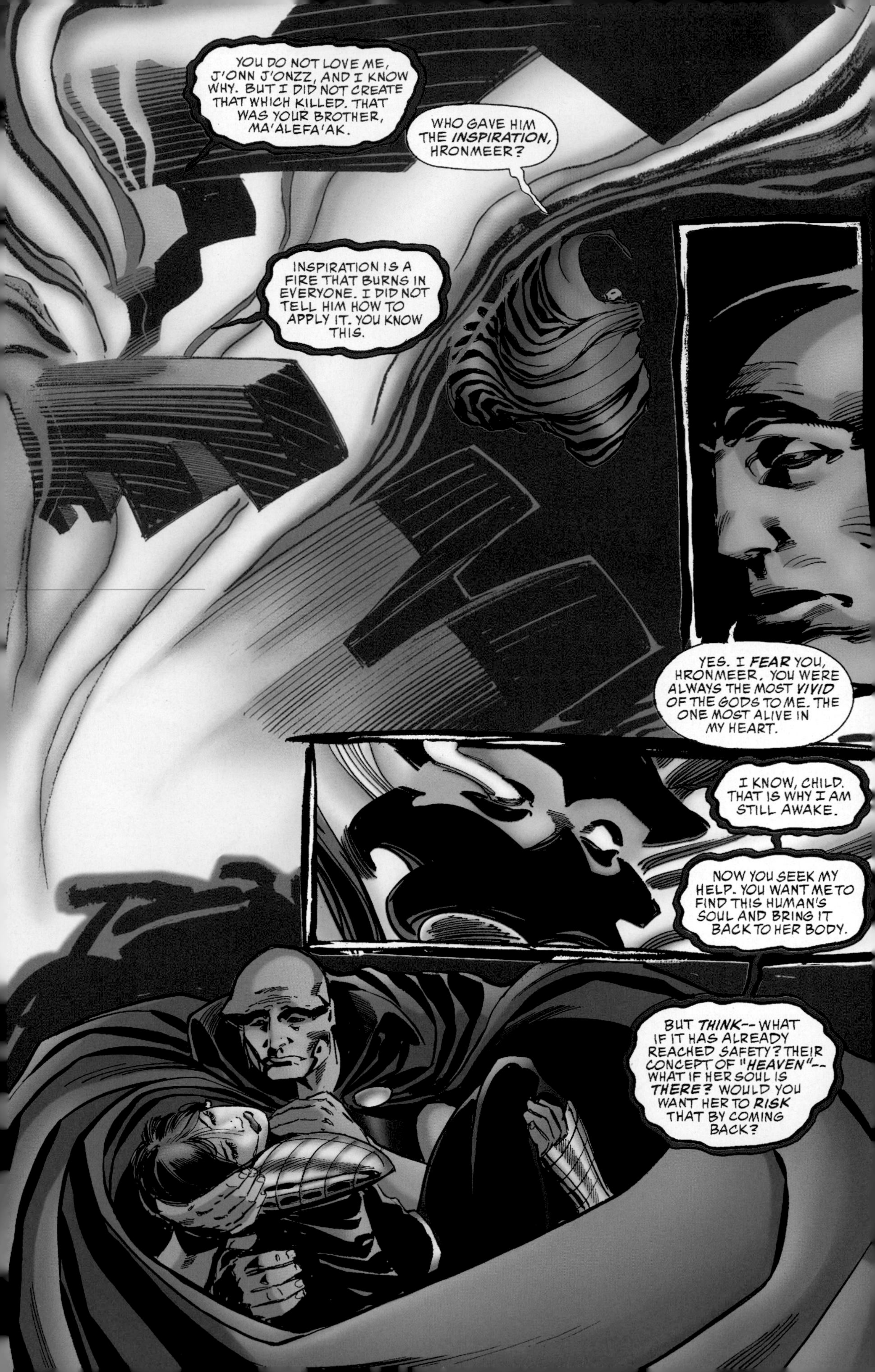
YOU DO NOT LOVE ME, J'ONN J'ONZZ, AND I KNOW WHY. BUT I DID NOT CREATE THAT WHICH KILLED. THAT WAS YOUR BROTHER, MA'ALEFA'AK.
WHO GAVE HIM THE *INSPIRATION*, HRONMEER?
INSPIRATION IS A FIRE THAT BURNS IN EVERYONE. I DID NOT TELL HIM HOW TO APPLY IT. YOU KNOW THIS.
YES. I *FEAR* YOU, HRONMEER. YOU WERE ALWAYS THE MOST *VIVID* OF THE GODS TO ME. THE ONE MOST ALIVE IN MY HEART.
I KNOW, CHILD. THAT IS WHY I AM STILL AWAKE.
NOW YOU SEEK MY HELP. YOU WANT ME TO FIND THIS HUMAN'S SOUL AND BRING IT BACK TO HER BODY.
BUT *THINK*-- WHAT IF IT HAS ALREADY REACHED SAFETY? THEIR CONCEPT OF "*HEAVEN*"-- WHAT IF HER SOUL IS *THERE*? WOULD YOU WANT HER TO *RISK* THAT BY COMING BACK?

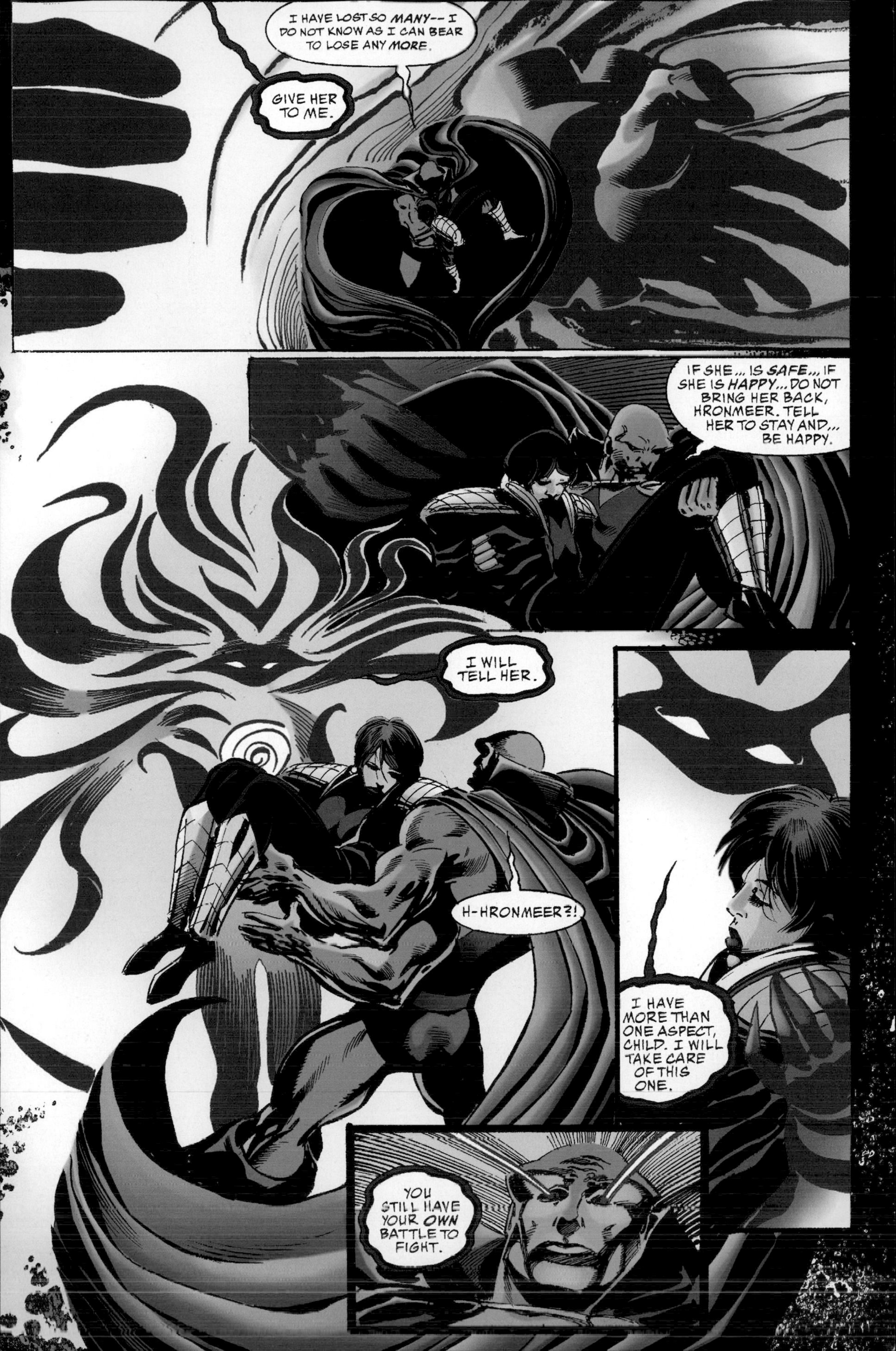
I HAVE LOST SO MANY-- I DO NOT KNOW AS I CAN BEAR TO LOSE ANY MORE.
GIVE HER TO ME.
IF SHE... IS SAFE... IF SHE IS HAPPY... DO NOT BRING HER BACK, HRONMEER. TELL HER TO STAY AND... BE HAPPY.
I WILL TELL HER.
H-HRONMEER?!
I HAVE MORE THAN ONE ASPECT, CHILD. I WILL TAKE CARE OF THIS ONE.
YOU STILL HAVE YOUR OWN BATTLE TO FIGHT.

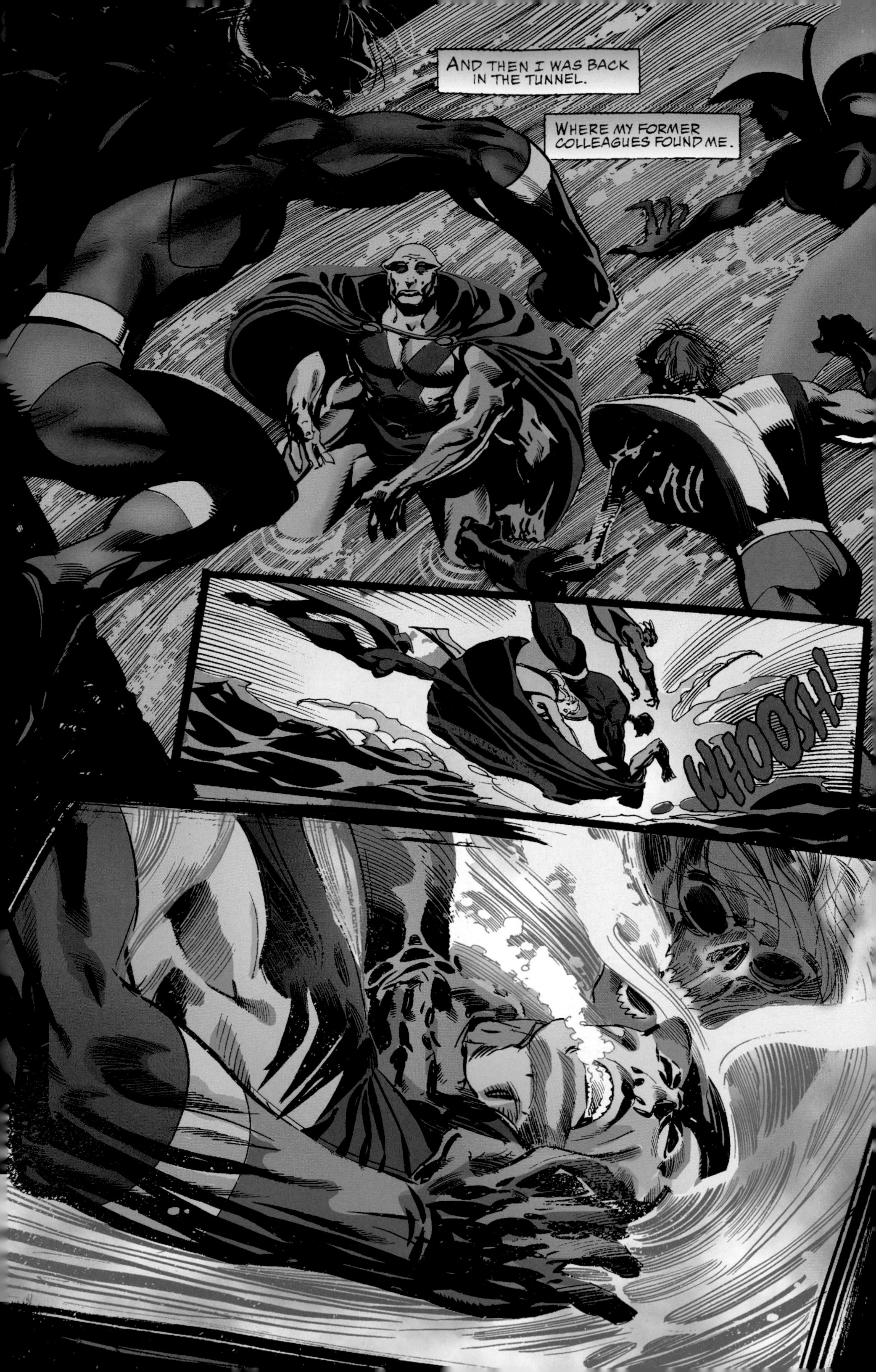
AND THEN I WAS BACK IN THE TUNNEL.
WHERE MY FORMER COLLEAGUES FOUND ME.
WHOOSH!

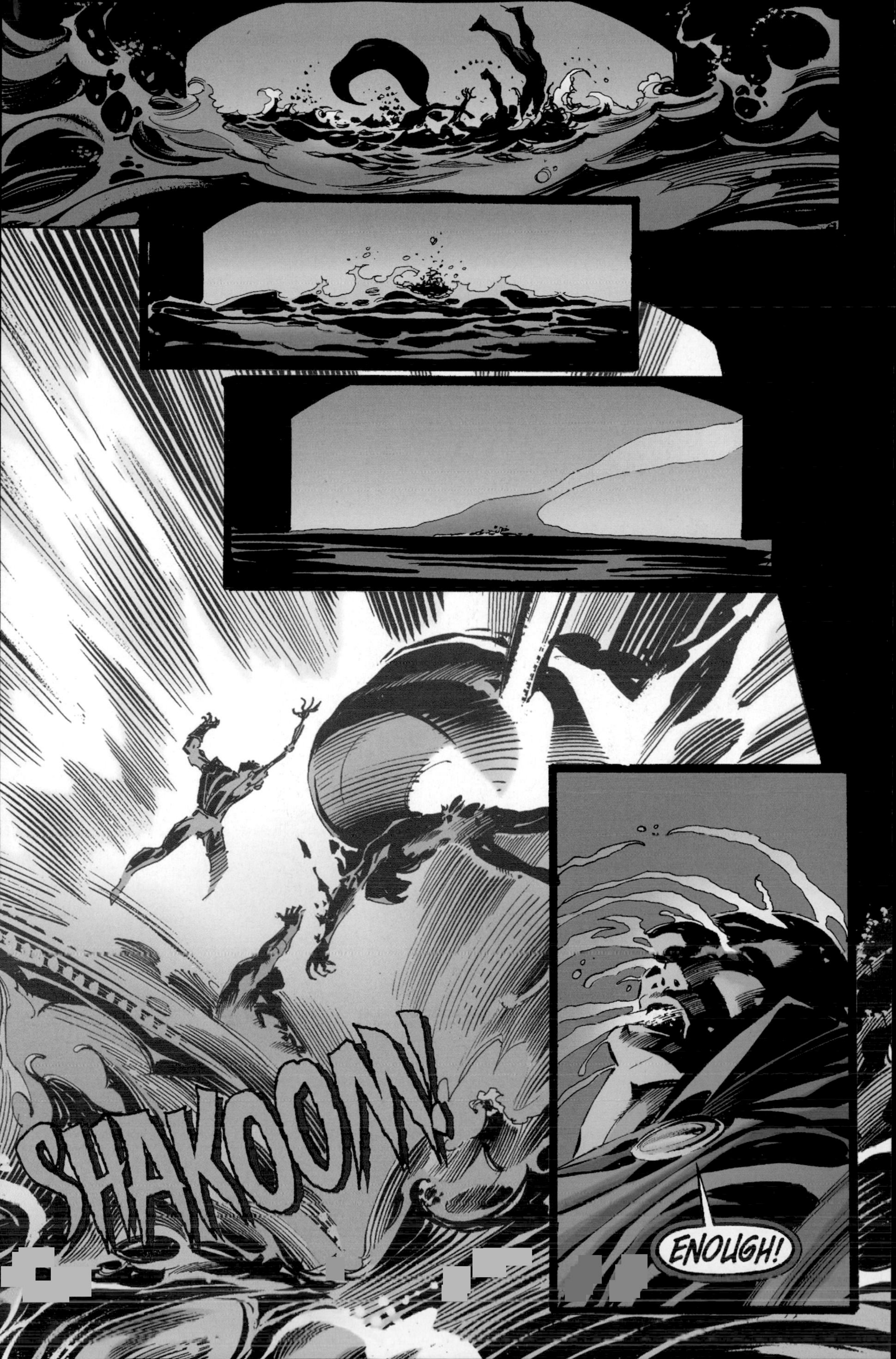
SHAKOOM!
ENOUGH!

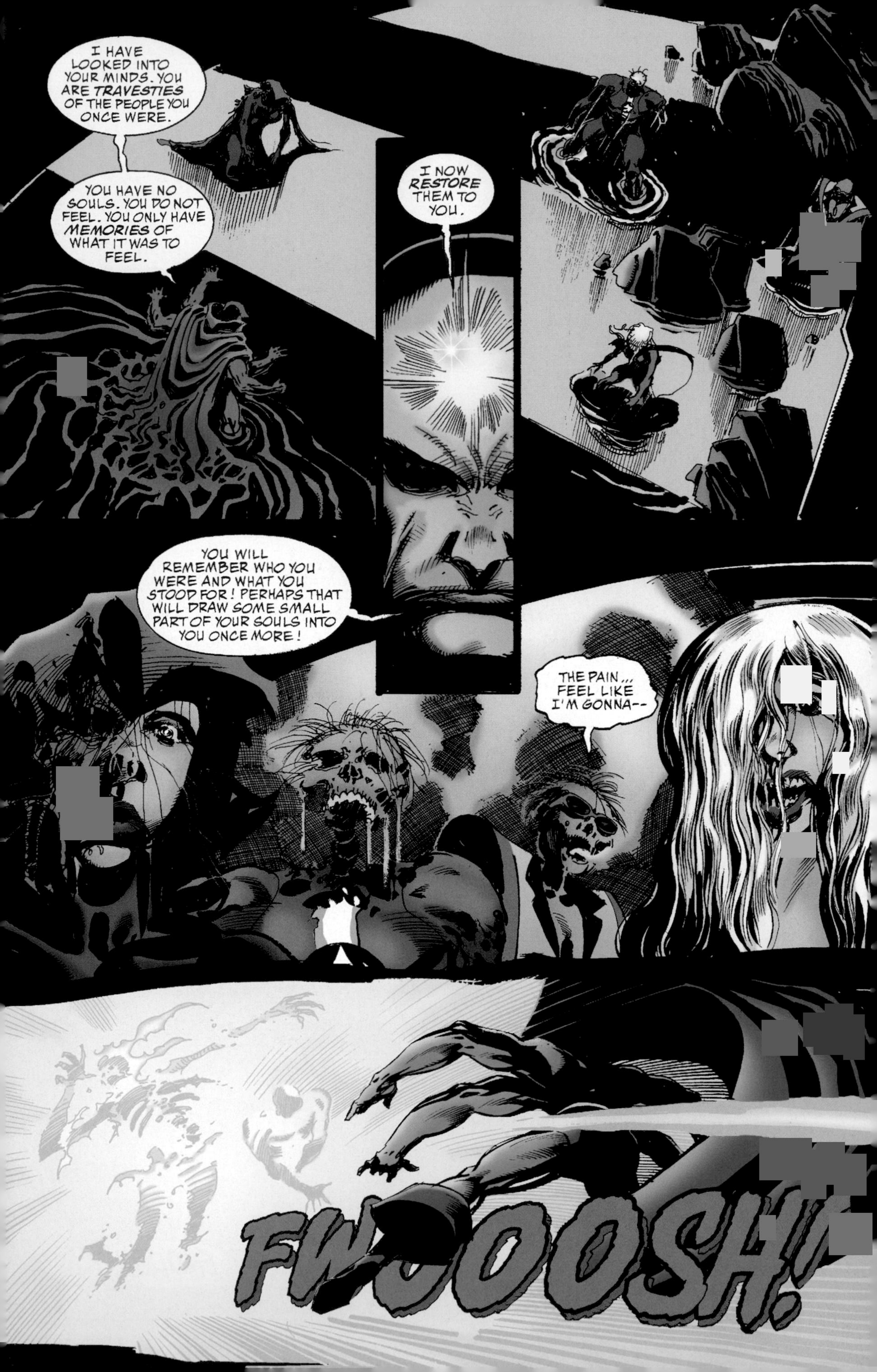
I HAVE LOOKED INTO YOUR MINDS. YOU ARE *TRAVESTIES* OF THE PEOPLE YOU ONCE WERE.
YOU HAVE NO SOULS. YOU DO NOT FEEL. YOU ONLY HAVE *MEMORIES* OF WHAT IT WAS TO FEEL.
I NOW *RESTORE* THEM TO YOU.
YOU WILL REMEMBER WHO YOU WERE AND WHAT YOU STOOD FOR! PERHAPS THAT WILL DRAW SOME SMALL PART OF YOUR SOULS INTO YOU ONCE MORE!
THE PAIN... FEEL LIKE I'M GONNA--
FWOOOOSH!

THE FRICTION BETWEEN THEIR INFERNAL PROGRAMMING AND THE PURITY OF THOSE MEMORIES CAUSED THEM TO BURST INTO FLAMES...

AND FIRE WAS MY WEAKNESS.

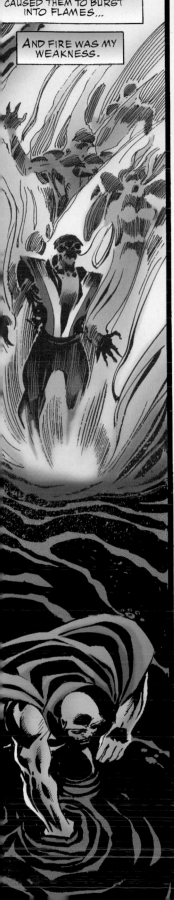

J'ONN! C'MON! YOU'VE GOT TO GET UP!

GYPSY?!

YEAH! NOW GET UP WHILE WE STILL CAN!

J'ONNNN...

THANK YOU, MAAAN... FOR REMINDING US... SAVING US... ONE LAST TIMMME...

VAYA CON DIOS...

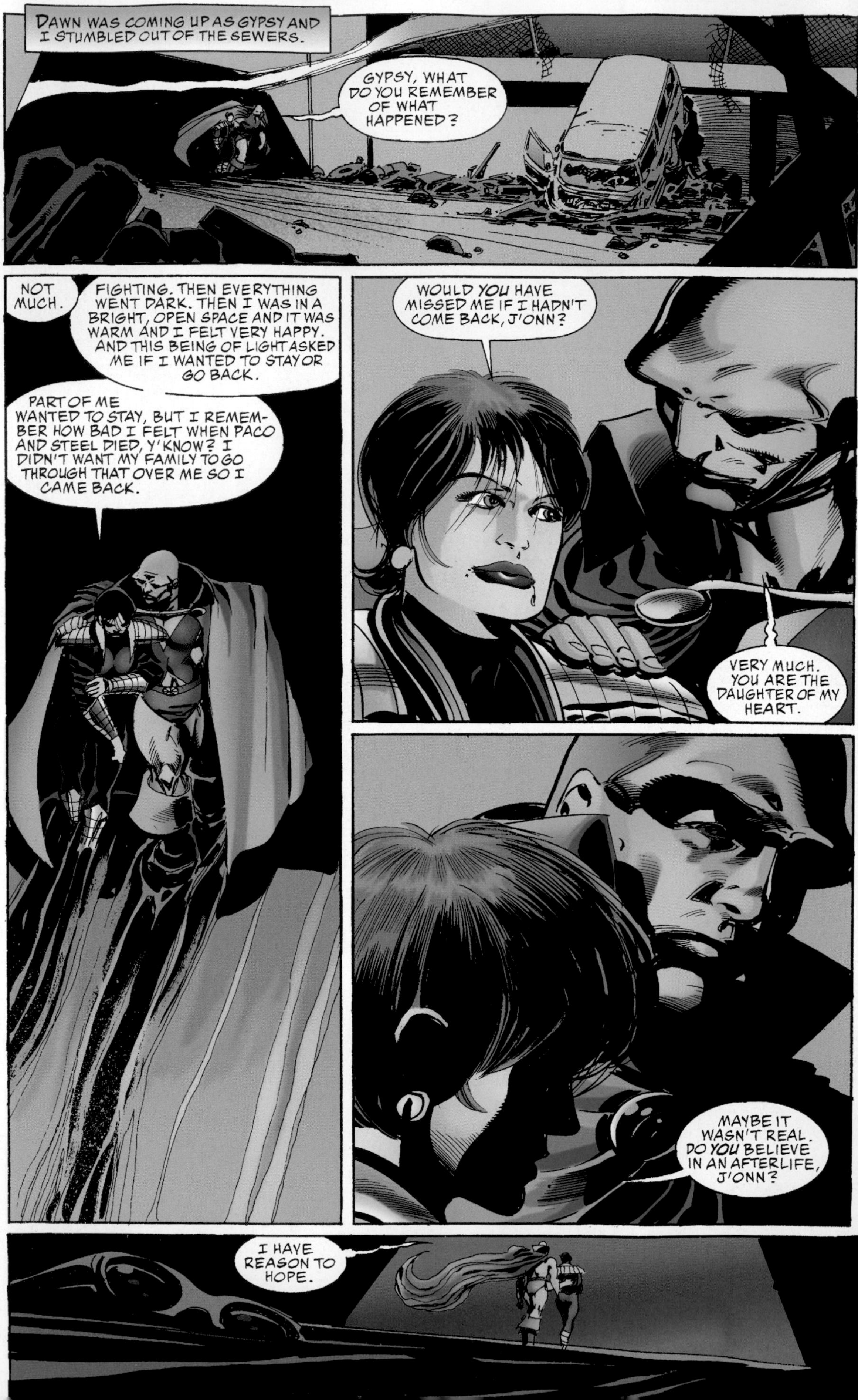
DAWN WAS COMING UP AS GYPSY AND I STUMBLED OUT OF THE SEWERS.
GYPSY, WHAT DO YOU REMEMBER OF WHAT HAPPENED?
NOT MUCH.
FIGHTING. THEN EVERYTHING WENT DARK. THEN I WAS IN A BRIGHT, OPEN SPACE AND IT WAS WARM AND I FELT VERY HAPPY. AND THIS BEING OF LIGHT ASKED ME IF I WANTED TO STAY OR GO BACK.
PART OF ME WANTED TO STAY, BUT I REMEMBER HOW BAD I FELT WHEN PACO AND STEEL DIED, Y'KNOW? I DIDN'T WANT MY FAMILY TO GO THROUGH THAT OVER ME SO I CAME BACK.
WOULD YOU HAVE MISSED ME IF I HADN'T COME BACK, J'ONN?
VERY MUCH. YOU ARE THE DAUGHTER OF MY HEART.
MAYBE IT WASN'T REAL. DO YOU BELIEVE IN AN AFTERLIFE, J'ONN?
I HAVE REASON TO HOPE.

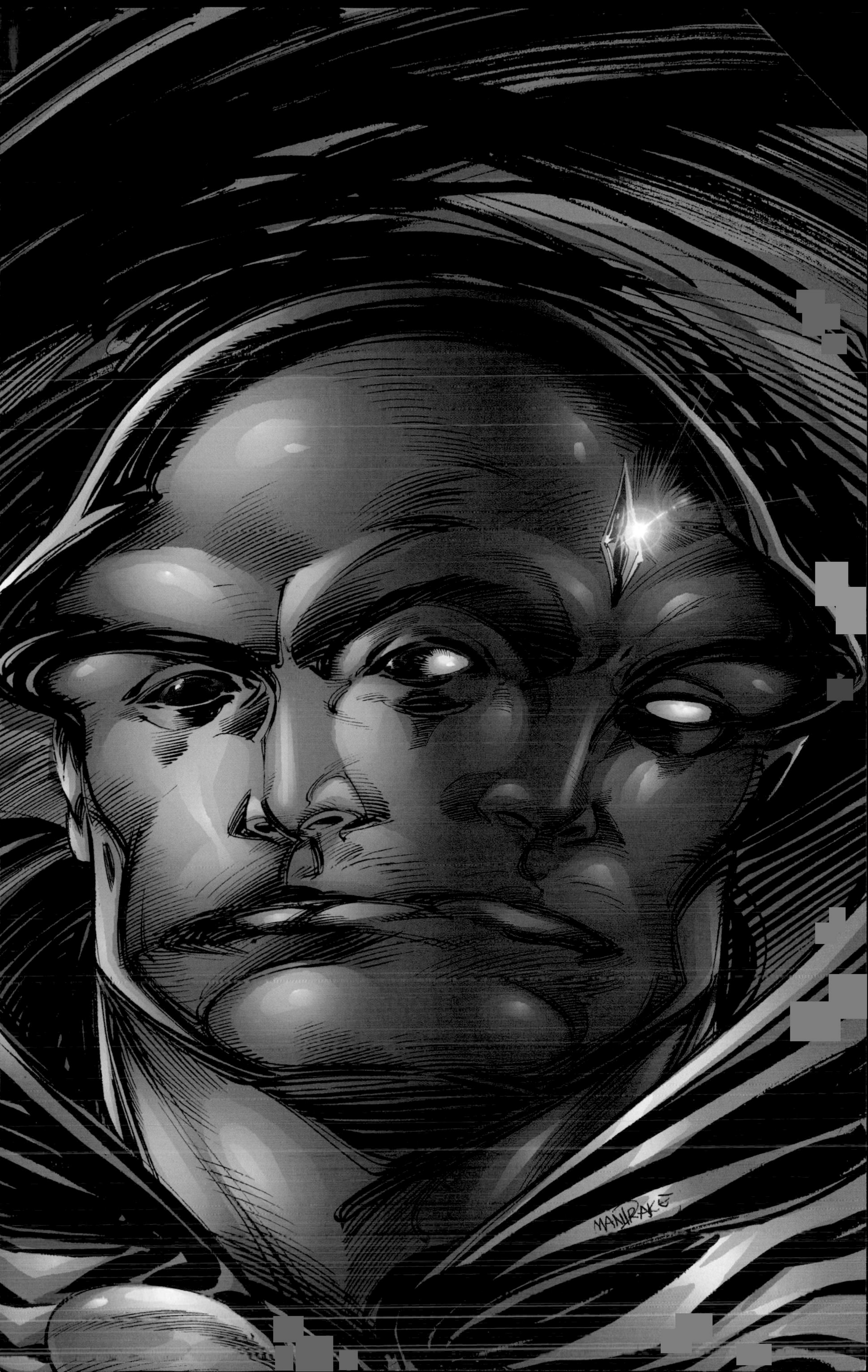
MANDRAKE

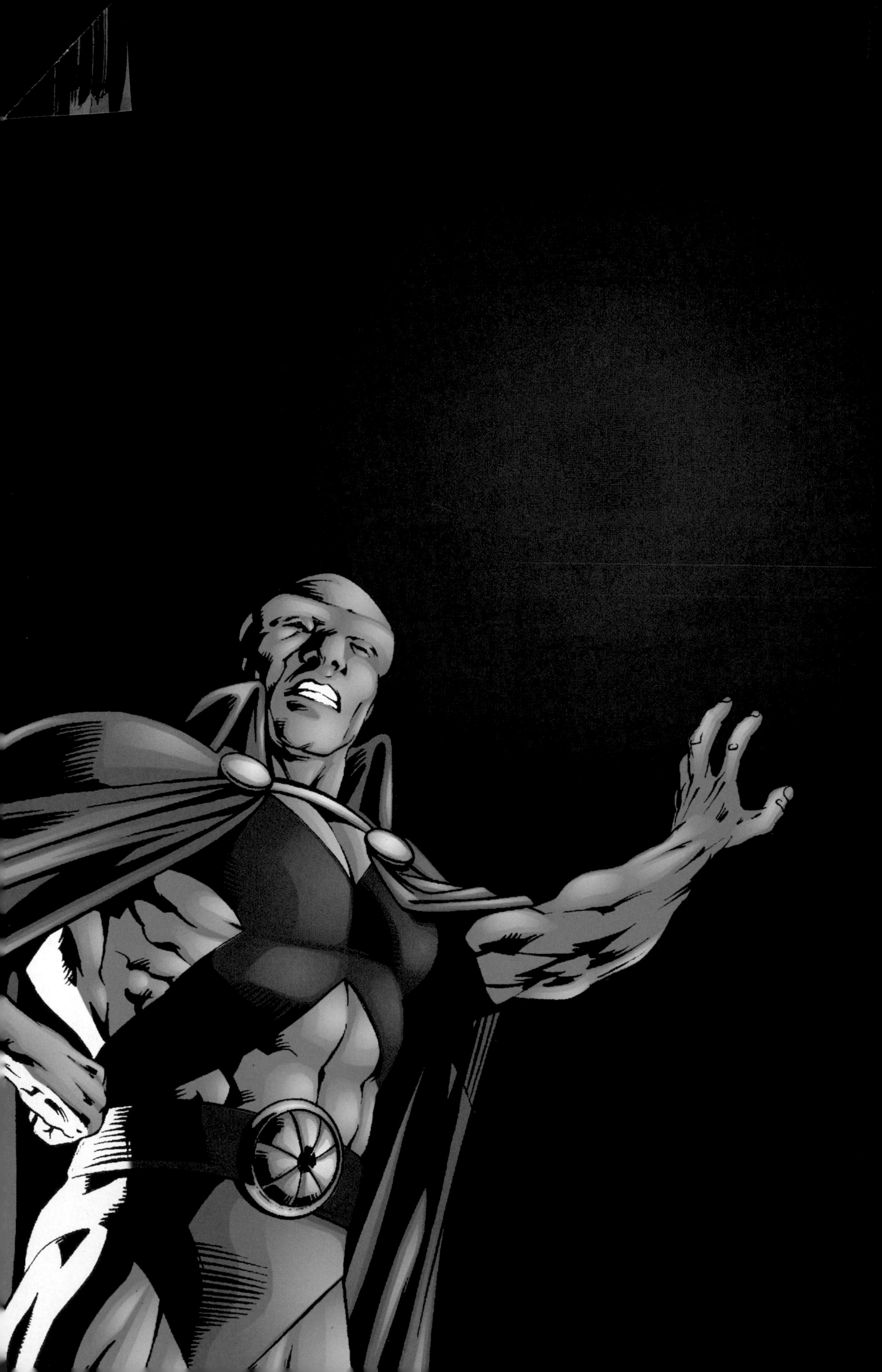

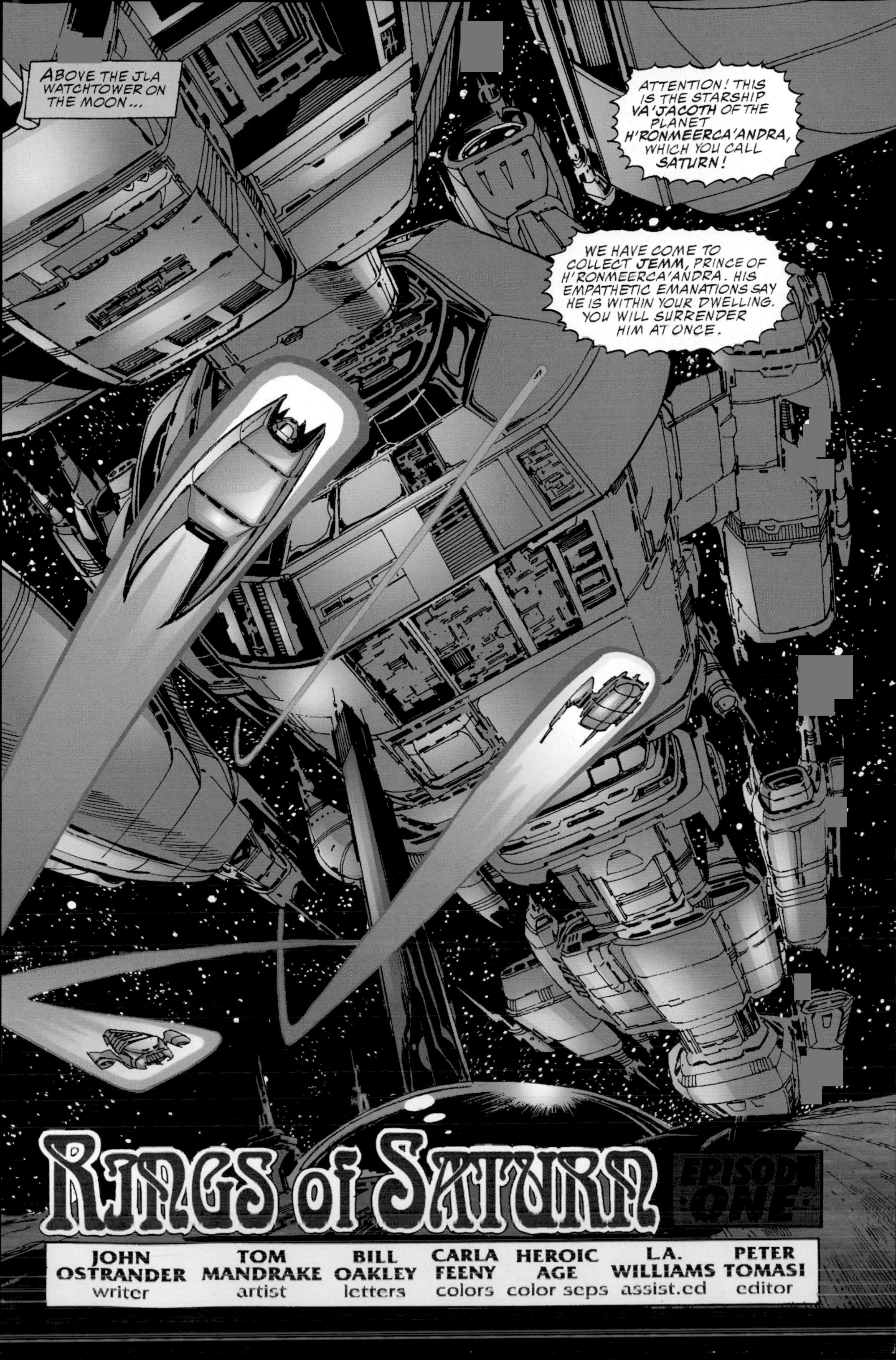
ABOVE THE JLA WATCHTOWER ON THE MOON...
ATTENTION! THIS IS THE STARSHIP VA'JACOTH OF THE PLANET H'RONMEERCA'ANDRA, WHICH YOU CALL SATURN!
WE HAVE COME TO COLLECT JEMM, PRINCE OF H'RONMEERCA'ANDRA. HIS EMPATHETIC EMANATIONS SAY HE IS WITHIN YOUR DWELLING. YOU WILL SURRENDER HIM AT ONCE.
RINGS of SATURN
EPISODE ONE
JOHN OSTRANDER writer
TOM MANDRAKE artist
BILL OAKLEY letters
CARLA FEENY colors
HEROIC AGE color seps
L.A. WILLIAMS assist.ed
PETER TOMASI editor

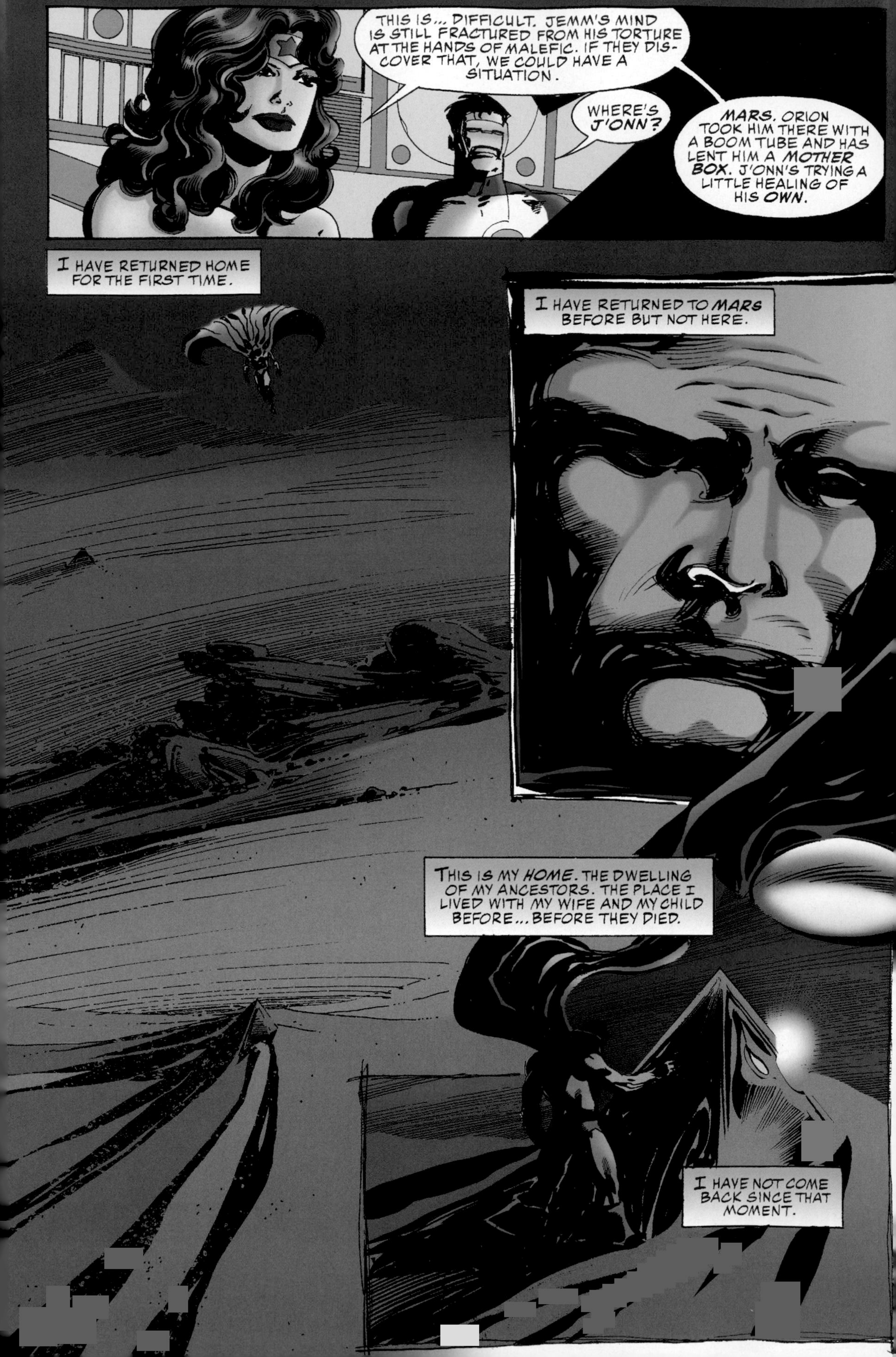
THIS IS... DIFFICULT. JEMM'S MIND IS STILL FRACTURED FROM HIS TORTURE AT THE HANDS OF MALEFIC. IF THEY DISCOVER THAT, WE COULD HAVE A SITUATION.
WHERE'S J'ONN?
MARS. ORION TOOK HIM THERE WITH A BOOM TUBE AND HAS LENT HIM A MOTHER BOX. J'ONN'S TRYING A LITTLE HEALING OF HIS OWN.
I HAVE RETURNED HOME FOR THE FIRST TIME.
I HAVE RETURNED TO MARS BEFORE BUT NOT HERE.
THIS IS MY HOME. THE DWELLING OF MY ANCESTORS. THE PLACE I LIVED WITH MY WIFE AND MY CHILD BEFORE... BEFORE THEY DIED.
I HAVE NOT COME BACK SINCE THAT MOMENT.

NOW-- I HAVE COME BACK IN SEARCH OF HEALING.

IT IS AS I REMEMBER IT-- SAVE THAT *THEY* ARE NOT HERE. M'YRI'AH AND K'HYM. WIFE AND DAUGHTER.

ONLY IN MEMORY ARE THEY HERE.

I DESCEND TO THE LOWEST LEVEL WHERE THE ASHES OF MY ANCESTORS MEET THE SANDS OF THE PLANET. THE HALL OF MEMORY.

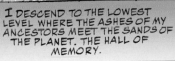

OH, MY ANCESTORS, HEAR ME!

I, J'ONN J'ONZZ, LAST OF THE LINE, COME TO KEEP FAITH WITH YOU. I REMEMBER AND REVERE YOU. YOUR MEMORIES ARE MINE. AND HERE I WILL RECLAIM MY HERITAGE OR MINGLE MY ASHES WITH YOU.

THE MOTHER BOX PINGS SOOTHINGLY. IT WILL HELP GUIDE ME THROUGH THIS TRANSFORMATION.

I CALL UP THE GOD OF FIRE, OF CHAOS, OF CREATION--H'RONMEER.

AND THEN I LET THE FLAME TAKE MY MIND.

AND THEN THE FIRE IS EVERYWHERE IN ME.

TO DEFEAT MY BROTHER MALEFIC, I TOOK A TERRIBLE CHANCE, ALLOWING ONE BODY TO DIE WHILE RECONSTITUTING ANOTHER.

BUT I USED *EARTH* MASS TO FILL THIS BODY OUT AND IT DOES NOT OBEY ME AS IT SHOULD.

I SEEK TO SWITCH THE EARTH MASS WITH MARTIAN MASS EVEN AS I SEEK TO CAGE THE FIRE IN MY MIND.

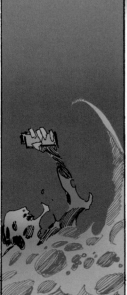

MOTHER BOX CALLS. IT SOOTHES. IT CAGES THE FIRE.

PING PING PING

IT CALLS ME BACK.

PING PING PING

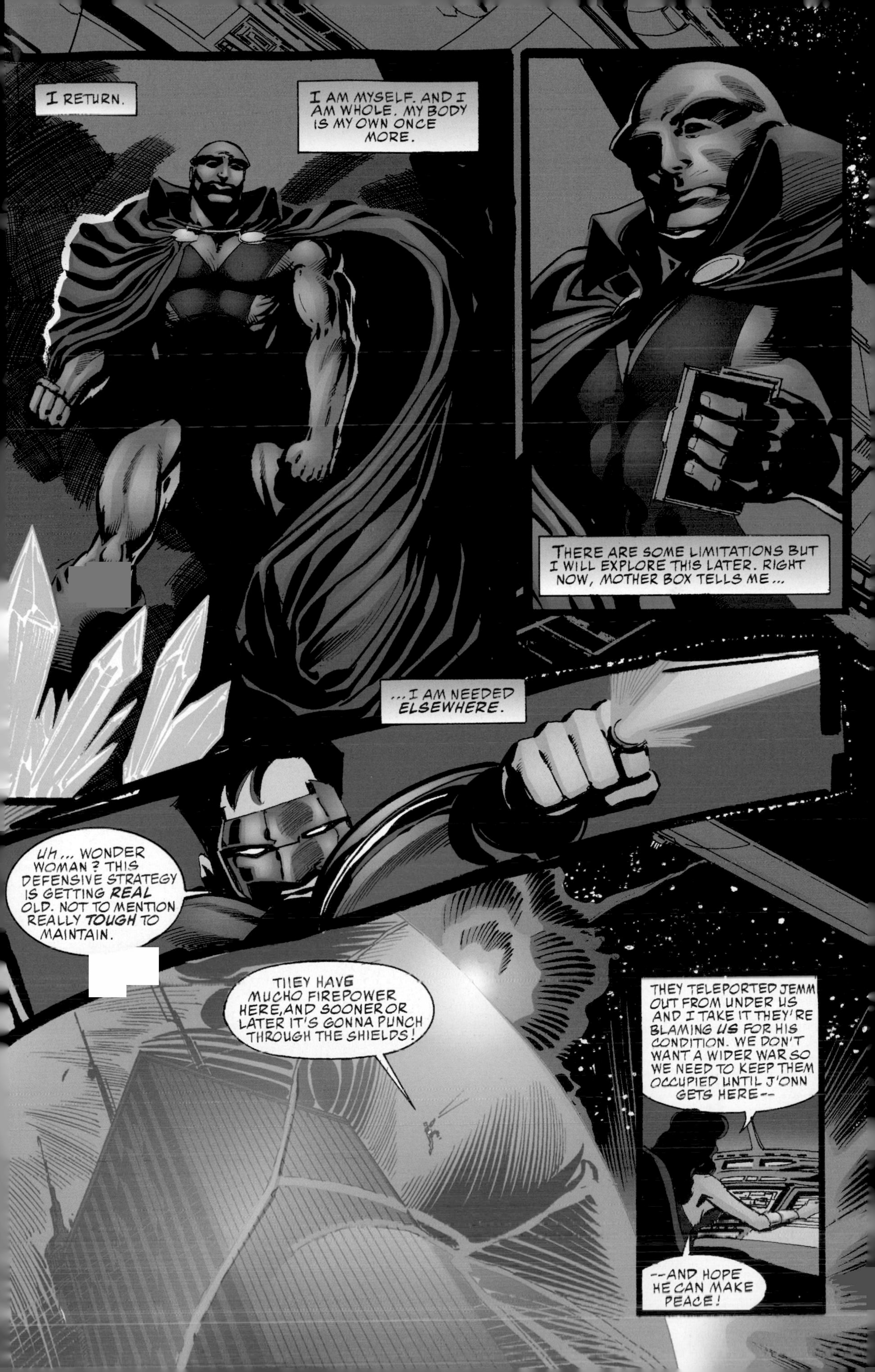
I RETURN.
I AM MYSELF. AND I AM WHOLE. MY BODY IS MY OWN ONCE MORE.
THERE ARE SOME LIMITATIONS BUT I WILL EXPLORE THIS LATER. RIGHT NOW, MOTHER BOX TELLS ME...
...I AM NEEDED *ELSEWHERE*.
UH... WONDER WOMAN? THIS DEFENSIVE STRATEGY IS GETTING *REAL* OLD. NOT TO MENTION REALLY *TOUGH* TO MAINTAIN.
THEY HAVE MUCHO FIREPOWER HERE, AND SOONER OR LATER IT'S GONNA PUNCH THROUGH THE SHIELDS!
THEY TELEPORTED JEMM OUT FROM UNDER US AND I TAKE IT THEY'RE BLAMING *US* FOR HIS CONDITION. WE DON'T WANT A WIDER WAR SO WE NEED TO KEEP THEM OCCUPIED UNTIL J'ONN GETS HERE--
--AND HOPE HE CAN MAKE PEACE!

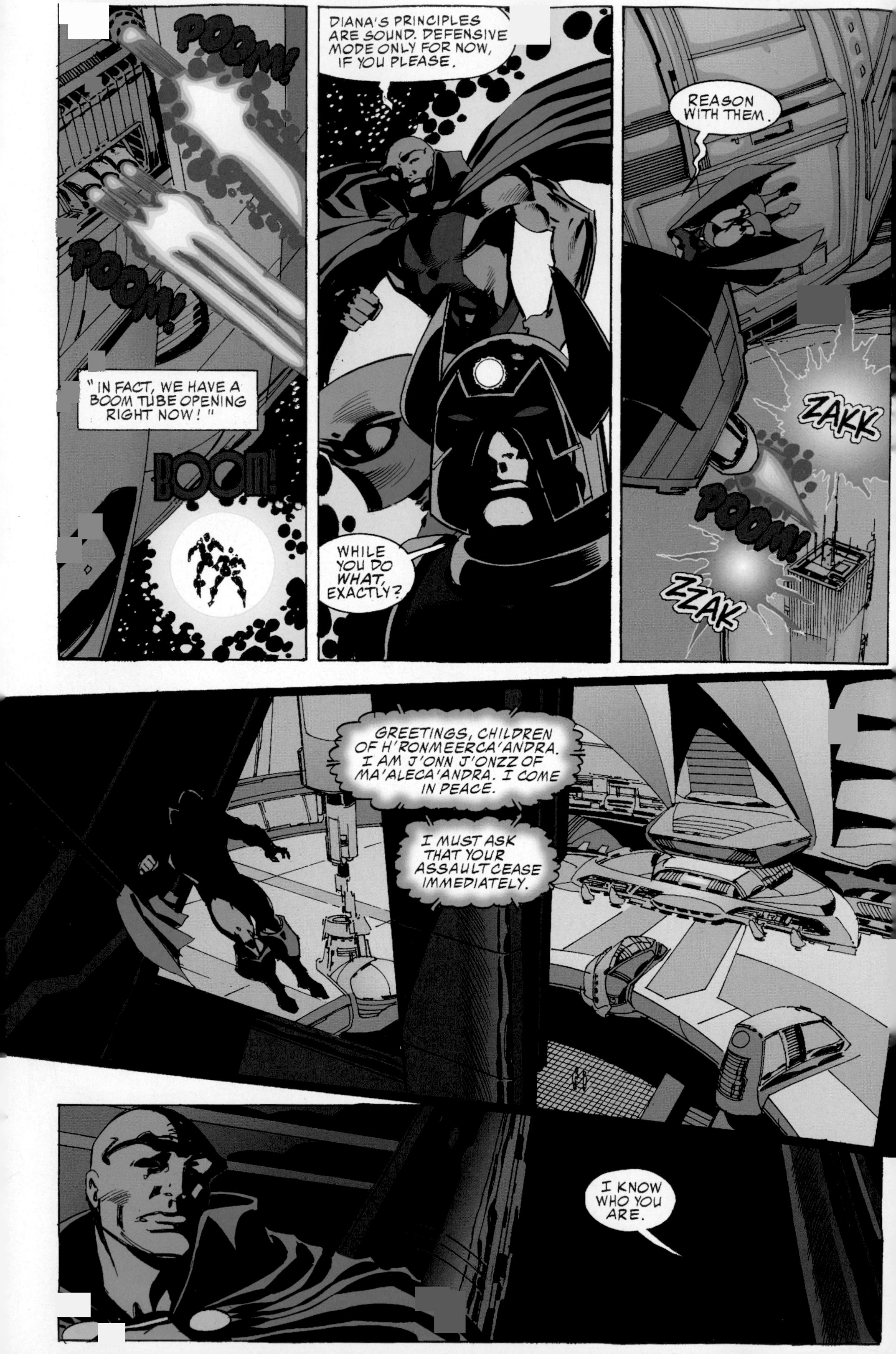
POOM!
POOM!
"IN FACT, WE HAVE A BOOM TUBE OPENING RIGHT NOW!"
BOOM!
DIANA'S PRINCIPLES ARE SOUND. DEFENSIVE MODE ONLY FOR NOW, IF YOU PLEASE.
WHILE YOU DO WHAT, EXACTLY?
REASON WITH THEM.
ZAKK
POOM!
ZZZAK
GREETINGS, CHILDREN OF H'RONMEERCA'ANDRA. I AM J'ONN J'ONZZ OF MA'ALECA'ANDRA. I COME IN PEACE.
I MUST ASK THAT YOUR ASSAULT CEASE IMMEDIATELY.
I KNOW WHO YOU ARE.

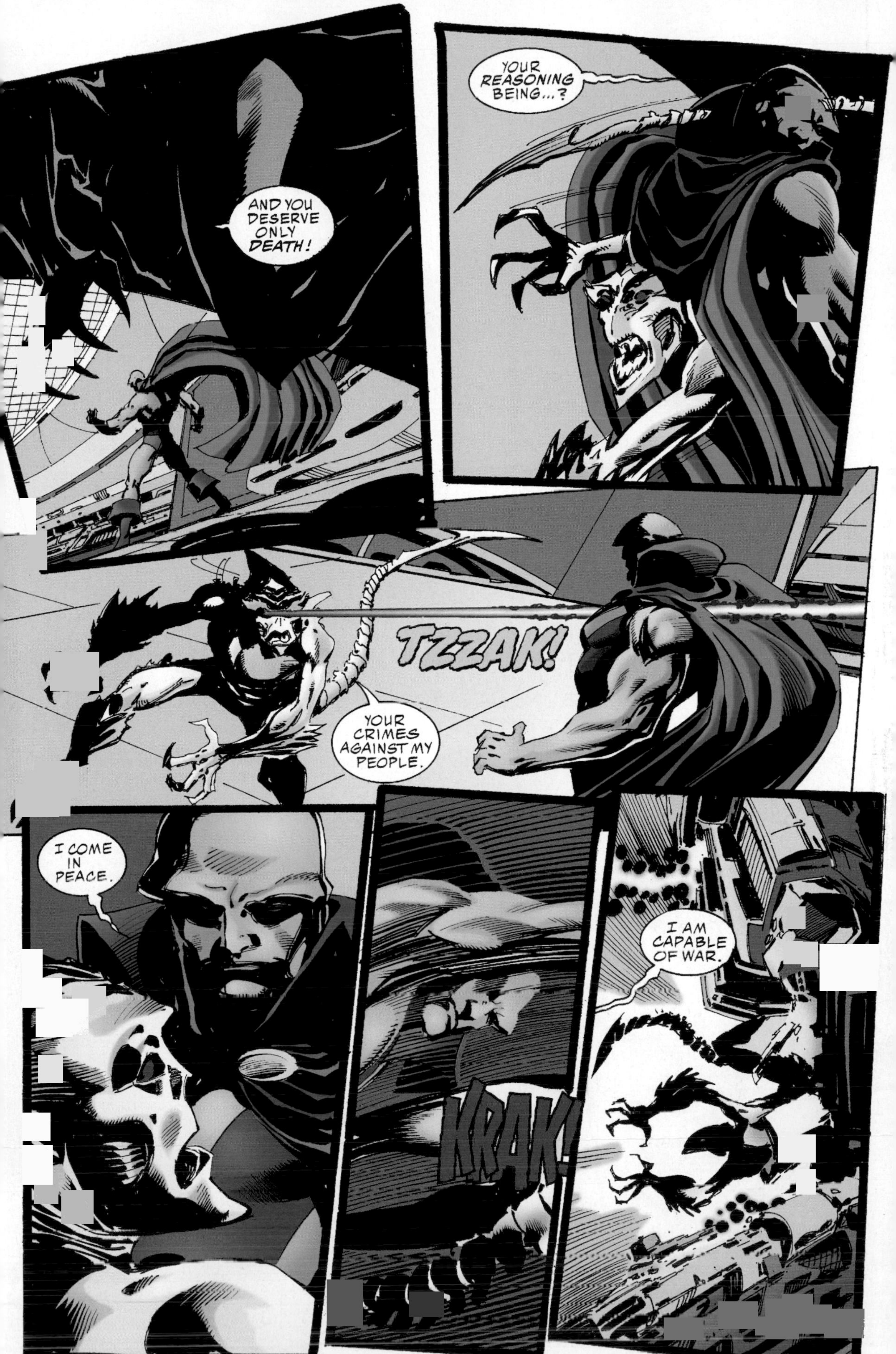
AND YOU DESERVE ONLY DEATH!
YOUR REASONING BEING...?
TZZAK!
YOUR CRIMES AGAINST MY PEOPLE.
I COME IN PEACE.
KRAK!
I AM CAPABLE OF WAR.

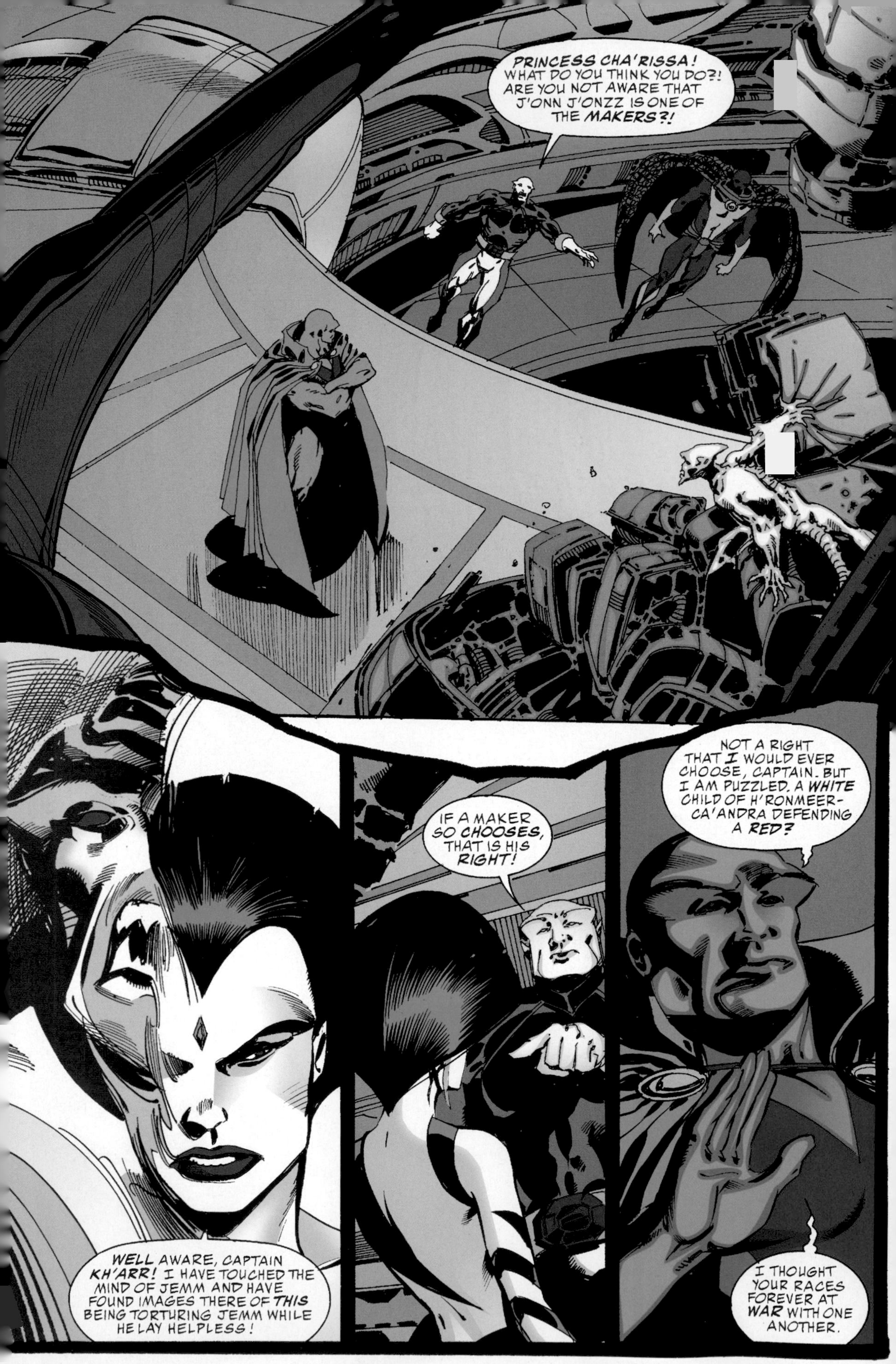
PRINCESS CHA'RISSA! WHAT DO YOU THINK YOU DO?! ARE YOU NOT AWARE THAT J'ONN J'ONZZ IS ONE OF THE MAKERS?!
WELL AWARE, CAPTAIN KH'ARR! I HAVE TOUCHED THE MIND OF JEMM AND HAVE FOUND IMAGES THERE OF THIS BEING TORTURING JEMM WHILE HE LAY HELPLESS!
IF A MAKER SO CHOOSES, THAT IS HIS RIGHT!
NOT A RIGHT THAT I WOULD EVER CHOOSE, CAPTAIN. BUT I AM PUZZLED. A WHITE CHILD OF H'RONMEER-CA'ANDRA DEFENDING A RED?
I THOUGHT YOUR RACES FOREVER AT WAR WITH ONE ANOTHER.

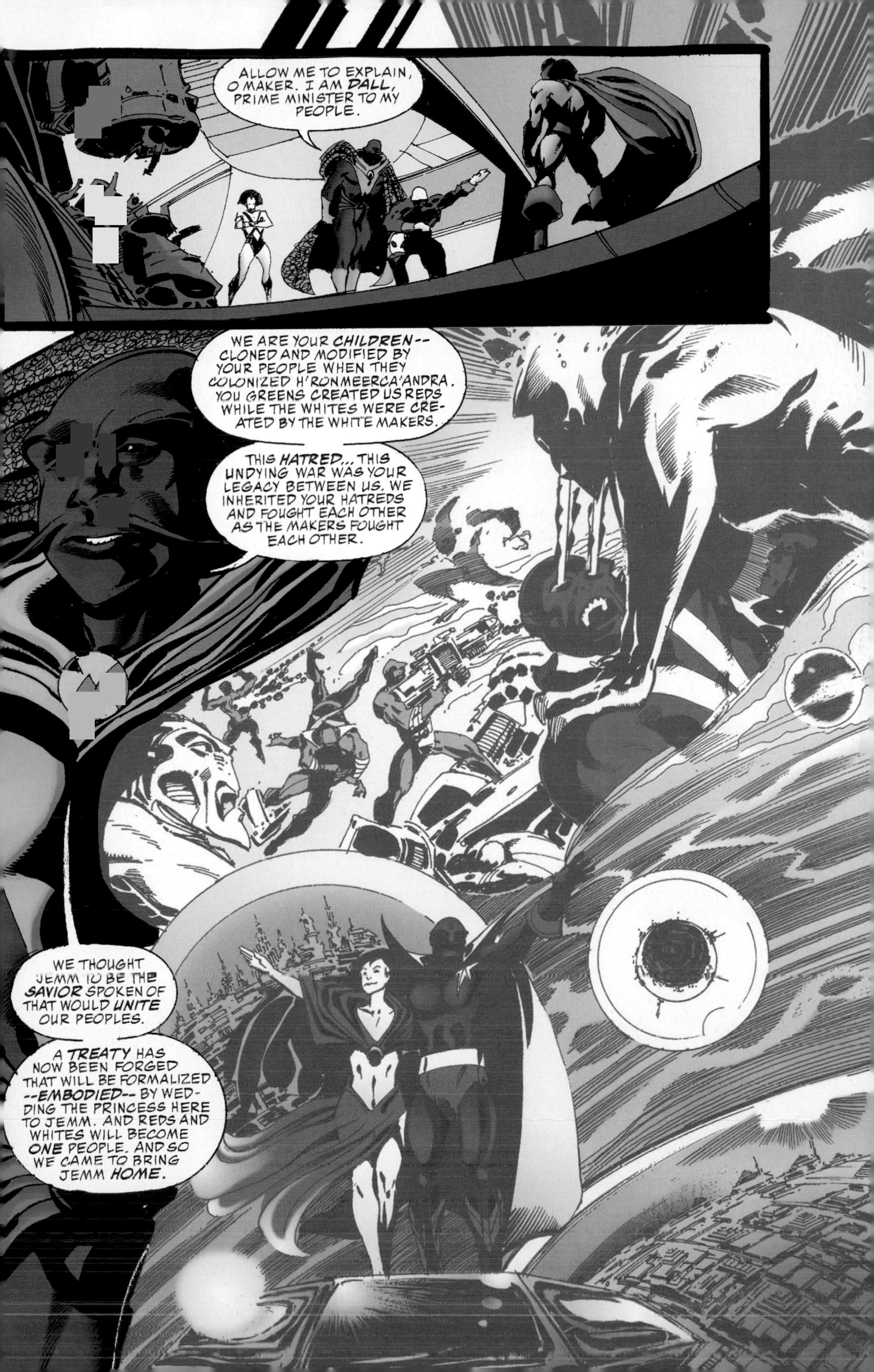
ALLOW ME TO EXPLAIN, O MAKER. I AM DALL, PRIME MINISTER TO MY PEOPLE.
WE ARE YOUR CHILDREN-- CLONED AND MODIFIED BY YOUR PEOPLE WHEN THEY COLONIZED H'RONMEERCA'ANDRA. YOU GREENS CREATED US REDS WHILE THE WHITES WERE CREATED BY THE WHITE MAKERS.
THIS HATRED... THIS UNDYING WAR WAS YOUR LEGACY BETWEEN US. WE INHERITED YOUR HATREDS AND FOUGHT EACH OTHER AS THE MAKERS FOUGHT EACH OTHER.
WE THOUGHT JEMM TO BE THE SAVIOR SPOKEN OF THAT WOULD UNITE OUR PEOPLES.
A TREATY HAS NOW BEEN FORGED THAT WILL BE FORMALIZED --EMBODIED-- BY WEDDING THE PRINCESS HERE TO JEMM. AND REDS AND WHITES WILL BECOME ONE PEOPLE. AND SO WE CAME TO BRING JEMM HOME.

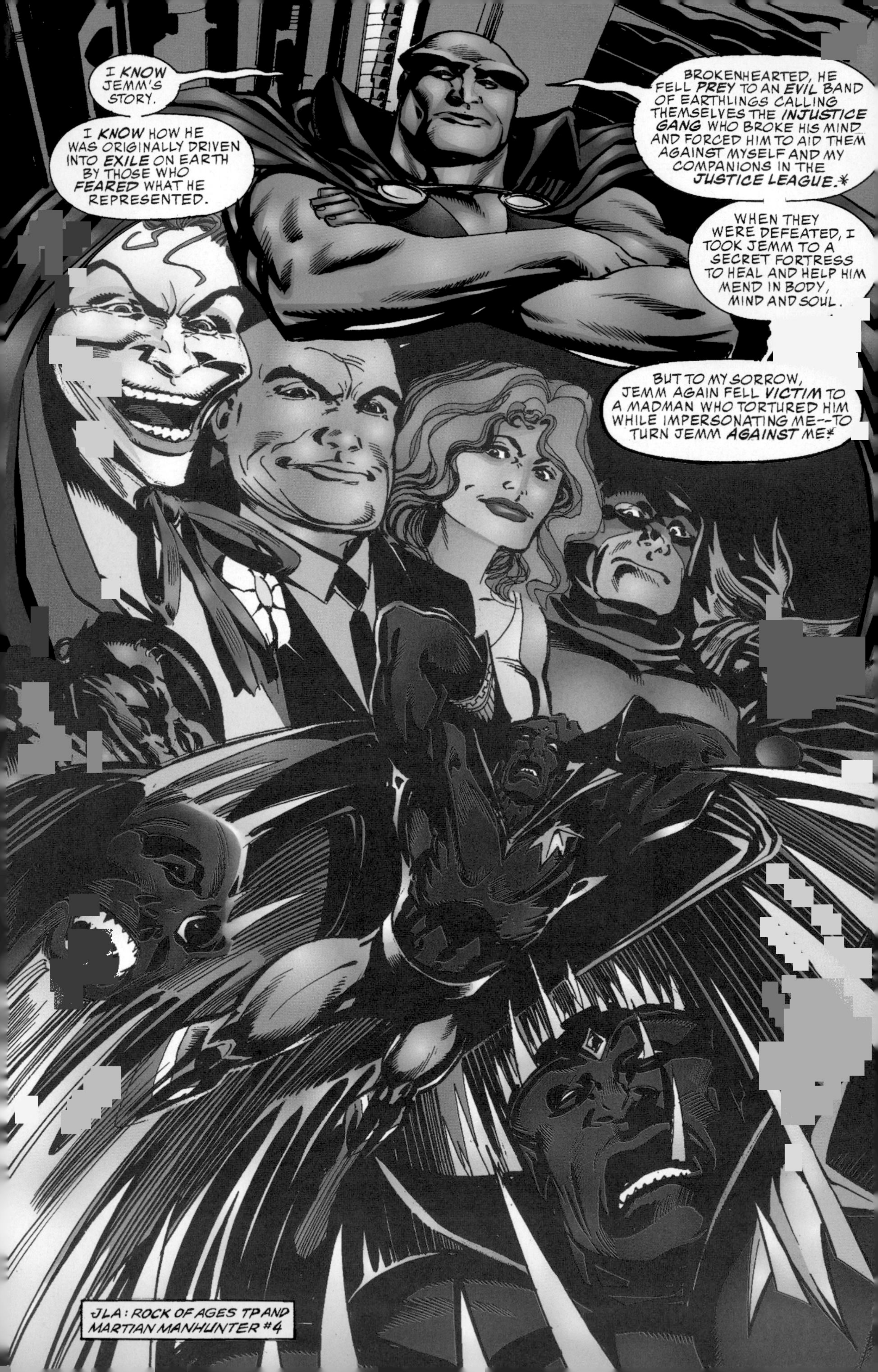
I KNOW JEMM'S STORY.
I KNOW HOW HE WAS ORIGINALLY DRIVEN INTO EXILE ON EARTH BY THOSE WHO FEARED WHAT HE REPRESENTED.
BROKENHEARTED, HE FELL PREY TO AN EVIL BAND OF EARTHLINGS CALLING THEMSELVES THE INJUSTICE GANG WHO BROKE HIS MIND AND FORCED HIM TO AID THEM AGAINST MYSELF AND MY COMPANIONS IN THE JUSTICE LEAGUE.*
WHEN THEY WERE DEFEATED, I TOOK JEMM TO A SECRET FORTRESS TO HEAL AND HELP HIM MEND IN BODY, MIND AND SOUL.
BUT TO MY SORROW, JEMM AGAIN FELL VICTIM TO A MADMAN WHO TORTURED HIM WHILE IMPERSONATING ME--TO TURN JEMM AGAINST ME*
JLA: ROCK OF AGES TP AND MARTIAN MANHUNTER #4

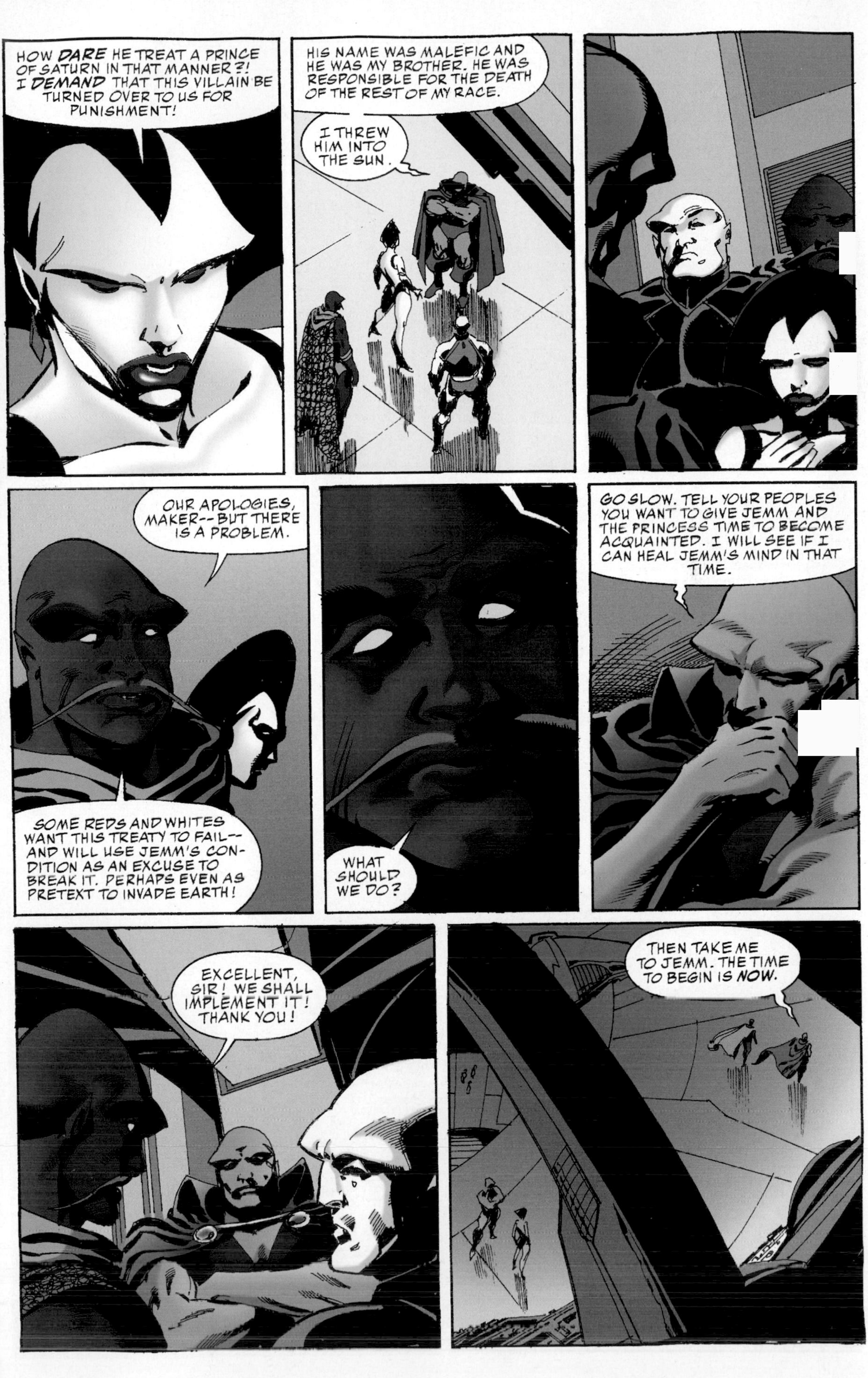
HOW DARE HE TREAT A PRINCE OF SATURN IN THAT MANNER?! I DEMAND THAT THIS VILLAIN BE TURNED OVER TO US FOR PUNISHMENT!
HIS NAME WAS MALEFIC AND HE WAS MY BROTHER. HE WAS RESPONSIBLE FOR THE DEATH OF THE REST OF MY RACE.
I THREW HIM INTO THE SUN.
OUR APOLOGIES, MAKER--BUT THERE IS A PROBLEM.
SOME REDS AND WHITES WANT THIS TREATY TO FAIL--AND WILL USE JEMM'S CONDITION AS AN EXCUSE TO BREAK IT. PERHAPS EVEN AS PRETEXT TO INVADE EARTH!
WHAT SHOULD WE DO?
GO SLOW. TELL YOUR PEOPLES YOU WANT TO GIVE JEMM AND THE PRINCESS TIME TO BECOME ACQUAINTED. I WILL SEE IF I CAN HEAL JEMM'S MIND IN THAT TIME.
EXCELLENT, SIR! WE SHALL IMPLEMENT IT! THANK YOU!
THEN TAKE ME TO JEMM. THE TIME TO BEGIN IS NOW.

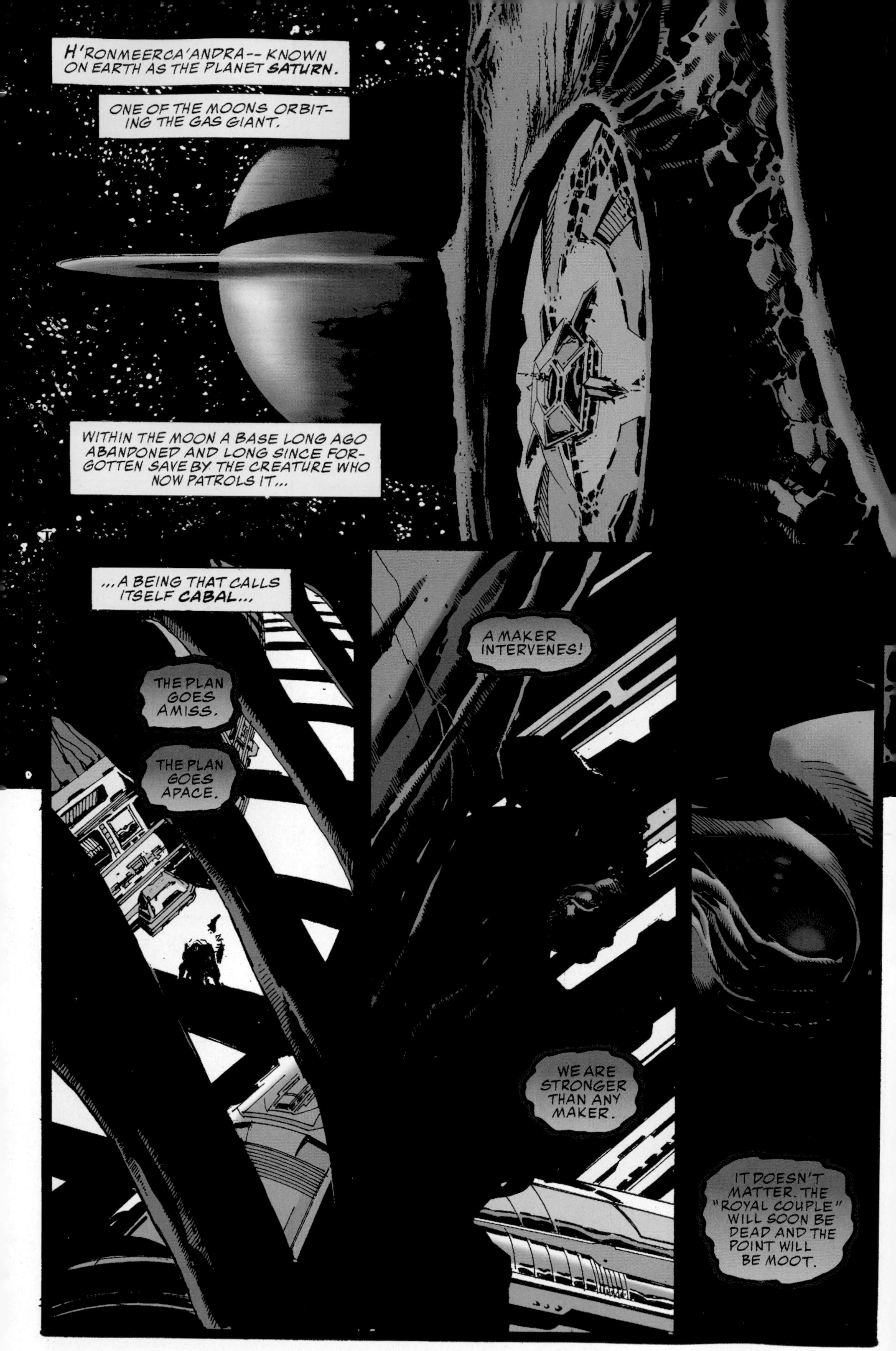
H'RONMEERCA'ANDRA-- KNOWN ON EARTH AS THE PLANET SATURN.
ONE OF THE MOONS ORBITING THE GAS GIANT.
WITHIN THE MOON A BASE LONG AGO ABANDONED AND LONG SINCE FORGOTTEN SAVE BY THE CREATURE WHO NOW PATROLS IT...
...A BEING THAT CALLS ITSELF CABAL...
THE PLAN GOES AMISS.
THE PLAN GOES APACE.
A MAKER INTERVENES!
WE ARE STRONGER THAN ANY MAKER.
IT DOESN'T MATTER. THE "ROYAL COUPLE" WILL SOON BE DEAD AND THE POINT WILL BE MOOT.

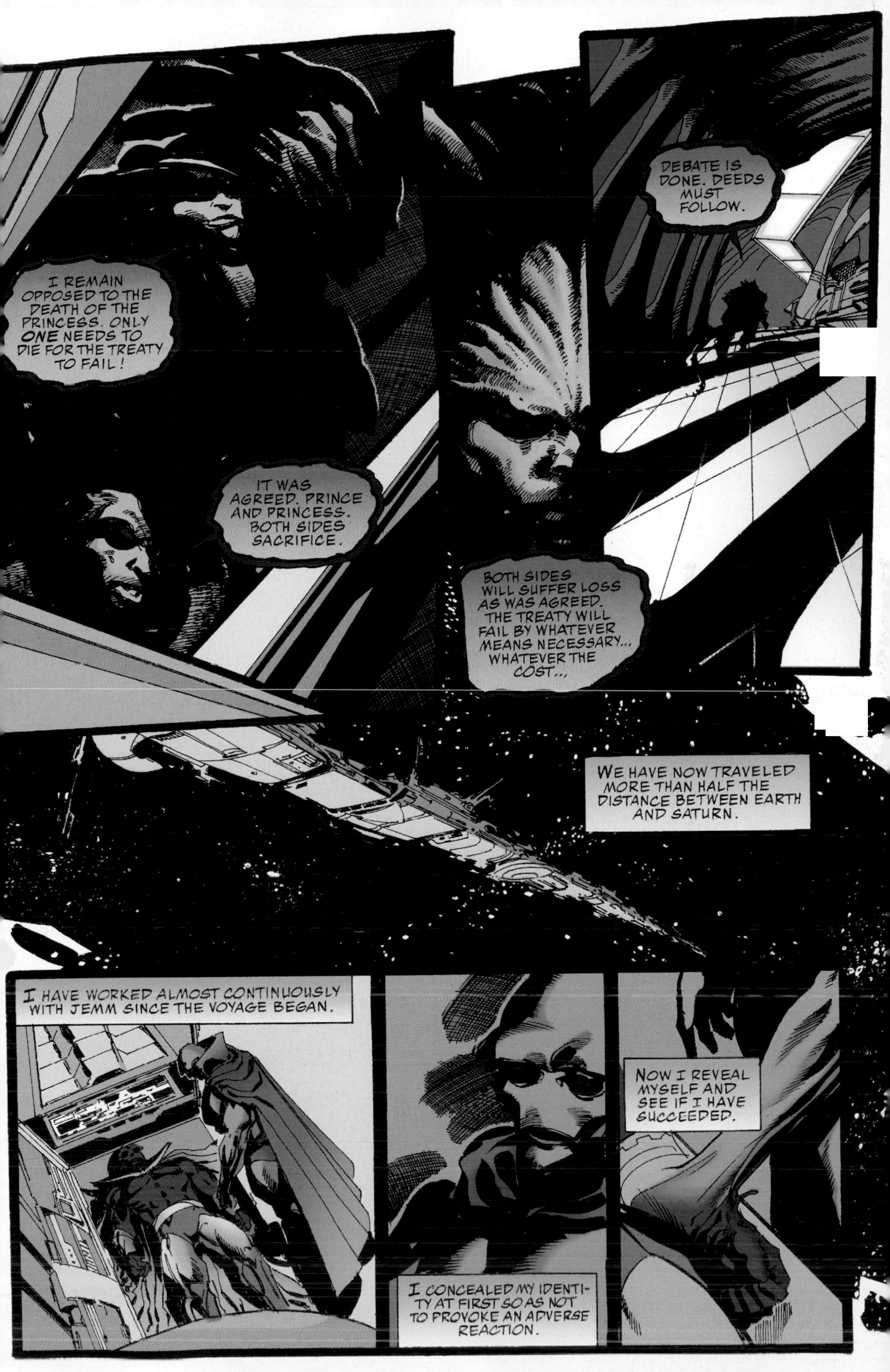

I REMAIN OPPOSED TO THE DEATH OF THE PRINCESS. ONLY ONE NEEDS TO DIE FOR THE TREATY TO FAIL!
IT WAS AGREED. PRINCE AND PRINCESS. BOTH SIDES SACRIFICE.
DEBATE IS DONE. DEEDS MUST FOLLOW.
BOTH SIDES WILL SUFFER LOSS AS WAS AGREED. THE TREATY WILL FAIL BY WHATEVER MEANS NECESSARY... WHATEVER THE COST...
WE HAVE NOW TRAVELED MORE THAN HALF THE DISTANCE BETWEEN EARTH AND SATURN.
I HAVE WORKED ALMOST CONTINUOUSLY WITH JEMM SINCE THE VOYAGE BEGAN.
I CONCEALED MY IDENTITY AT FIRST SO AS NOT TO PROVOKE AN ADVERSE REACTION.
NOW I REVEAL MYSELF AND SEE IF I HAVE SUCCEEDED.

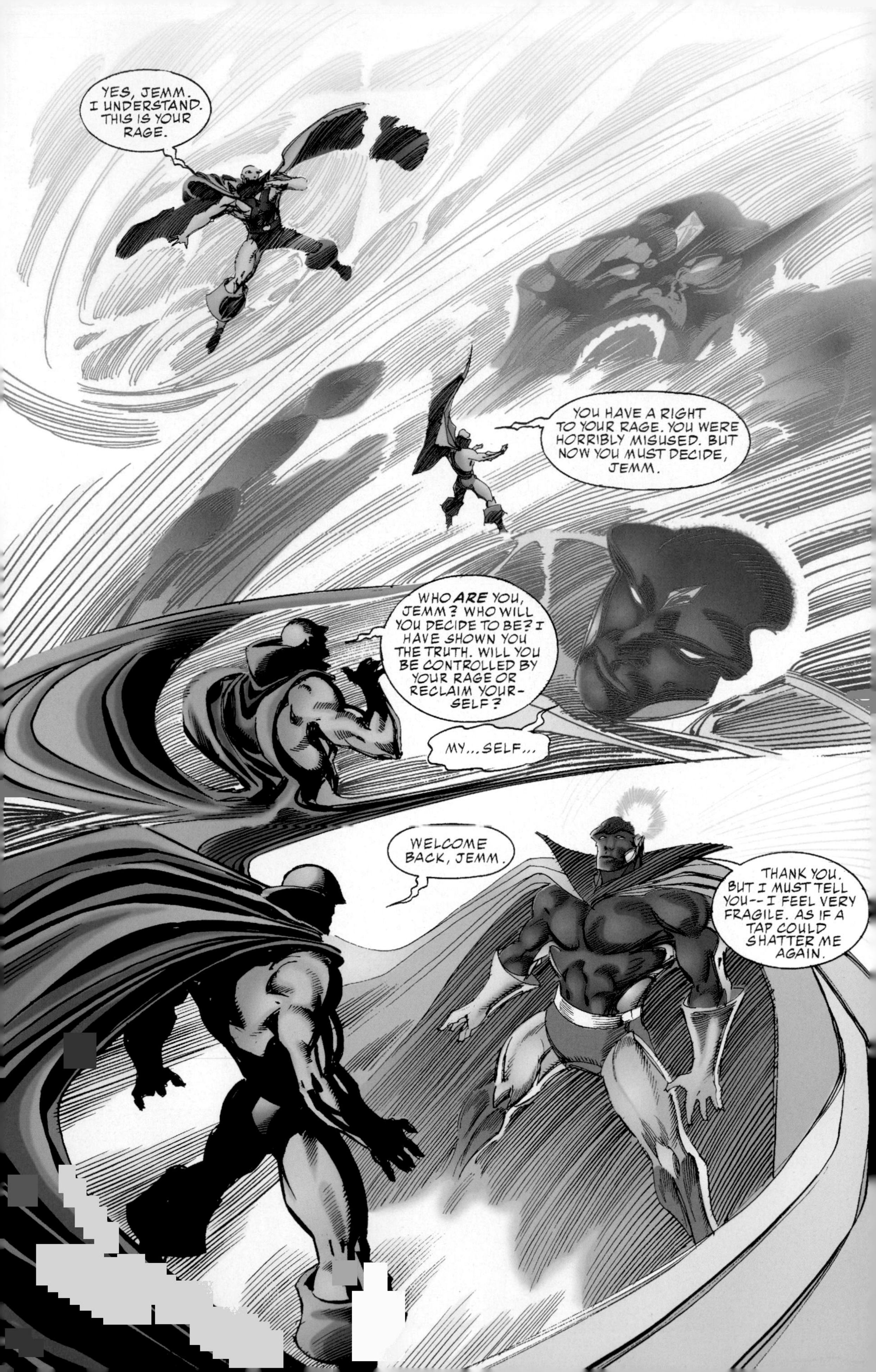
YES, JEMM. I UNDERSTAND. THIS IS YOUR RAGE.
YOU HAVE A RIGHT TO YOUR RAGE. YOU WERE HORRIBLY MISUSED. BUT NOW YOU MUST DECIDE, JEMM.
WHO ARE YOU, JEMM? WHO WILL YOU DECIDE TO BE? I HAVE SHOWN YOU THE TRUTH. WILL YOU BE CONTROLLED BY YOUR RAGE OR RECLAIM YOUR-SELF?
MY... SELF...
WELCOME BACK, JEMM.
THANK YOU. BUT I MUST TELL YOU-- I FEEL VERY FRAGILE. AS IF A TAP COULD SHATTER ME AGAIN.

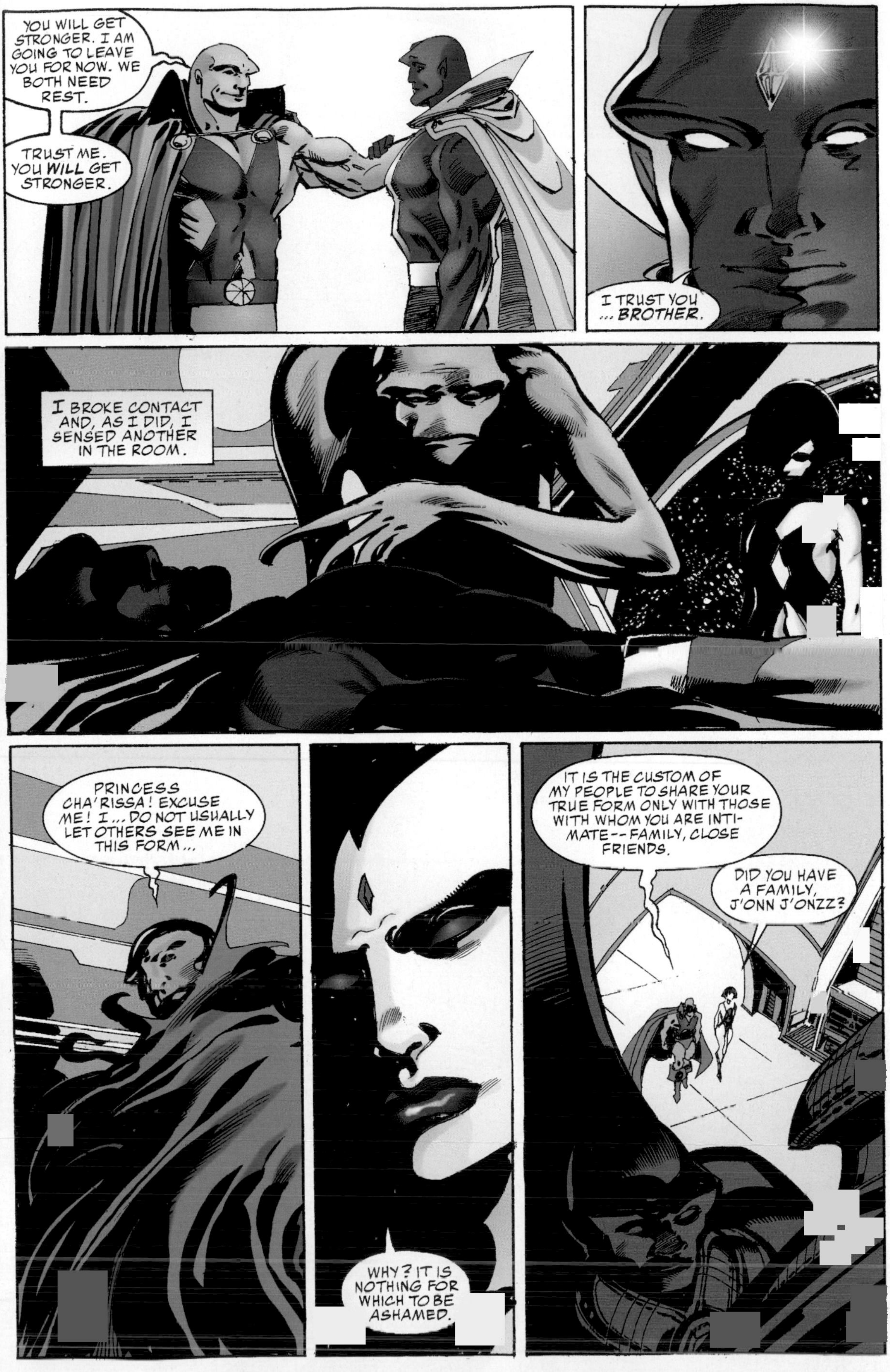
YOU WILL GET STRONGER. I AM GOING TO LEAVE YOU FOR NOW. WE BOTH NEED REST.
TRUST ME. YOU WILL GET STRONGER.
I TRUST YOU ...BROTHER.
I BROKE CONTACT AND, AS I DID, I SENSED ANOTHER IN THE ROOM.
PRINCESS CHA'RISSA! EXCUSE ME! I... DO NOT USUALLY LET OTHERS SEE ME IN THIS FORM...
WHY? IT IS NOTHING FOR WHICH TO BE ASHAMED.
IT IS THE CUSTOM OF MY PEOPLE TO SHARE YOUR TRUE FORM ONLY WITH THOSE WITH WHOM YOU ARE INTI-MATE--FAMILY, CLOSE FRIENDS.
DID YOU HAVE A FAMILY, J'ONN J'ONZZ?

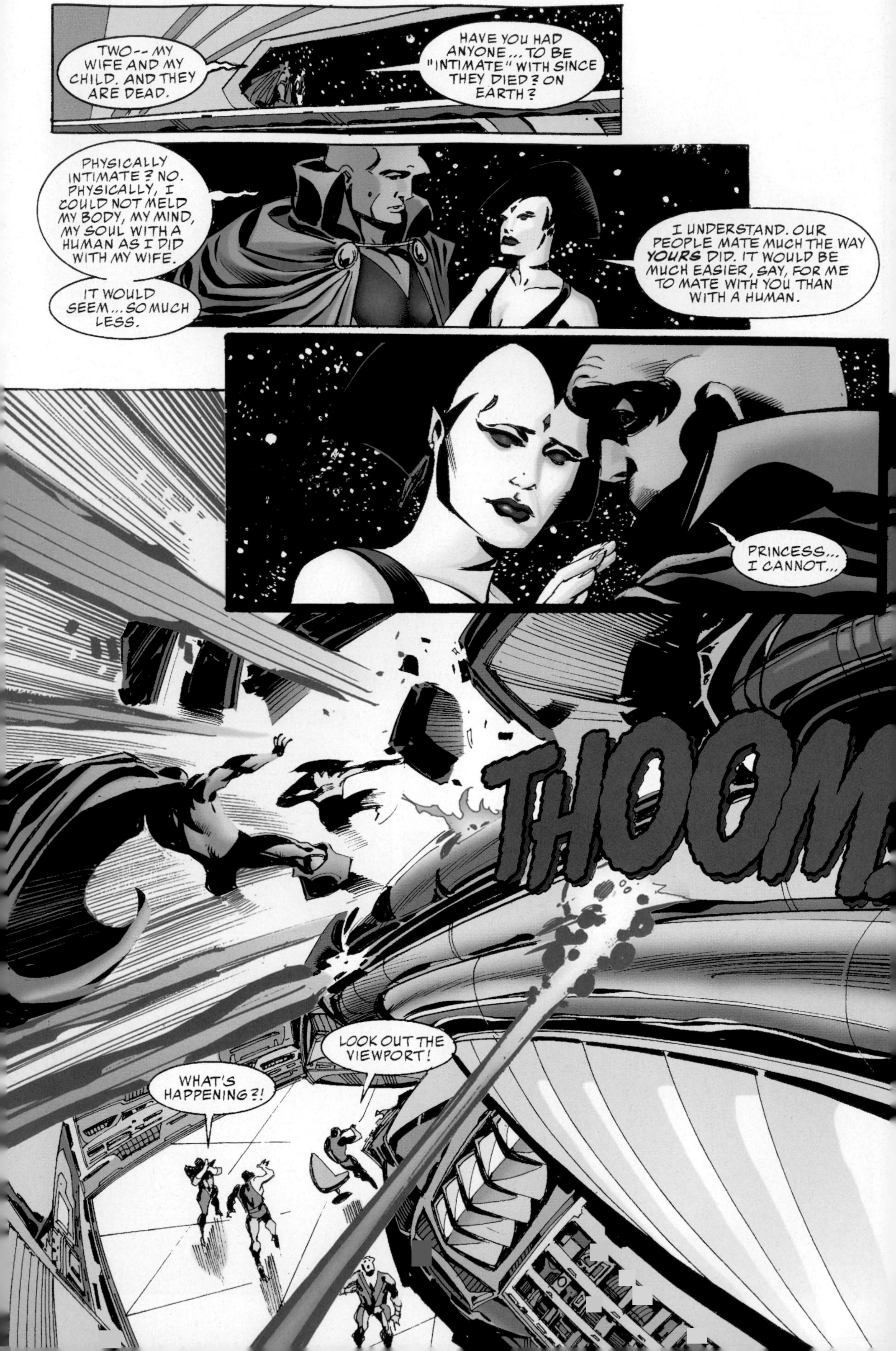

TWO-- MY WIFE AND MY CHILD. AND THEY ARE DEAD.
HAVE YOU HAD ANYONE... TO BE "INTIMATE" WITH SINCE THEY DIED? ON EARTH?
PHYSICALLY INTIMATE? NO. PHYSICALLY, I COULD NOT MELD MY BODY, MY MIND, MY SOUL WITH A HUMAN AS I DID WITH MY WIFE.
IT WOULD SEEM... SO MUCH LESS.
I UNDERSTAND. OUR PEOPLE MATE MUCH THE WAY YOURS DID. IT WOULD BE MUCH EASIER, SAY, FOR ME TO MATE WITH YOU THAN WITH A HUMAN.
PRINCESS... I CANNOT...
THOOM!
LOOK OUT THE VIEWPORT!
WHAT'S HAPPENING?!

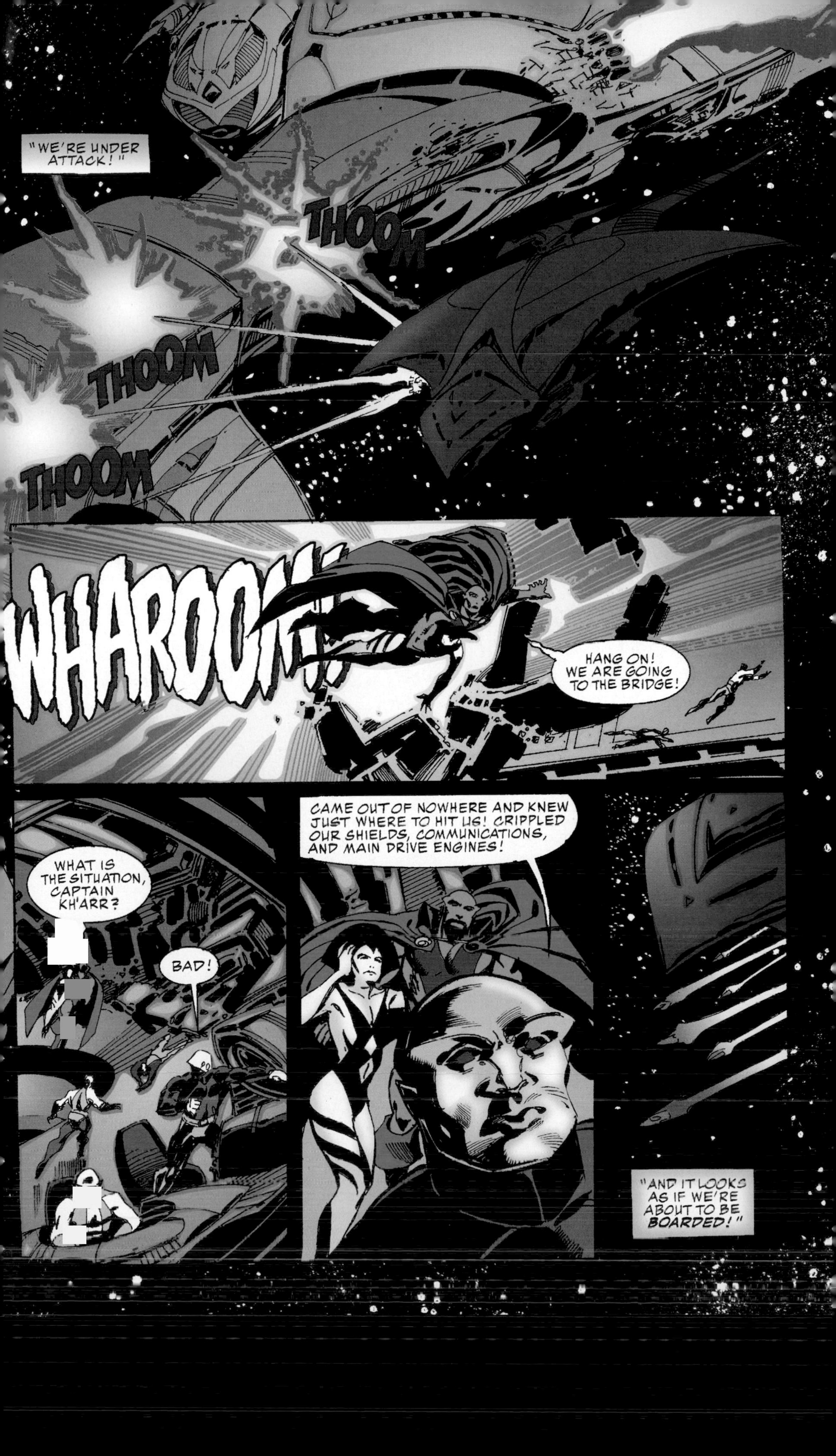
"WE'RE UNDER ATTACK!"
THOOM
THOOM
THOOM
WHAROO
HANG ON! WE ARE GOING TO THE BRIDGE!
WHAT IS THE SITUATION, CAPTAIN KH'ARR?
BAD!
CAME OUT OF NOWHERE AND KNEW JUST WHERE TO HIT US! CRIPPLED OUR SHIELDS, COMMUNICATIONS, AND MAIN DRIVE ENGINES!
"AND IT LOOKS AS IF WE'RE ABOUT TO BE BOARDED!"

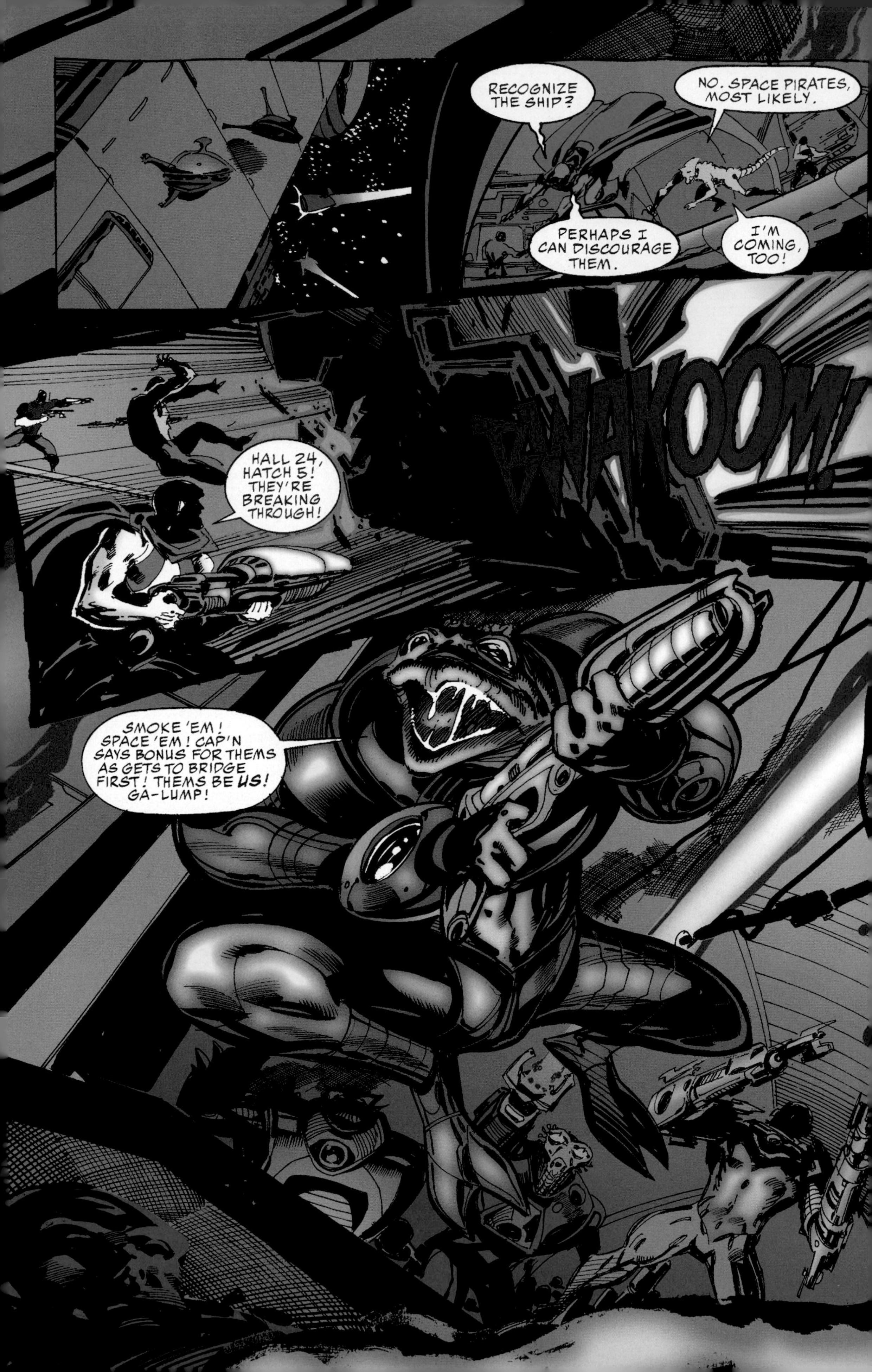
RECOGNIZE THE SHIP?
NO. SPACE PIRATES, MOST LIKELY.
PERHAPS I CAN DISCOURAGE THEM.
I'M COMING, TOO!
WAKOOM!
HALL 24, HATCH 5! THEY'RE BREAKING THROUGH!
SMOKE 'EM! SPACE 'EM! CAP'N SAYS BONUS FOR THEMS AS GETS TO BRIDGE FIRST! THEMS BE US! GA-LUMP!

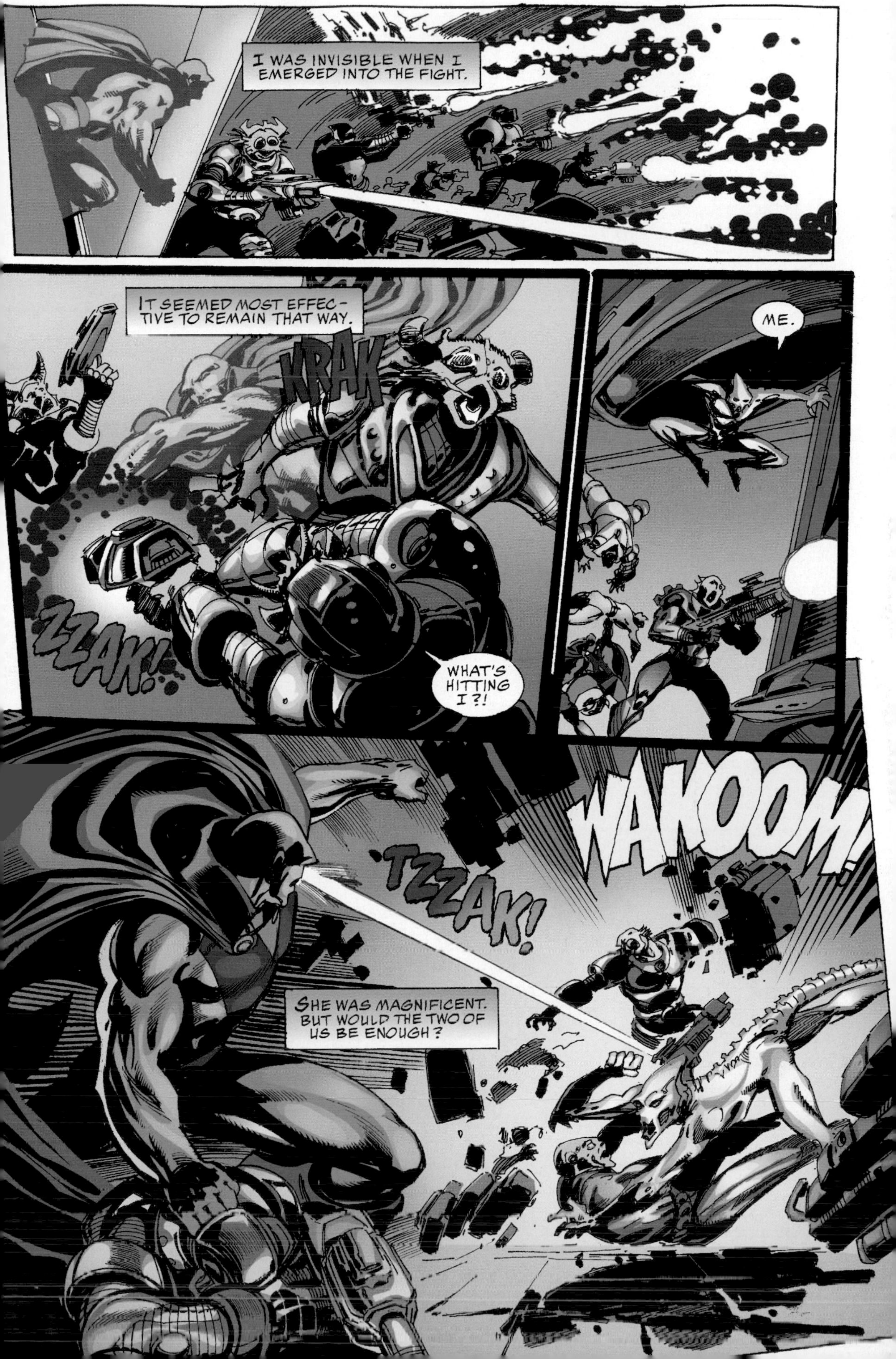
I WAS INVISIBLE WHEN I EMERGED INTO THE FIGHT.
IT SEEMED MOST EFFECTIVE TO REMAIN THAT WAY.
KRAK
ZZAK!
WHAT'S HITTING I?!
ME.
WAKOOM!
TZZAK!
SHE WAS MAGNIFICENT. BUT WOULD THE TWO OF US BE ENOUGH?

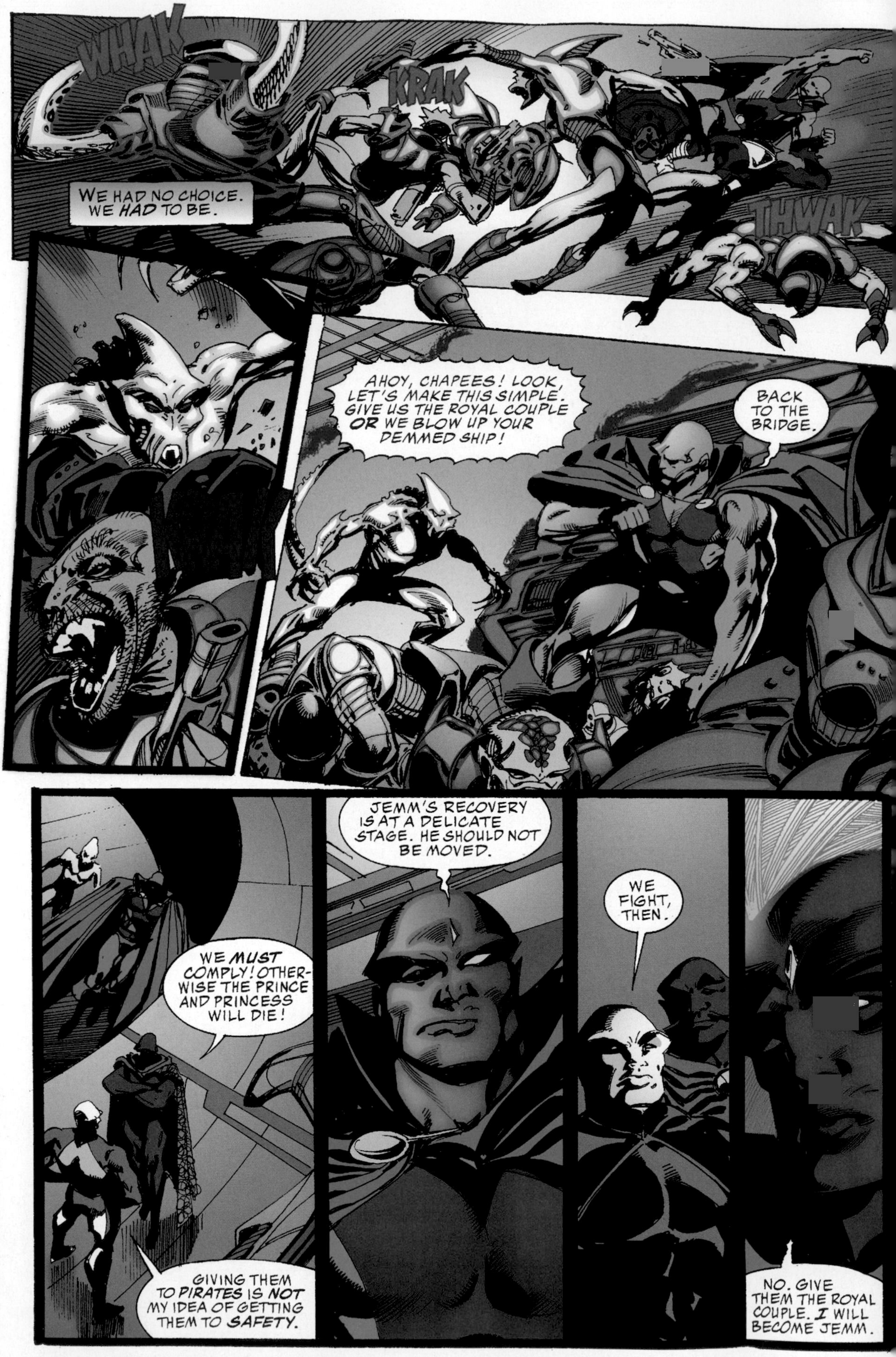
WHAK
KRAK
WE HAD NO CHOICE. WE HAD TO BE.
THWAK
AHOY, CHAPEES! LOOK, LET'S MAKE THIS SIMPLE. GIVE US THE ROYAL COUPLE OR WE BLOW UP YOUR DEMMED SHIP!
BACK TO THE BRIDGE.
WE MUST COMPLY! OTHERWISE THE PRINCE AND PRINCESS WILL DIE!
GIVING THEM TO PIRATES IS NOT MY IDEA OF GETTING THEM TO SAFETY.
JEMM'S RECOVERY IS AT A DELICATE STAGE. HE SHOULD NOT BE MOVED.
WE FIGHT, THEN.
NO. GIVE THEM THE ROYAL COUPLE. I WILL BECOME JEMM.

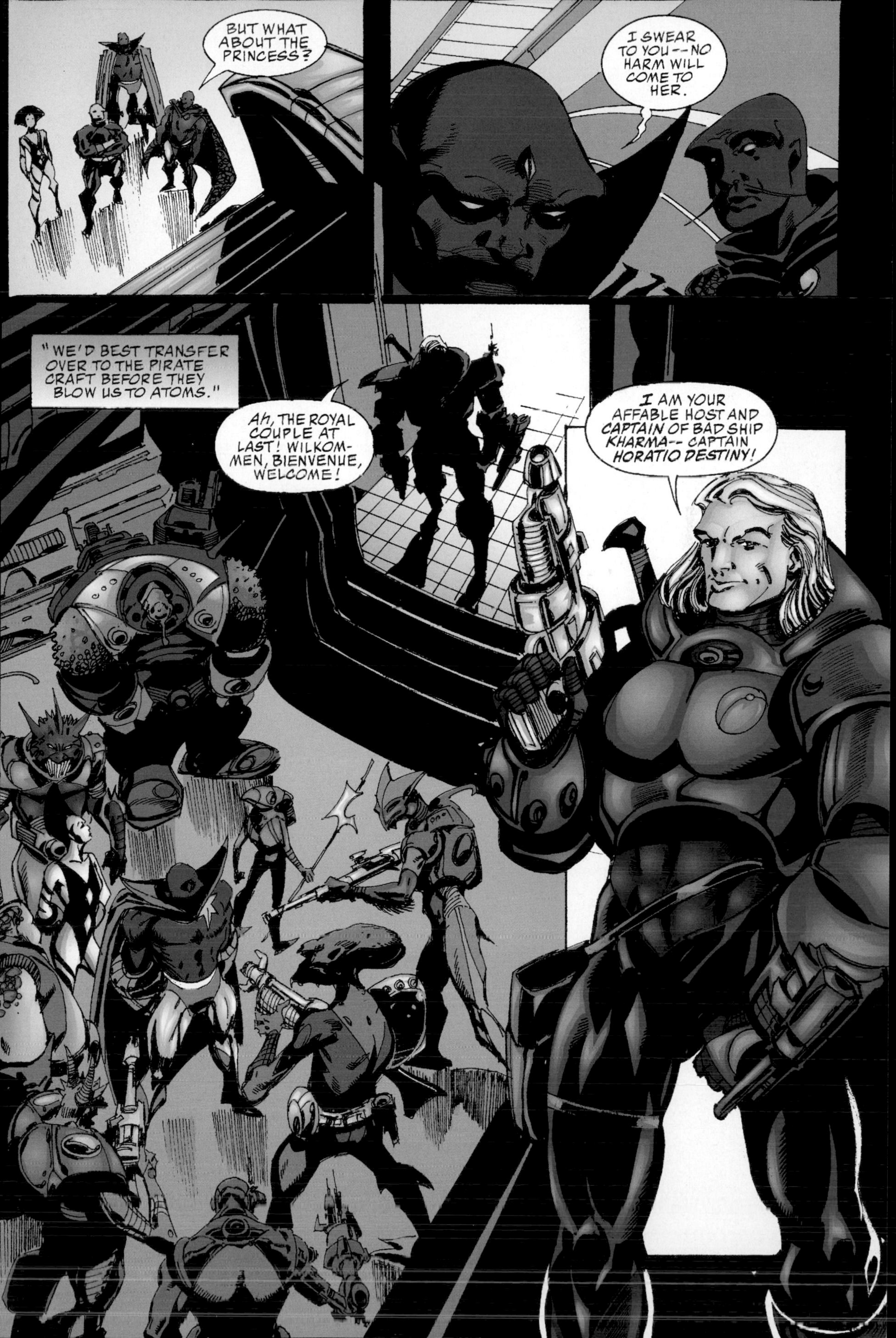
BUT WHAT ABOUT THE PRINCESS?
I SWEAR TO YOU--NO HARM WILL COME TO HER.
"WE'D BEST TRANSFER OVER TO THE PIRATE CRAFT BEFORE THEY BLOW US TO ATOMS."
AH, THE ROYAL COUPLE AT LAST! WILKOMMEN, BIENVENUE, WELCOME!
I AM YOUR AFFABLE HOST AND CAPTAIN OF BAD SHIP KHARMA-- CAPTAIN HORATIO DESTINY!

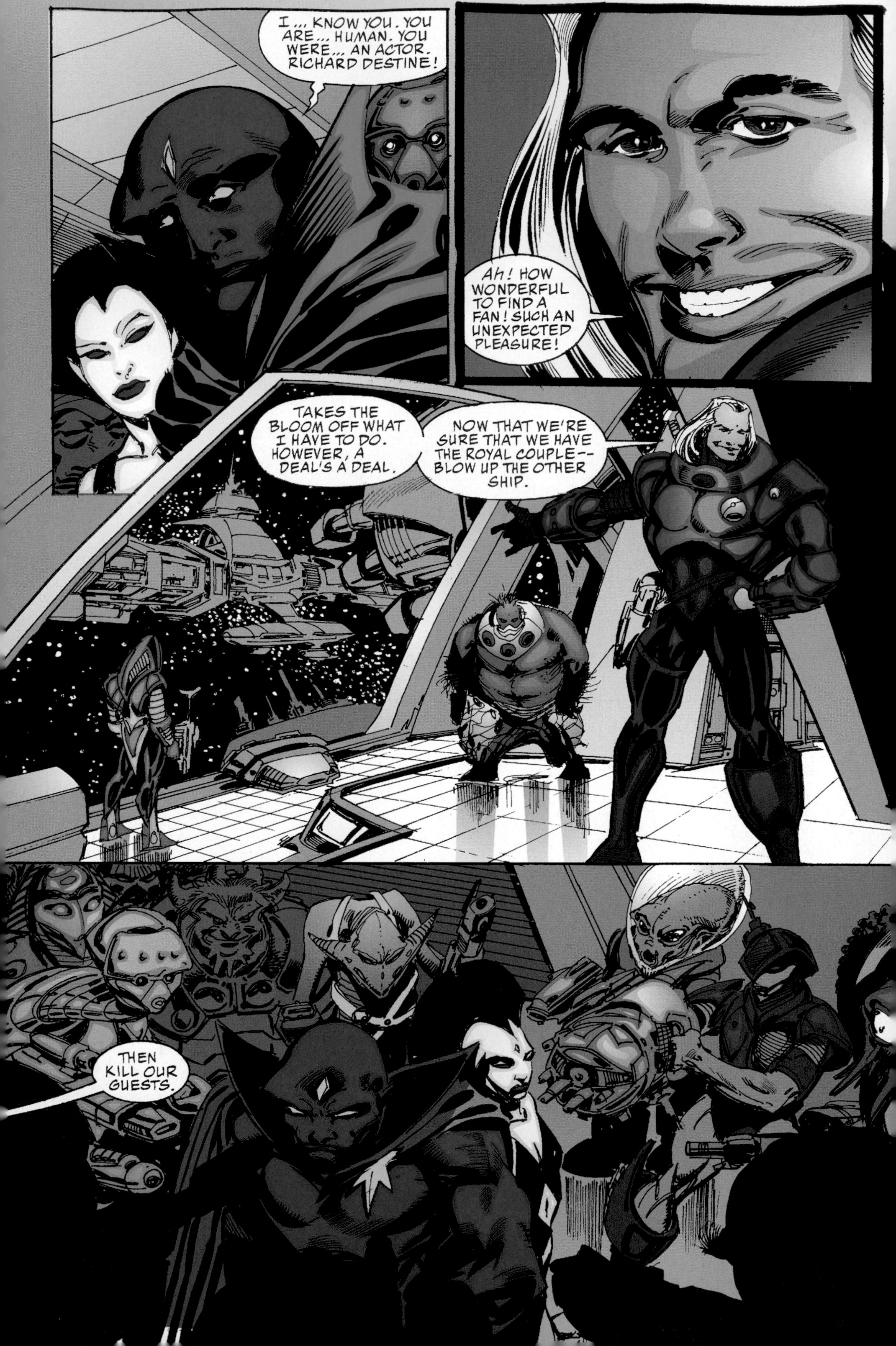
I... KNOW YOU. YOU ARE... HUMAN. YOU WERE... AN ACTOR. RICHARD DESTINE!
Ah! HOW WONDERFUL TO FIND A FAN! SUCH AN UNEXPECTED PLEASURE!
TAKES THE BLOOM OFF WHAT I HAVE TO DO. HOWEVER, A DEAL'S A DEAL.
NOW THAT WE'RE SURE THAT WE HAVE THE ROYAL COUPLE-- BLOW UP THE OTHER SHIP.
THEN KILL OUR GUESTS.

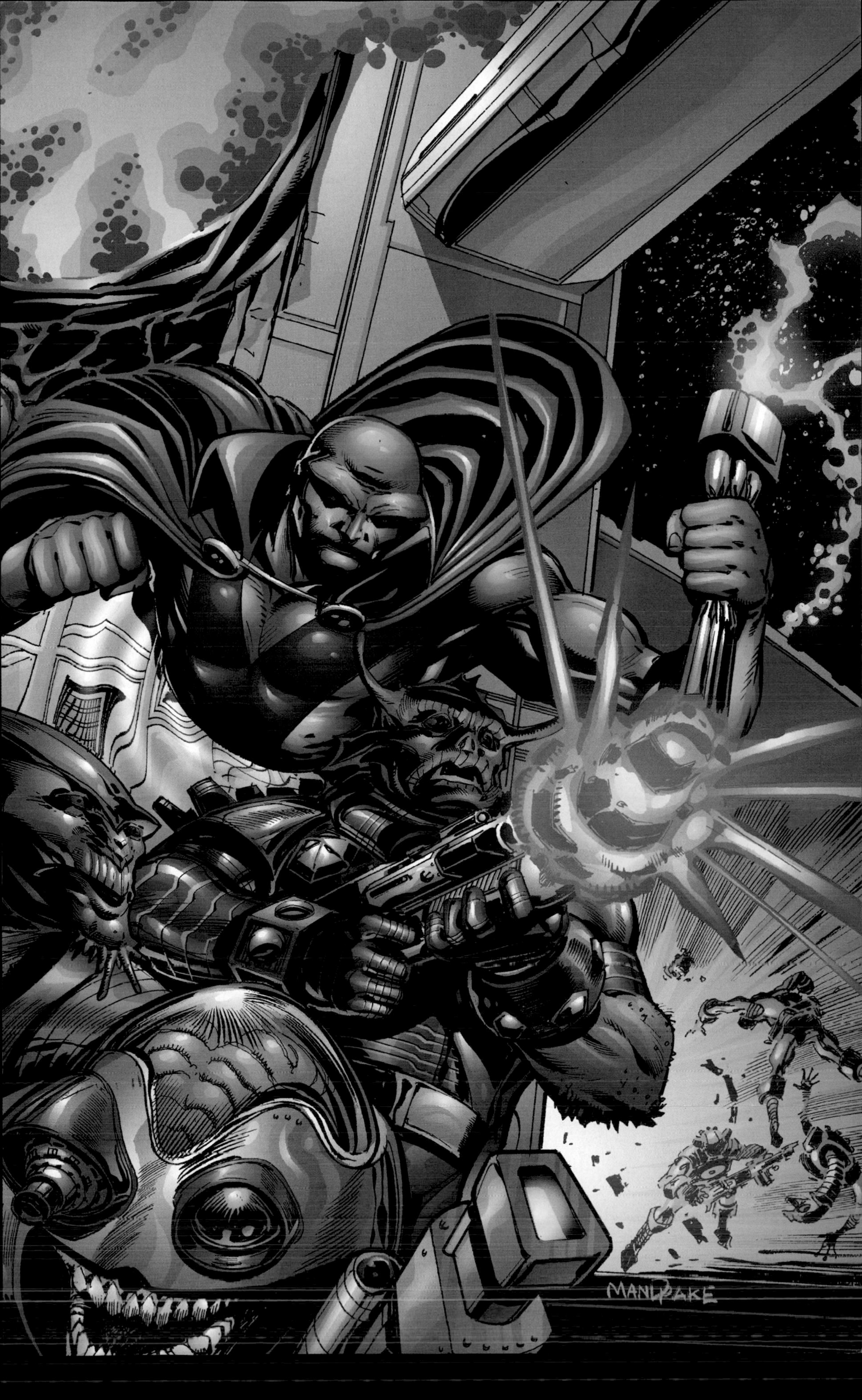
MANDRAKE

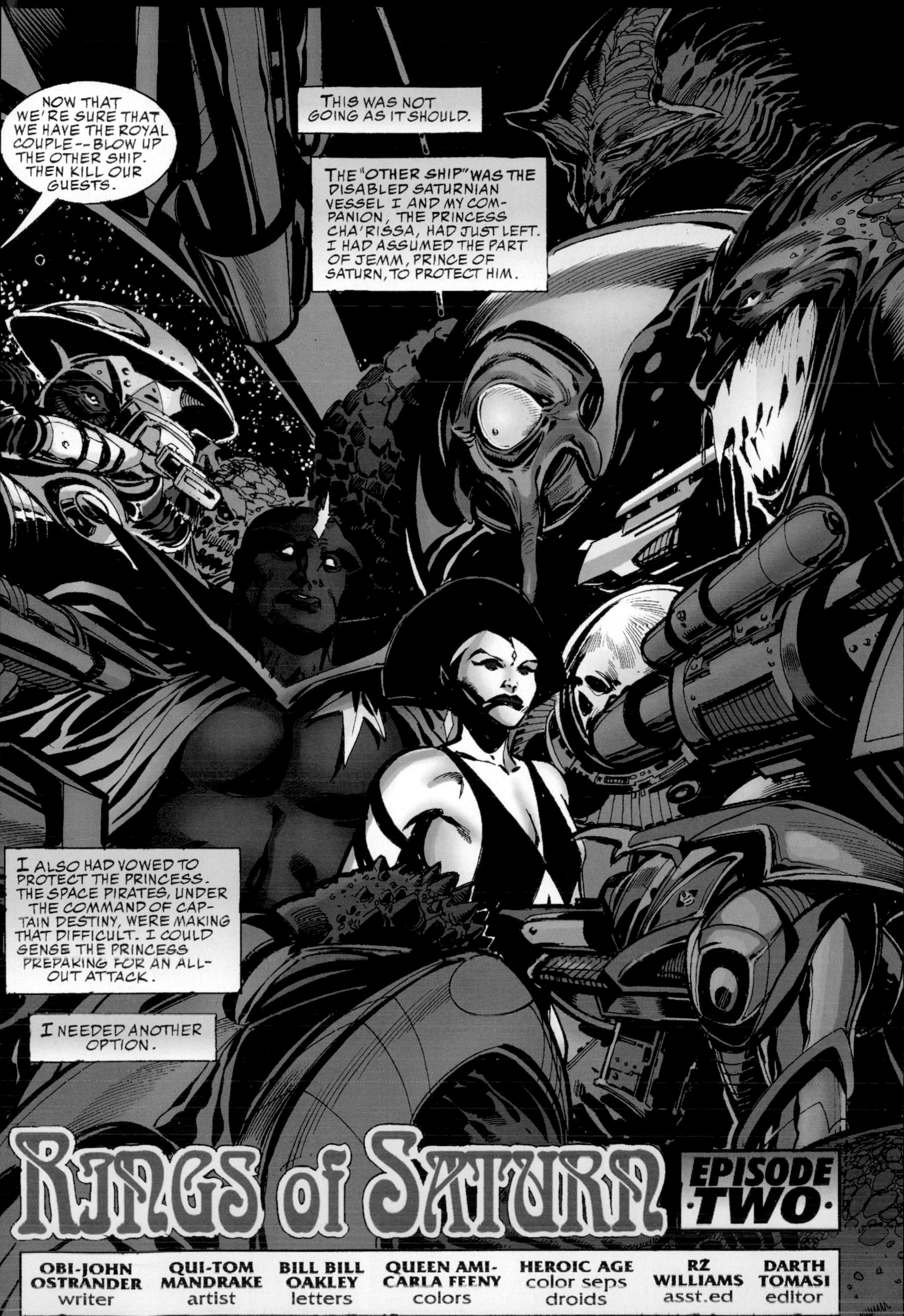

NOW THAT WE'RE SURE THAT WE HAVE THE ROYAL COUPLE--BLOW UP THE OTHER SHIP. THEN KILL OUR GUESTS.
THIS WAS NOT GOING AS IT SHOULD.
THE "OTHER SHIP" WAS THE DISABLED SATURNIAN VESSEL I AND MY COMPANION, THE PRINCESS CHA'RISSA, HAD JUST LEFT. I HAD ASSUMED THE PART OF JEMM, PRINCE OF SATURN, TO PROTECT HIM.
I ALSO HAD VOWED TO PROTECT THE PRINCESS. THE SPACE PIRATES, UNDER THE COMMAND OF CAPTAIN DESTINY, WERE MAKING THAT DIFFICULT. I COULD SENSE THE PRINCESS PREPARING FOR AN ALL-OUT ATTACK.
I NEEDED ANOTHER OPTION.
RINGS of SATURN
EPISODE TWO
OBI-JOHN OSTRANDER writer
QUI-TOM MANDRAKE artist
BILL BILL OAKLEY letters
QUEEN AMI-CARLA FEENY colors
HEROIC AGE color seps droids
R2 WILLIAMS asst.ed
DARTH TOMASI editor

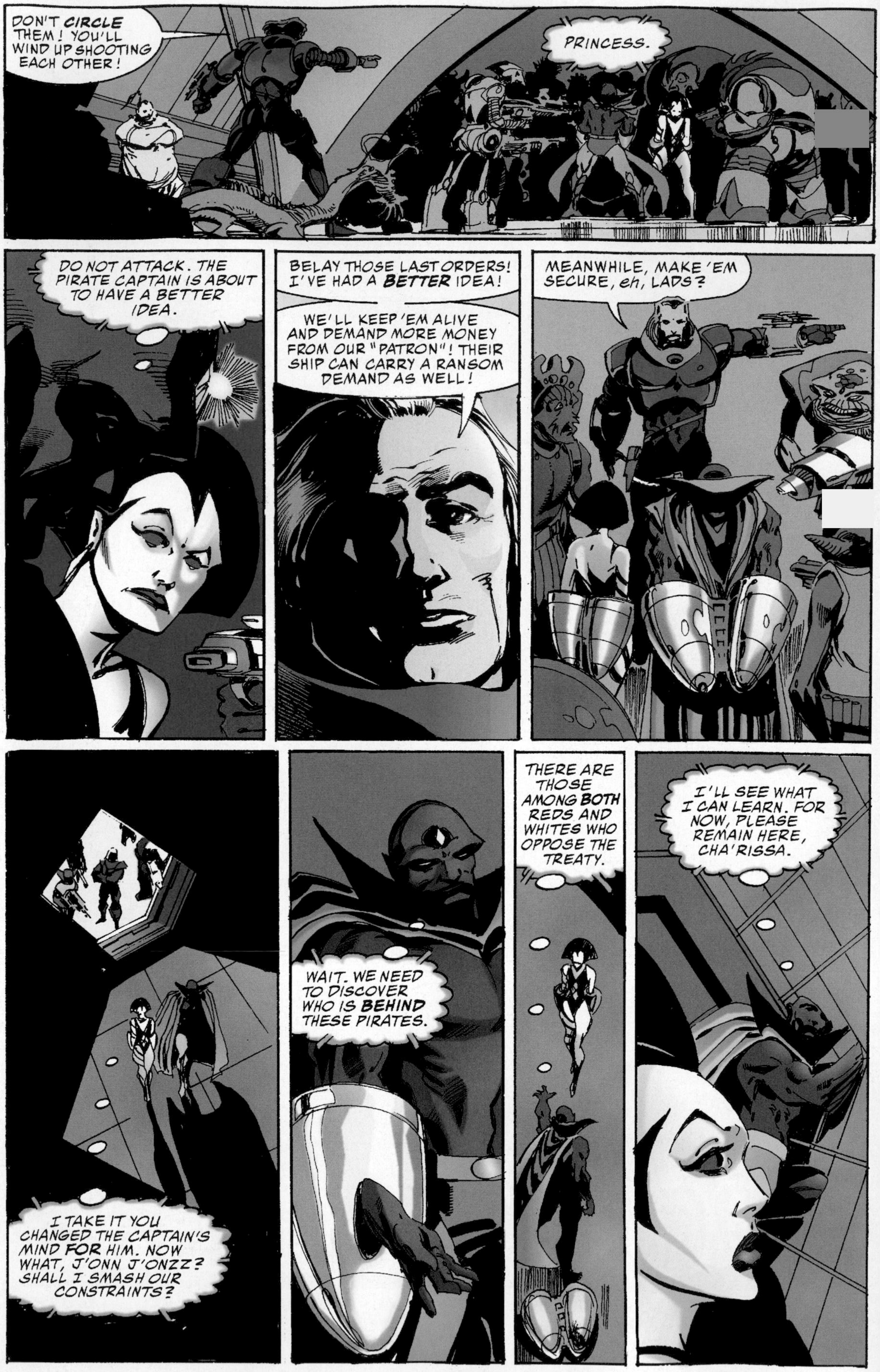
DON'T CIRCLE THEM! YOU'LL WIND UP SHOOTING EACH OTHER!
PRINCESS.
DO NOT ATTACK. THE PIRATE CAPTAIN IS ABOUT TO HAVE A BETTER IDEA.
BELAY THOSE LAST ORDERS! I'VE HAD A BETTER IDEA!
WE'LL KEEP 'EM ALIVE AND DEMAND MORE MONEY FROM OUR "PATRON"! THEIR SHIP CAN CARRY A RANSOM DEMAND AS WELL!
MEANWHILE, MAKE 'EM SECURE, eh, LADS?
I TAKE IT YOU CHANGED THE CAPTAIN'S MIND FOR HIM. NOW WHAT, J'ONN J'ONZZ? SHALL I SMASH OUR CONSTRAINTS?
WAIT. WE NEED TO DISCOVER WHO IS BEHIND THESE PIRATES.
THERE ARE THOSE AMONG BOTH REDS AND WHITES WHO OPPOSE THE TREATY.
I'LL SEE WHAT I CAN LEARN. FOR NOW, PLEASE REMAIN HERE, CHA'RISSA.

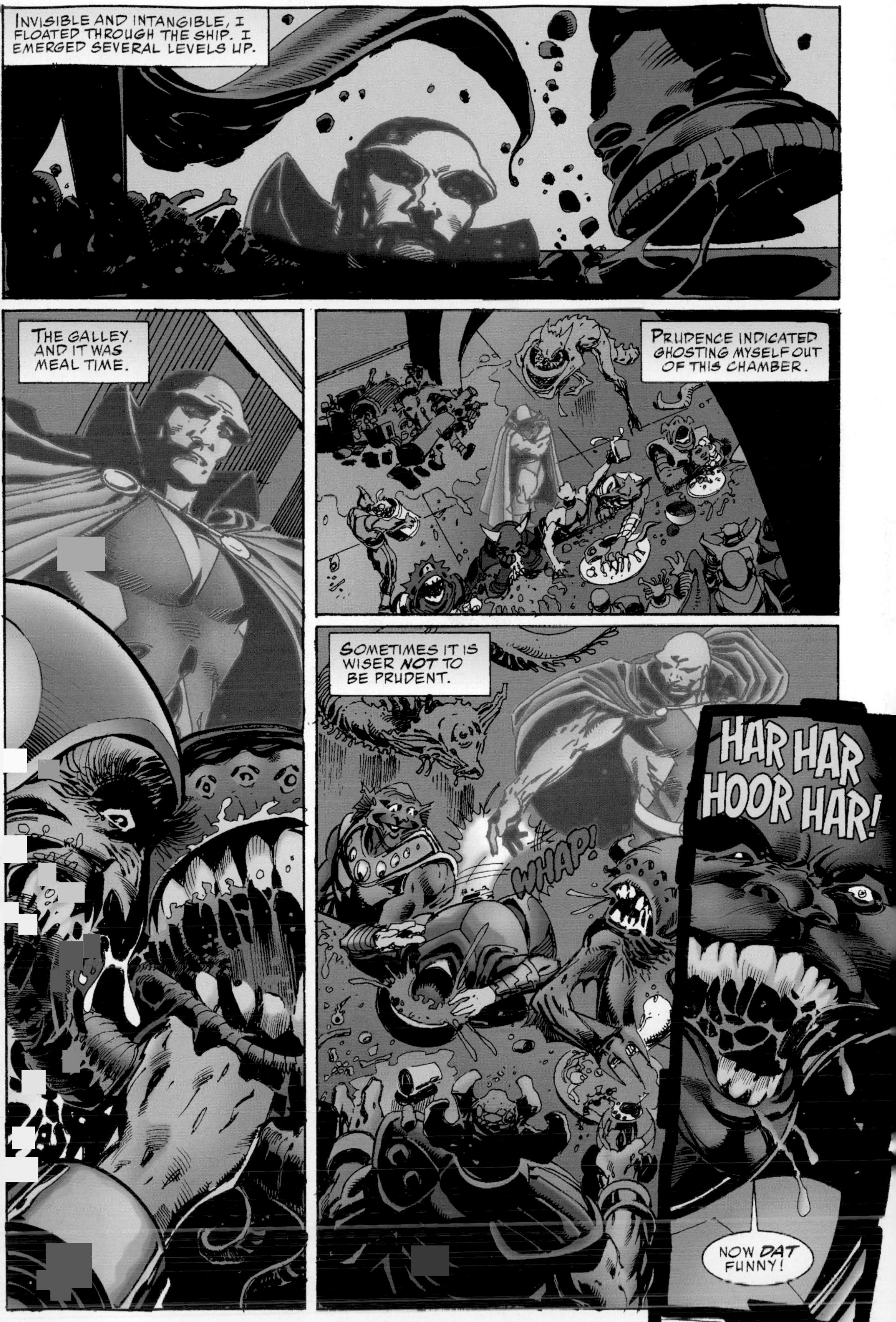

INVISIBLE AND INTANGIBLE, I FLOATED THROUGH THE SHIP. I EMERGED SEVERAL LEVELS UP.
THE GALLEY. AND IT WAS MEAL TIME.
PRUDENCE INDICATED GHOSTING MYSELF OUT OF THIS CHAMBER.
SOMETIMES IT IS WISER NOT TO BE PRUDENT.
WHAP!
HAR HAR HOOR HAR!
NOW DAT FUNNY!

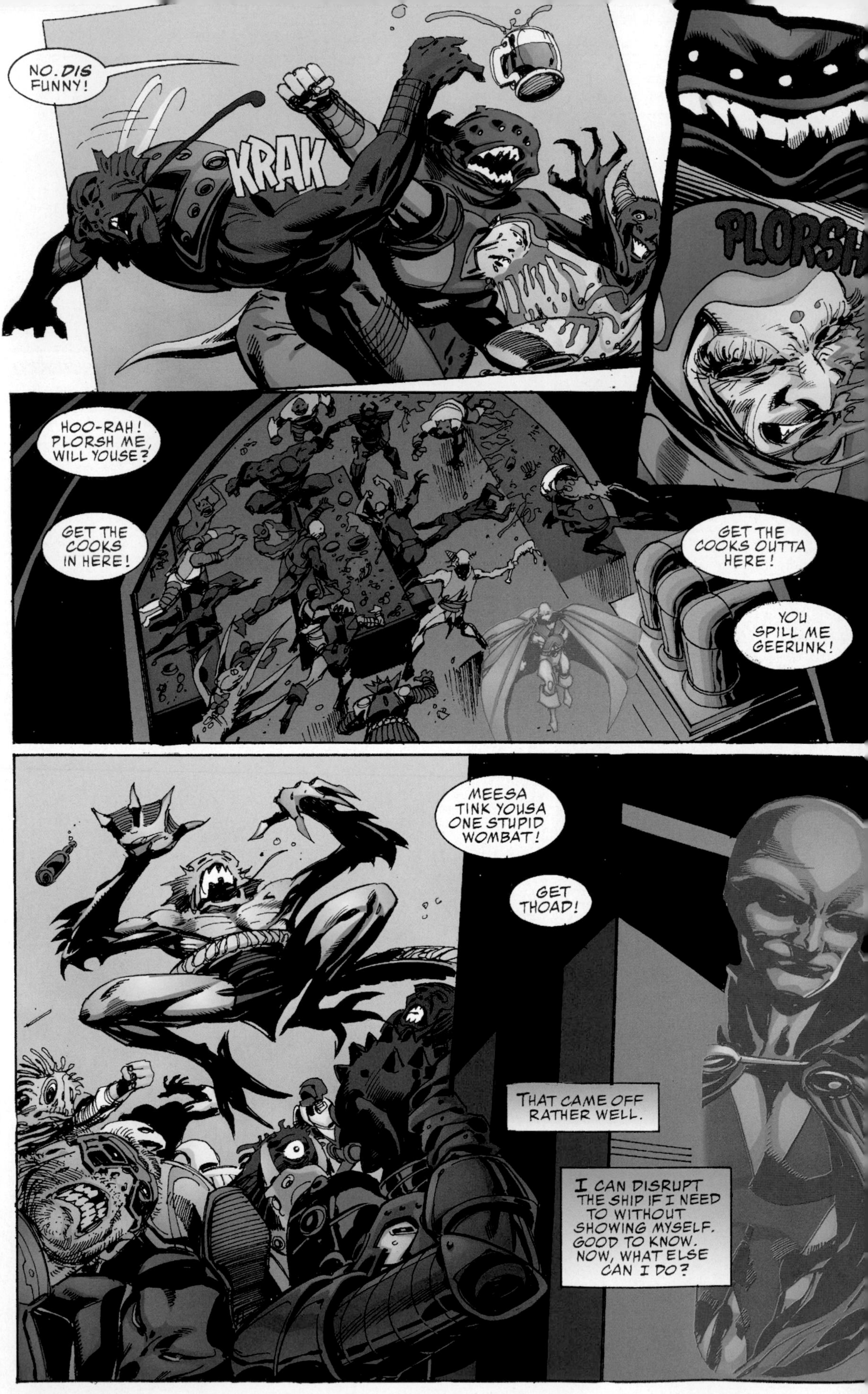
NO. DIS FUNNY!
KRAK
PLORSH
HOO-RAH! PLORSH ME, WILL YOUSE?
GET THE COOKS IN HERE!
GET THE COOKS OUTTA HERE!
YOU SPILL ME GEERUNK!
MEESA TINK YOUSA ONE STUPID WOMBAT!
GET THOAD!
THAT CAME OFF RATHER WELL.
I CAN DISRUPT THE SHIP IF I NEED TO WITHOUT SHOWING MYSELF. GOOD TO KNOW. NOW, WHAT ELSE CAN I DO?

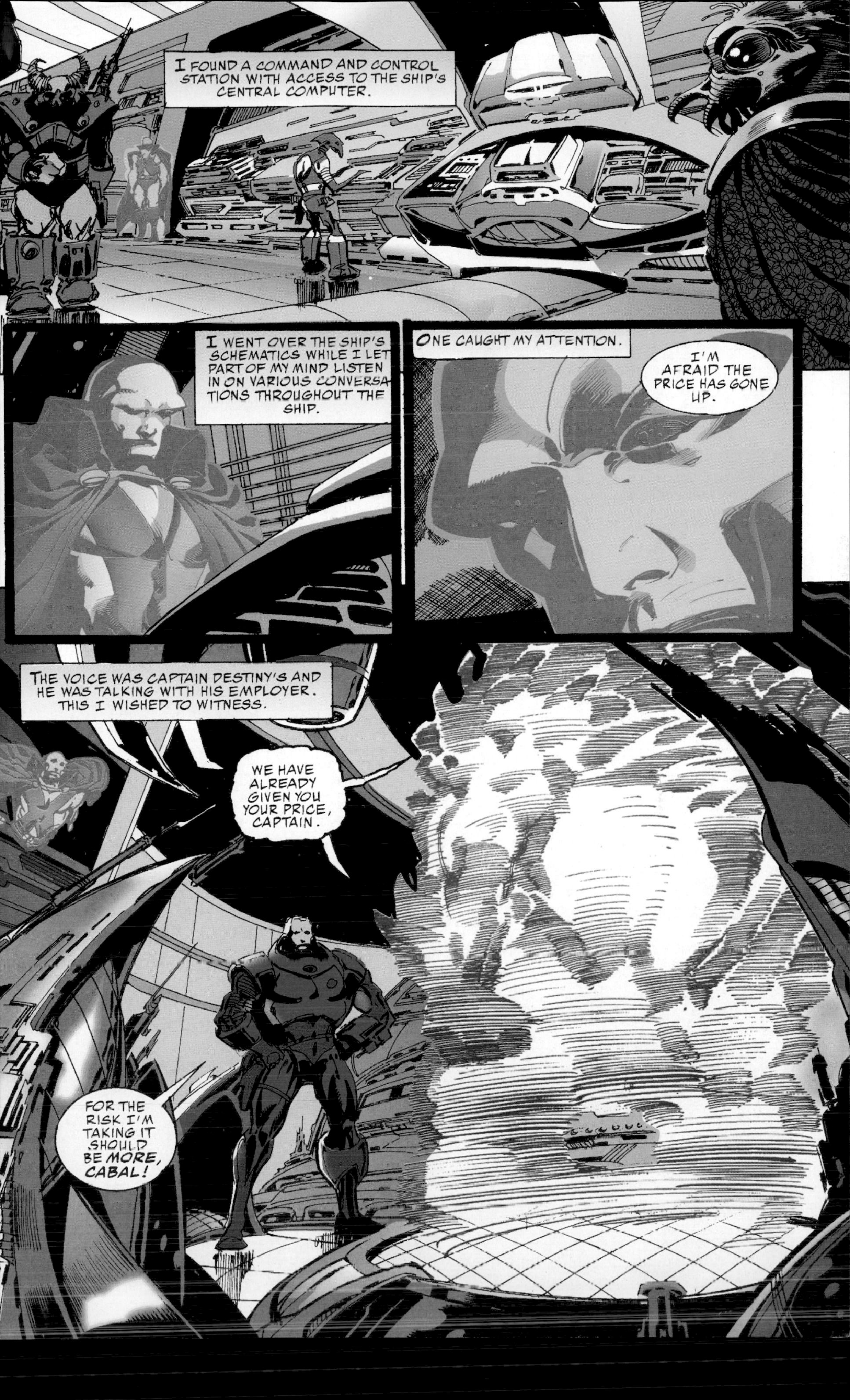
I FOUND A COMMAND AND CONTROL STATION WITH ACCESS TO THE SHIP'S CENTRAL COMPUTER.
I WENT OVER THE SHIP'S SCHEMATICS WHILE I LET PART OF MY MIND LISTEN IN ON VARIOUS CONVERSATIONS THROUGHOUT THE SHIP.
ONE CAUGHT MY ATTENTION.
I'M AFRAID THE PRICE HAS GONE UP.
THE VOICE WAS CAPTAIN DESTINY'S AND HE WAS TALKING WITH HIS EMPLOYER. THIS I WISHED TO WITNESS.
WE HAVE ALREADY GIVEN YOU YOUR PRICE, CAPTAIN.
FOR THE RISK I'M TAKING IT SHOULD BE *MORE*, CABAL!

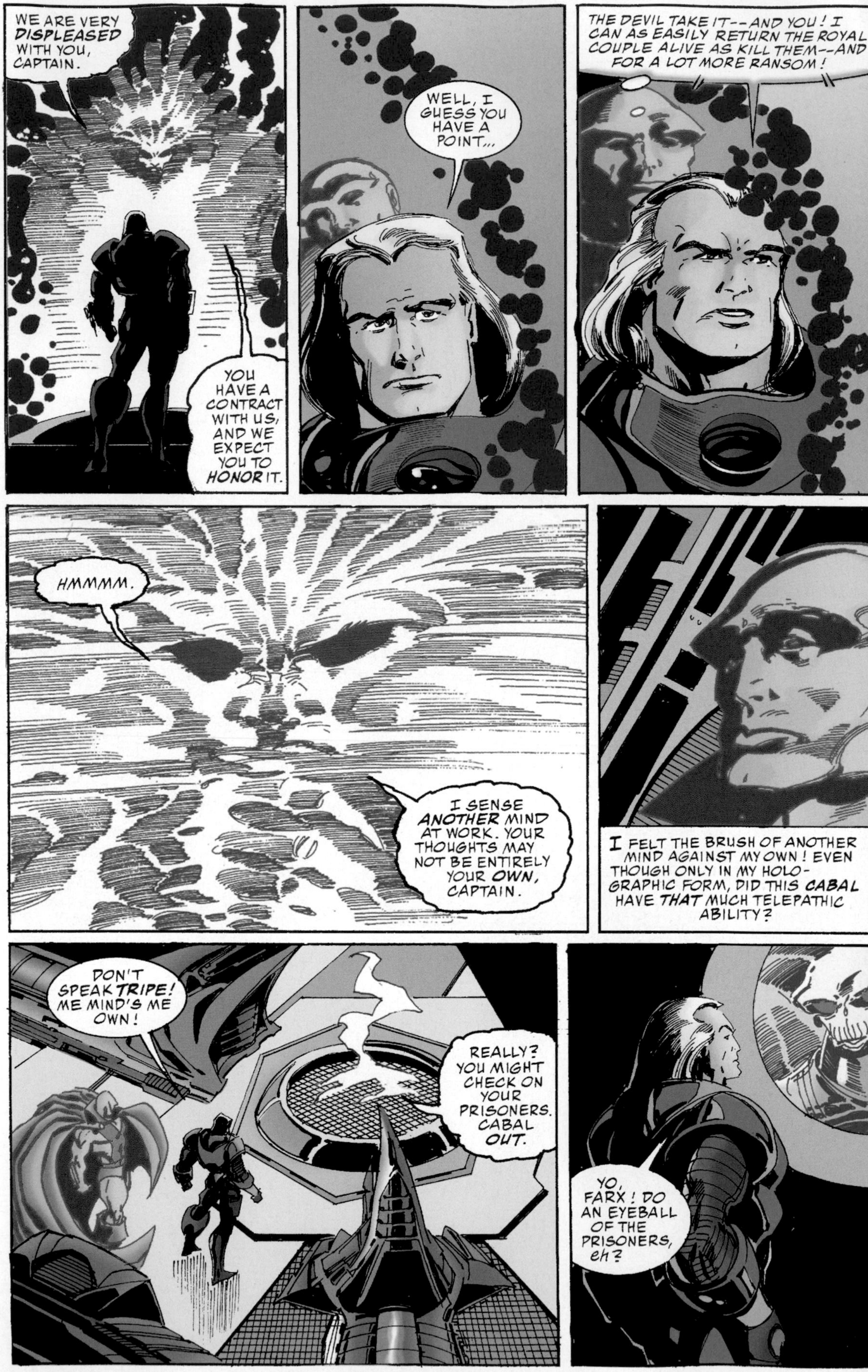
WE ARE VERY DISPLEASED WITH YOU, CAPTAIN.
YOU HAVE A CONTRACT WITH US, AND WE EXPECT YOU TO HONOR IT.
WELL, I GUESS YOU HAVE A POINT...
THE DEVIL TAKE IT--AND YOU! I CAN AS EASILY RETURN THE ROYAL COUPLE ALIVE AS KILL THEM--AND FOR A LOT MORE RANSOM!
HMMMM.
I SENSE ANOTHER MIND AT WORK. YOUR THOUGHTS MAY NOT BE ENTIRELY YOUR OWN, CAPTAIN.
I FELT THE BRUSH OF ANOTHER MIND AGAINST MY OWN! EVEN THOUGH ONLY IN MY HOLOGRAPHIC FORM, DID THIS CABAL HAVE THAT MUCH TELEPATHIC ABILITY?
DON'T SPEAK TRIPE! ME MIND'S ME OWN!
REALLY? YOU MIGHT CHECK ON YOUR PRISONERS. CABAL OUT.
YO, FARX! DO AN EYEBALL OF THE PRISONERS, eh?

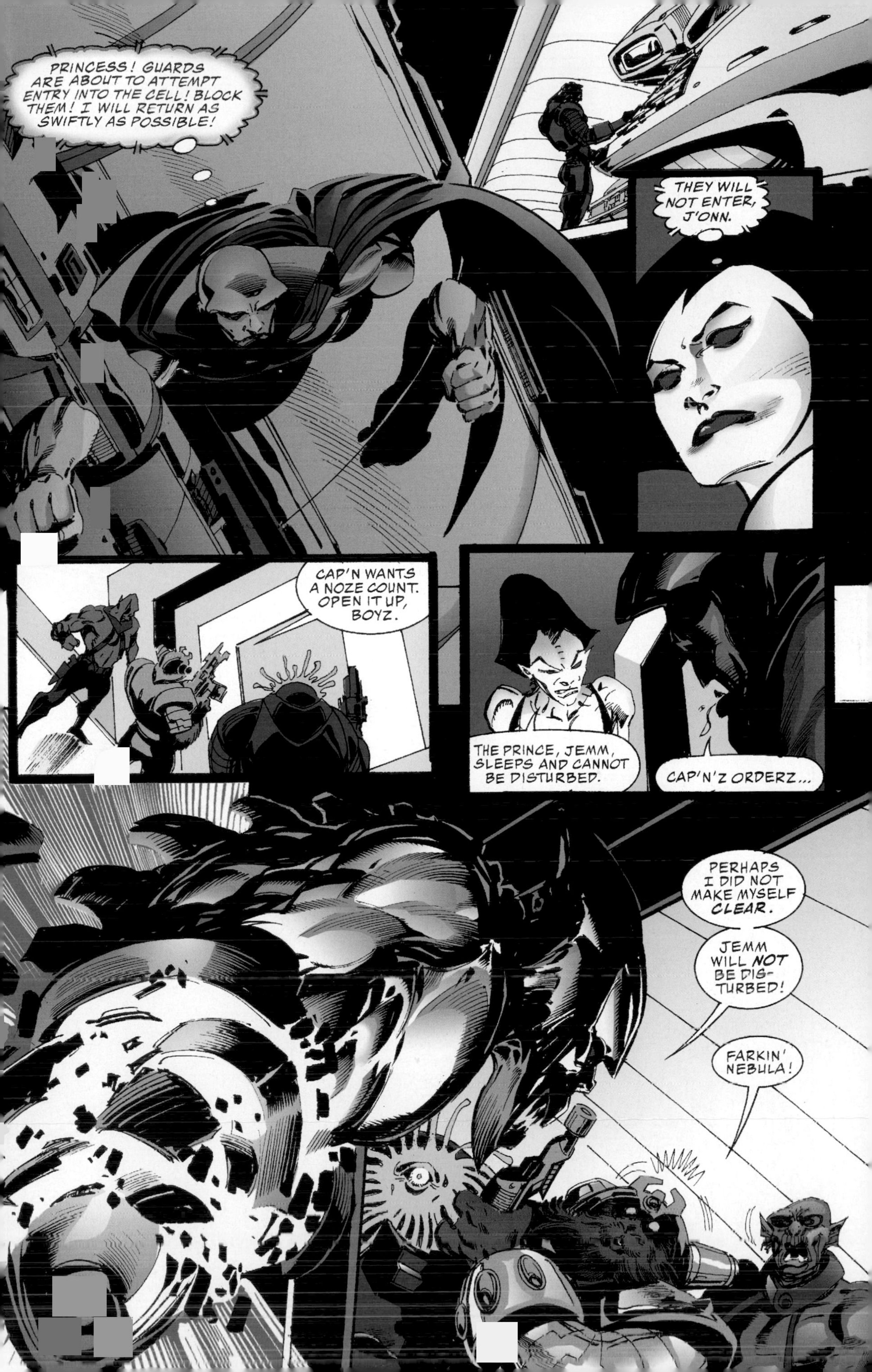
PRINCESS! GUARDS ARE ABOUT TO ATTEMPT ENTRY INTO THE CELL! BLOCK THEM! I WILL RETURN AS SWIFTLY AS POSSIBLE!
THEY WILL NOT ENTER, J'ONN.
CAP'N WANTS A NOZE COUNT. OPEN IT UP, BOYZ.
THE PRINCE, JEMM, SLEEPS AND CANNOT BE DISTURBED.
CAP'N'Z ORDERZ...
PERHAPS I DID NOT MAKE MYSELF CLEAR.
JEMM WILL NOT BE DISTURBED!
FARKIN' NEBULA!

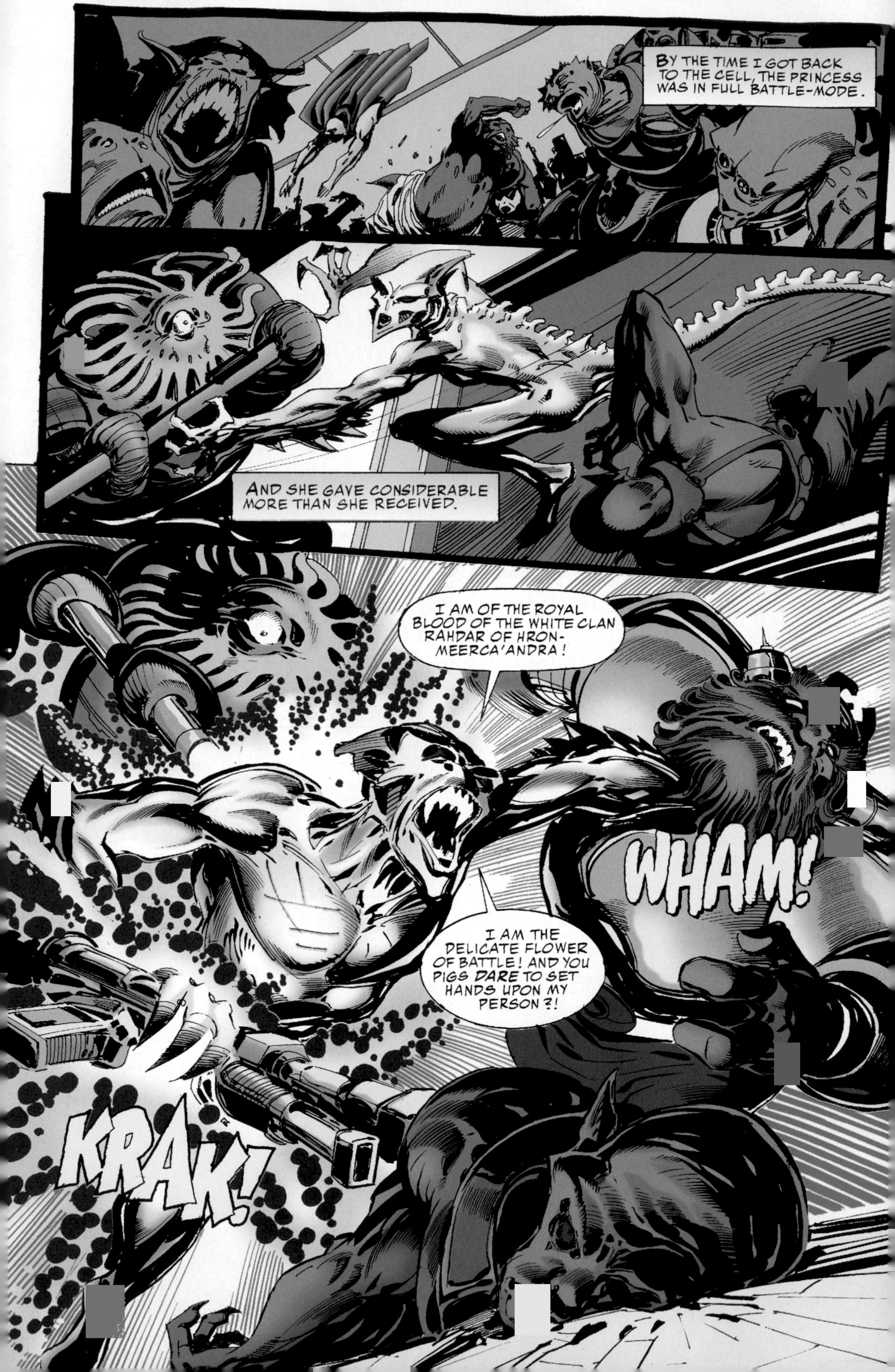
BY THE TIME I GOT BACK TO THE CELL, THE PRINCESS WAS IN FULL BATTLE-MODE.
AND SHE GAVE CONSIDERABLE MORE THAN SHE RECEIVED.
I AM OF THE ROYAL BLOOD OF THE WHITE CLAN RAHDAR OF HRON-MEERCA'ANDRA!
WHAM!
I AM THE DELICATE FLOWER OF BATTLE! AND YOU PIGS DARE TO SET HANDS UPON MY PERSON?!
KRAK!

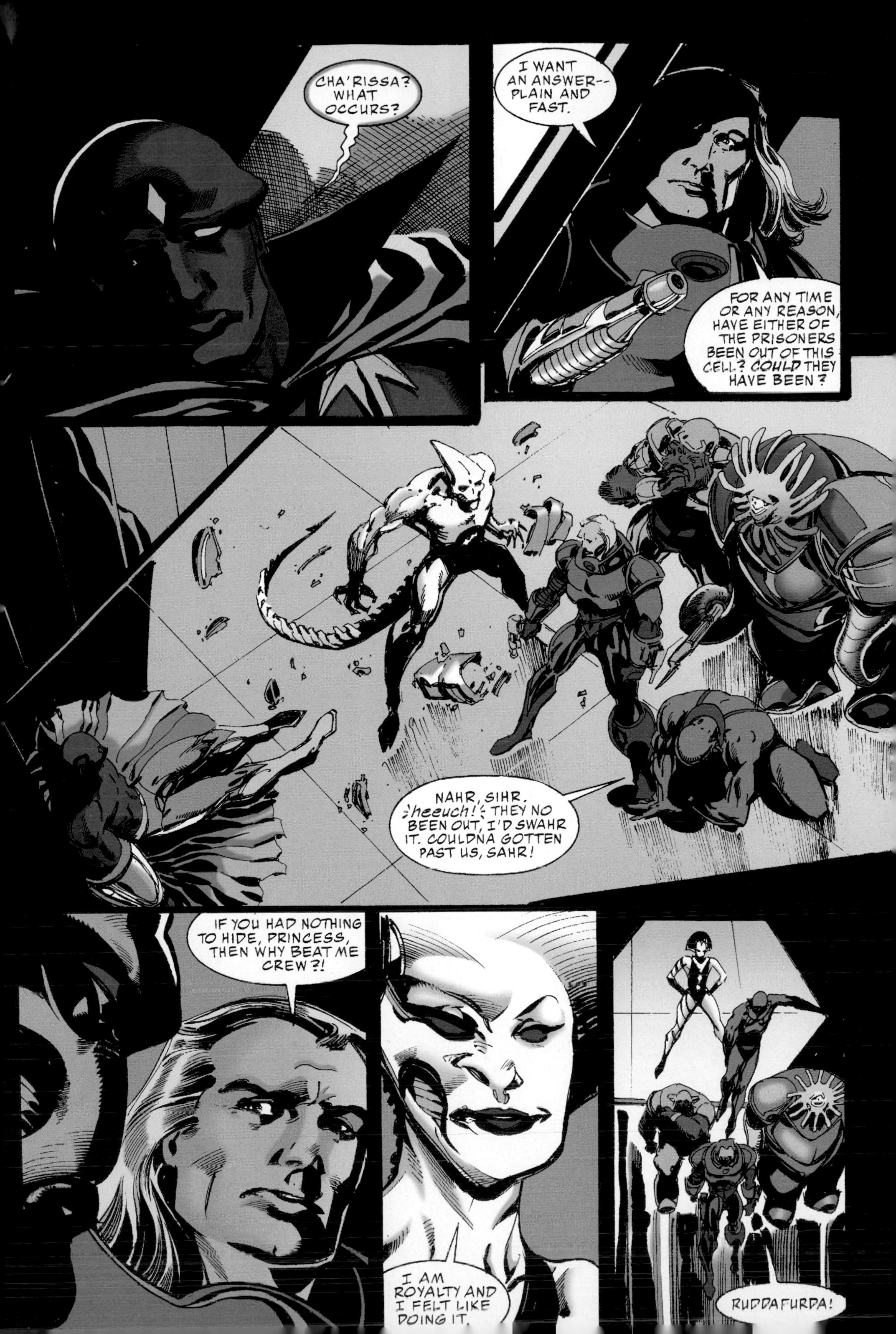
CHA'RISSA? WHAT OCCURS?
I WANT AN ANSWER-- PLAIN AND FAST.
FOR ANY TIME OR ANY REASON, HAVE EITHER OF THE PRISONERS BEEN OUT OF THIS CELL? COULD THEY HAVE BEEN?
NAHR, SIHR. ;heeuch!; THEY NO BEEN OUT, I'D SWAHR IT. COULDNA GOTTEN PAST US, SAHR!
IF YOU HAD NOTHING TO HIDE, PRINCESS, THEN WHY BEAT ME CREW?!
I AM ROYALTY AND I FELT LIKE DOING IT.
RUDDAFURDA!

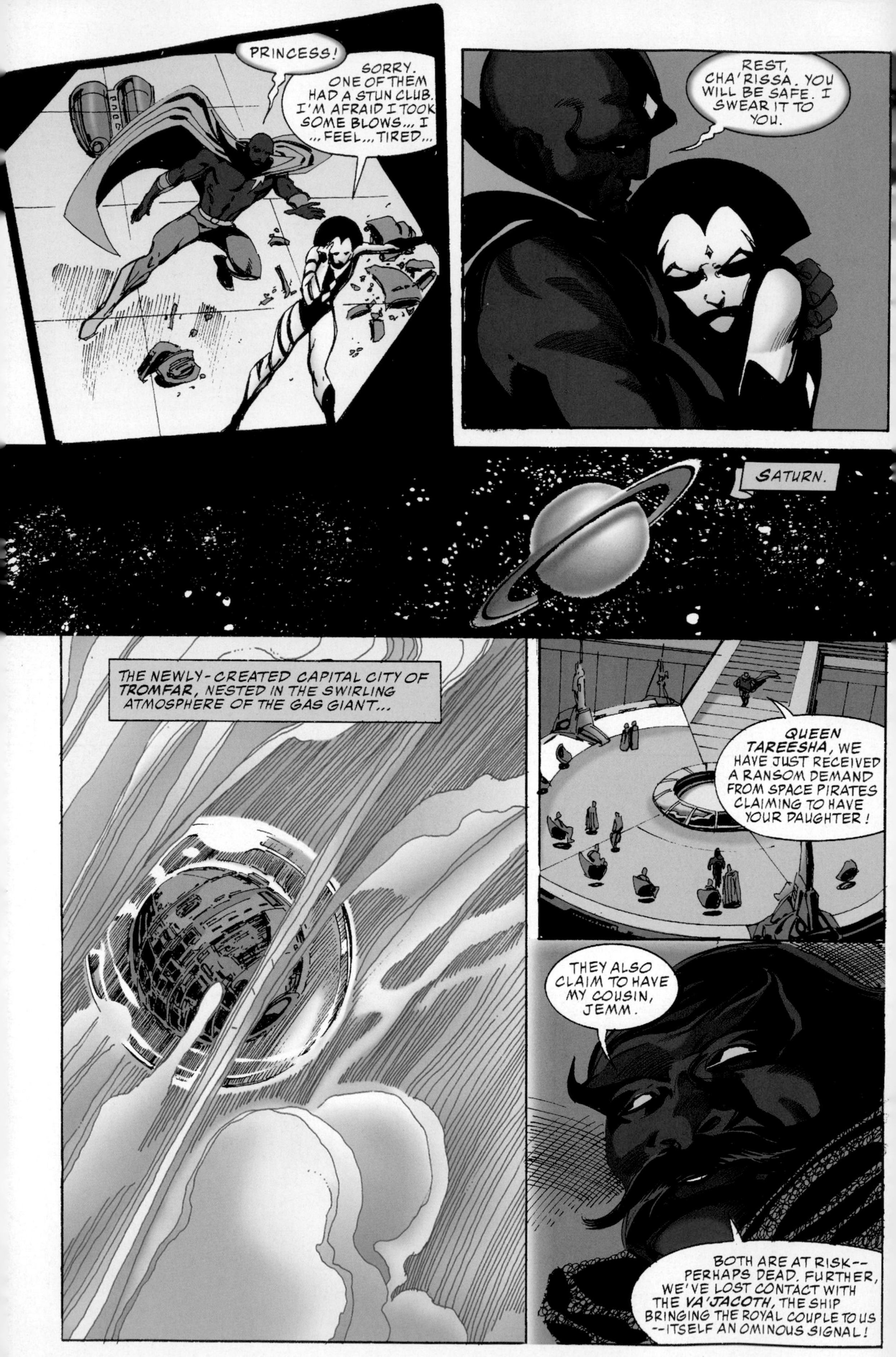
PRINCESS!
SORRY. ONE OF THEM HAD A STUN CLUB. I'M AFRAID I TOOK SOME BLOWS... I ...FEEL...TIRED...
REST, CHA'RISSA. YOU WILL BE SAFE. I SWEAR IT TO YOU.
SATURN.
THE NEWLY-CREATED CAPITAL CITY OF TROMFAR, NESTED IN THE SWIRLING ATMOSPHERE OF THE GAS GIANT...
QUEEN TAREESHA, WE HAVE JUST RECEIVED A RANSOM DEMAND FROM SPACE PIRATES CLAIMING TO HAVE YOUR DAUGHTER!
THEY ALSO CLAIM TO HAVE MY COUSIN, JEMM.
BOTH ARE AT RISK-- PERHAPS DEAD. FURTHER, WE'VE LOST CONTACT WITH THE VA'JACOTH, THE SHIP BRINGING THE ROYAL COUPLE TO US --ITSELF AN OMINOUS SIGNAL!

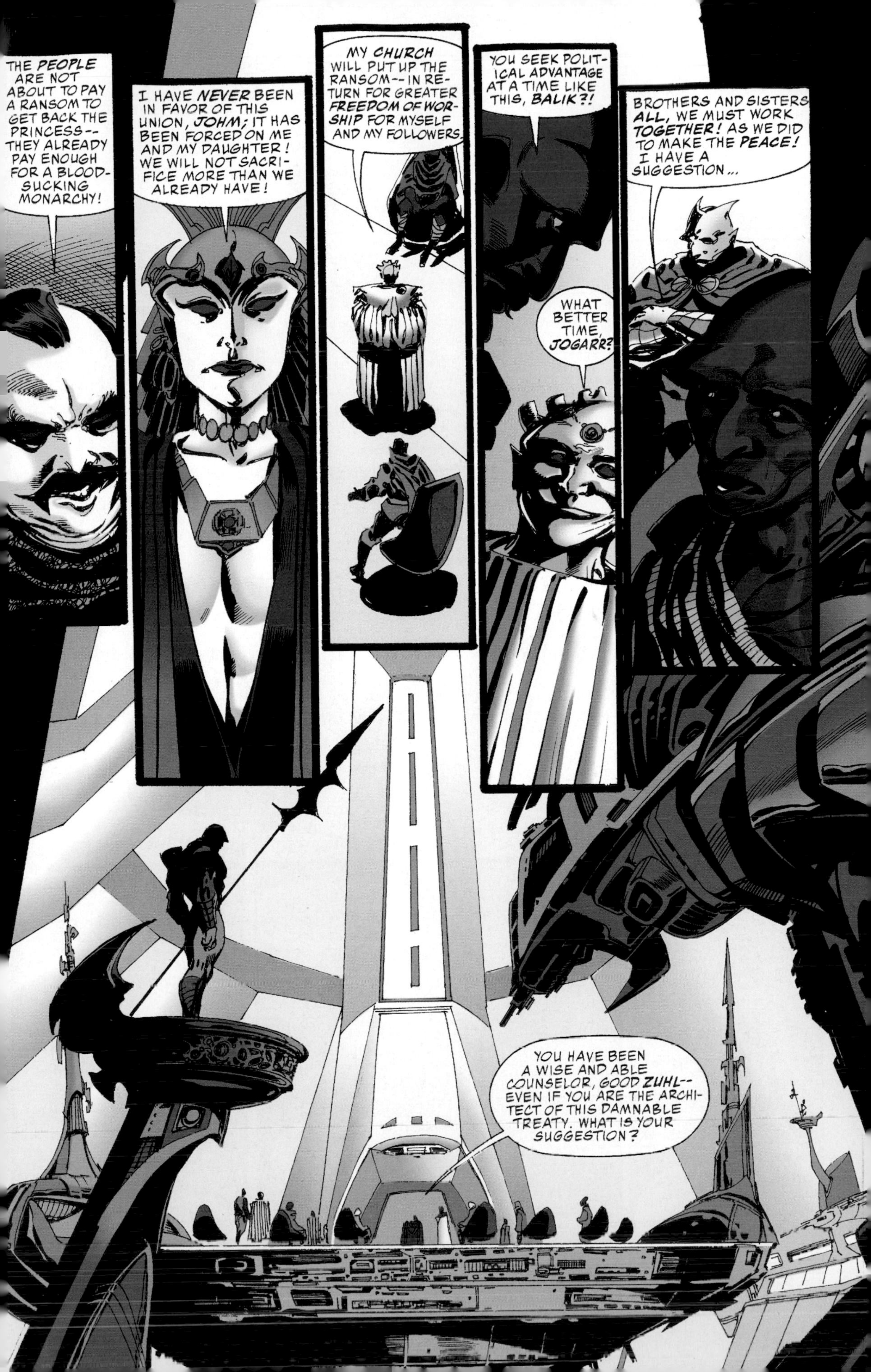
THE *PEOPLE* ARE NOT ABOUT TO PAY A RANSOM TO GET BACK THE PRINCESS-- THEY ALREADY PAY ENOUGH FOR A BLOOD-SUCKING MONARCHY!
I HAVE *NEVER* BEEN IN FAVOR OF THIS UNION, *JOHM;* IT HAS BEEN FORCED ON ME AND MY DAUGHTER! WE WILL NOT SACRIFICE MORE THAN WE ALREADY HAVE!
MY *CHURCH* WILL PUT UP THE RANSOM-- IN RETURN FOR GREATER *FREEDOM OF WORSHIP* FOR MYSELF AND MY FOLLOWERS.
YOU SEEK POLITICAL ADVANTAGE AT A TIME LIKE THIS, *BALIK?!*
WHAT BETTER TIME, *JOGARR?*
BROTHERS AND SISTERS *ALL*, WE MUST WORK *TOGETHER!* AS WE DID TO MAKE THE *PEACE!* I HAVE A SUGGESTION...
YOU HAVE BEEN A WISE AND ABLE COUNSELOR, GOOD *ZUHL*-- EVEN IF YOU ARE THE ARCHITECT OF THIS DAMNABLE TREATY. WHAT IS YOUR SUGGESTION?

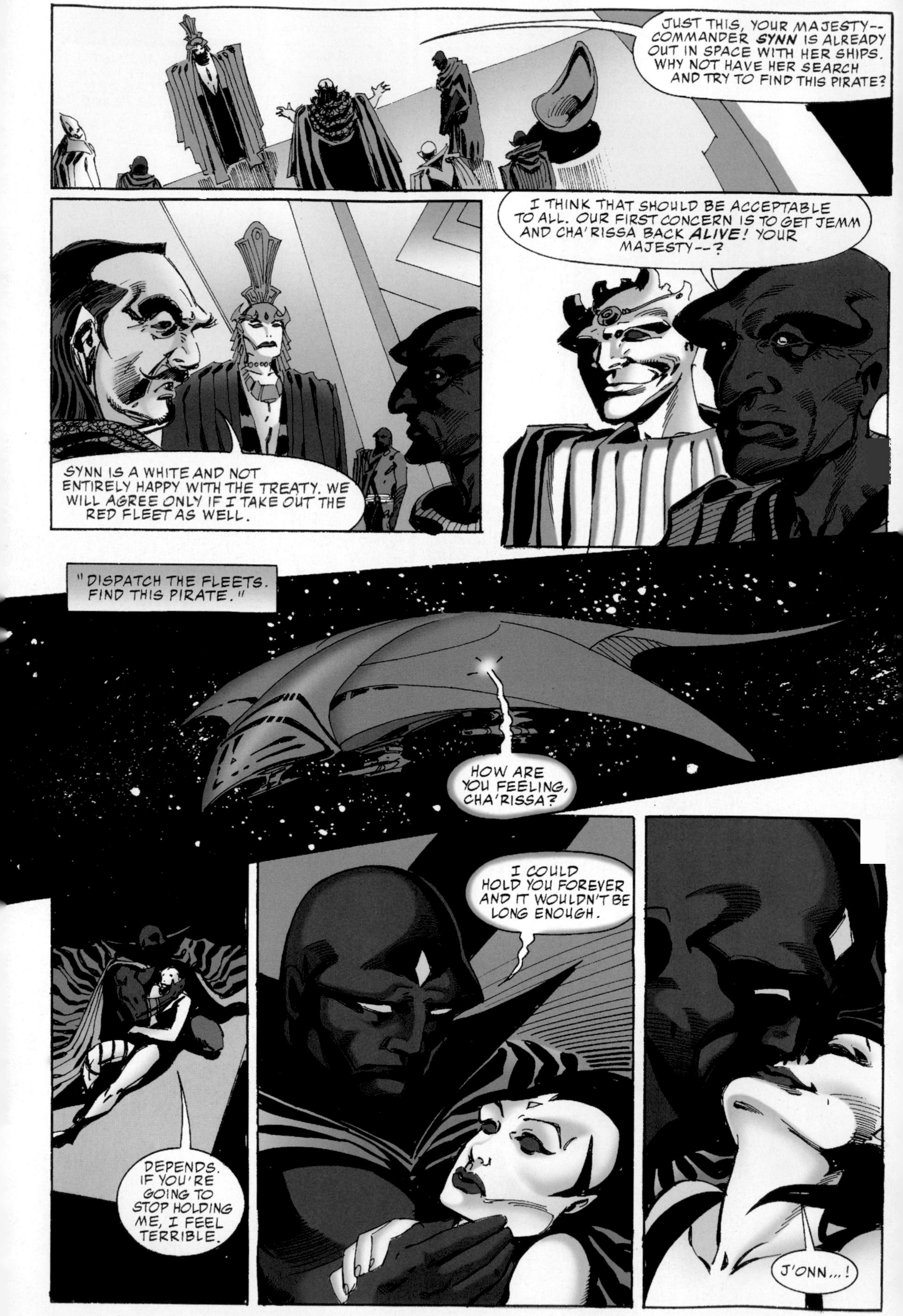
JUST THIS, YOUR MAJESTY-- COMMANDER SYNN IS ALREADY OUT IN SPACE WITH HER SHIPS. WHY NOT HAVE HER SEARCH AND TRY TO FIND THIS PIRATE?
SYNN IS A WHITE AND NOT ENTIRELY HAPPY WITH THE TREATY. WE WILL AGREE ONLY IF I TAKE OUT THE RED FLEET AS WELL.
I THINK THAT SHOULD BE ACCEPTABLE TO ALL. OUR FIRST CONCERN IS TO GET JEMM AND CHA'RISSA BACK ALIVE! YOUR MAJESTY--?
"DISPATCH THE FLEETS. FIND THIS PIRATE."
HOW ARE YOU FEELING, CHA'RISSA?
DEPENDS. IF YOU'RE GOING TO STOP HOLDING ME, I FEEL TERRIBLE.
I COULD HOLD YOU FOREVER AND IT WOULDN'T BE LONG ENOUGH.
J'ONN...!

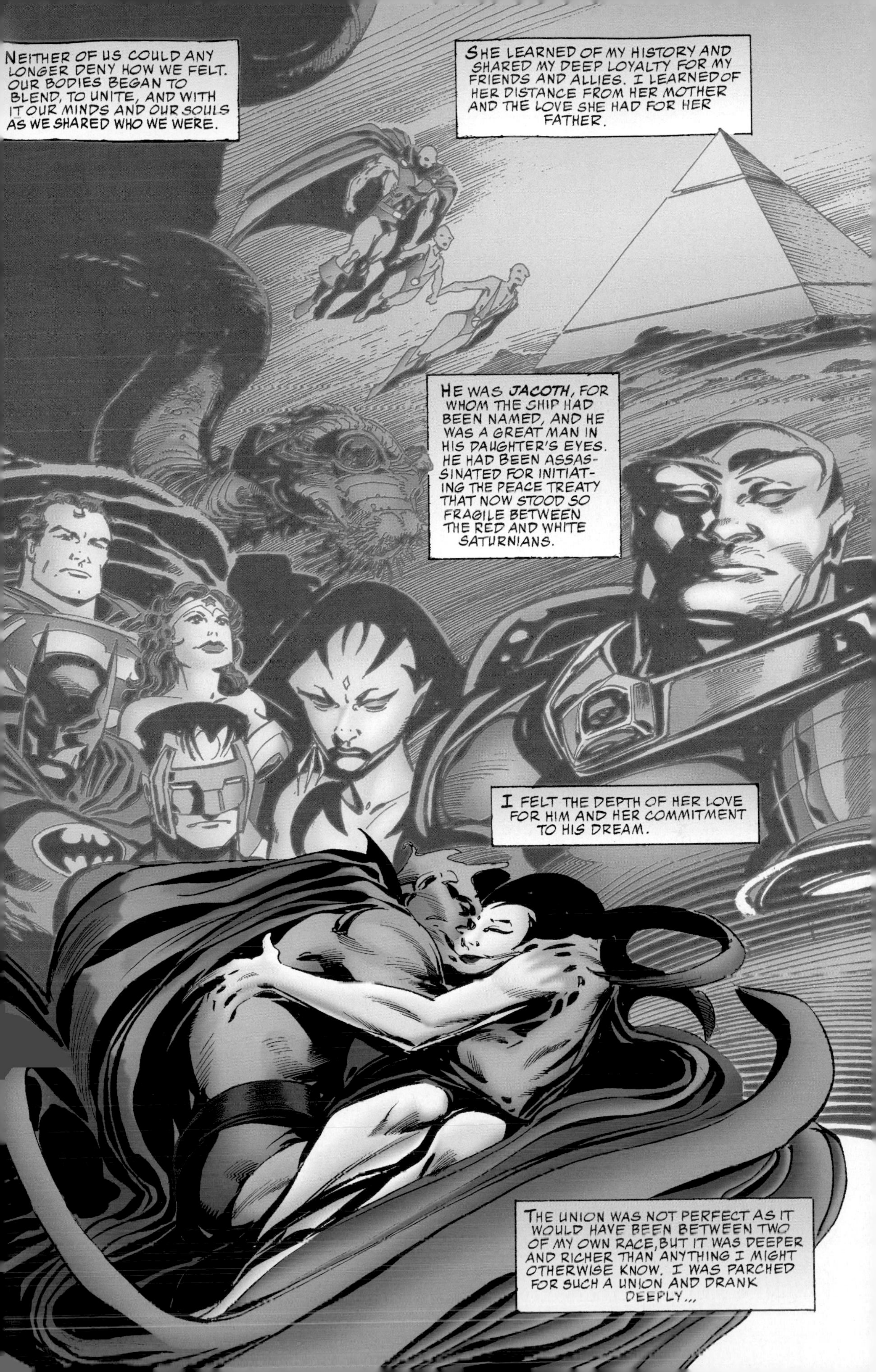
NEITHER OF US COULD ANY LONGER DENY HOW WE FELT. OUR BODIES BEGAN TO BLEND, TO UNITE, AND WITH IT OUR MINDS AND OUR SOULS AS WE SHARED WHO WE WERE.
SHE LEARNED OF MY HISTORY AND SHARED MY DEEP LOYALTY FOR MY FRIENDS AND ALLIES. I LEARNED OF HER DISTANCE FROM HER MOTHER AND THE LOVE SHE HAD FOR HER FATHER.
HE WAS JACOTH, FOR WHOM THE SHIP HAD BEEN NAMED, AND HE WAS A GREAT MAN IN HIS DAUGHTER'S EYES. HE HAD BEEN ASSAS-SINATED FOR INITIAT-ING THE PEACE TREATY THAT NOW STOOD SO FRAGILE BETWEEN THE RED AND WHITE SATURNIANS.
I FELT THE DEPTH OF HER LOVE FOR HIM AND HER COMMITMENT TO HIS DREAM.
THE UNION WAS NOT PERFECT AS IT WOULD HAVE BEEN BETWEEN TWO OF MY OWN RACE, BUT IT WAS DEEPER AND RICHER THAN ANYTHING I MIGHT OTHERWISE KNOW. I WAS PARCHED FOR SUCH A UNION AND DRANK DEEPLY...

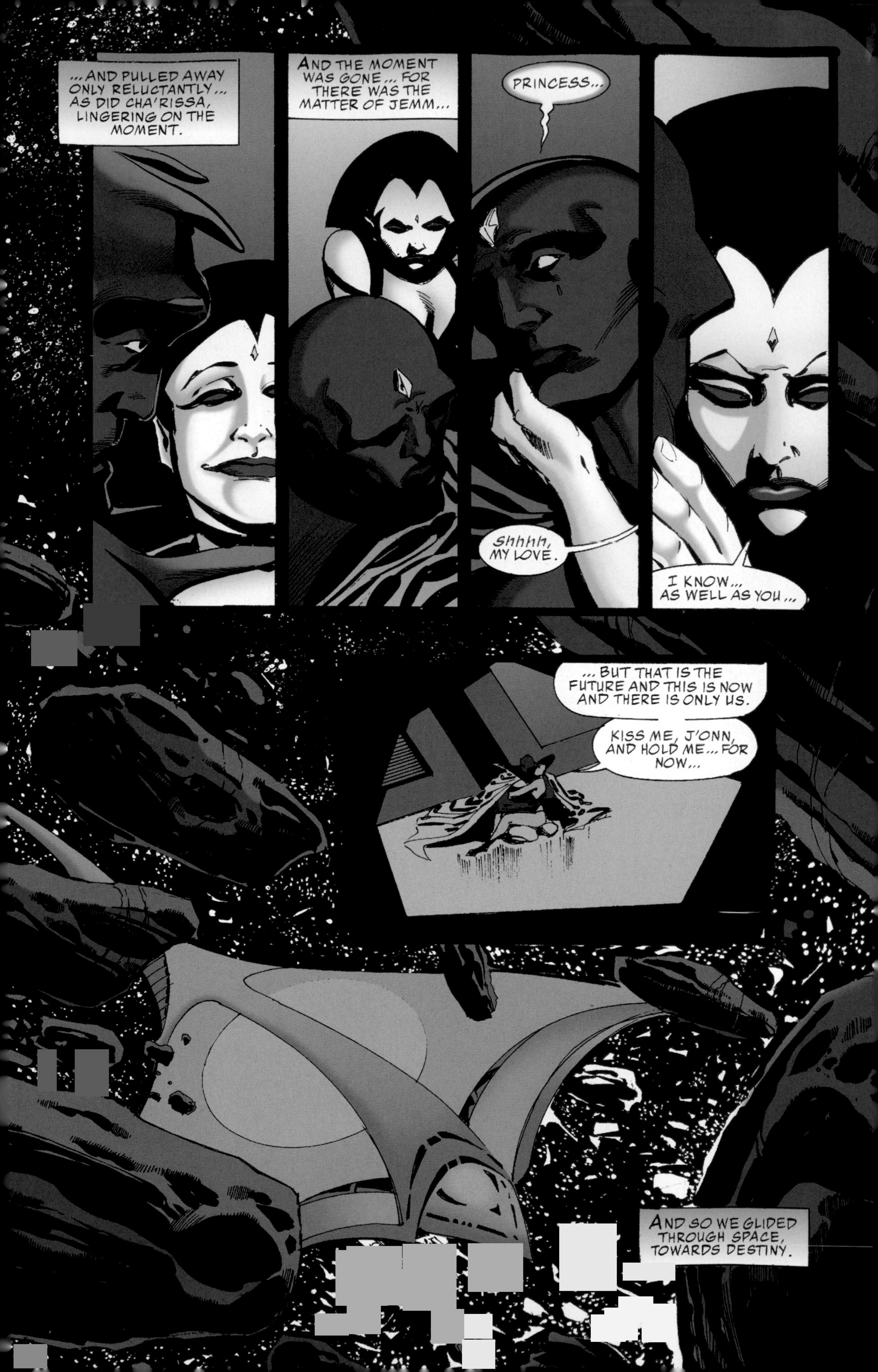
...AND PULLED AWAY ONLY RELUCTANTLY... AS DID CHA'RISSA, LINGERING ON THE MOMENT.
AND THE MOMENT WAS GONE... FOR THERE WAS THE MATTER OF JEMM...
PRINCESS...
Shhhh, MY LOVE.
I KNOW... AS WELL AS YOU...
...BUT THAT IS THE FUTURE AND THIS IS NOW AND THERE IS ONLY US.
KISS ME, J'ONN, AND HOLD ME... FOR NOW...
AND SO WE GLIDED THROUGH SPACE, TOWARDS DESTINY.

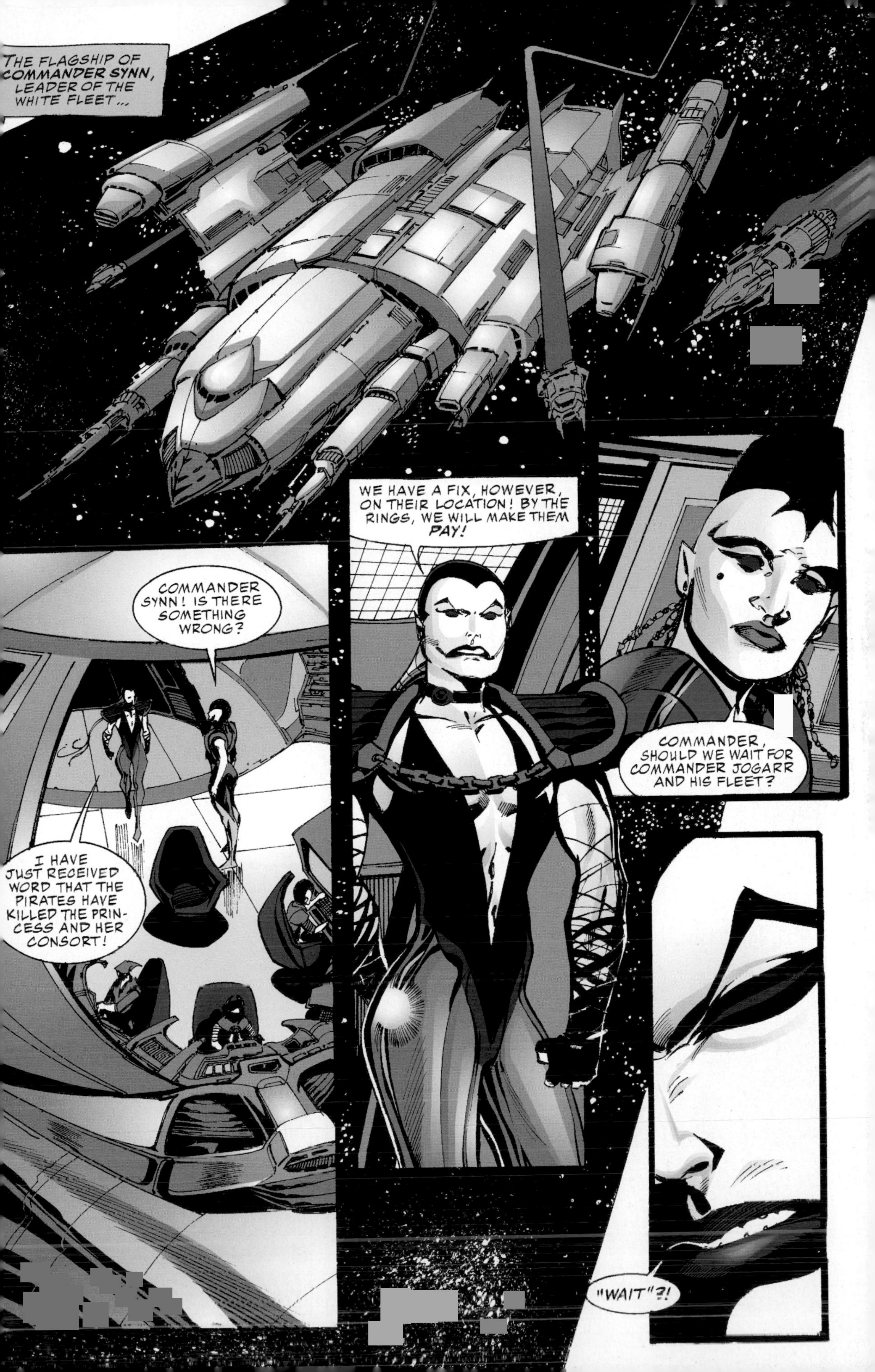
THE FLAGSHIP OF COMMANDER SYNN, LEADER OF THE WHITE FLEET...
COMMANDER SYNN! IS THERE SOMETHING WRONG?
I HAVE JUST RECEIVED WORD THAT THE PIRATES HAVE KILLED THE PRINCESS AND HER CONSORT!
WE HAVE A FIX, HOWEVER, ON THEIR LOCATION! BY THE RINGS, WE WILL MAKE THEM PAY!
COMMANDER, SHOULD WE WAIT FOR COMMANDER JOGARR AND HIS FLEET?
"WAIT"?!

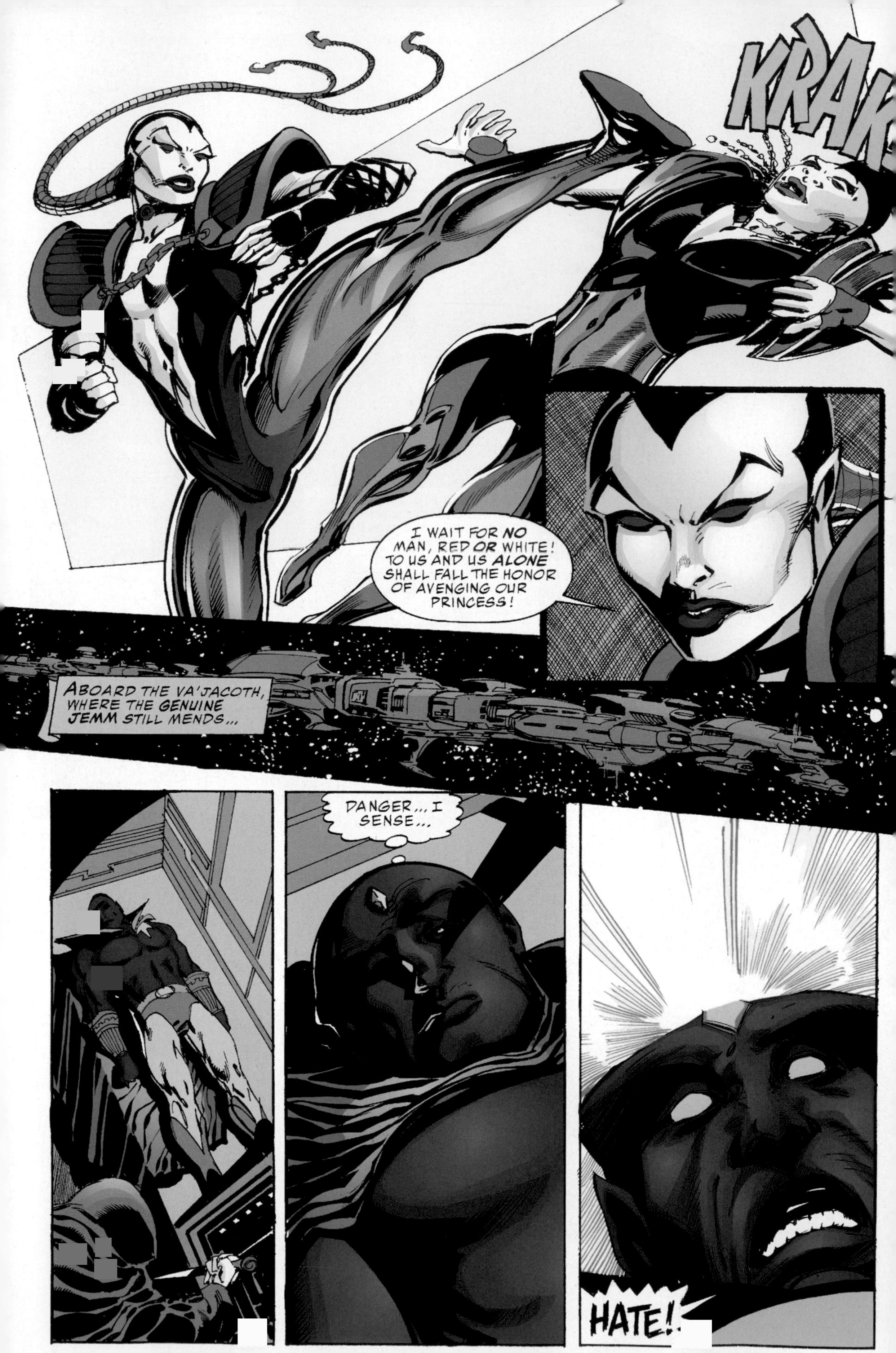
KRAK
I WAIT FOR NO MAN, RED OR WHITE! TO US AND US ALONE SHALL FALL THE HONOR OF AVENGING OUR PRINCESS!
ABOARD THE VA'JACOTH, WHERE THE GENUINE JEMM STILL MENDS...
DANGER... I SENSE...
HATE!

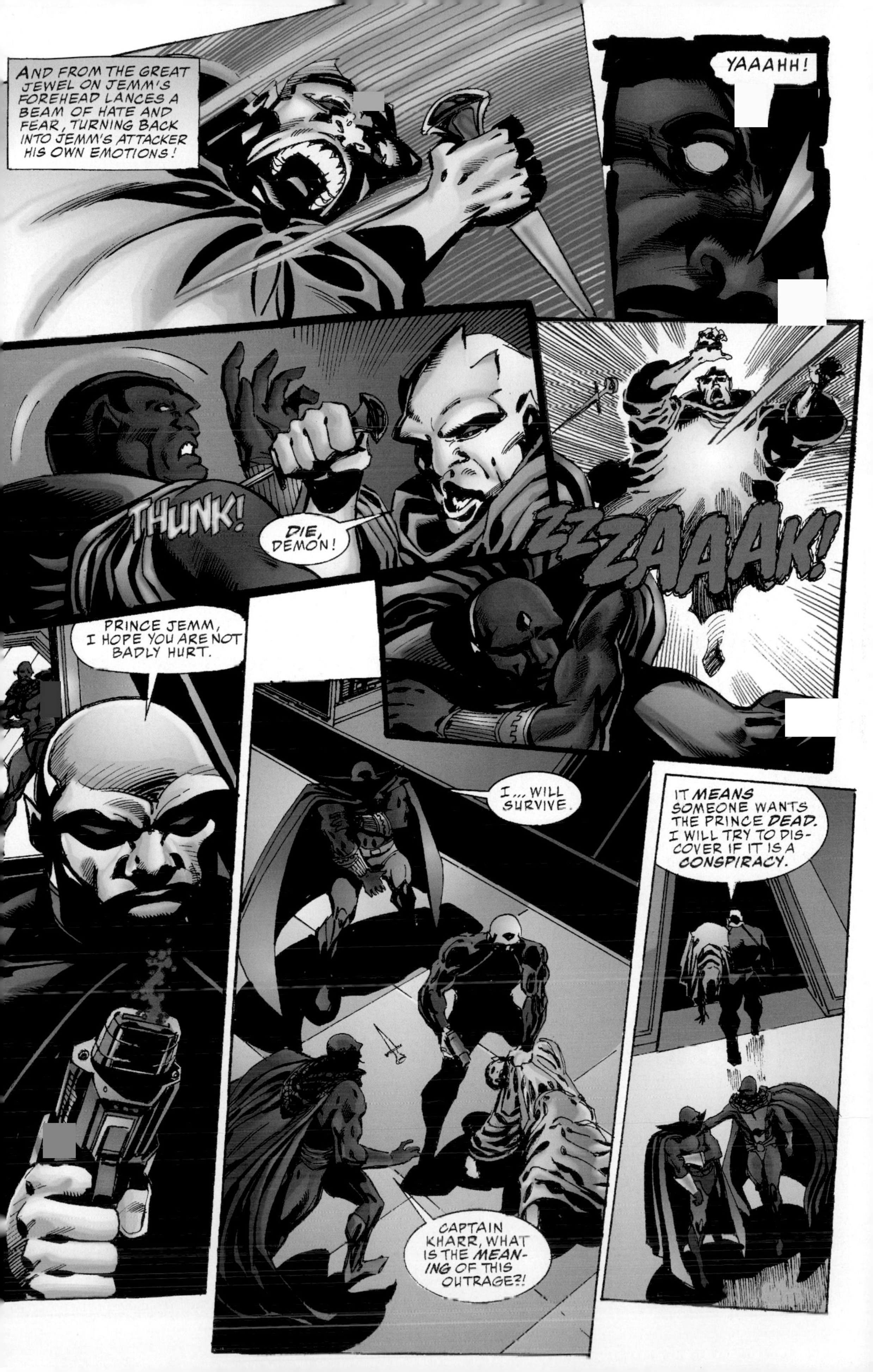
AND FROM THE GREAT JEWEL ON JEMM'S FOREHEAD LANCES A BEAM OF HATE AND FEAR, TURNING BACK INTO JEMM'S ATTACKER HIS OWN EMOTIONS!
YAAAHH!
THUNK!
DIE, DEMON!
ZZZAAAK!
PRINCE JEMM, I HOPE YOU ARE NOT BADLY HURT.
I... WILL SURVIVE.
CAPTAIN KHARR, WHAT IS THE MEANING OF THIS OUTRAGE?!
IT MEANS SOMEONE WANTS THE PRINCE DEAD. I WILL TRY TO DISCOVER IF IT IS A CONSPIRACY.

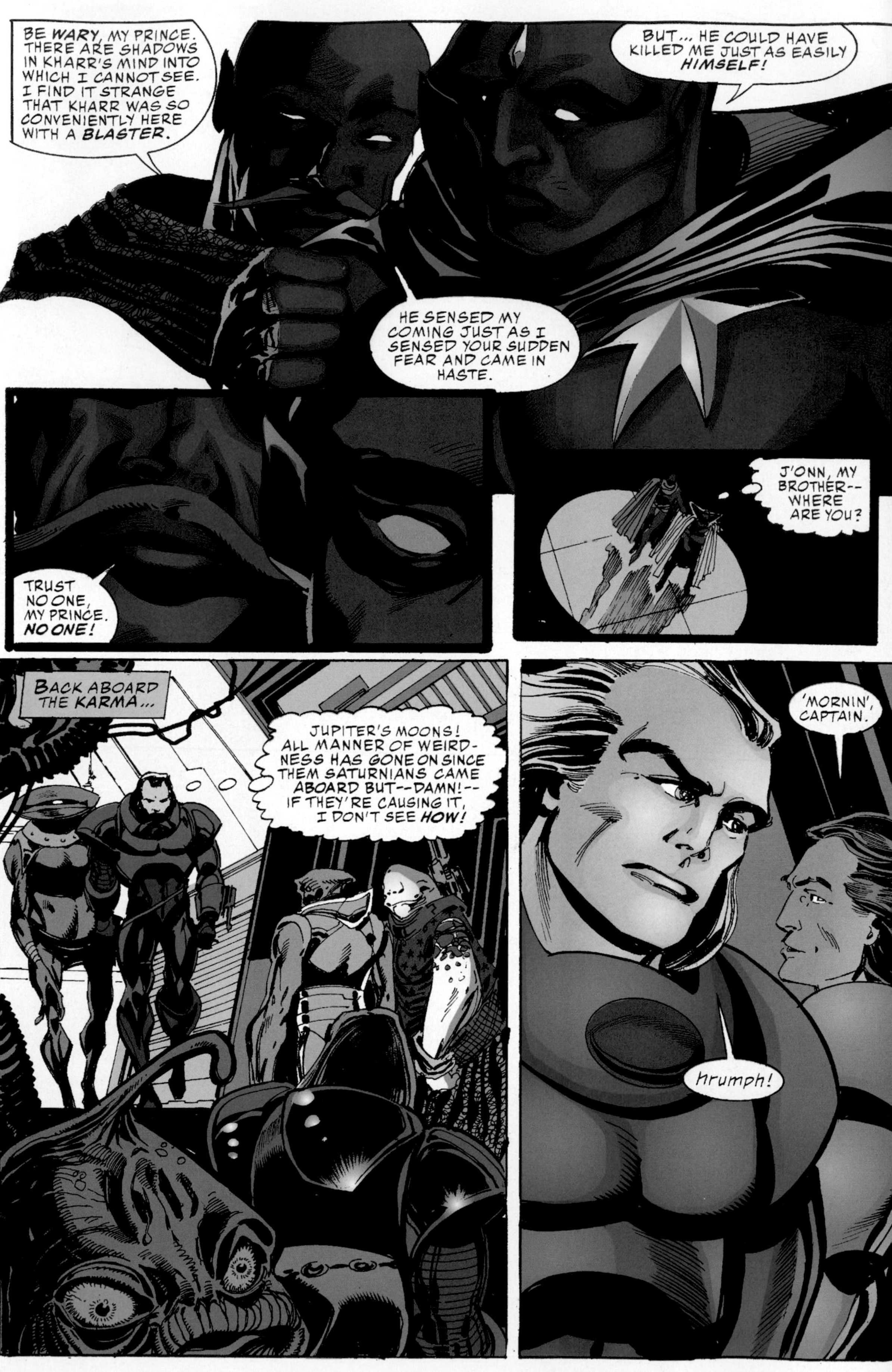
BE WARY, MY PRINCE. THERE ARE SHADOWS IN KHARR'S MIND INTO WHICH I CANNOT SEE. I FIND IT STRANGE THAT KHARR WAS SO CONVENIENTLY HERE WITH A BLASTER.
BUT... HE COULD HAVE KILLED ME JUST AS EASILY HIMSELF!
HE SENSED MY COMING JUST AS I SENSED YOUR SUDDEN FEAR AND CAME IN HASTE.
TRUST NO ONE, MY PRINCE. NO ONE!
J'ONN, MY BROTHER-- WHERE ARE YOU?
BACK ABOARD THE KARMA...
JUPITER'S MOONS! ALL MANNER OF WEIRDNESS HAS GONE ON SINCE THEM SATURNIANS CAME ABOARD BUT--DAMN!-- IF THEY'RE CAUSING IT, I DON'T SEE HOW!
'MORNIN', CAPTAIN.
hrumph!

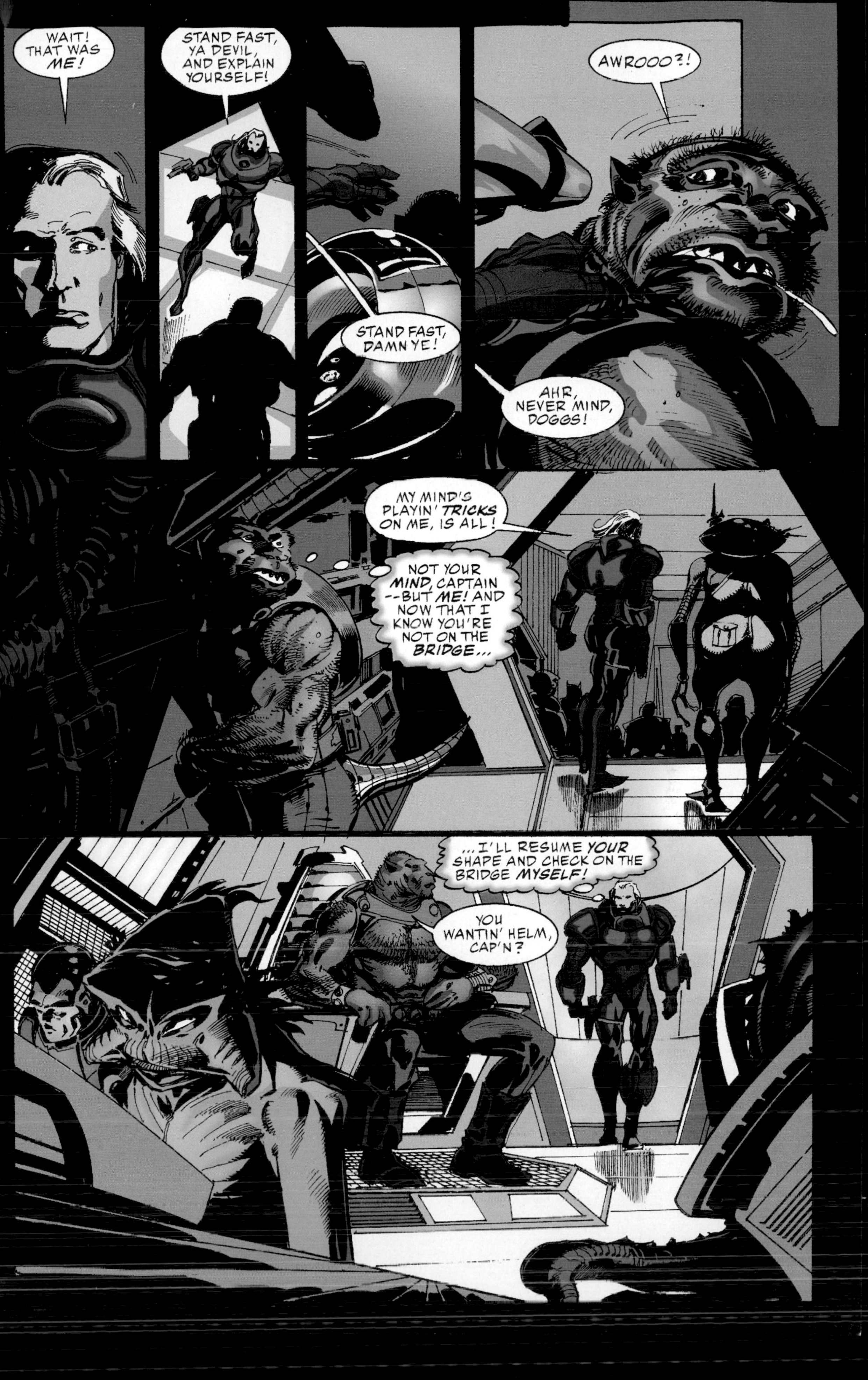
WAIT! THAT WAS ME!
STAND FAST, YA DEVIL, AND EXPLAIN YOURSELF!
STAND FAST, DAMN YE!
AWROOO?!
AHR, NEVER MIND, DOGGS!
MY MIND'S PLAYIN' TRICKS ON ME, IS ALL!
NOT YOUR MIND, CAPTAIN --BUT ME! AND NOW THAT I KNOW YOU'RE NOT ON THE BRIDGE...
...I'LL RESUME YOUR SHAPE AND CHECK ON THE BRIDGE MYSELF!
YOU WANTIN' HELM, CAP'N?

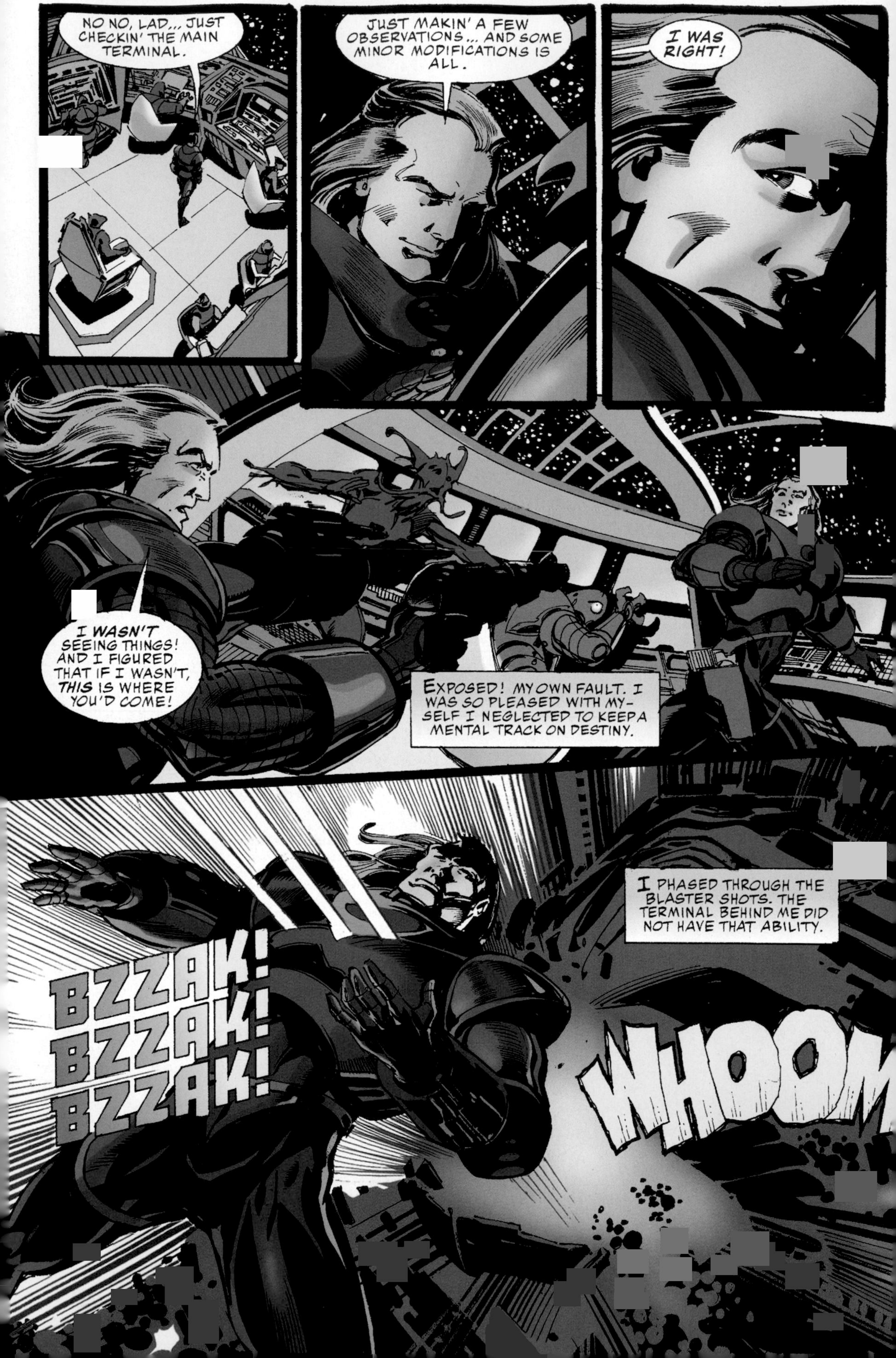

NO NO, LAD... JUST CHECKIN' THE MAIN TERMINAL.
JUST MAKIN' A FEW OBSERVATIONS... AND SOME MINOR MODIFICATIONS IS ALL.
I WAS RIGHT!
I WASN'T SEEING THINGS! AND I FIGURED THAT IF I WASN'T, THIS IS WHERE YOU'D COME!
EXPOSED! MY OWN FAULT. I WAS SO PLEASED WITH MYSELF I NEGLECTED TO KEEP A MENTAL TRACK ON DESTINY.
I PHASED THROUGH THE BLASTER SHOTS. THE TERMINAL BEHIND ME DID NOT HAVE THAT ABILITY.
BZZAK! BZZAK! BZZAK!
WHOOM

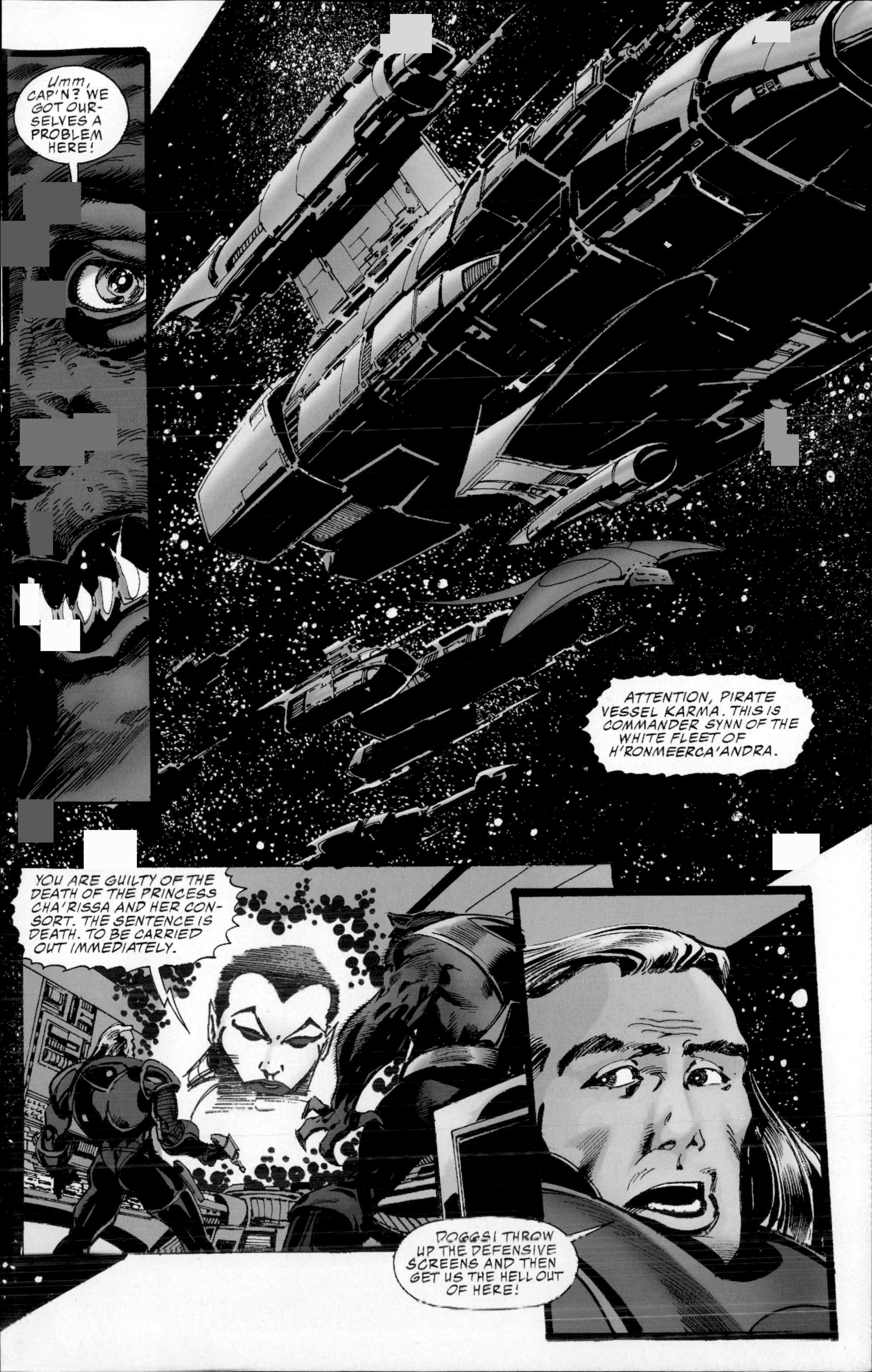
Umm, CAP'N? WE GOT OURSELVES A PROBLEM HERE!
ATTENTION, PIRATE VESSEL KARMA. THIS IS COMMANDER SYNN OF THE WHITE FLEET OF H'RONMEERCA'ANDRA.
YOU ARE GUILTY OF THE DEATH OF THE PRINCESS CHA'RISSA AND HER CONSORT. THE SENTENCE IS DEATH. TO BE CARRIED OUT IMMEDIATELY.
DOGGS! THROW UP THE DEFENSIVE SCREENS AND THEN GET US THE HELL OUT OF HERE!

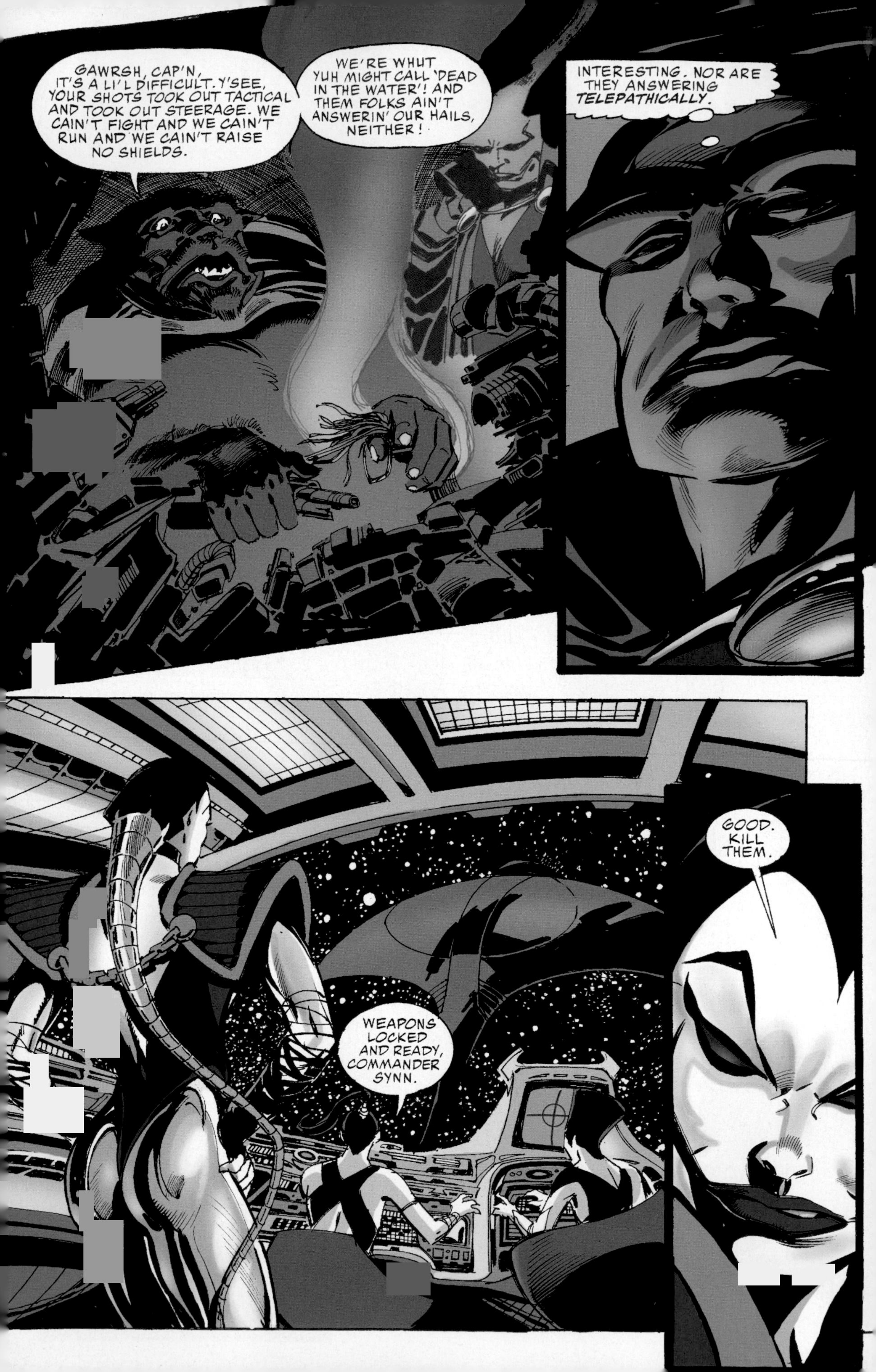
GAWRSH, CAP'N, IT'S A LI'L DIFFICULT. Y'SEE, YOUR SHOTS TOOK OUT TACTICAL AND TOOK OUT STEERAGE. WE CAIN'T FIGHT AND WE CAIN'T RUN AND WE CAIN'T RAISE NO SHIELDS.
WE'RE WHUT YUH MIGHT CALL 'DEAD IN THE WATER'! AND THEM FOLKS AIN'T ANSWERIN' OUR HAILS, NEITHER!
INTERESTING. NOR ARE THEY ANSWERING *TELEPATHICALLY*.
WEAPONS LOCKED AND READY, COMMANDER SYNN.
GOOD. KILL THEM.

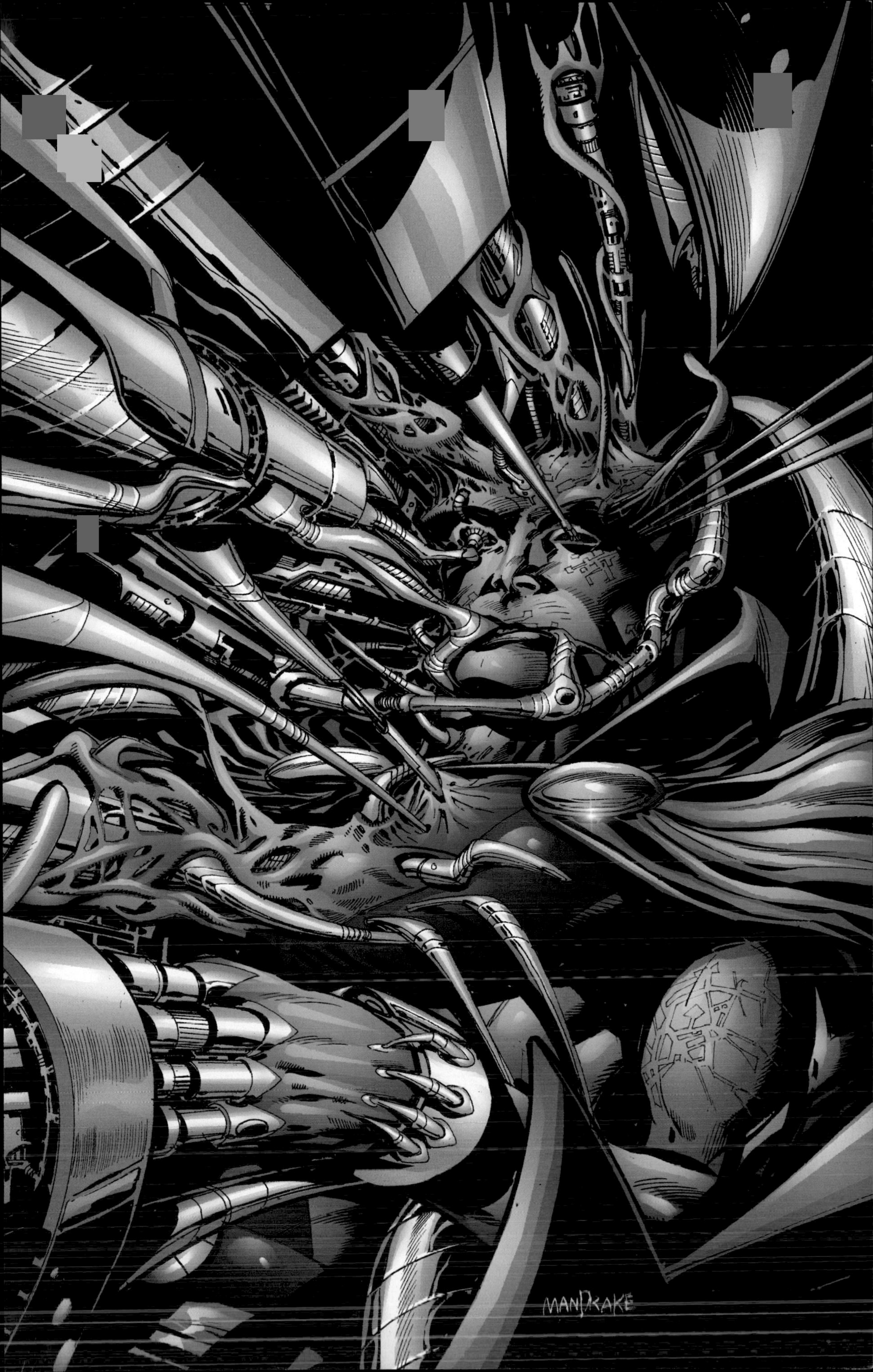
MANDRAKE

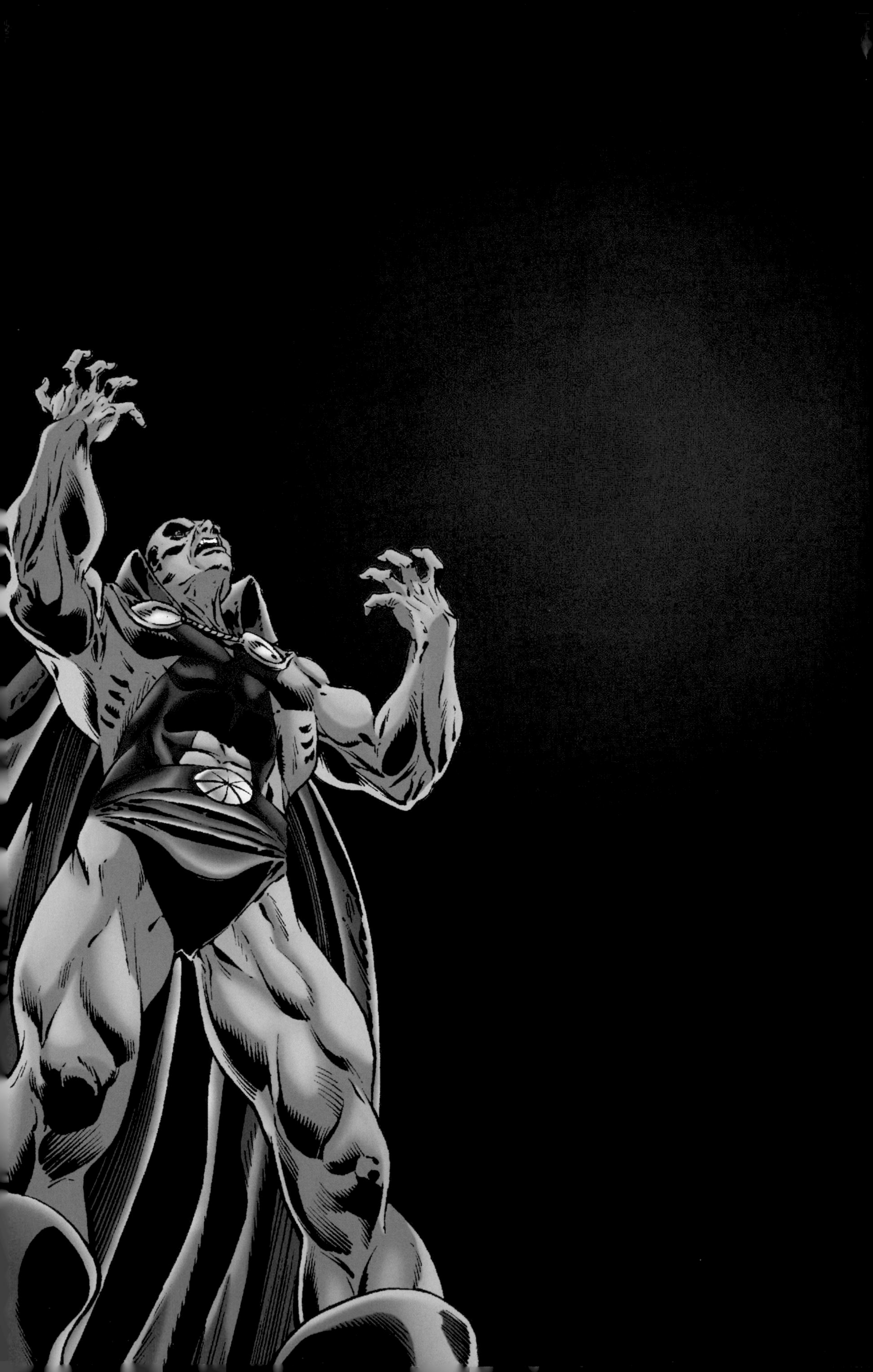

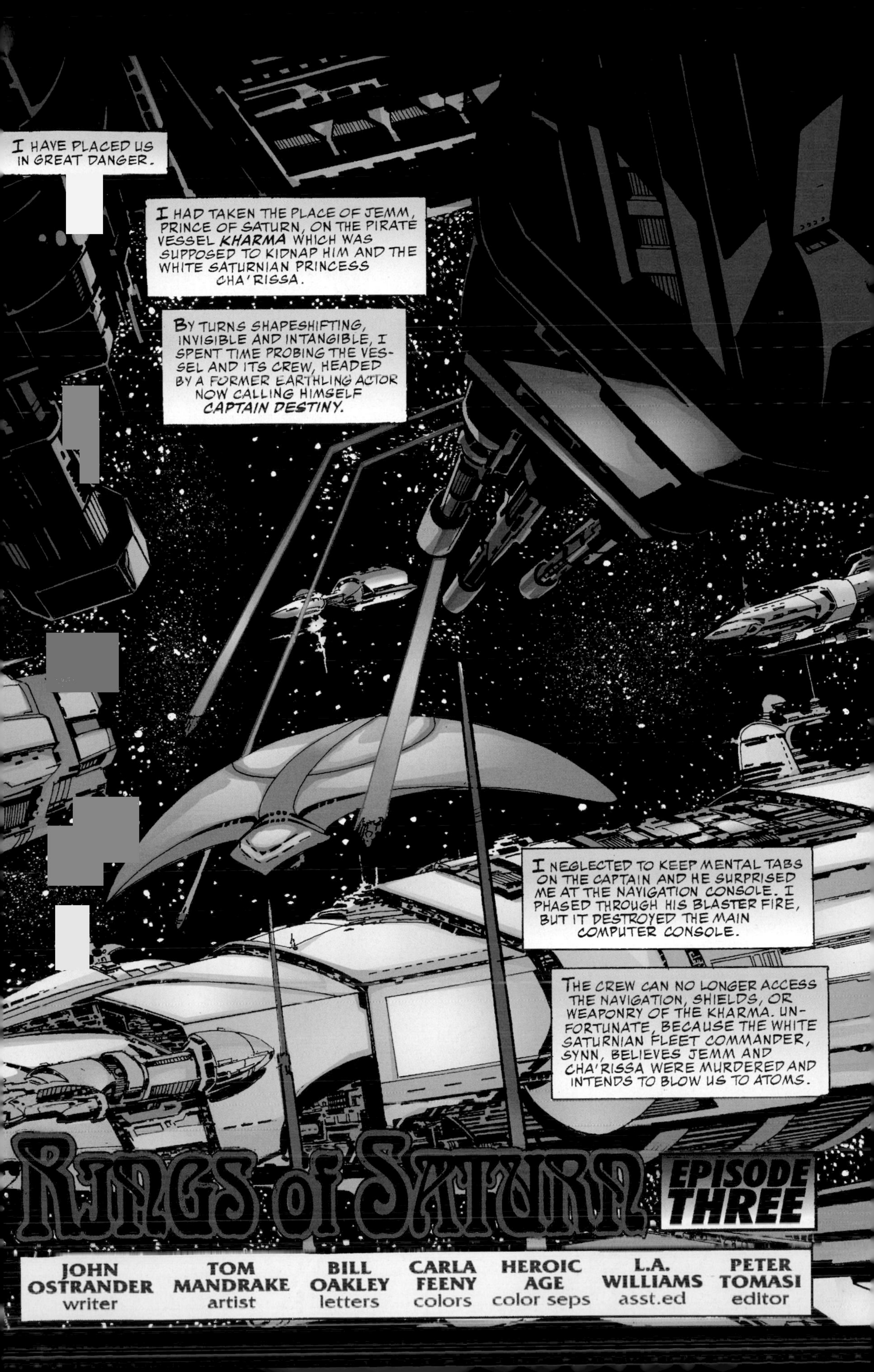
I HAVE PLACED US IN GREAT DANGER.
I HAD TAKEN THE PLACE OF JEMM, PRINCE OF SATURN, ON THE PIRATE VESSEL KHARMA WHICH WAS SUPPOSED TO KIDNAP HIM AND THE WHITE SATURNIAN PRINCESS CHA'RISSA.
BY TURNS SHAPESHIFTING, INVISIBLE AND INTANGIBLE, I SPENT TIME PROBING THE VESSEL AND ITS CREW, HEADED BY A FORMER EARTHLING ACTOR NOW CALLING HIMSELF CAPTAIN DESTINY.
I NEGLECTED TO KEEP MENTAL TABS ON THE CAPTAIN AND HE SURPRISED ME AT THE NAVIGATION CONSOLE. I PHASED THROUGH HIS BLASTER FIRE, BUT IT DESTROYED THE MAIN COMPUTER CONSOLE.
THE CREW CAN NO LONGER ACCESS THE NAVIGATION, SHIELDS, OR WEAPONRY OF THE KHARMA. UNFORTUNATE, BECAUSE THE WHITE SATURNIAN FLEET COMMANDER, SYNN, BELIEVES JEMM AND CHA'RISSA WERE MURDERED AND INTENDS TO BLOW US TO ATOMS.
RINGS of SATURN
EPISODE THREE
JOHN OSTRANDER writer
TOM MANDRAKE artist
BILL OAKLEY letters
CARLA FEENY colors
HEROIC AGE color seps
L.A. WILLIAMS asst.ed
PETER TOMASI editor

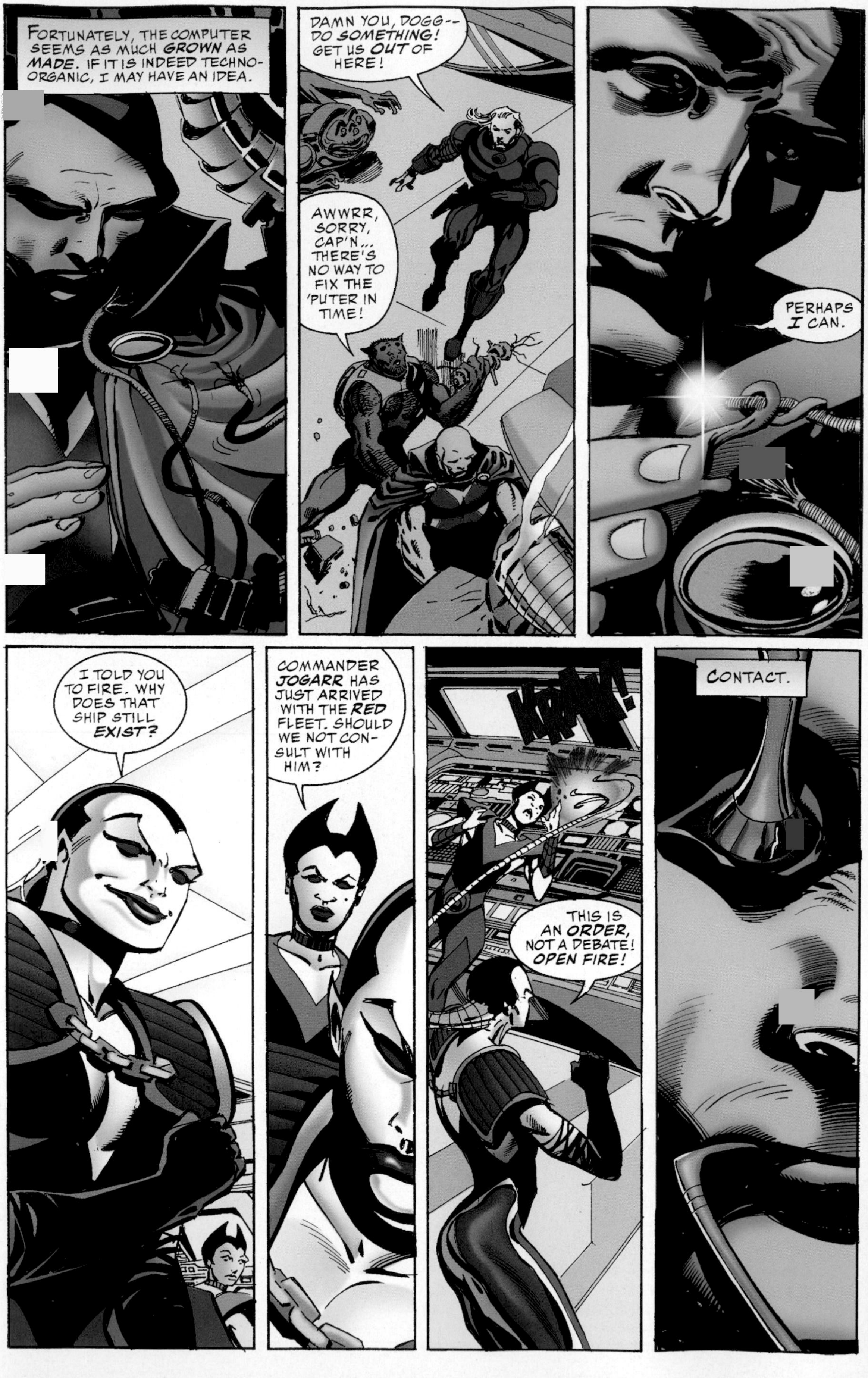

FORTUNATELY, THE COMPUTER SEEMS AS MUCH GROWN AS MADE. IF IT IS INDEED TECHNO-ORGANIC, I MAY HAVE AN IDEA.
DAMN YOU, DOGG-- DO SOMETHING! GET US OUT OF HERE!
AWWRR, SORRY, CAP'N... THERE'S NO WAY TO FIX THE 'PUTER IN TIME!
PERHAPS I CAN.
I TOLD YOU TO FIRE. WHY DOES THAT SHIP STILL EXIST?
COMMANDER JOGARR HAS JUST ARRIVED WITH THE RED FLEET. SHOULD WE NOT CONSULT WITH HIM?
KRAK!
THIS IS AN ORDER, NOT A DEBATE! OPEN FIRE!
CONTACT.

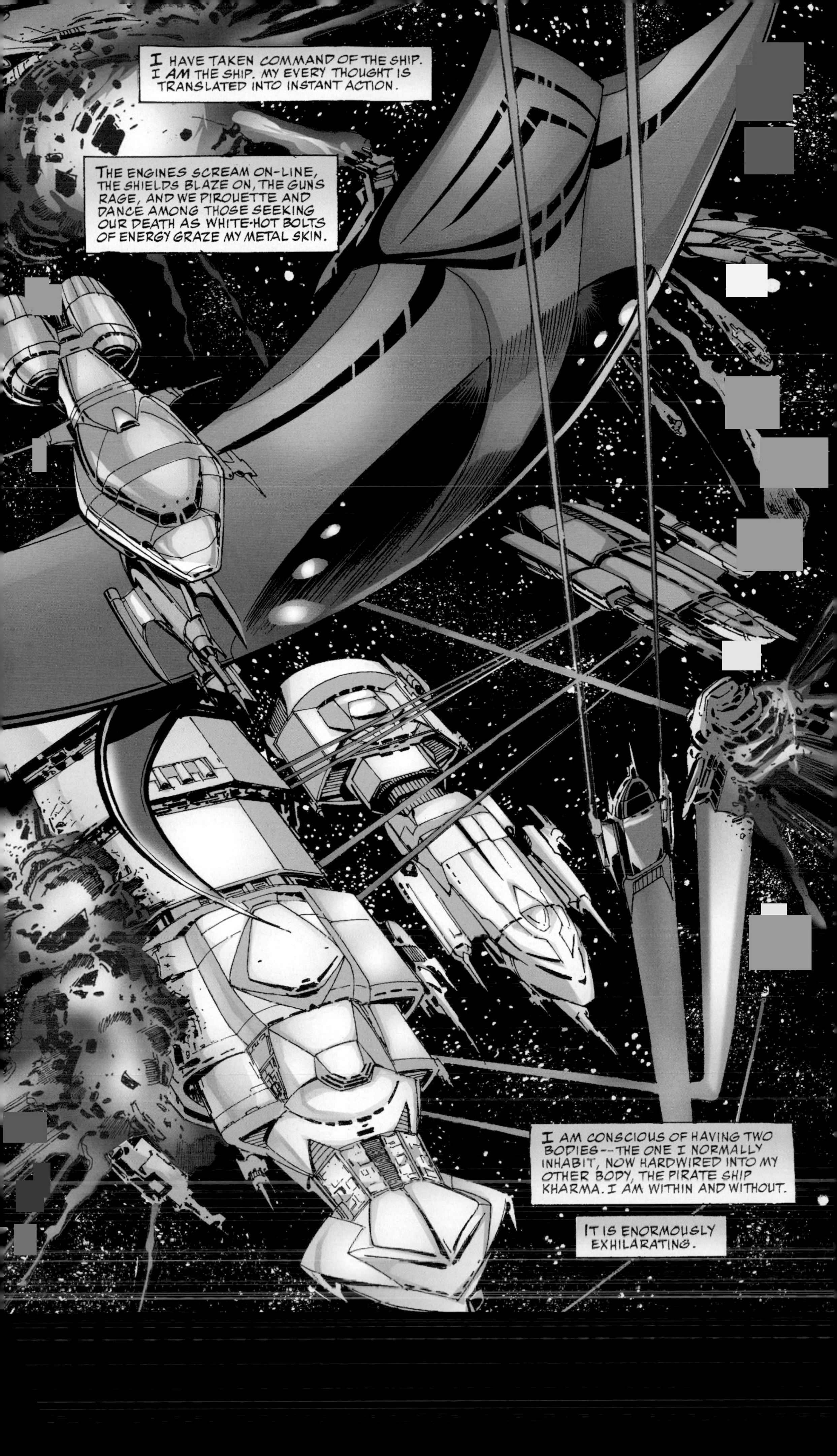
I HAVE TAKEN COMMAND OF THE SHIP. I AM THE SHIP. MY EVERY THOUGHT IS TRANSLATED INTO INSTANT ACTION.
THE ENGINES SCREAM ON-LINE, THE SHIELDS BLAZE ON, THE GUNS RAGE, AND WE PIROUETTE AND DANCE AMONG THOSE SEEKING OUR DEATH AS WHITE-HOT BOLTS OF ENERGY GRAZE MY METAL SKIN.
I AM CONSCIOUS OF HAVING TWO BODIES--THE ONE I NORMALLY INHABIT, NOW HARDWIRED INTO MY OTHER BODY, THE PIRATE SHIP KHARMA. I AM WITHIN AND WITHOUT.
IT IS ENORMOUSLY EXHILARATING.

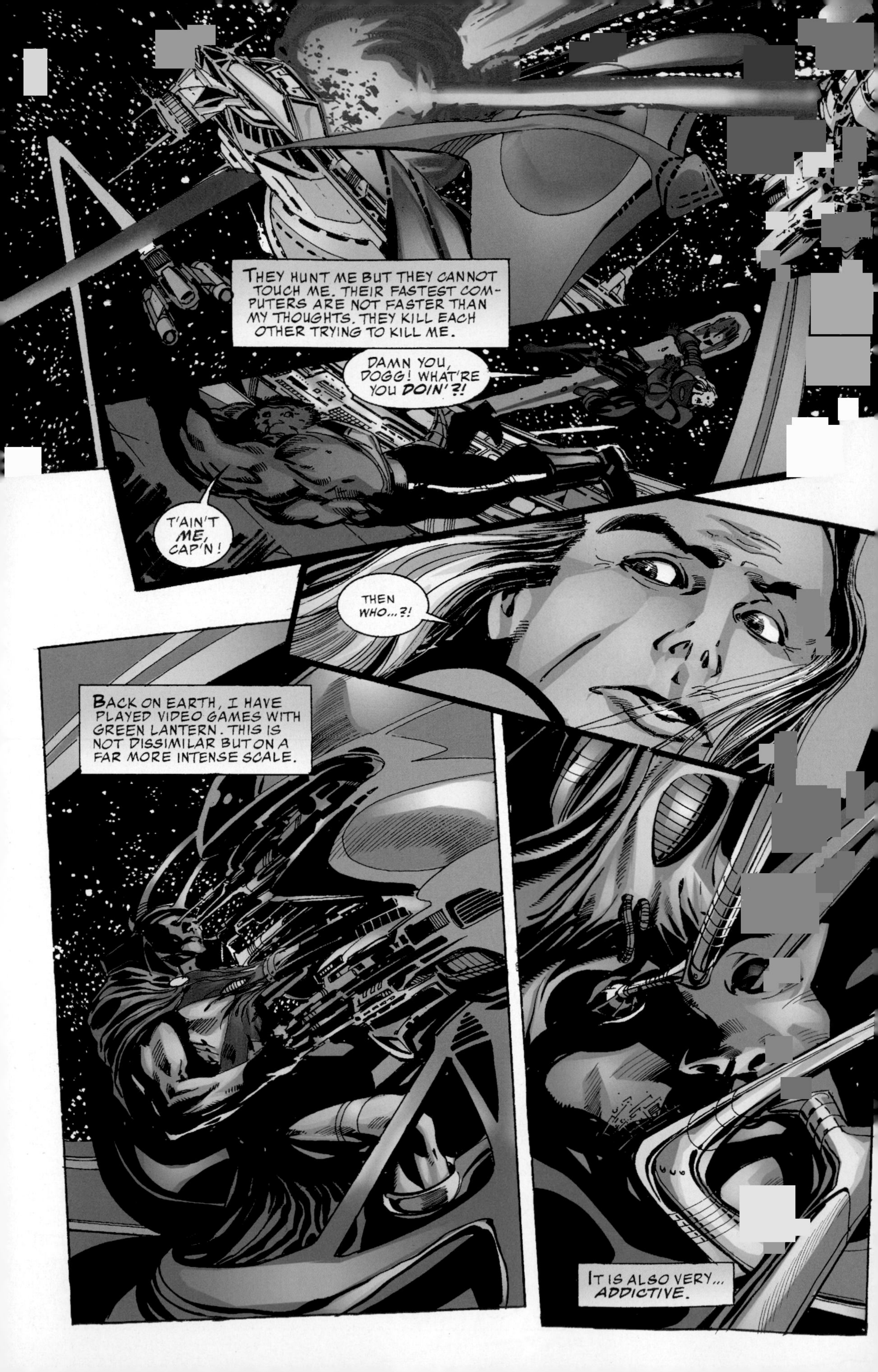
THEY HUNT ME BUT THEY CANNOT TOUCH ME. THEIR FASTEST COMPUTERS ARE NOT FASTER THAN MY THOUGHTS. THEY KILL EACH OTHER TRYING TO KILL ME.
DAMN YOU, DOGG! WHAT'RE YOU DOIN'?!
T'AIN'T ME, CAP'N!
THEN WHO...?!
BACK ON EARTH, I HAVE PLAYED VIDEO GAMES WITH GREEN LANTERN. THIS IS NOT DISSIMILAR BUT ON A FAR MORE INTENSE SCALE.
IT IS ALSO VERY... ADDICTIVE.

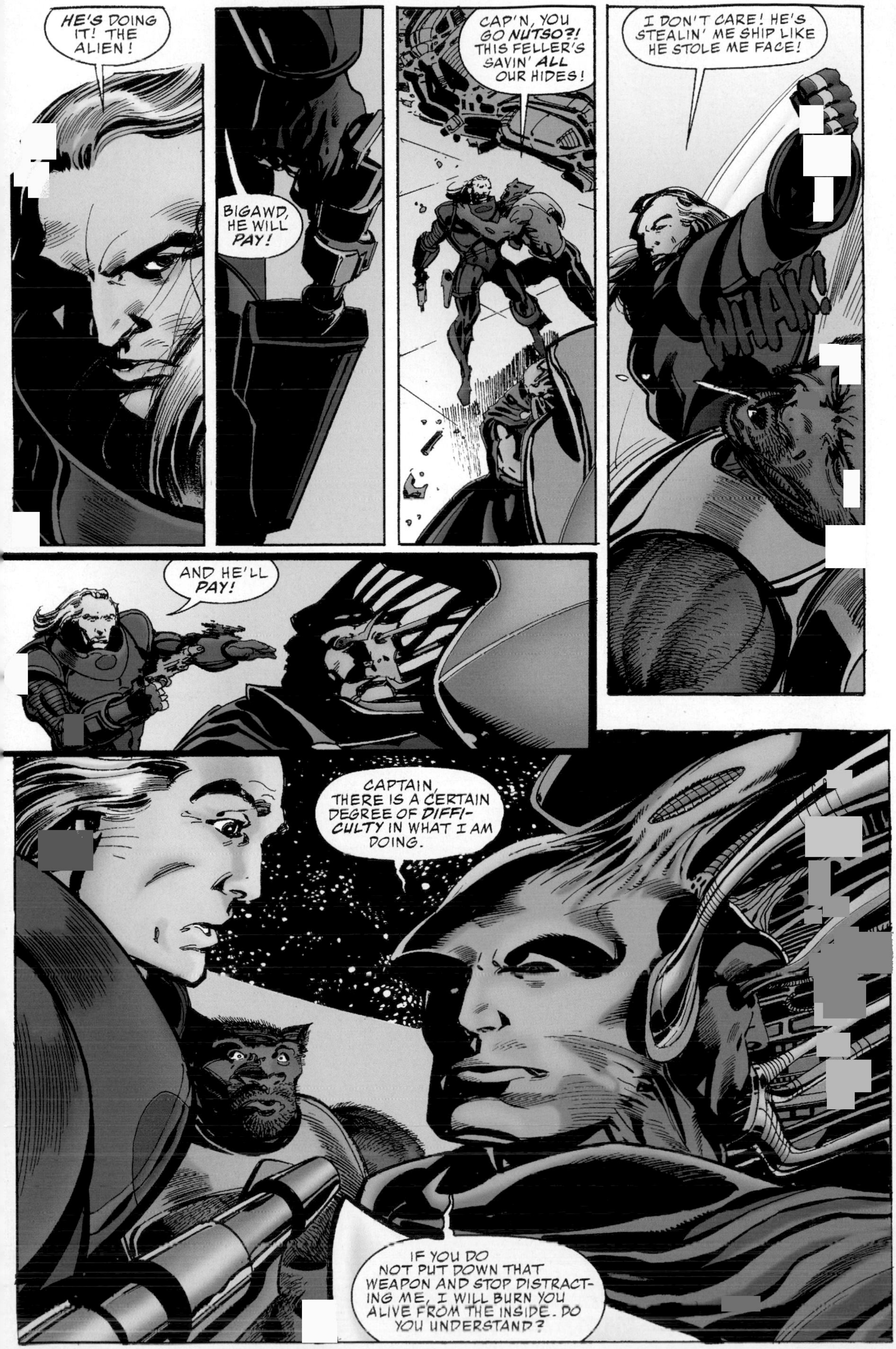
HE'S DOING IT! THE ALIEN!
BIGAWD, HE WILL PAY!
CAP'N, YOU GO NUTSO?! THIS FELLER'S SAVIN' ALL OUR HIDES!
I DON'T CARE! HE'S STEALIN' ME SHIP LIKE HE STOLE ME FACE!
WHAK!
AND HE'LL PAY!
CAPTAIN, THERE IS A CERTAIN DEGREE OF DIFFI-CULTY IN WHAT I AM DOING.
IF YOU DO NOT PUT DOWN THAT WEAPON AND STOP DISTRACT-ING ME, I WILL BURN YOU ALIVE FROM THE INSIDE. DO YOU UNDERSTAND?

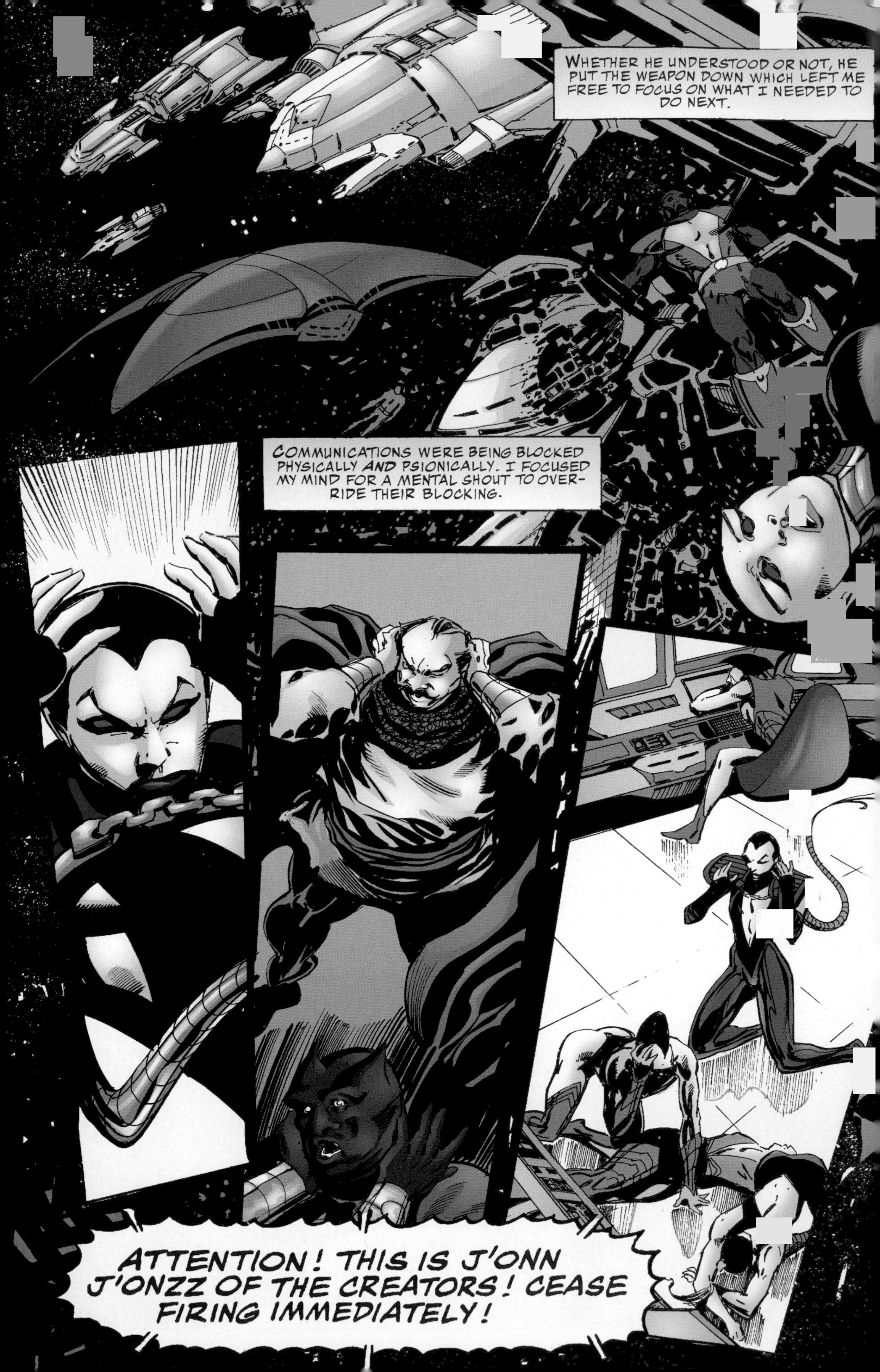

WHETHER HE UNDERSTOOD OR NOT, HE PUT THE WEAPON DOWN WHICH LEFT ME FREE TO FOCUS ON WHAT I NEEDED TO DO NEXT.
COMMUNICATIONS WERE BEING BLOCKED PHYSICALLY AND PSIONICALLY. I FOCUSED MY MIND FOR A MENTAL SHOUT TO OVER-RIDE THEIR BLOCKING.
ATTENTION! THIS IS J'ONN J'ONZZ OF THE CREATORS! CEASE FIRING IMMEDIATELY!

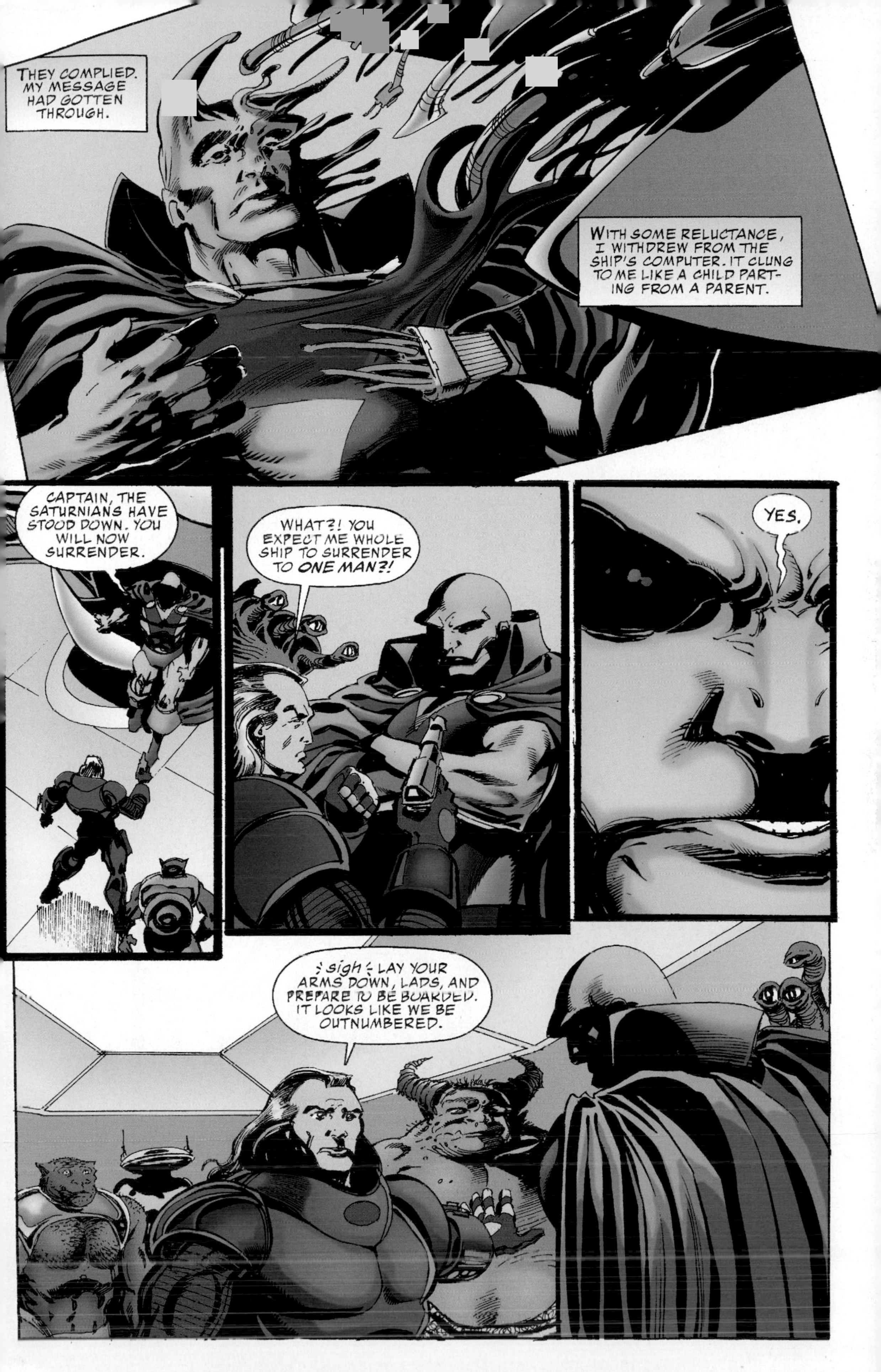
THEY COMPLIED. MY MESSAGE HAD GOTTEN THROUGH.
WITH SOME RELUCTANCE, I WITHDREW FROM THE SHIP'S COMPUTER. IT CLUNG TO ME LIKE A CHILD PARTING FROM A PARENT.
CAPTAIN, THE SATURNIANS HAVE STOOD DOWN. YOU WILL NOW SURRENDER.
WHAT?! YOU EXPECT ME WHOLE SHIP TO SURRENDER TO ONE MAN?!
YES.
sigh LAY YOUR ARMS DOWN, LADS, AND PREPARE TO BE BOARDED. IT LOOKS LIKE WE BE OUTNUMBERED.

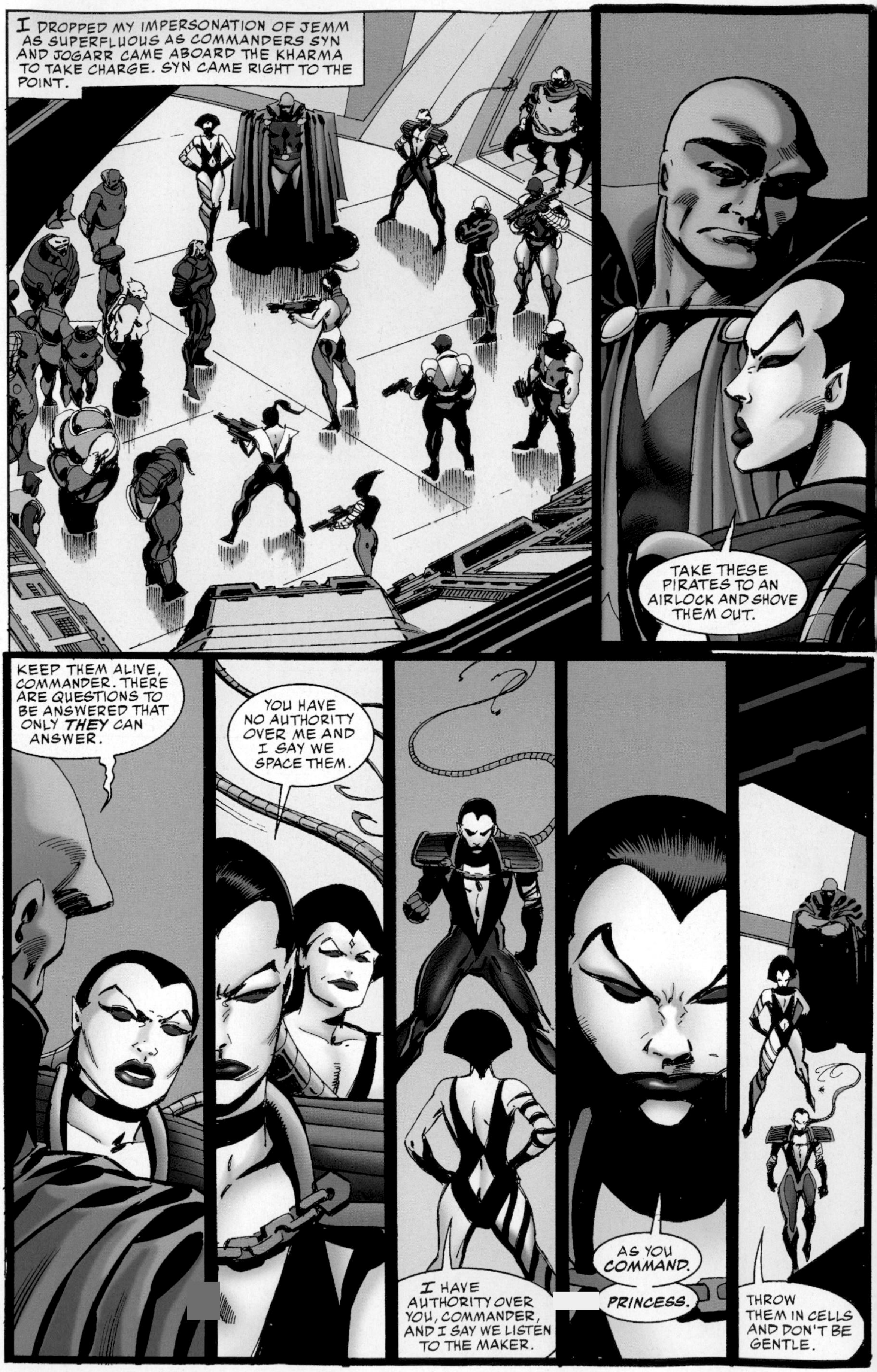
I DROPPED MY IMPERSONATION OF JEMM AS SUPERFLUOUS AS COMMANDERS SYN AND JOGARR CAME ABOARD THE KHARMA TO TAKE CHARGE. SYN CAME RIGHT TO THE POINT.
TAKE THESE PIRATES TO AN AIRLOCK AND SHOVE THEM OUT.
KEEP THEM ALIVE, COMMANDER. THERE ARE QUESTIONS TO BE ANSWERED THAT ONLY *THEY* CAN ANSWER.
YOU HAVE NO AUTHORITY OVER ME AND I SAY WE SPACE THEM.
I HAVE AUTHORITY OVER YOU, COMMANDER, AND I SAY WE LISTEN TO THE MAKER.
AS YOU **COMMAND.**
PRINCESS.
THROW THEM IN CELLS AND DON'T BE GENTLE.

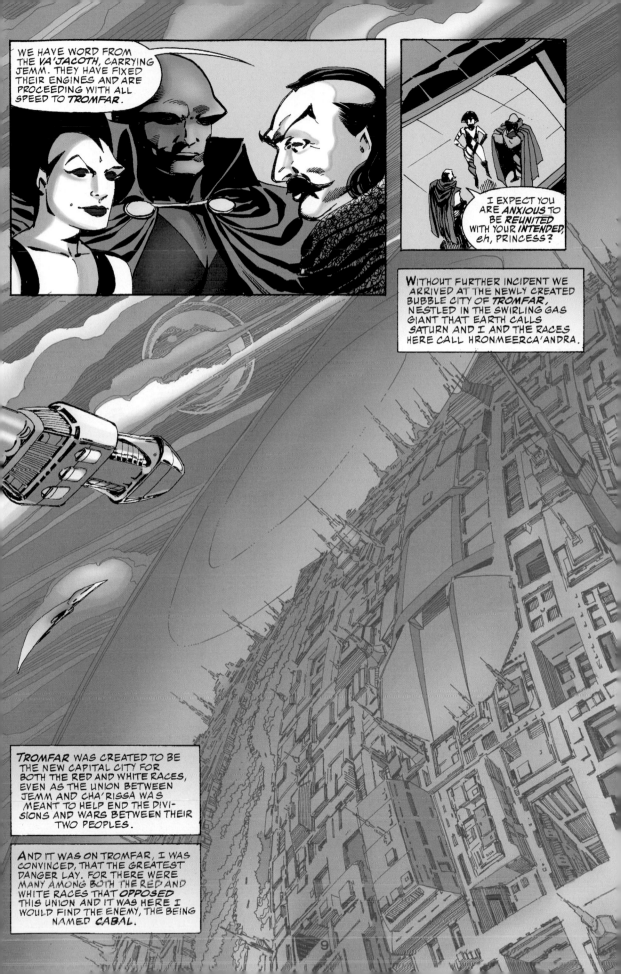

WE HAVE WORD FROM THE *VA'JACOTH*, CARRYING JEMM. THEY HAVE FIXED THEIR ENGINES AND ARE PROCEEDING WITH ALL SPEED TO *TROMFAR*.

I EXPECT YOU ARE *ANXIOUS* TO BE *REUNITED* WITH YOUR *INTENDED*, eh, PRINCESS?

WITHOUT FURTHER INCIDENT WE ARRIVED AT THE NEWLY CREATED BUBBLE CITY OF *TROMFAR*, NESTLED IN THE SWIRLING GAS GIANT THAT EARTH CALLS *SATURN* AND I AND THE RACES HERE CALL *HRONMEERCA'ANDRA*.

TROMFAR WAS CREATED TO BE THE NEW CAPITAL CITY FOR BOTH THE RED AND WHITE RACES, EVEN AS THE UNION BETWEEN JEMM AND CHA'RISSA WAS MEANT TO HELP END THE DIVISIONS AND WARS BETWEEN THEIR TWO PEOPLES.

AND IT WAS ON TROMFAR, I WAS CONVINCED, THAT THE GREATEST DANGER LAY. FOR THERE WERE MANY AMONG BOTH THE RED AND WHITE RACES THAT *OPPOSED* THIS UNION AND IT WAS HERE I WOULD FIND THE ENEMY, THE BEING NAMED *CABAL*.

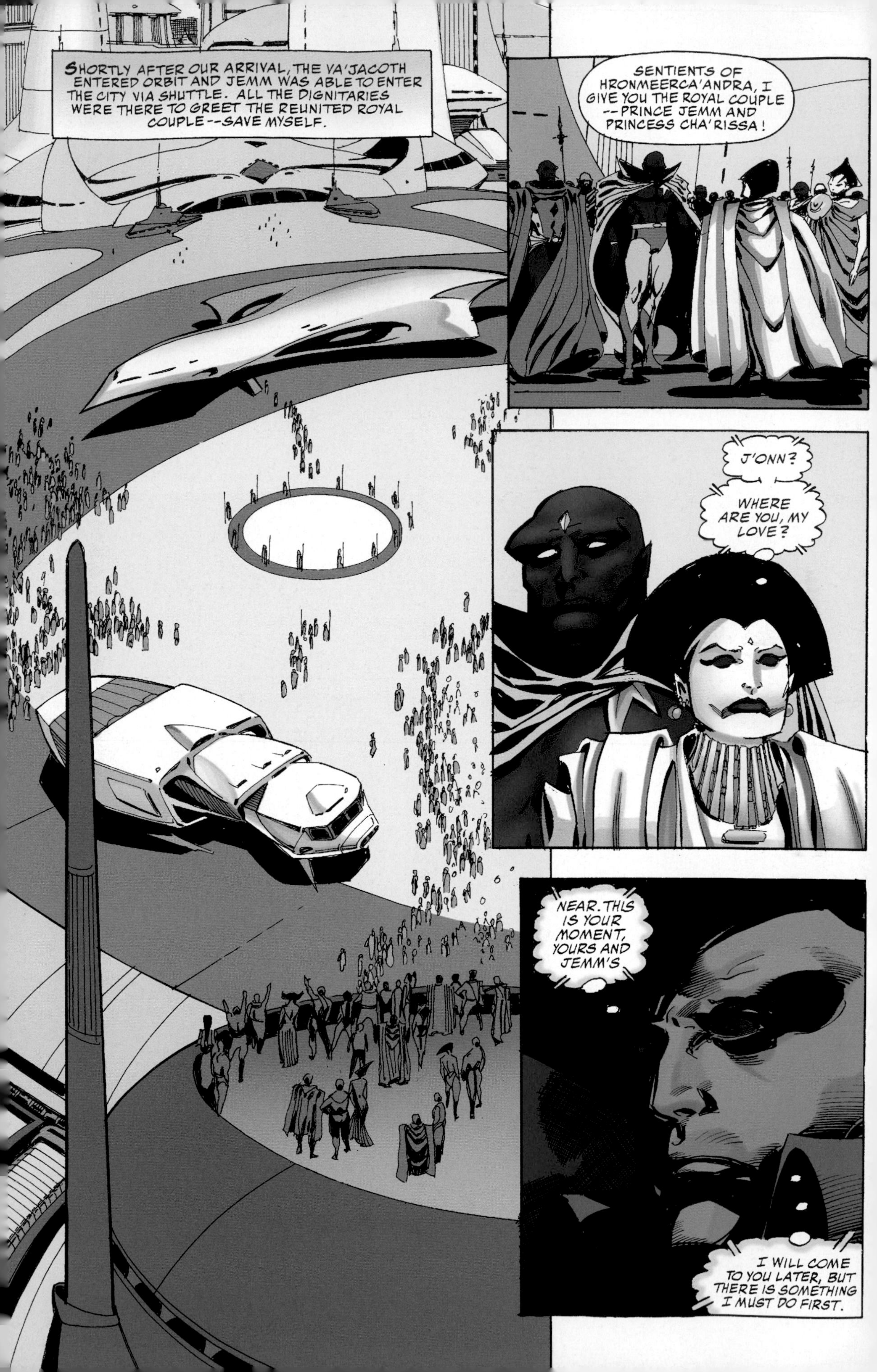
SHORTLY AFTER OUR ARRIVAL, THE VA'JACOTH ENTERED ORBIT AND JEMM WAS ABLE TO ENTER THE CITY VIA SHUTTLE. ALL THE DIGNITARIES WERE THERE TO GREET THE REUNITED ROYAL COUPLE--SAVE MYSELF.
SENTIENTS OF HRONMEERCA'ANDRA, I GIVE YOU THE ROYAL COUPLE --PRINCE JEMM AND PRINCESS CHA'RISSA!
J'ONN?
WHERE ARE YOU, MY LOVE?
NEAR. THIS IS YOUR MOMENT, YOURS AND JEMM'S
I WILL COME TO YOU LATER, BUT THERE IS SOMETHING I MUST DO FIRST.

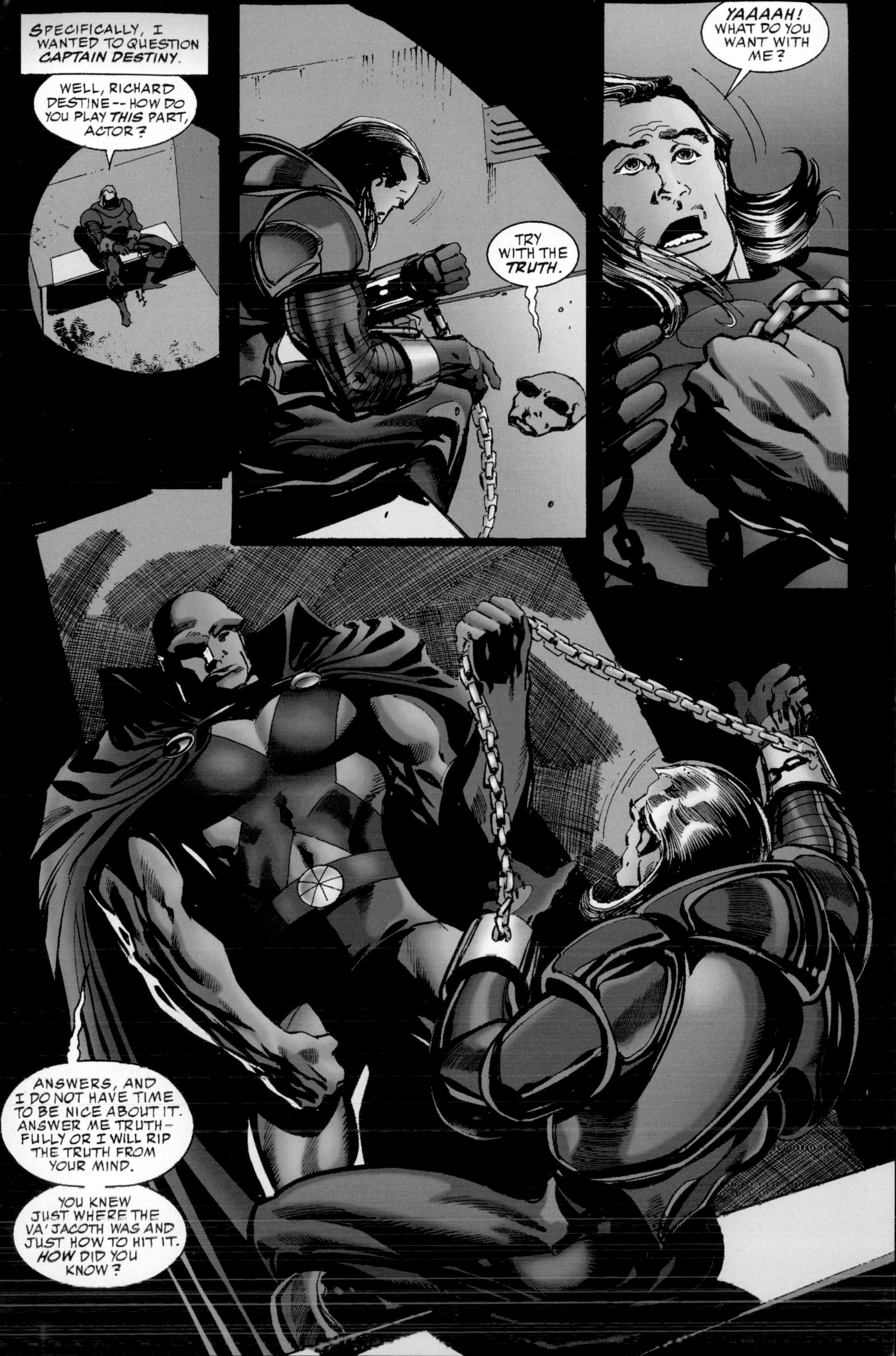

SPECIFICALLY, I WANTED TO QUESTION CAPTAIN DESTINY.
WELL, RICHARD DESTINE-- HOW DO YOU PLAY THIS PART, ACTOR?
TRY WITH THE TRUTH.
YAAAAH! WHAT DO YOU WANT WITH ME?
ANSWERS, AND I DO NOT HAVE TIME TO BE NICE ABOUT IT. ANSWER ME TRUTHFULLY OR I WILL RIP THE TRUTH FROM YOUR MIND.
YOU KNEW JUST WHERE THE VA'JACOTH WAS AND JUST HOW TO HIT IT. HOW DID YOU KNOW?

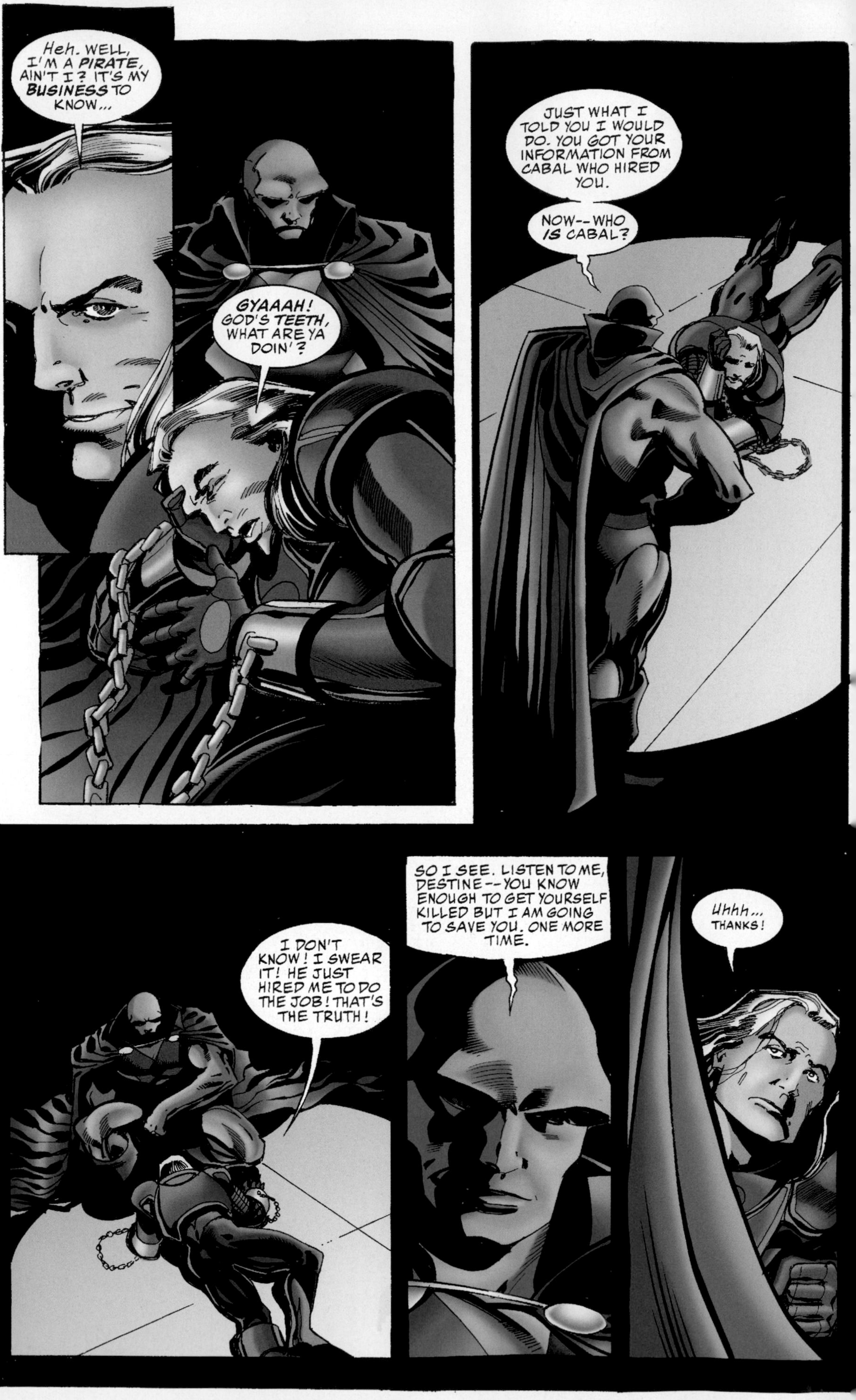
Heh. WELL, I'M A PIRATE, AIN'T I? IT'S MY BUSINESS TO KNOW...
GYAAAH! GOD'S TEETH, WHAT ARE YA DOIN'?
JUST WHAT I TOLD YOU I WOULD DO. YOU GOT YOUR INFORMATION FROM CABAL WHO HIRED YOU.
NOW--WHO IS CABAL?
I DON'T KNOW! I SWEAR IT! HE JUST HIRED ME TO DO THE JOB! THAT'S THE TRUTH!
SO I SEE. LISTEN TO ME, DESTINE--YOU KNOW ENOUGH TO GET YOURSELF KILLED BUT I AM GOING TO SAVE YOU. ONE MORE TIME.
Uhhh... THANKS!

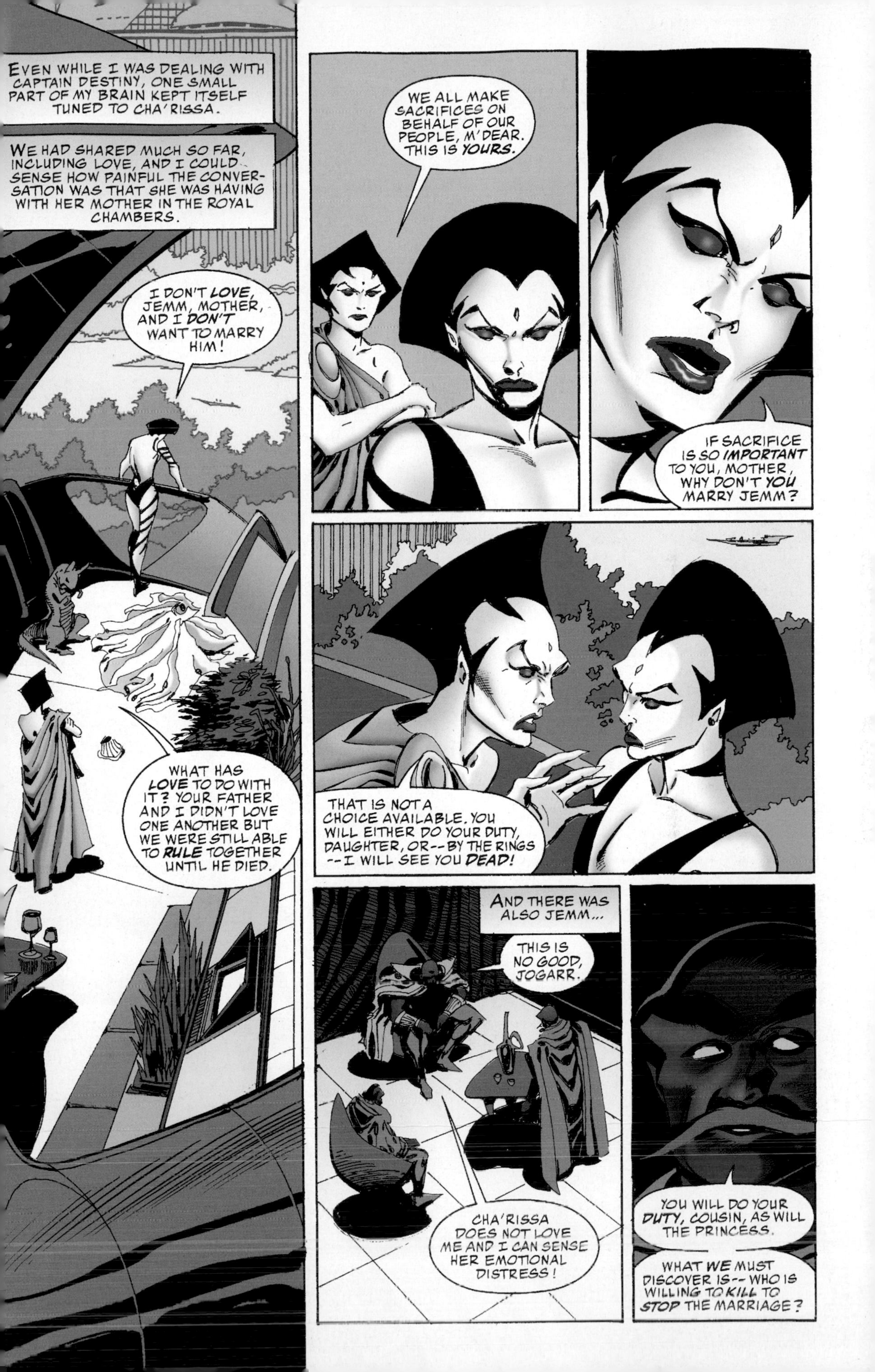
EVEN WHILE I WAS DEALING WITH CAPTAIN DESTINY, ONE SMALL PART OF MY BRAIN KEPT ITSELF TUNED TO CHA'RISSA.
WE HAD SHARED MUCH SO FAR, INCLUDING LOVE, AND I COULD SENSE HOW PAINFUL THE CONVERSATION WAS THAT SHE WAS HAVING WITH HER MOTHER IN THE ROYAL CHAMBERS.
I DON'T LOVE, JEMM, MOTHER, AND I DON'T WANT TO MARRY HIM!
WHAT HAS LOVE TO DO WITH IT? YOUR FATHER AND I DIDN'T LOVE ONE ANOTHER BUT WE WERE STILL ABLE TO RULE TOGETHER UNTIL HE DIED.
WE ALL MAKE SACRIFICES ON BEHALF OF OUR PEOPLE, M'DEAR. THIS IS YOURS.
IF SACRIFICE IS SO IMPORTANT TO YOU, MOTHER, WHY DON'T YOU MARRY JEMM?
THAT IS NOT A CHOICE AVAILABLE. YOU WILL EITHER DO YOUR DUTY, DAUGHTER, OR--BY THE RINGS --I WILL SEE YOU DEAD!
AND THERE WAS ALSO JEMM...
THIS IS NO GOOD, JOGARR.
CHA'RISSA DOES NOT LOVE ME AND I CAN SENSE HER EMOTIONAL DISTRESS!
YOU WILL DO YOUR DUTY, COUSIN, AS WILL THE PRINCESS.
WHAT WE MUST DISCOVER IS-- WHO IS WILLING TO KILL TO STOP THE MARRIAGE?

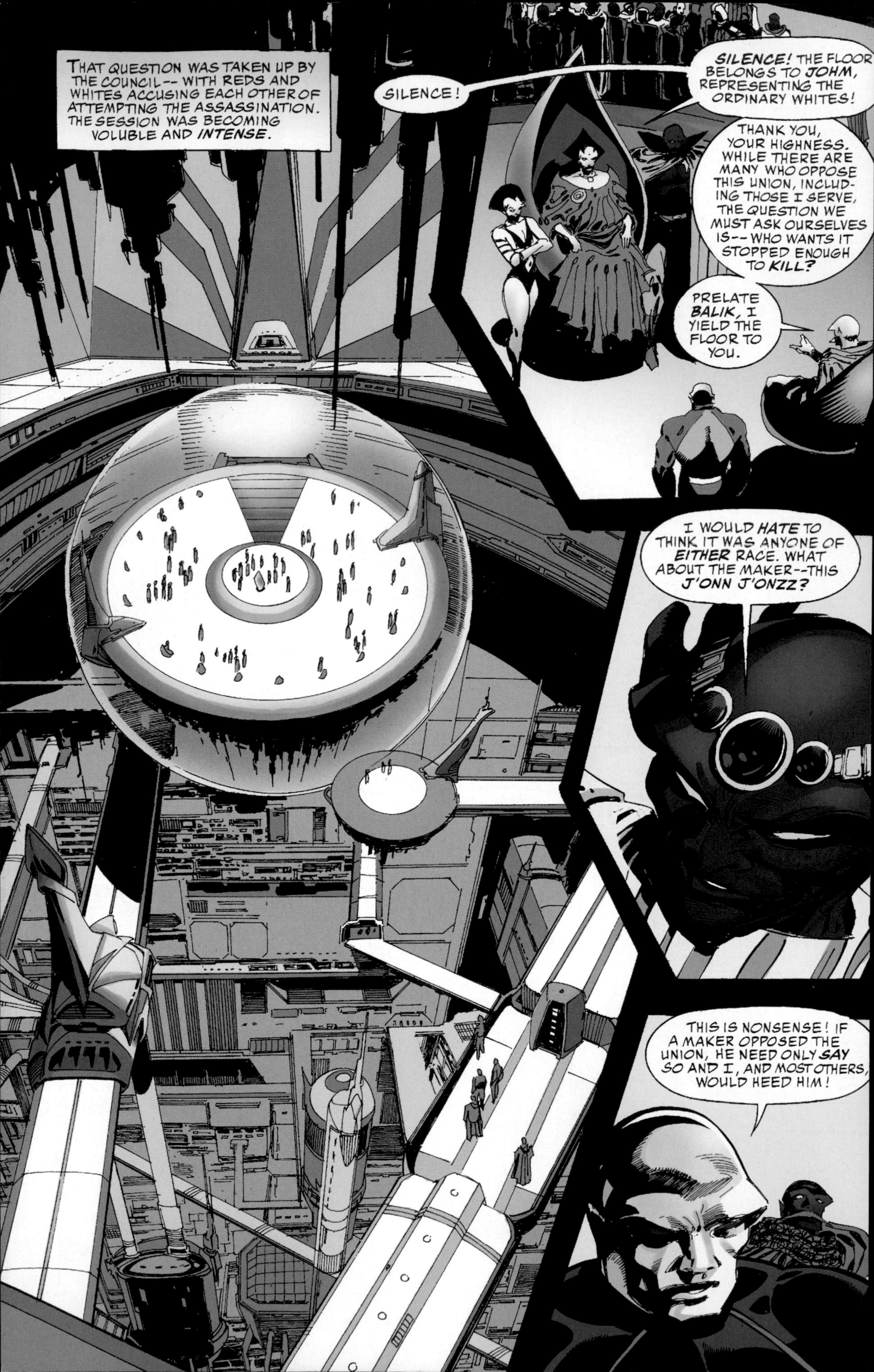
THAT QUESTION WAS TAKEN UP BY THE COUNCIL-- WITH REDS AND WHITES ACCUSING EACH OTHER OF ATTEMPTING THE ASSASSINATION. THE SESSION WAS BECOMING VOLUBLE AND INTENSE.
SILENCE!
SILENCE! THE FLOOR BELONGS TO JOHM, REPRESENTING THE ORDINARY WHITES!
THANK YOU, YOUR HIGHNESS. WHILE THERE ARE MANY WHO OPPOSE THIS UNION, INCLUDING THOSE I SERVE, THE QUESTION WE MUST ASK OURSELVES IS-- WHO WANTS IT STOPPED ENOUGH TO KILL?
PRELATE BALIK, I YIELD THE FLOOR TO YOU.
I WOULD HATE TO THINK IT WAS ANYONE OF EITHER RACE. WHAT ABOUT THE MAKER--THIS J'ONN J'ONZZ?
THIS IS NONSENSE! IF A MAKER OPPOSED THE UNION, HE NEED ONLY SAY SO AND I, AND MOST OTHERS, WOULD HEED HIM!

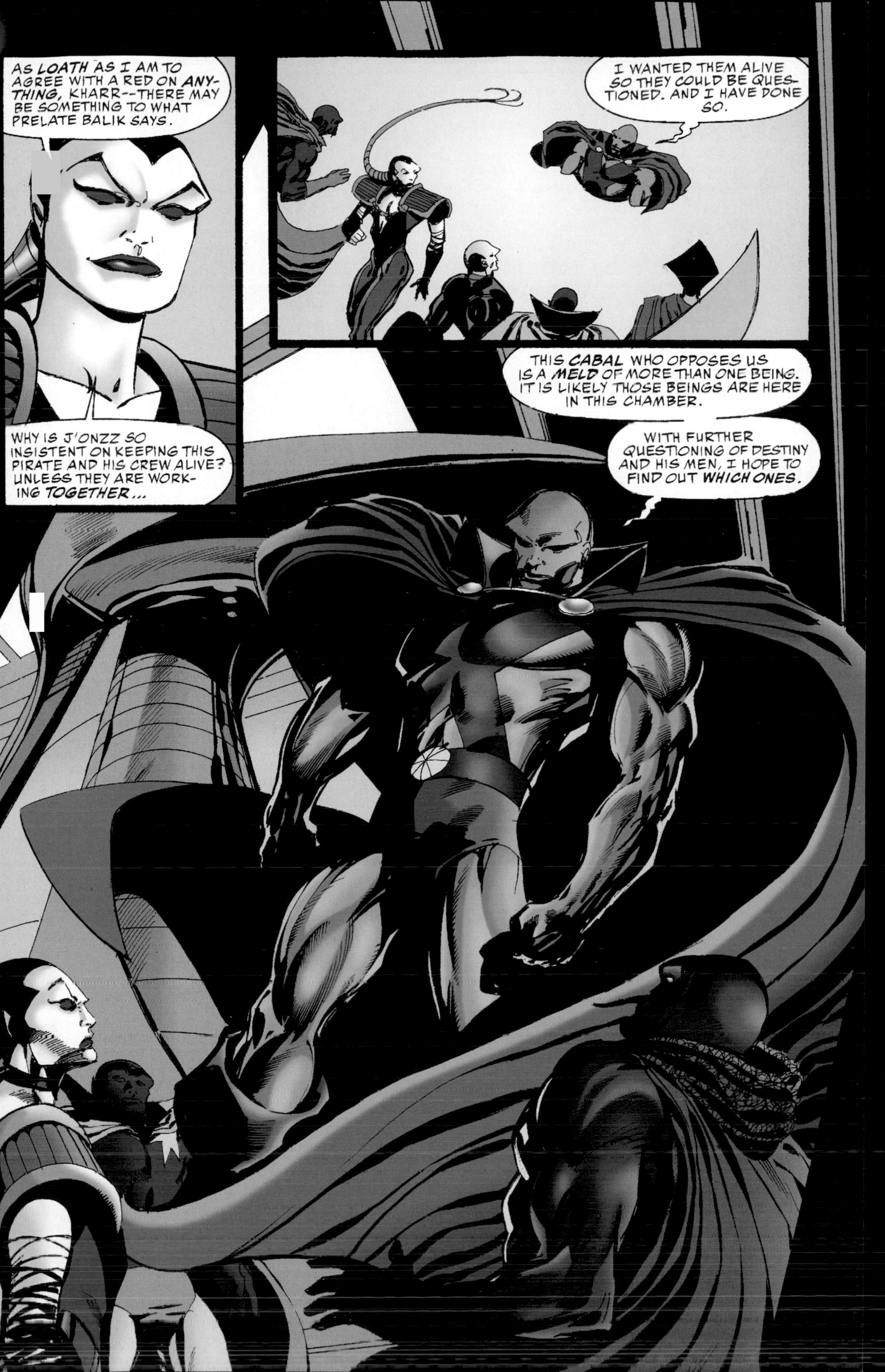
AS LOATH AS I AM TO AGREE WITH A RED ON ANYTHING, KHARR--THERE MAY BE SOMETHING TO WHAT PRELATE BALIK SAYS.
WHY IS J'ONZZ SO INSISTENT ON KEEPING THIS PIRATE AND HIS CREW ALIVE? UNLESS THEY ARE WORKING TOGETHER...
I WANTED THEM ALIVE SO THEY COULD BE QUESTIONED. AND I HAVE DONE SO.
THIS CABAL WHO OPPOSES US IS A MELD OF MORE THAN ONE BEING. IT IS LIKELY THOSE BEINGS ARE HERE IN THIS CHAMBER.
WITH FURTHER QUESTIONING OF DESTINY AND HIS MEN, I HOPE TO FIND OUT WHICH ONES.

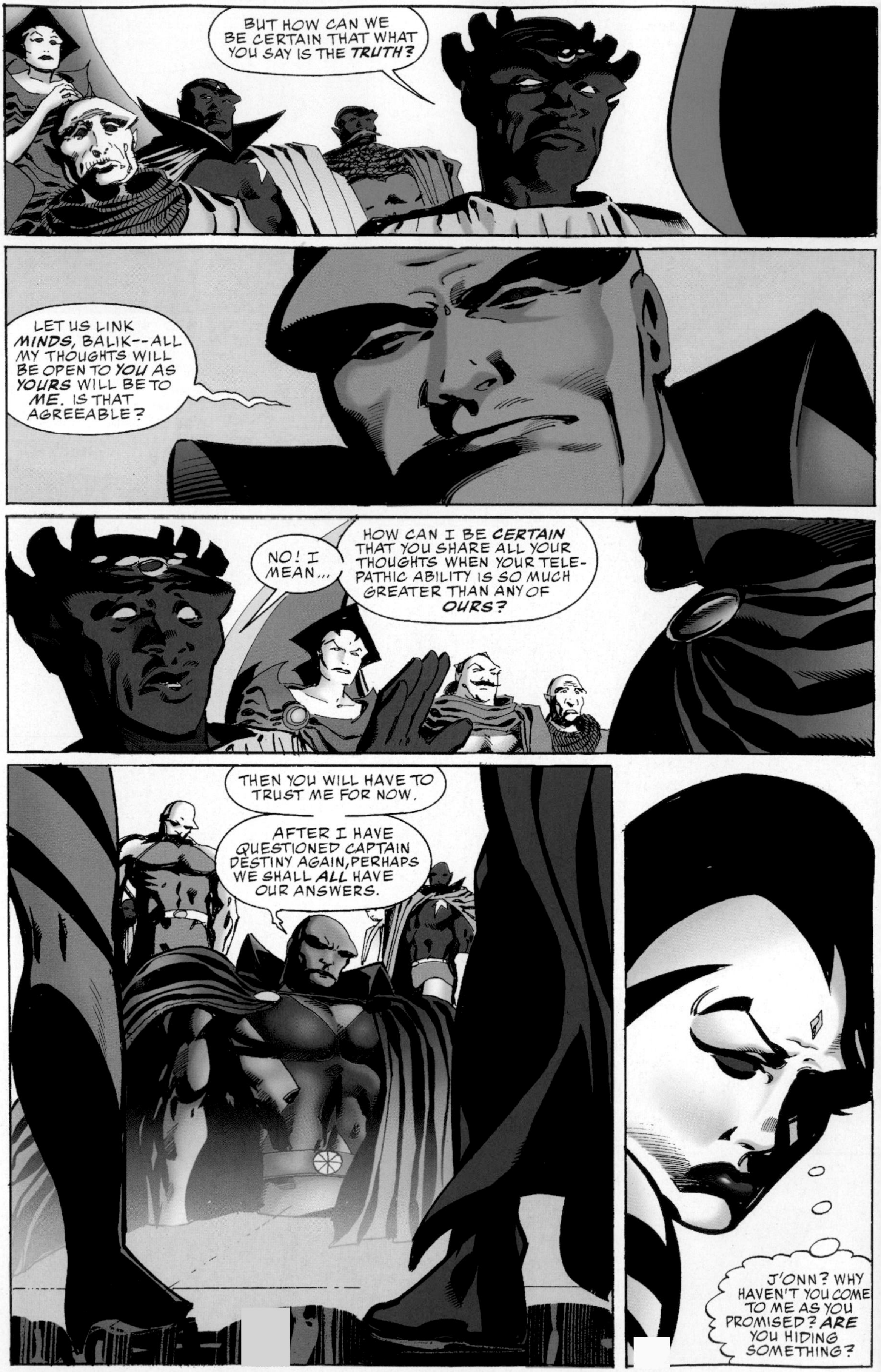
BUT HOW CAN WE BE CERTAIN THAT WHAT YOU SAY IS THE TRUTH?
LET US LINK MINDS, BALIK--ALL MY THOUGHTS WILL BE OPEN TO YOU AS YOURS WILL BE TO ME. IS THAT AGREEABLE?
NO! I MEAN...
HOW CAN I BE CERTAIN THAT YOU SHARE ALL YOUR THOUGHTS WHEN YOUR TELEPATHIC ABILITY IS SO MUCH GREATER THAN ANY OF OURS?
THEN YOU WILL HAVE TO TRUST ME FOR NOW.
AFTER I HAVE QUESTIONED CAPTAIN DESTINY AGAIN, PERHAPS WE SHALL ALL HAVE OUR ANSWERS.
J'ONN? WHY HAVEN'T YOU COME TO ME AS YOU PROMISED? ARE YOU HIDING SOMETHING?

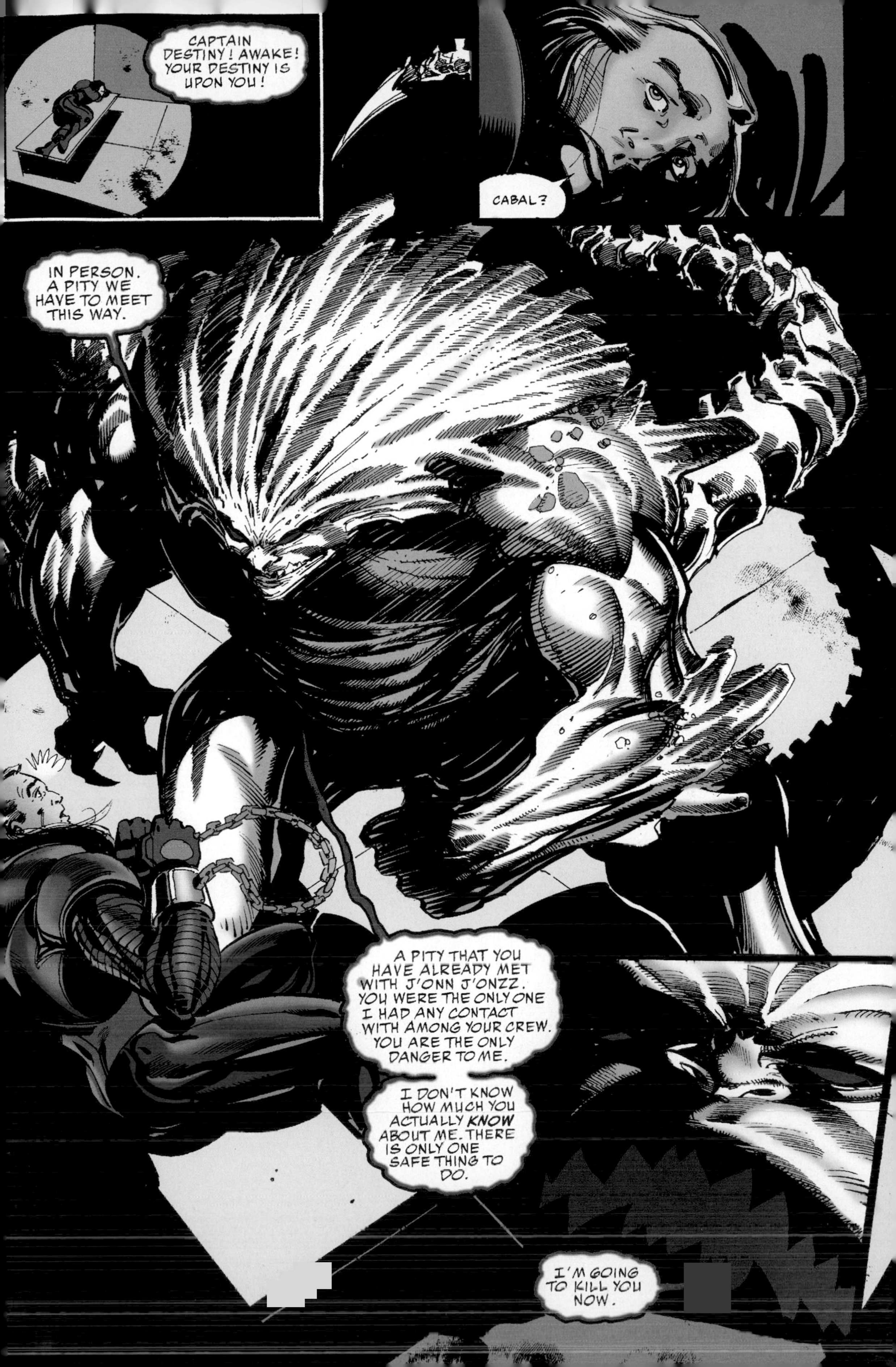
CAPTAIN DESTINY! AWAKE! YOUR DESTINY IS UPON YOU!
CABAL?
IN PERSON. A PITY WE HAVE TO MEET THIS WAY.
A PITY THAT YOU HAVE ALREADY MET WITH J'ONN J'ONZZ. YOU WERE THE ONLY ONE I HAD ANY CONTACT WITH AMONG YOUR CREW. YOU ARE THE ONLY DANGER TO ME.
I DON'T KNOW HOW MUCH YOU ACTUALLY KNOW ABOUT ME. THERE IS ONLY ONE SAFE THING TO DO.
I'M GOING TO KILL YOU NOW.

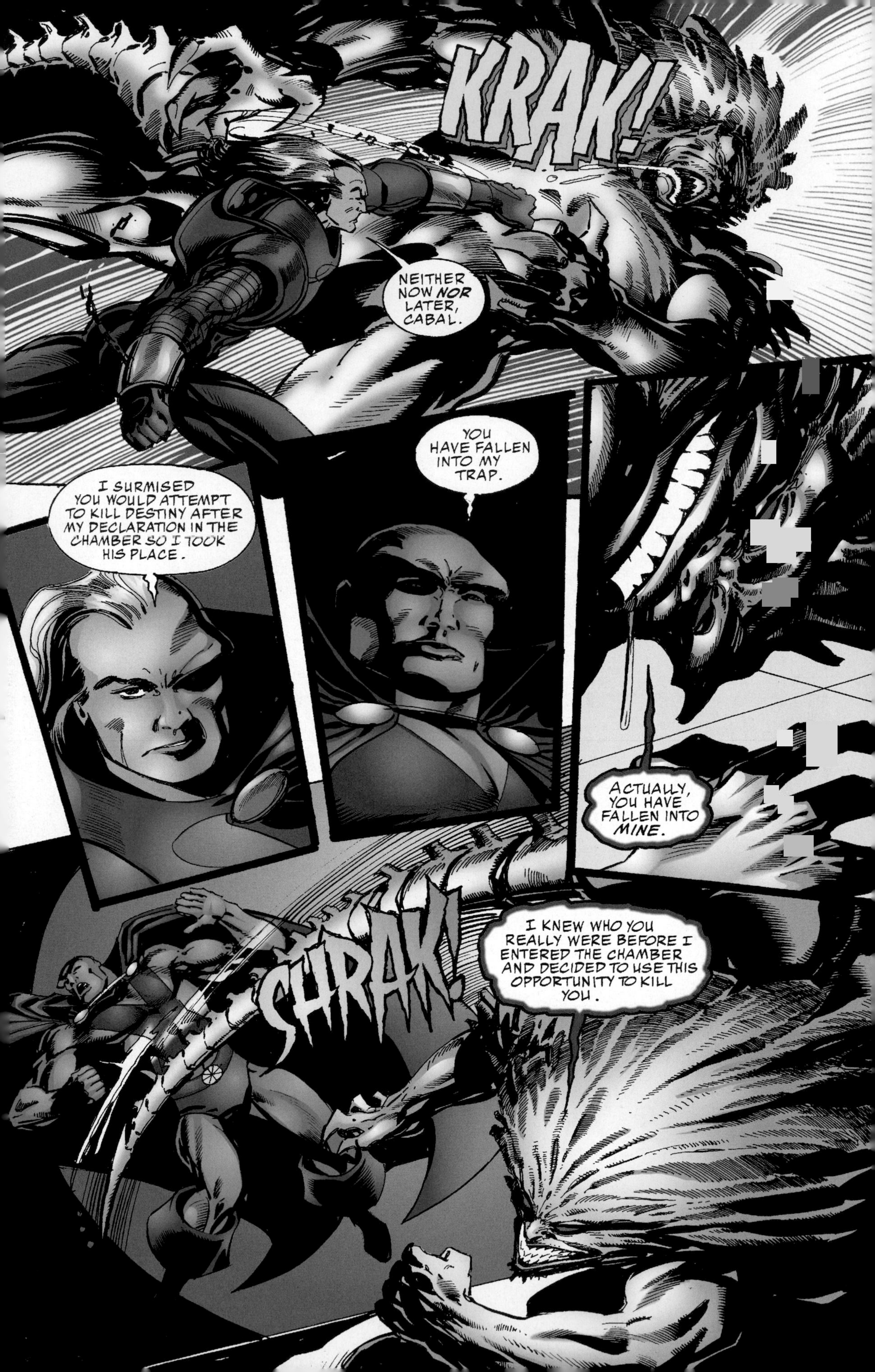
KRAK!
NEITHER NOW NOR LATER, CABAL.
I SURMISED YOU WOULD ATTEMPT TO KILL DESTINY AFTER MY DECLARATION IN THE CHAMBER SO I TOOK HIS PLACE.
YOU HAVE FALLEN INTO MY TRAP.
ACTUALLY, YOU HAVE FALLEN INTO MINE.
SHRAK!
I KNEW WHO YOU REALLY WERE BEFORE I ENTERED THE CHAMBER AND DECIDED TO USE THIS OPPORTUNITY TO KILL YOU.

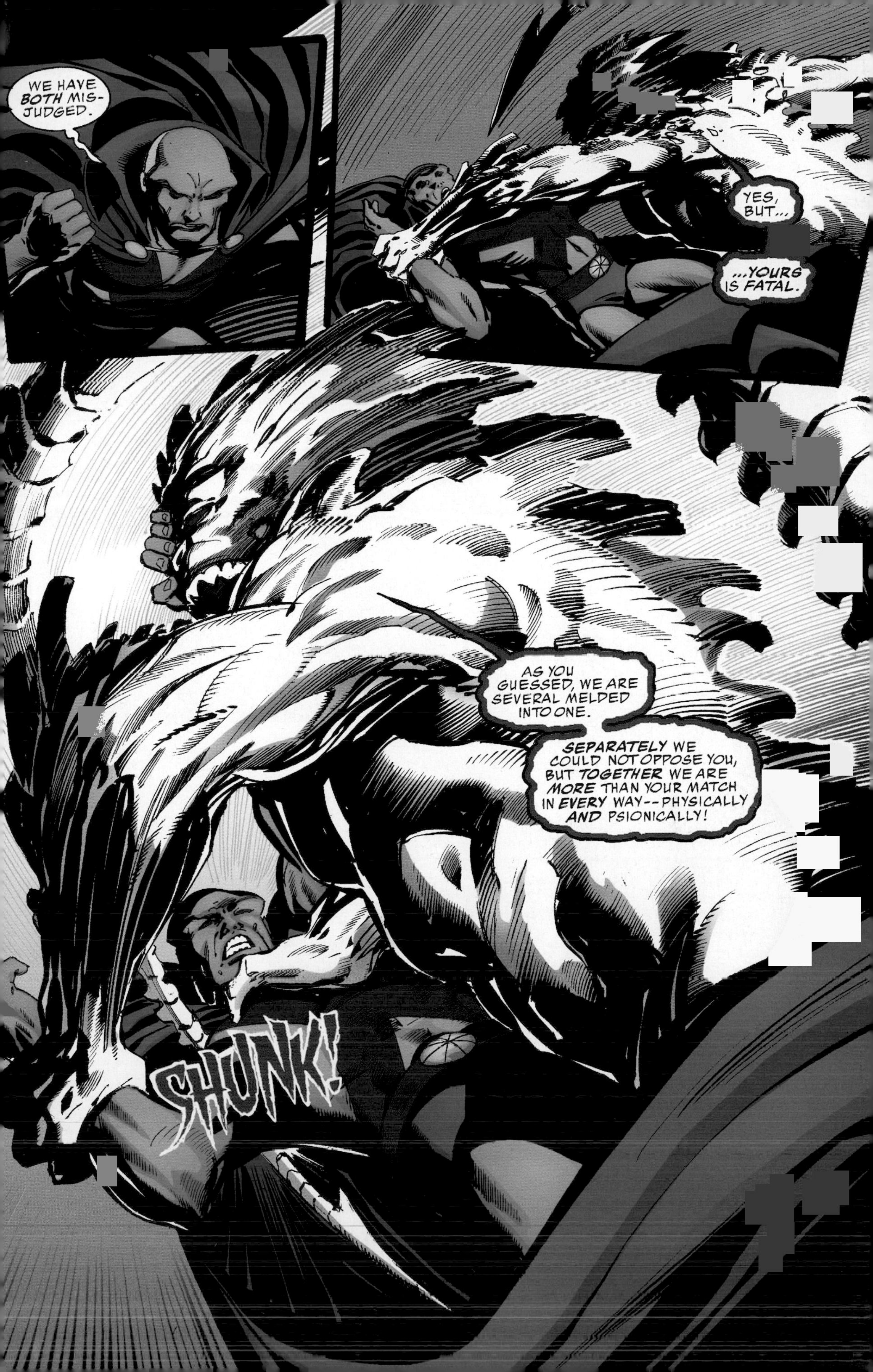
WE HAVE BOTH MIS-JUDGED.
YES, BUT...
...YOURS IS FATAL.
AS YOU GUESSED, WE ARE SEVERAL MELDED INTO ONE.
SEPARATELY WE COULD NOT OPPOSE YOU, BUT TOGETHER WE ARE MORE THAN YOUR MATCH IN EVERY WAY--PHYSICALLY AND PSIONICALLY!
SHUNK!

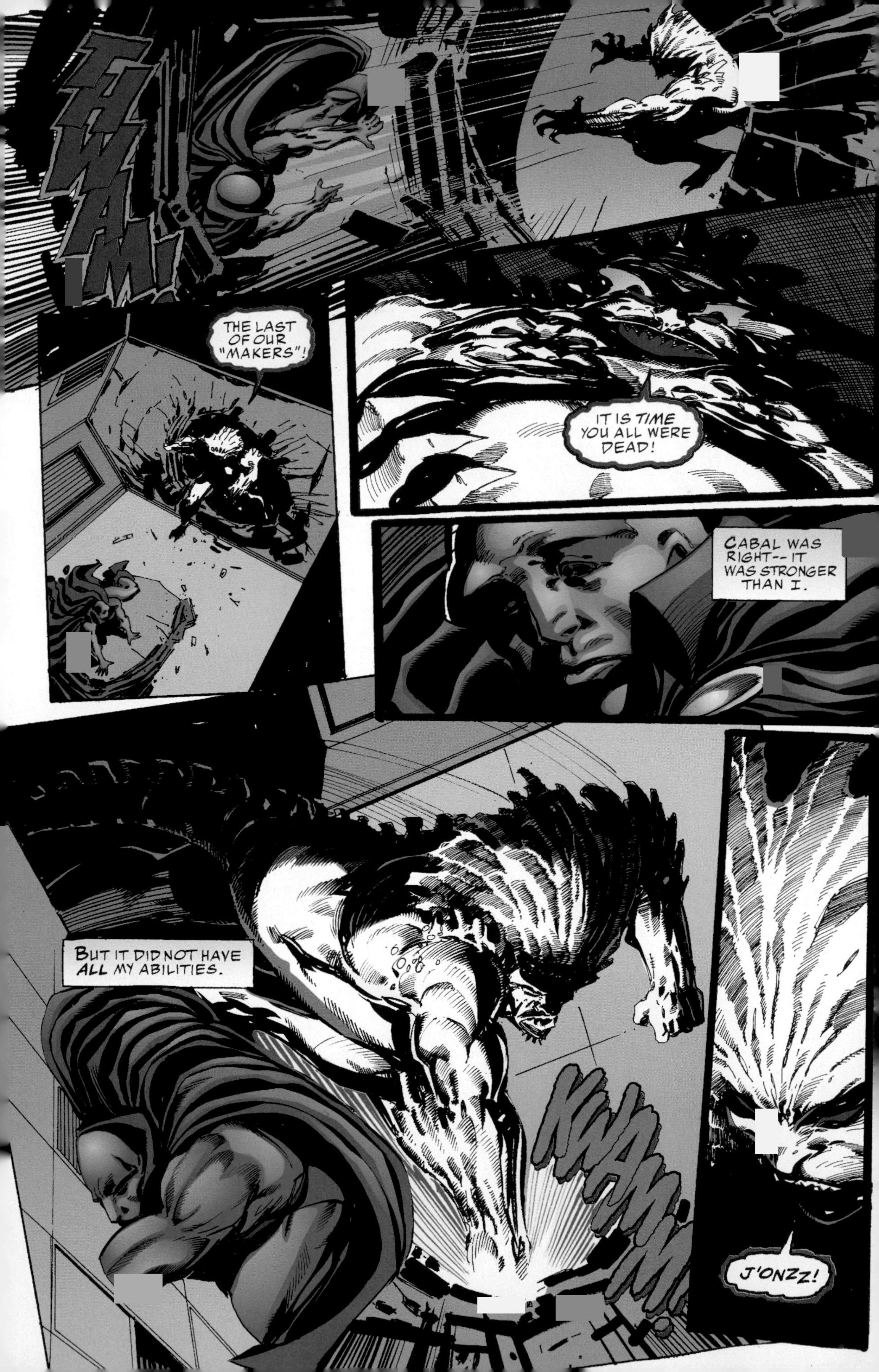
THWAM!
THE LAST OF OUR "MAKERS"!
IT IS TIME YOU ALL WERE DEAD!
CABAL WAS RIGHT-- IT WAS STRONGER THAN I.
BUT IT DID NOT HAVE ALL MY ABILITIES.
KWAM!
J'ONZZ!

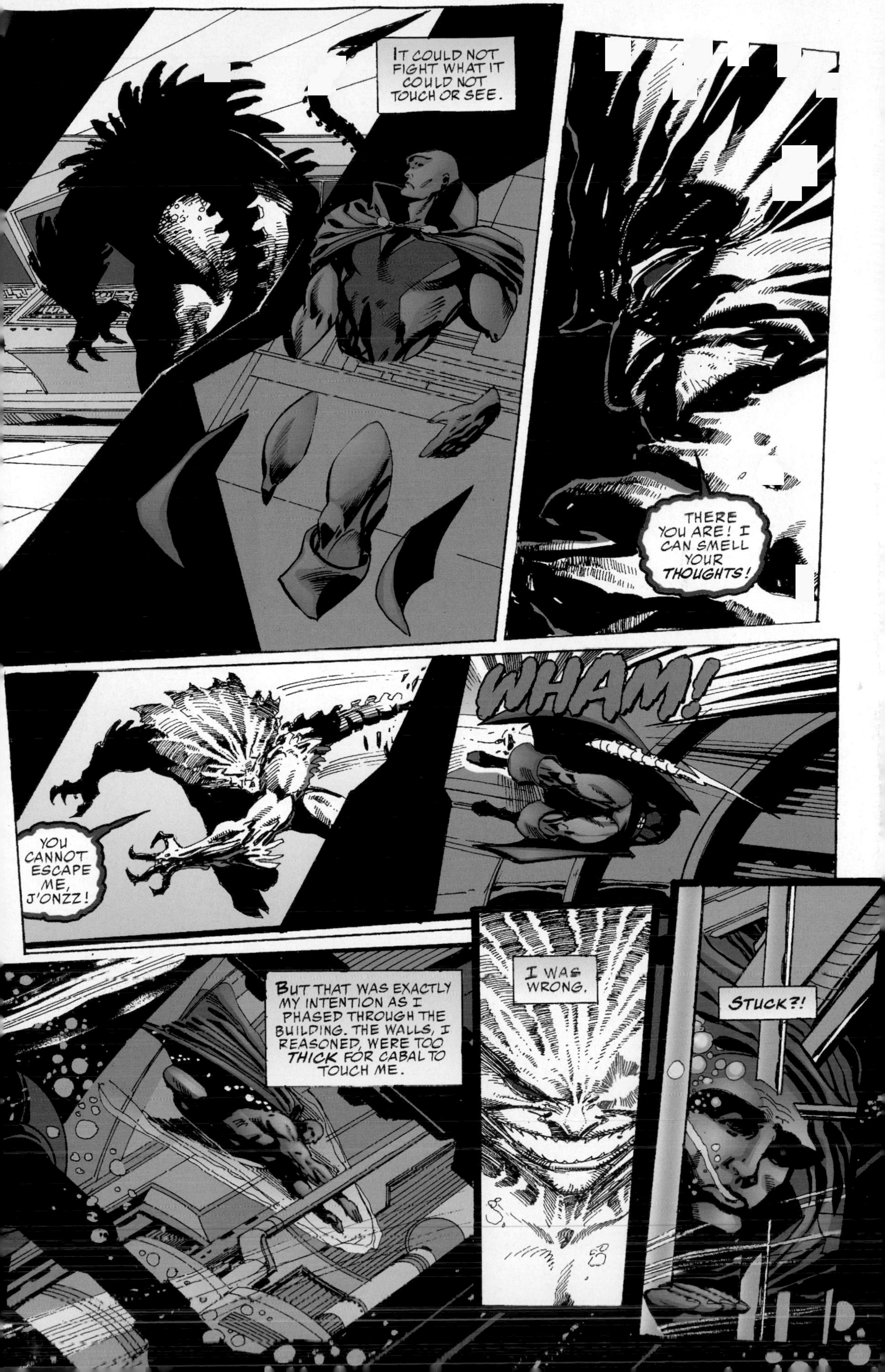
IT COULD NOT FIGHT WHAT IT COULD NOT TOUCH OR SEE.
THERE YOU ARE! I CAN SMELL YOUR THOUGHTS!
YOU CANNOT ESCAPE ME, J'ONZZ!
WHAM!
BUT THAT WAS EXACTLY MY INTENTION AS I PHASED THROUGH THE BUILDING. THE WALLS, I REASONED, WERE TOO THICK FOR CABAL TO TOUCH ME.
I WAS WRONG.
STUCK?!

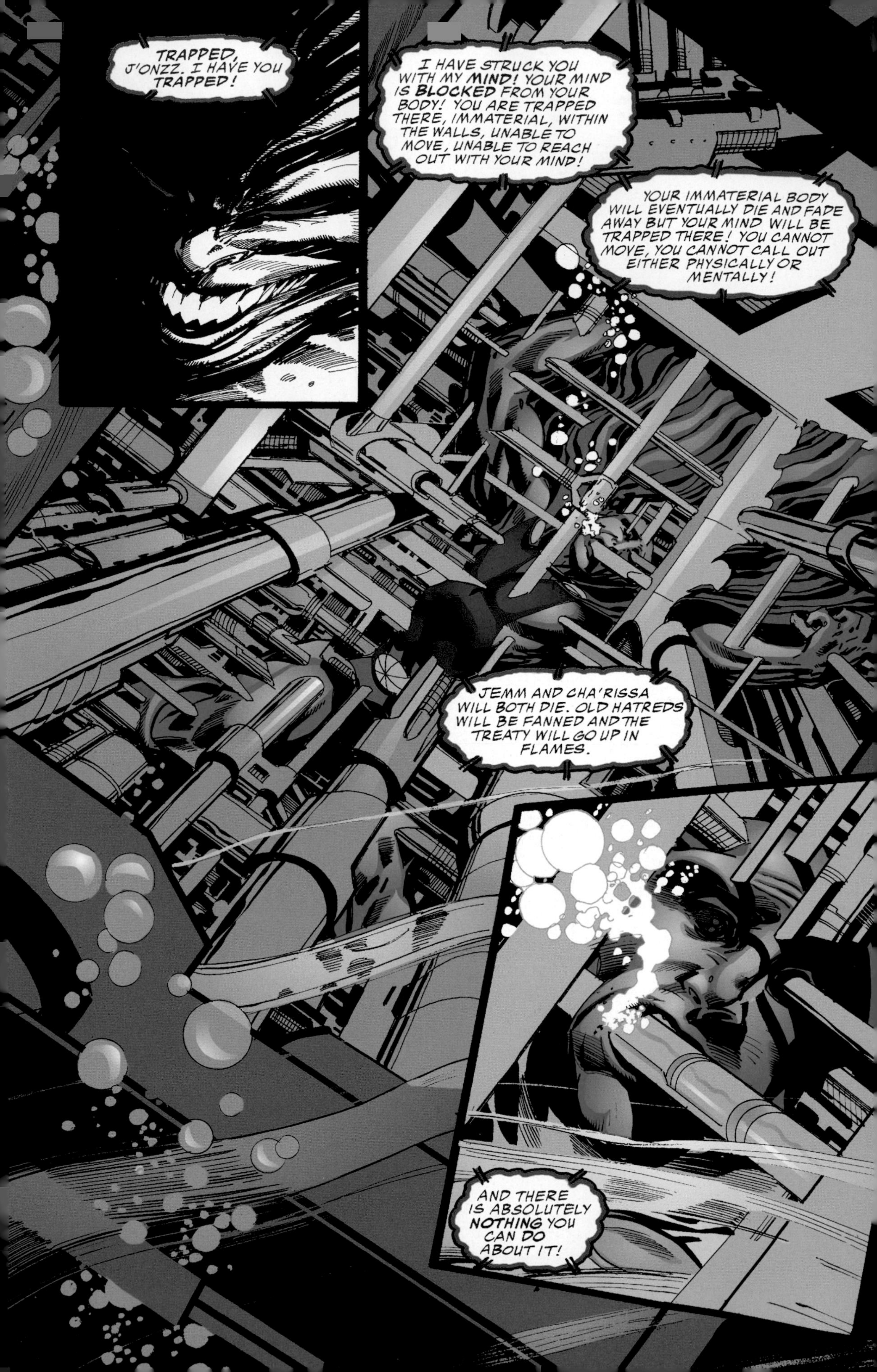
TRAPPED, J'ONZZ. I HAVE YOU TRAPPED!
I HAVE STRUCK YOU WITH MY MIND! YOUR MIND IS BLOCKED FROM YOUR BODY! YOU ARE TRAPPED THERE, IMMATERIAL, WITHIN THE WALLS, UNABLE TO MOVE, UNABLE TO REACH OUT WITH YOUR MIND!
YOUR IMMATERIAL BODY WILL EVENTUALLY DIE AND FADE AWAY BUT YOUR MIND WILL BE TRAPPED THERE! YOU CANNOT MOVE, YOU CANNOT CALL OUT EITHER PHYSICALLY OR MENTALLY!
JEMM AND CHA'RISSA WILL BOTH DIE. OLD HATREDS WILL BE FANNED AND THE TREATY WILL GO UP IN FLAMES.
AND THERE IS ABSOLUTELY NOTHING YOU CAN DO ABOUT IT!

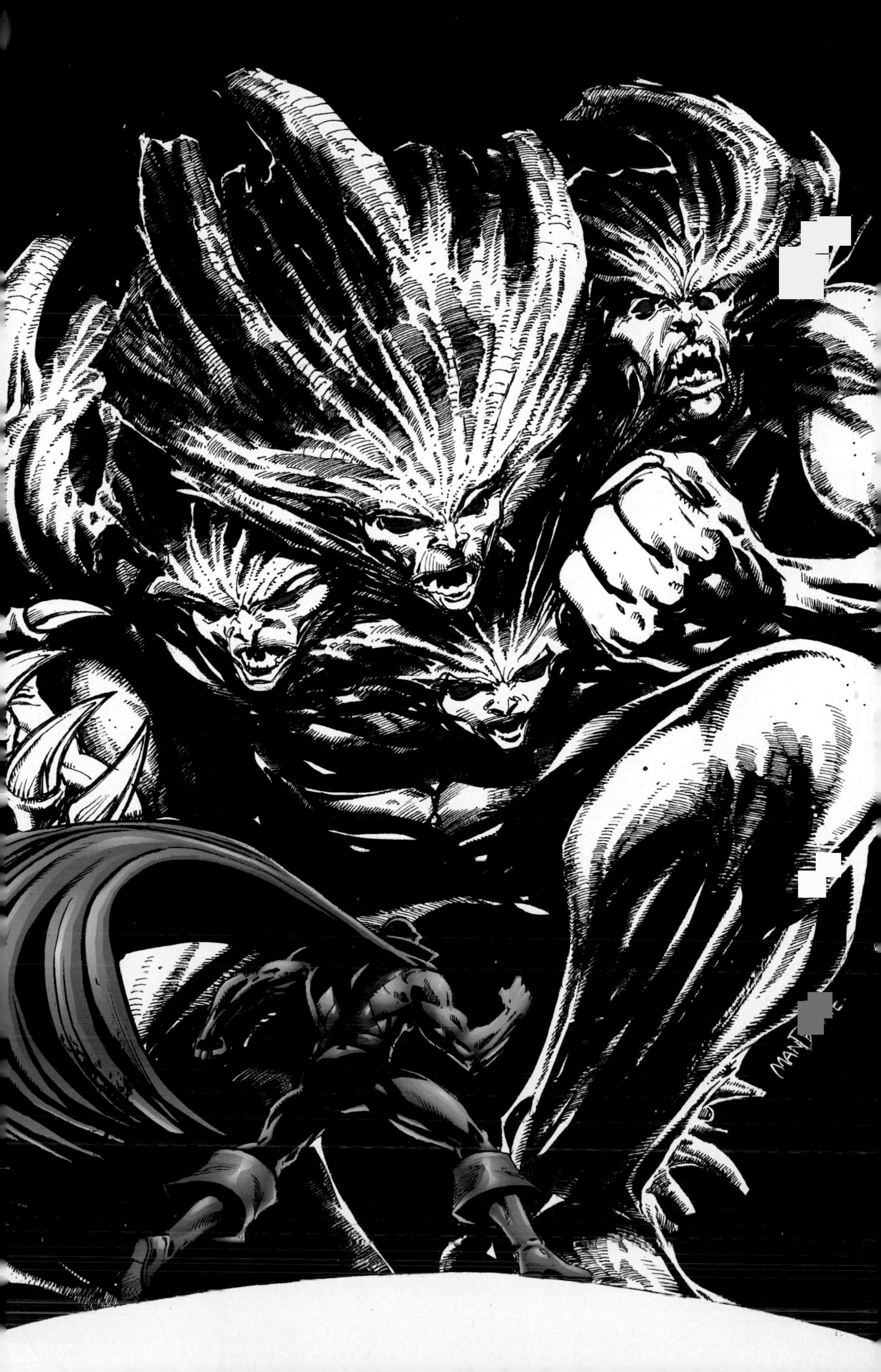

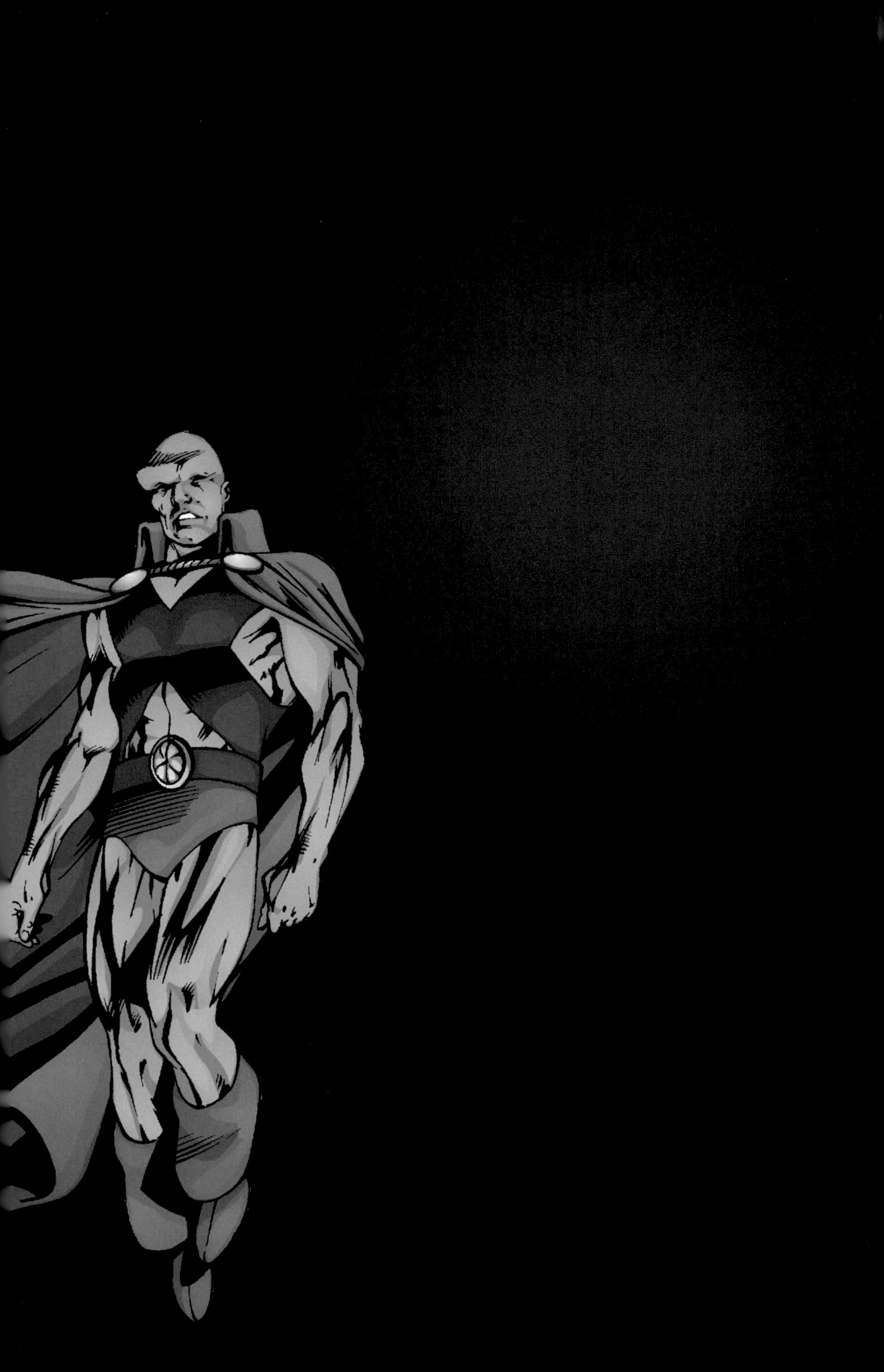

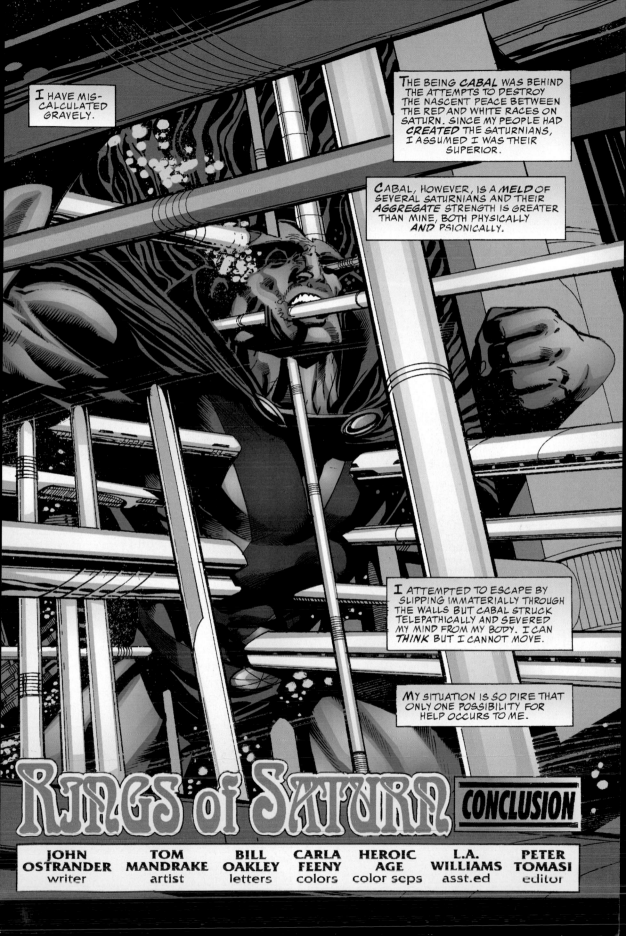

I HAVE MIS-CALCULATED GRAVELY.

THE BEING *CABAL* WAS BEHIND THE ATTEMPTS TO DESTROY THE NASCENT PEACE BETWEEN THE RED AND WHITE RACES ON SATURN. SINCE MY PEOPLE HAD *CREATED* THE SATURNIANS, I ASSUMED I WAS THEIR SUPERIOR.

CABAL, HOWEVER, IS A *MELD* OF SEVERAL SATURNIANS AND THEIR *AGGREGATE* STRENGTH IS GREATER THAN MINE, BOTH PHYSICALLY *AND* PSIONICALLY.

I ATTEMPTED TO ESCAPE BY SLIPPING IMMATERIALLY THROUGH THE WALLS BUT CABAL STRUCK TELEPATHICALLY AND SEVERED MY MIND FROM MY BODY. I CAN *THINK* BUT I CANNOT MOVE.

MY SITUATION IS SO DIRE THAT ONLY ONE POSSIBILITY FOR HELP OCCURS TO ME.

RINGS of SATURN CONCLUSION

JOHN OSTRANDER writer
TOM MANDRAKE artist
BILL OAKLEY letters
CARLA FEENY colors
HEROIC AGE color seps
L.A. WILLIAMS asst.ed
PETER TOMASI editor

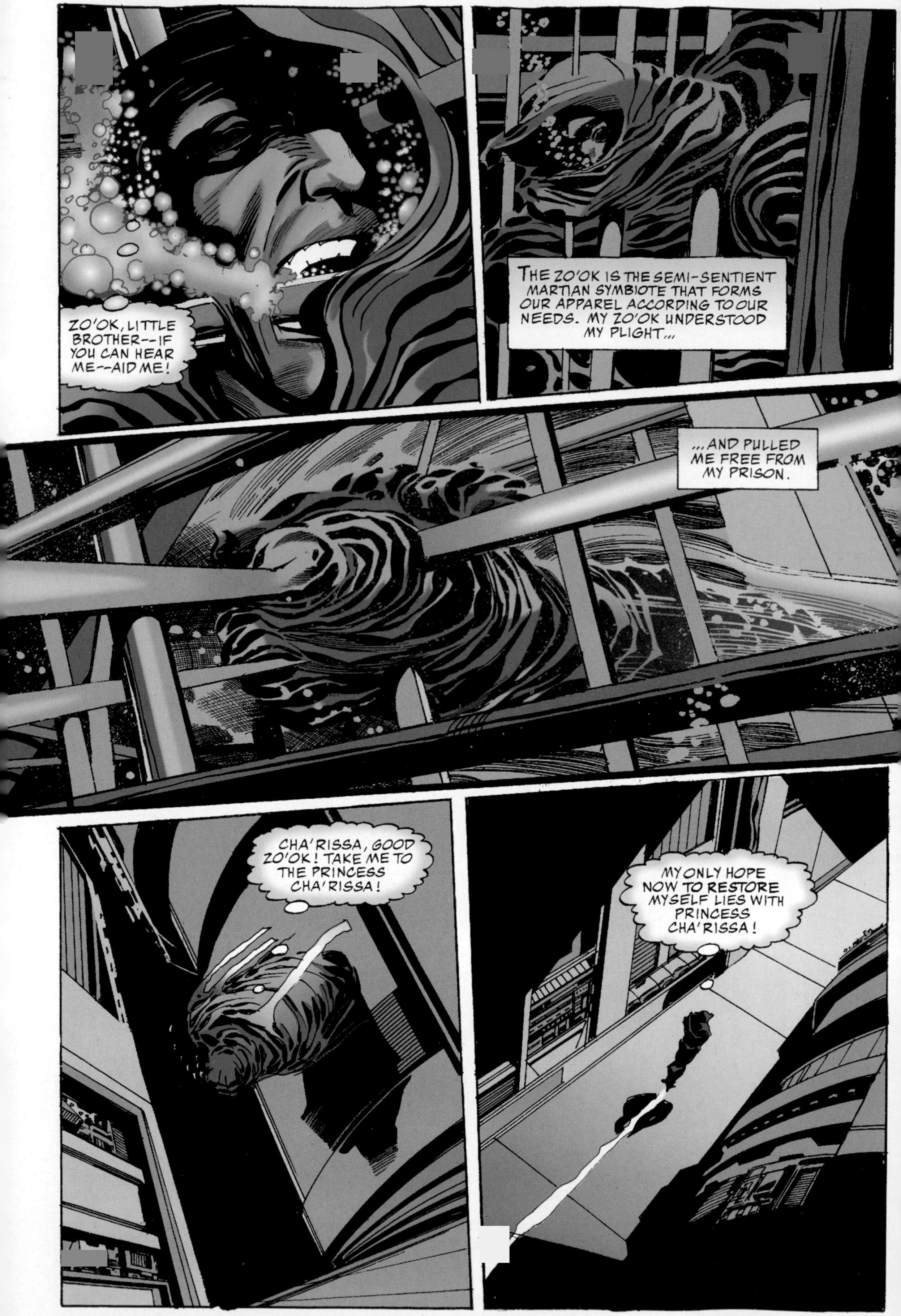
ZO'OK, LITTLE BROTHER--IF YOU CAN HEAR ME--AID ME!
THE ZO'OK IS THE SEMI-SENTIENT MARTIAN SYMBIOTE THAT FORMS OUR APPAREL ACCORDING TO OUR NEEDS. MY ZO'OK UNDERSTOOD MY PLIGHT...
...AND PULLED ME FREE FROM MY PRISON.
CHA'RISSA, GOOD ZO'OK! TAKE ME TO THE PRINCESS CHA'RISSA!
MY ONLY HOPE NOW TO RESTORE MYSELF LIES WITH PRINCESS CHA'RISSA!

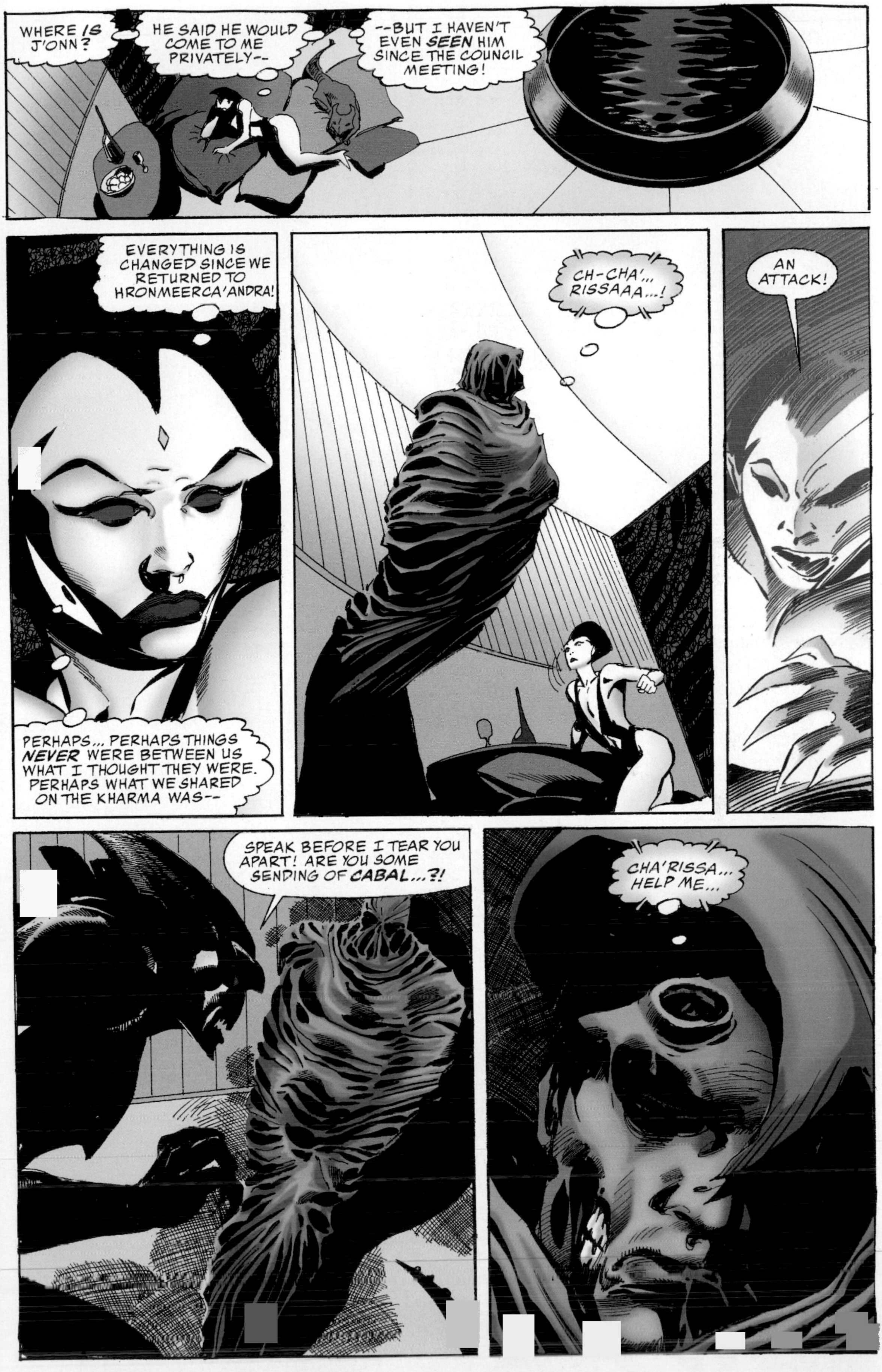
WHERE IS J'ONN?
HE SAID HE WOULD COME TO ME PRIVATELY--
--BUT I HAVEN'T EVEN SEEN HIM SINCE THE COUNCIL MEETING!
EVERYTHING IS CHANGED SINCE WE RETURNED TO HRONMEERCA'ANDRA!
PERHAPS... PERHAPS THINGS NEVER WERE BETWEEN US WHAT I THOUGHT THEY WERE. PERHAPS WHAT WE SHARED ON THE KHARMA WAS--
CH-CHA'... RISSAAA...!
AN ATTACK!
SPEAK BEFORE I TEAR YOU APART! ARE YOU SOME SENDING OF CABAL...?!
CHA'RISSA... HELP ME...

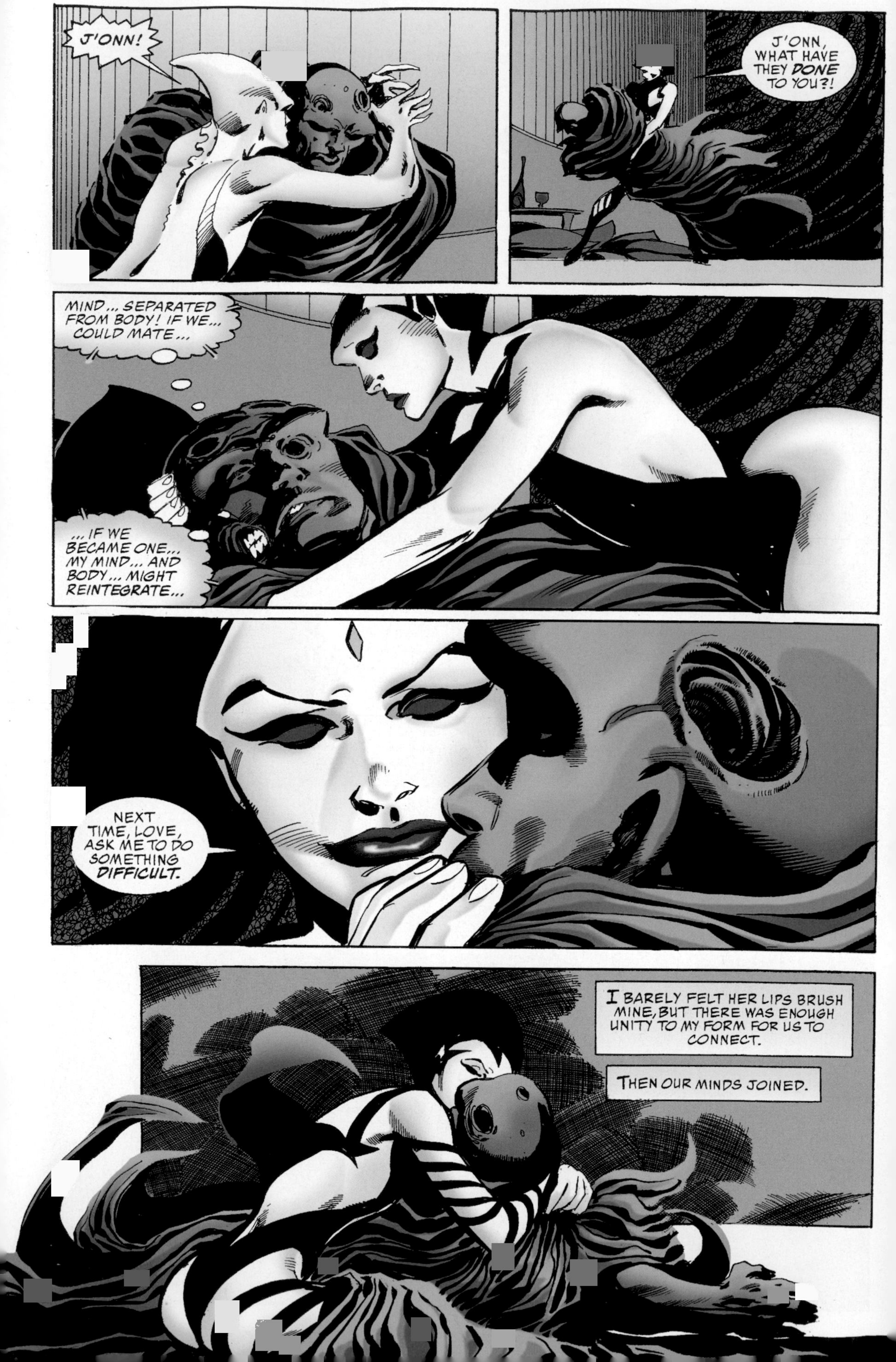
J'ONN!
J'ONN, WHAT HAVE THEY *DONE* TO YOU?!
MIND... SEPARATED FROM BODY! IF WE... COULD MATE...
...IF WE BECAME ONE... MY MIND... AND BODY... MIGHT REINTEGRATE...
NEXT TIME, LOVE, ASK ME TO DO SOMETHING *DIFFICULT.*
I BARELY FELT HER LIPS BRUSH MINE, BUT THERE WAS ENOUGH UNITY TO MY FORM FOR US TO CONNECT.
THEN OUR MINDS JOINED.

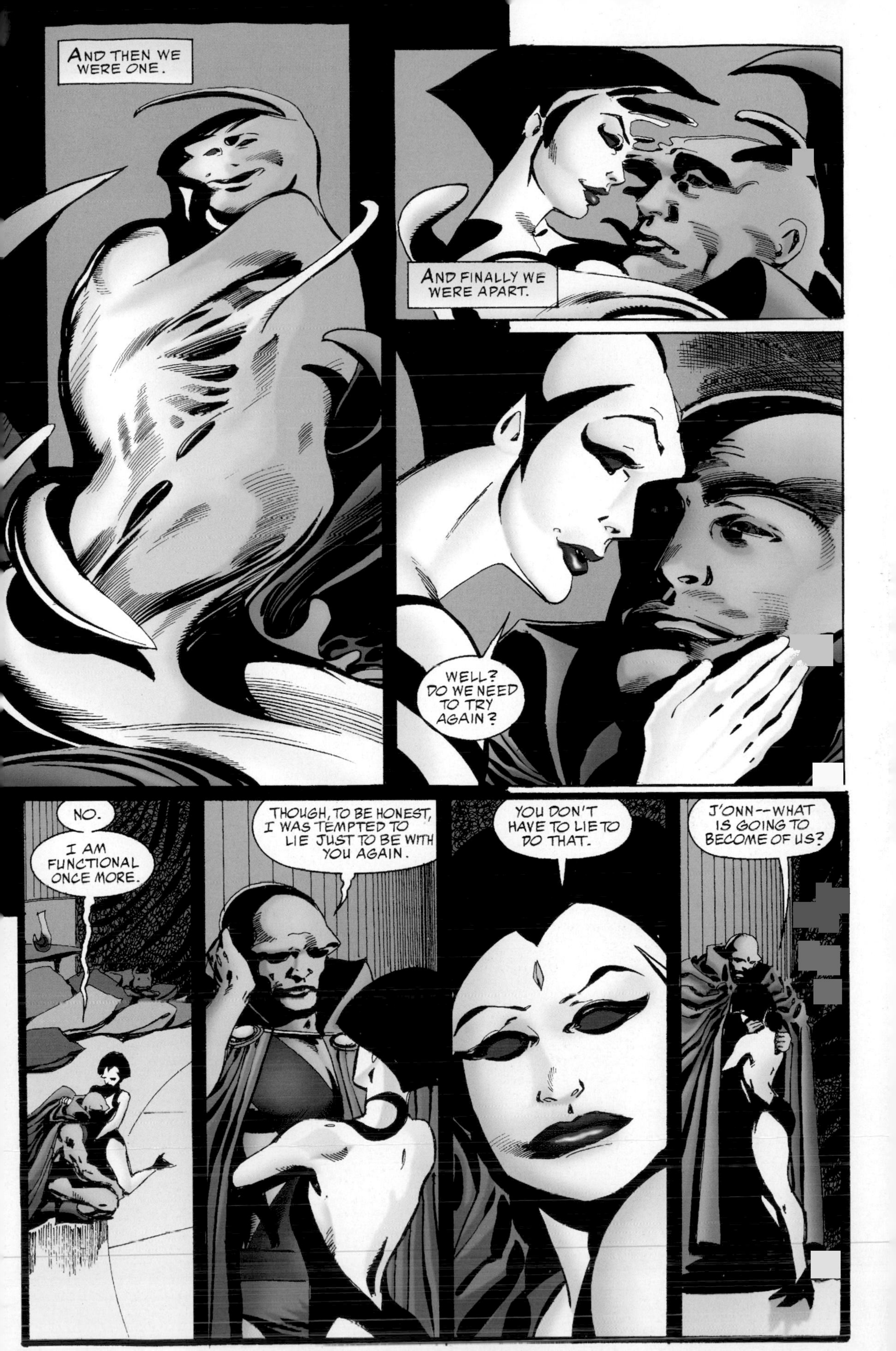
AND THEN WE WERE ONE.
AND FINALLY WE WERE APART.
WELL? DO WE NEED TO TRY AGAIN?
NO.
I AM FUNCTIONAL ONCE MORE.
THOUGH, TO BE HONEST, I WAS TEMPTED TO LIE JUST TO BE WITH YOU AGAIN.
YOU DON'T HAVE TO LIE TO DO THAT.
J'ONN--WHAT IS GOING TO BECOME OF US?

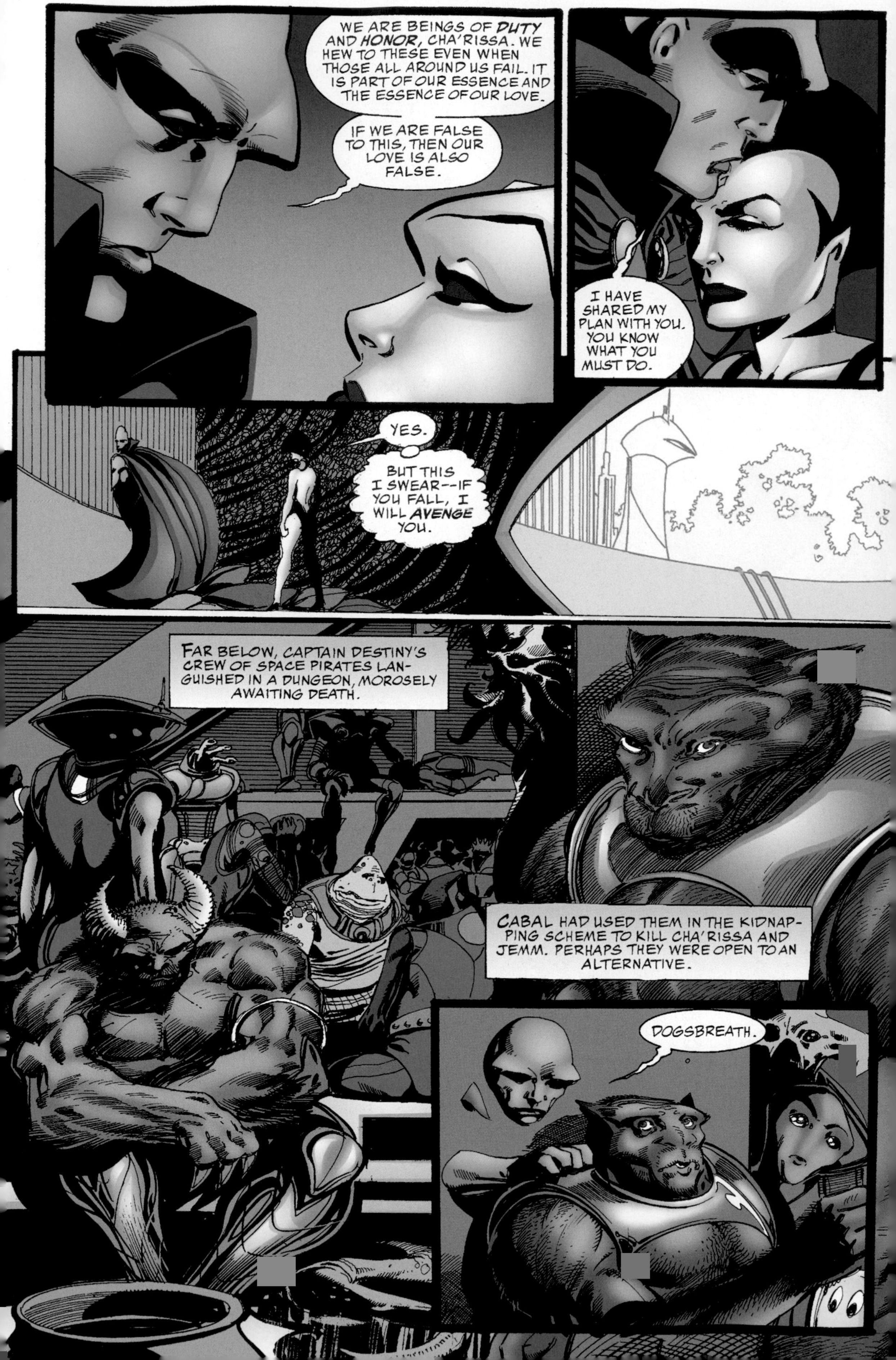
WE ARE BEINGS OF DUTY AND HONOR, CHA'RISSA. WE HEW TO THESE EVEN WHEN THOSE ALL AROUND US FAIL. IT IS PART OF OUR ESSENCE AND THE ESSENCE OF OUR LOVE.
IF WE ARE FALSE TO THIS, THEN OUR LOVE IS ALSO FALSE.
I HAVE SHARED MY PLAN WITH YOU. YOU KNOW WHAT YOU MUST DO.
YES.
BUT THIS I SWEAR--IF YOU FALL, I WILL AVENGE YOU.
FAR BELOW, CAPTAIN DESTINY'S CREW OF SPACE PIRATES LANGUISHED IN A DUNGEON, MOROSELY AWAITING DEATH.
CABAL HAD USED THEM IN THE KIDNAPPING SCHEME TO KILL CHA'RISSA AND JEMM. PERHAPS THEY WERE OPEN TO AN ALTERNATIVE.
DOGSBREATH.

BRING ME CAPTAIN DESTINY.

DON'T KNOW WHY WE'RE BOTHERING TO HIDE HIS BODY, SEEIN' HOW HE'S *DEAD*.

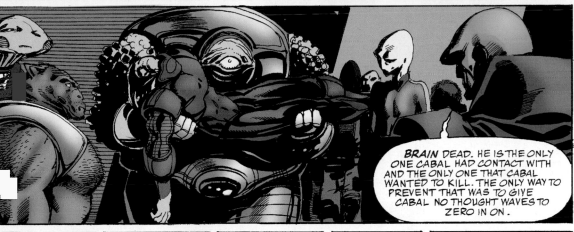

BRAIN DEAD. HE IS THE ONLY ONE CABAL HAD CONTACT WITH AND THE ONLY ONE THAT CABAL WANTED TO KILL. THE ONLY WAY TO PREVENT THAT WAS TO GIVE CABAL NO THOUGHT WAVES TO ZERO IN ON.

WAKE UP, DESTINY.

OOK.

LET'S NOT DO THAT AGAIN, ALIEN. MIGHTY BAD DREAMS I HAD!

I HAVE A DEAL TO OFFER YOU LOT. DEFEND JEMM AND CHA'RISSA. IF I FALL, GET THEM TO EARTH AND THE JLA.

YOUR SHIP IS PREPARED, BUT LEAVE NOW AND YOU WILL DIE.

YOU PLAYED RIGHT BY US, UNLIKE CABAL. WE'RE WITH YOU!

I HAVE INSERTED THE PLAN IN YOUR MIND, CAPTAIN. THE WAY IS OPEN AND THE GUARDS ARE ASLEEP. GET IN PLACE. YOU WILL BE NEEDED VERY SOON.

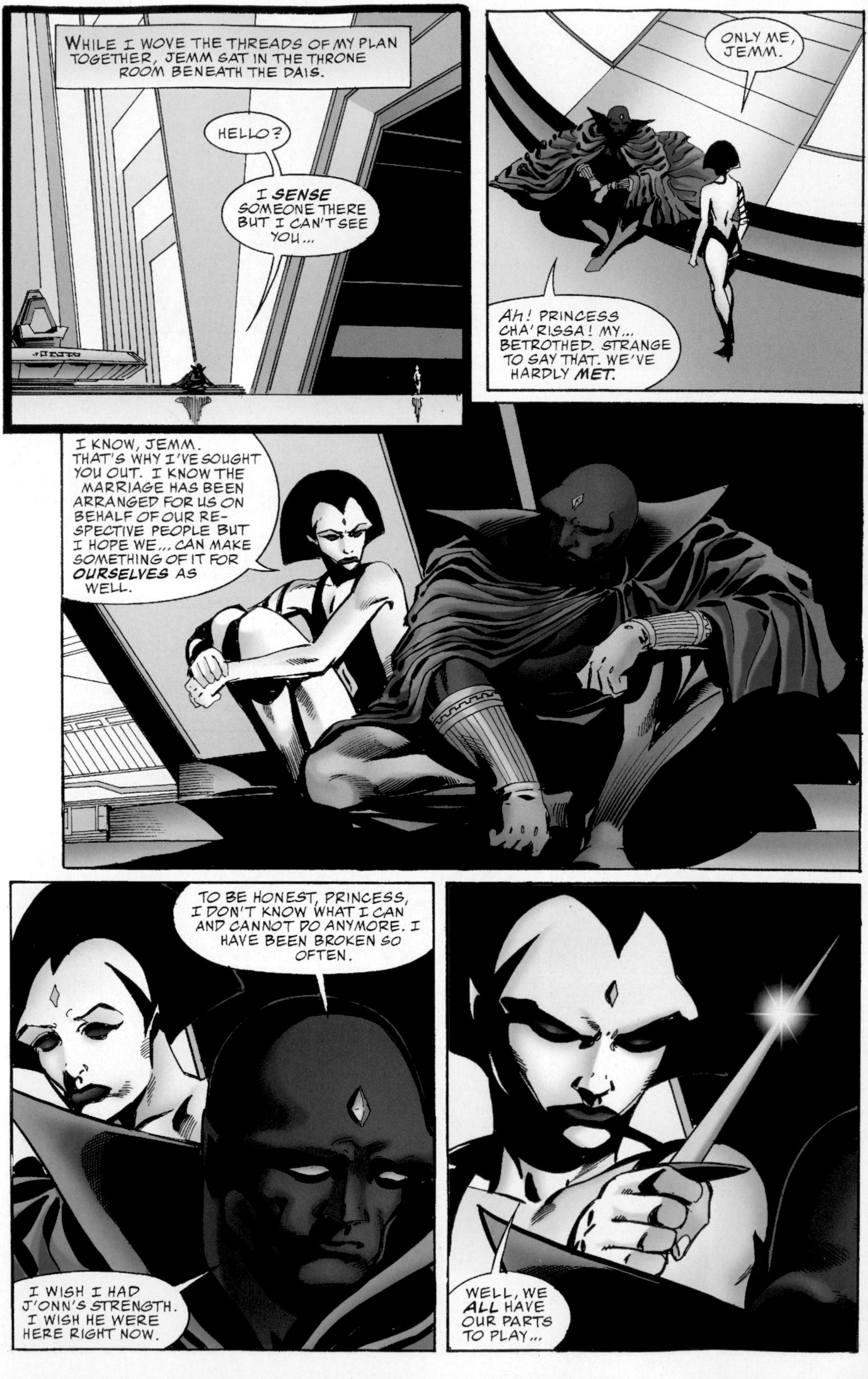
WHILE I WOVE THE THREADS OF MY PLAN TOGETHER, JEMM SAT IN THE THRONE ROOM BENEATH THE DAIS.
HELLO?
I SENSE SOMEONE THERE BUT I CAN'T SEE YOU...
ONLY ME, JEMM.
AH! PRINCESS CHA'RISSA! MY... BETROTHED. STRANGE TO SAY THAT. WE'VE HARDLY MET.
I KNOW, JEMM. THAT'S WHY I'VE SOUGHT YOU OUT. I KNOW THE MARRIAGE HAS BEEN ARRANGED FOR US ON BEHALF OF OUR RESPECTIVE PEOPLE BUT I HOPE WE... CAN MAKE SOMETHING OF IT FOR OURSELVES AS WELL.
TO BE HONEST, PRINCESS, I DON'T KNOW WHAT I CAN AND CANNOT DO ANYMORE. I HAVE BEEN BROKEN SO OFTEN.
I WISH I HAD J'ONN'S STRENGTH. I WISH HE WERE HERE RIGHT NOW.
WELL, WE ALL HAVE OUR PARTS TO PLAY...

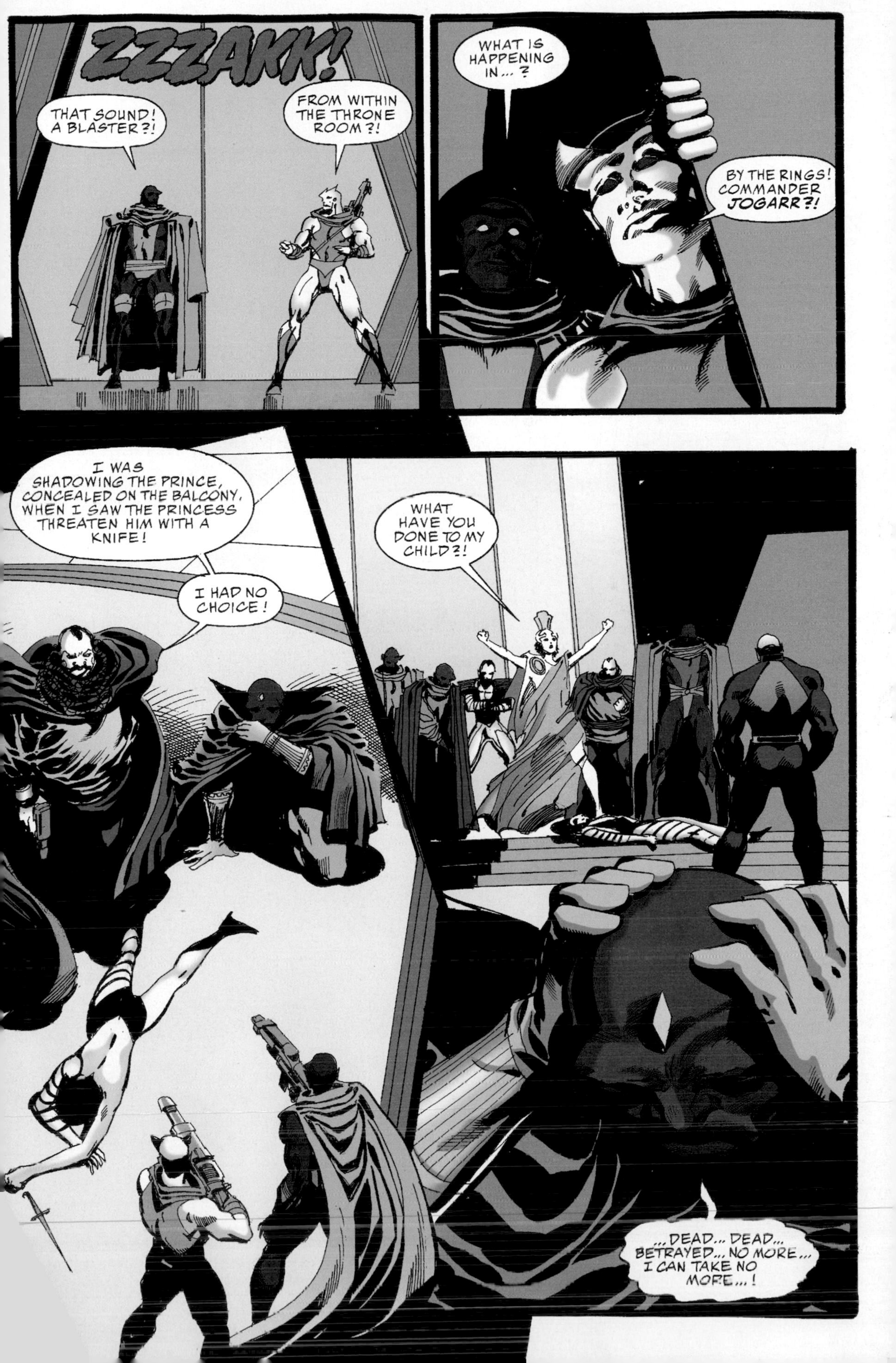
ZZZAKK!
THAT SOUND! A BLASTER?!
FROM WITHIN THE THRONE ROOM?!
WHAT IS HAPPENING IN...?
BY THE RINGS! COMMANDER JOGARR?!
I WAS SHADOWING THE PRINCE, CONCEALED ON THE BALCONY, WHEN I SAW THE PRINCESS THREATEN HIM WITH A KNIFE!
I HAD NO CHOICE!
WHAT HAVE YOU DONE TO MY CHILD?!
...DEAD... DEAD... BETRAYED... NO MORE... I CAN TAKE NO MORE...!

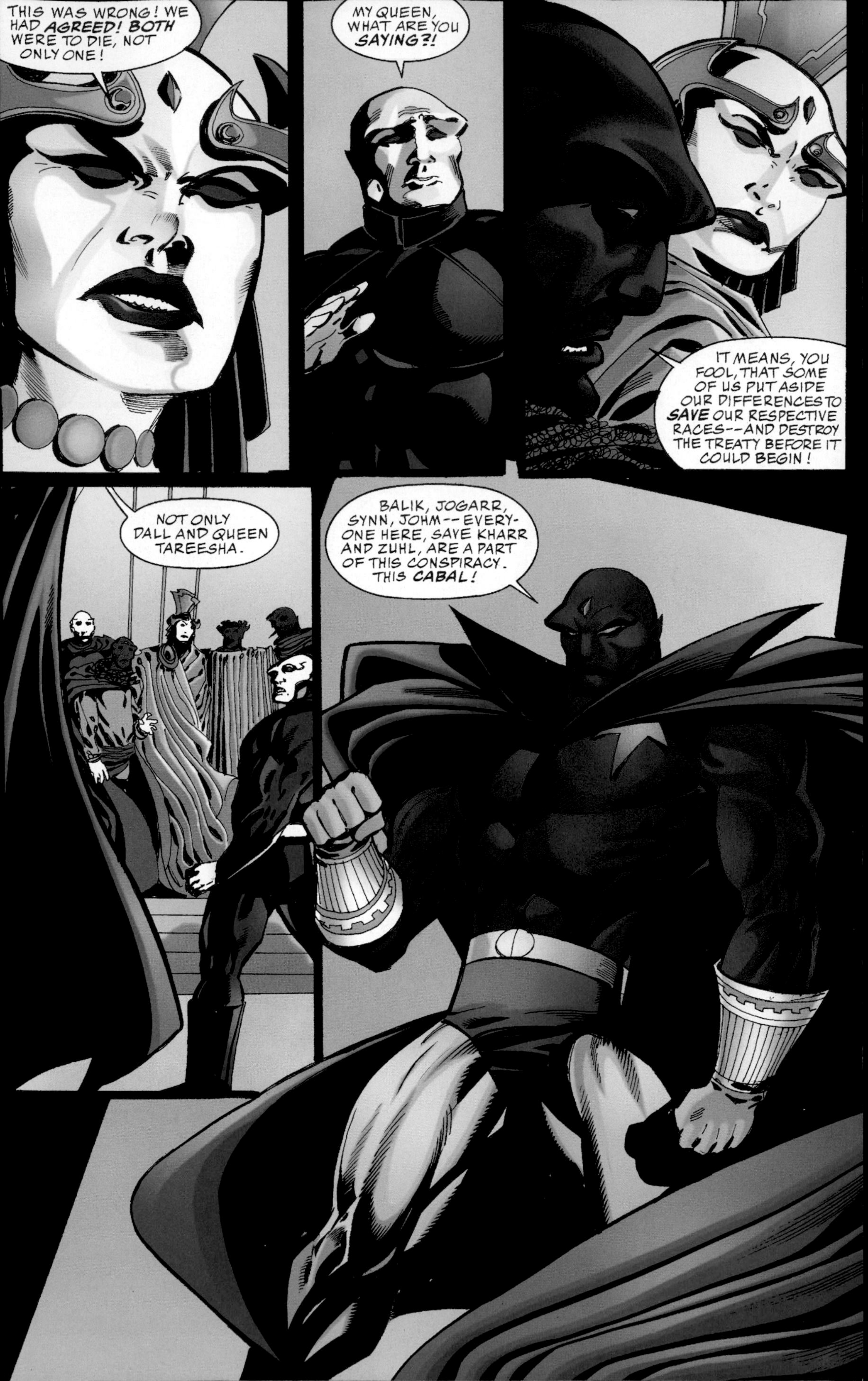
THIS WAS WRONG! WE HAD AGREED! BOTH WERE TO DIE, NOT ONLY ONE!
MY QUEEN, WHAT ARE YOU SAYING?!
IT MEANS, YOU FOOL, THAT SOME OF US PUT ASIDE OUR DIFFERENCES TO SAVE OUR RESPECTIVE RACES--AND DESTROY THE TREATY BEFORE IT COULD BEGIN!
NOT ONLY DALL AND QUEEN TAREESHA.
BALIK, JOGARR, SYNN, JOHM--EVERY-ONE HERE, SAVE KHARR AND ZUHL, ARE A PART OF THIS CONSPIRACY. THIS CABAL!

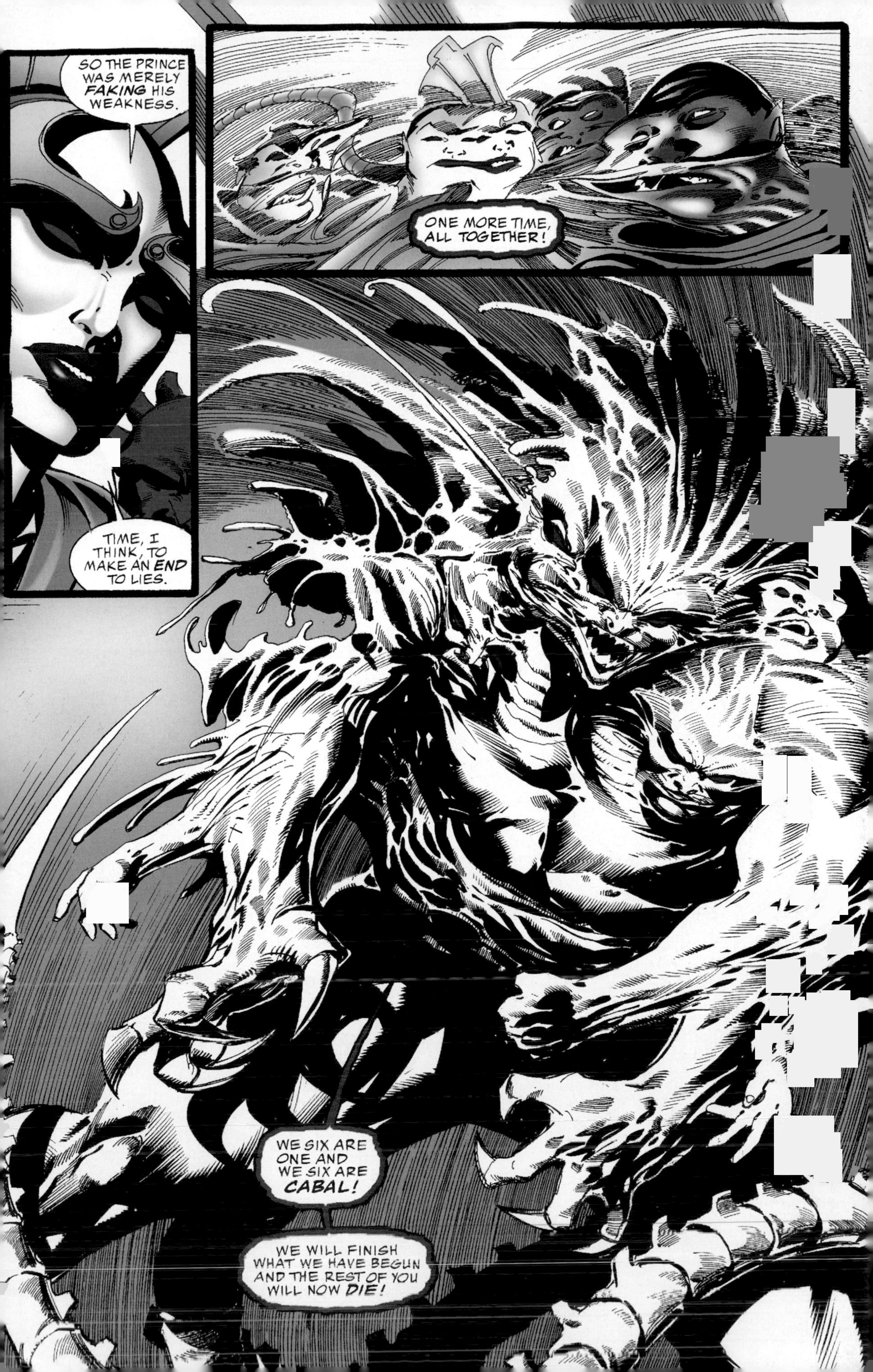
SO THE PRINCE WAS MERELY FAKING HIS WEAKNESS.
TIME, I THINK, TO MAKE AN END TO LIES.
ONE MORE TIME, ALL TOGETHER!
WE SIX ARE ONE AND WE SIX ARE CABAL!
WE WILL FINISH WHAT WE HAVE BEGUN AND THE REST OF YOU WILL NOW DIE!

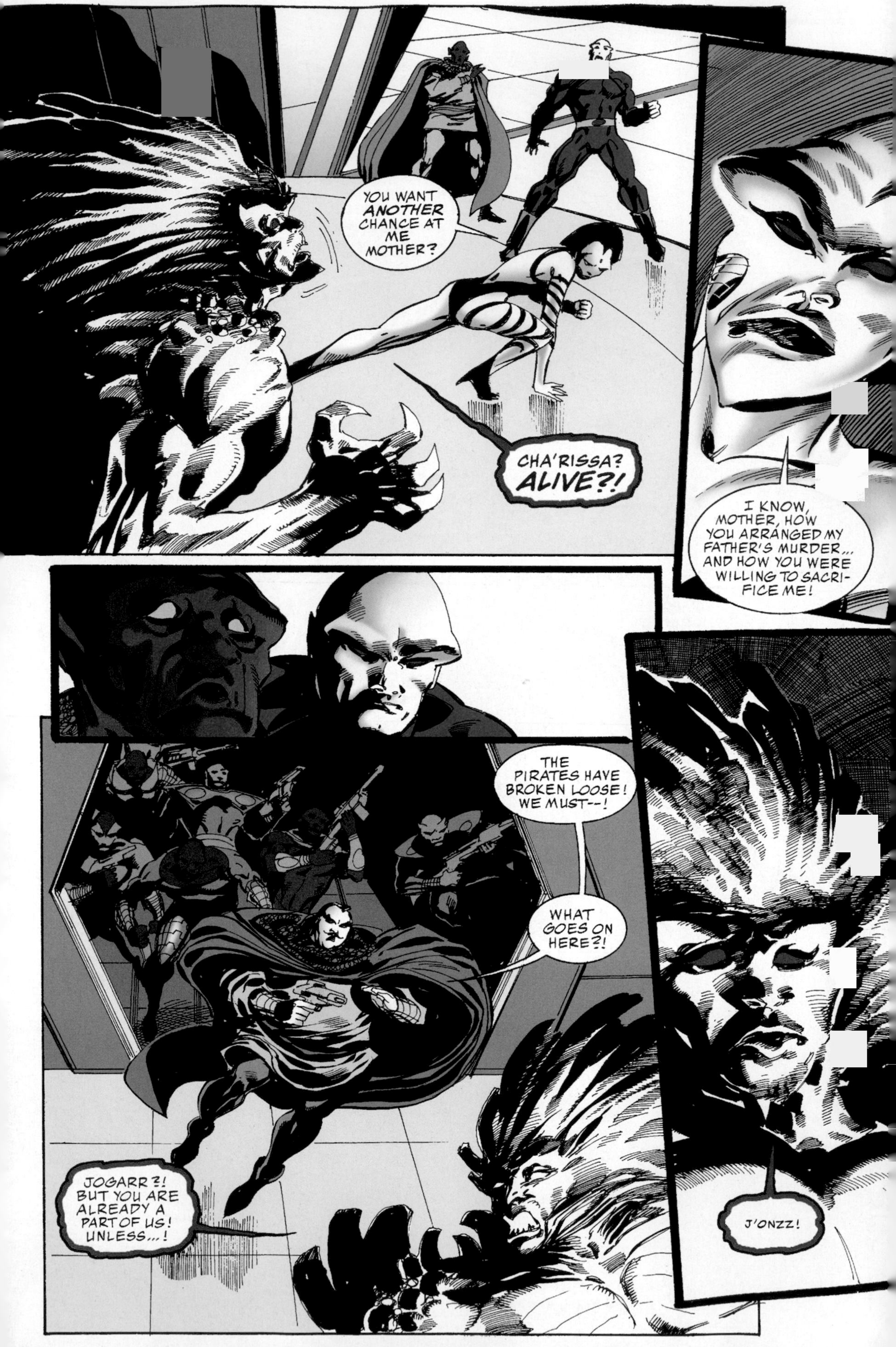
YOU WANT ANOTHER CHANCE AT ME MOTHER?
CHA'RISSA? ALIVE?!
I KNOW, MOTHER, HOW YOU ARRANGED MY FATHER'S MURDER... AND HOW YOU WERE WILLING TO SACRIFICE ME!
THE PIRATES HAVE BROKEN LOOSE! WE MUST--!
WHAT GOES ON HERE?!
JOGARR?! BUT YOU ARE ALREADY A PART OF US! UNLESS...!
J'ONZZ!

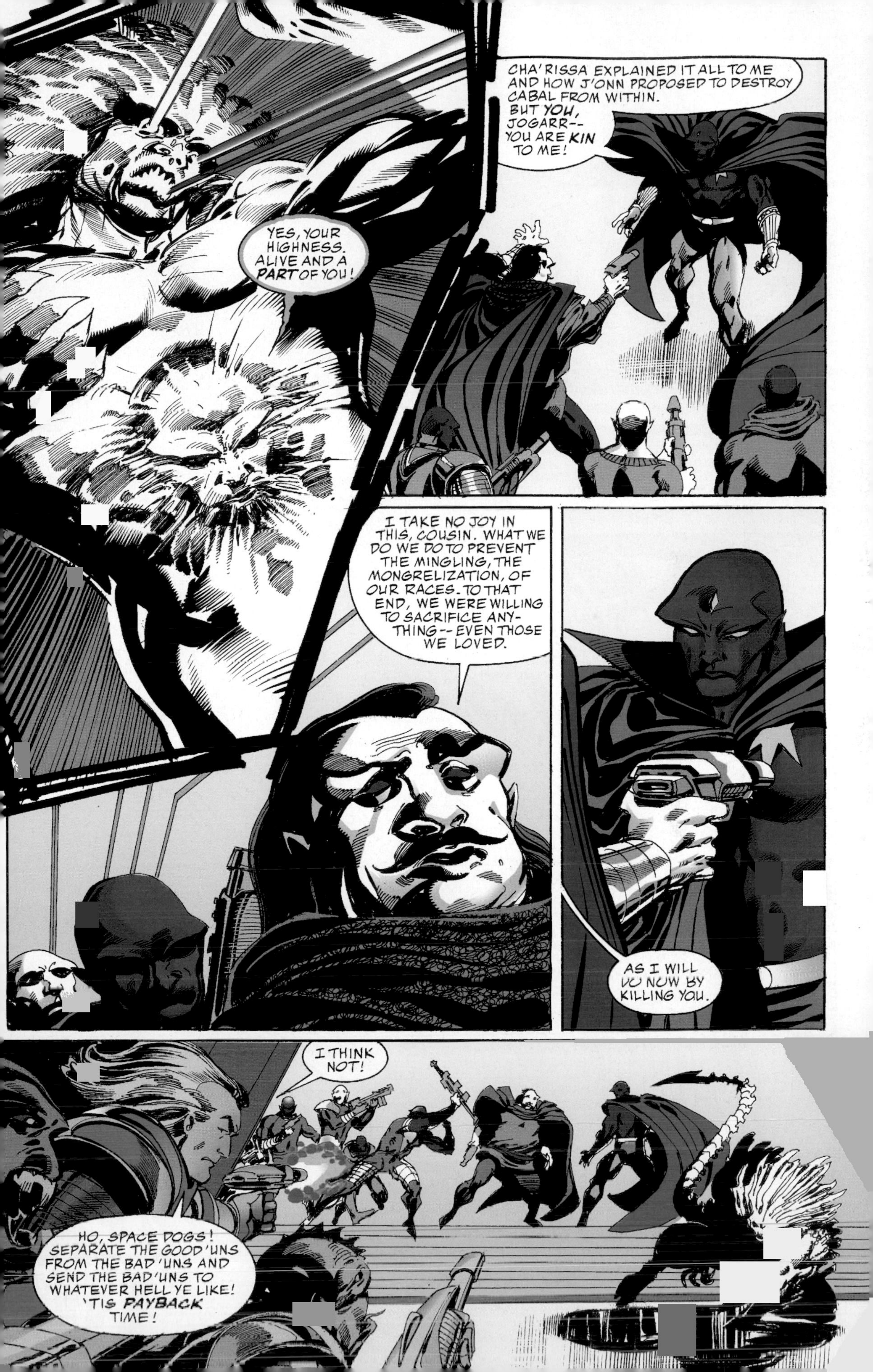
CHA'RISSA EXPLAINED IT ALL TO ME AND HOW J'ONN PROPOSED TO DESTROY CABAL FROM WITHIN.
BUT YOU, JOGARR-- YOU ARE KIN TO ME!
YES, YOUR HIGHNESS. ALIVE AND A PART OF YOU!
I TAKE NO JOY IN THIS, COUSIN. WHAT WE DO WE DO TO PREVENT THE MINGLING, THE MONGRELIZATION, OF OUR RACES. TO THAT END, WE WERE WILLING TO SACRIFICE ANYTHING-- EVEN THOSE WE LOVED.
AS I WILL DO NOW BY KILLING YOU.
I THINK NOT!
HO, SPACE DOGS! SEPARATE THE GOOD'UNS FROM THE BAD'UNS AND SEND THE BAD'UNS TO WHATEVER HELL YE LIKE! 'TIS PAYBACK TIME!

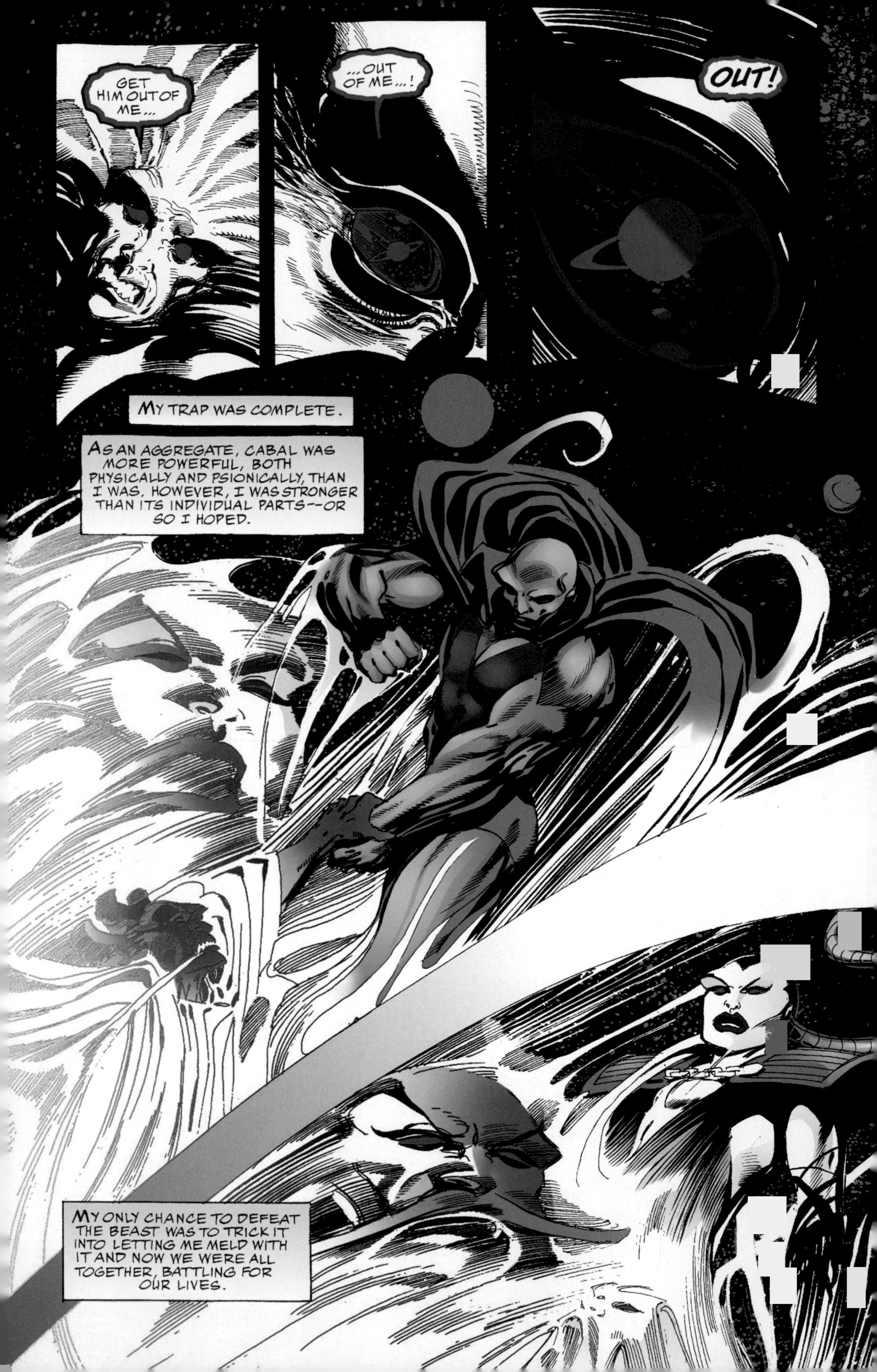
GET HIM OUT OF ME...
...OUT OF ME...!
OUT!
MY TRAP WAS COMPLETE.
AS AN AGGREGATE, CABAL WAS MORE POWERFUL, BOTH PHYSICALLY AND PSIONICALLY, THAN I WAS. HOWEVER, I WAS STRONGER THAN ITS INDIVIDUAL PARTS--OR SO I HOPED.
MY ONLY CHANCE TO DEFEAT THE BEAST WAS TO TRICK IT INTO LETTING ME MELD WITH IT AND NOW WE WERE ALL TOGETHER, BATTLING FOR OUR LIVES.

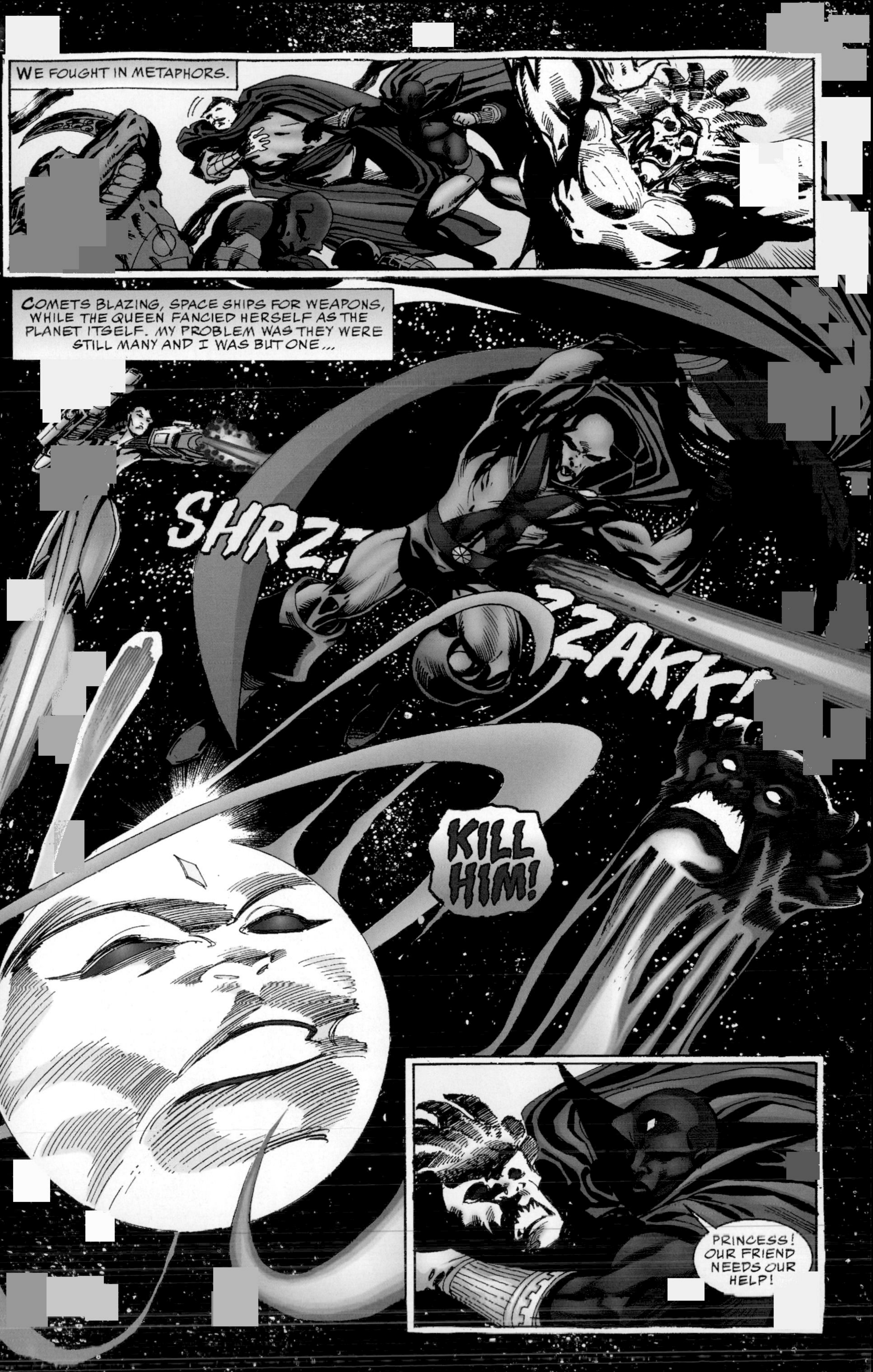
WE FOUGHT IN METAPHORS.
COMETS BLAZING, SPACE SHIPS FOR WEAPONS, WHILE THE QUEEN FANCIED HERSELF AS THE PLANET ITSELF. MY PROBLEM WAS THEY WERE STILL MANY AND I WAS BUT ONE...
SHRZZ
ZZAKK!
KILL HIM!
PRINCESS! OUR FRIEND NEEDS OUR HELP!

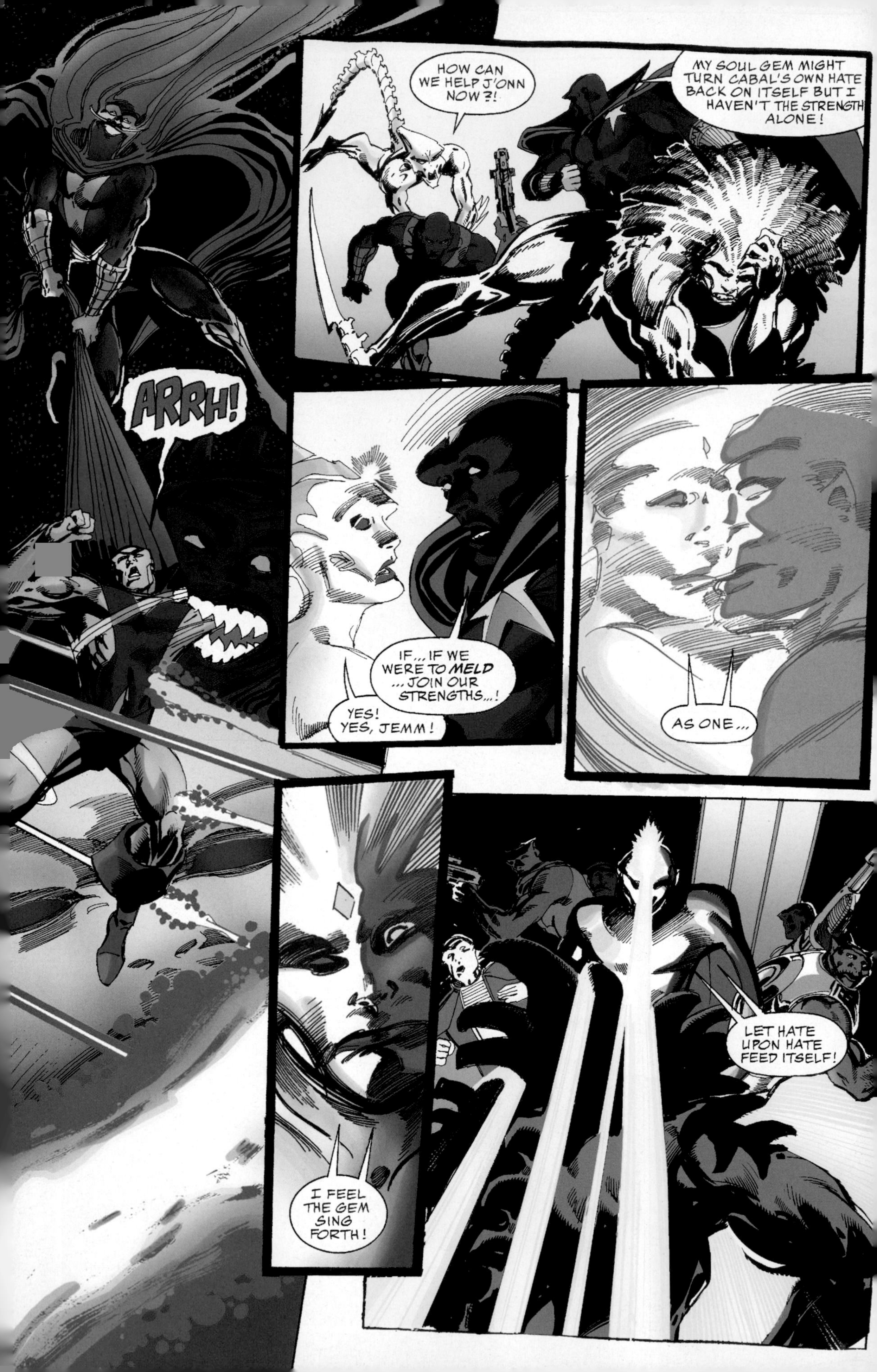
ARRH!
HOW CAN WE HELP J'ONN NOW?!
MY SOUL GEM MIGHT TURN CABAL'S OWN HATE BACK ON ITSELF BUT I HAVEN'T THE STRENGTH ALONE!
IF... IF WE WERE TO MELD ...JOIN OUR STRENGTHS...!
YES! YES, JEMM!
AS ONE...
I FEEL THE GEM SING FORTH!
LET HATE UPON HATE FEED ITSELF!

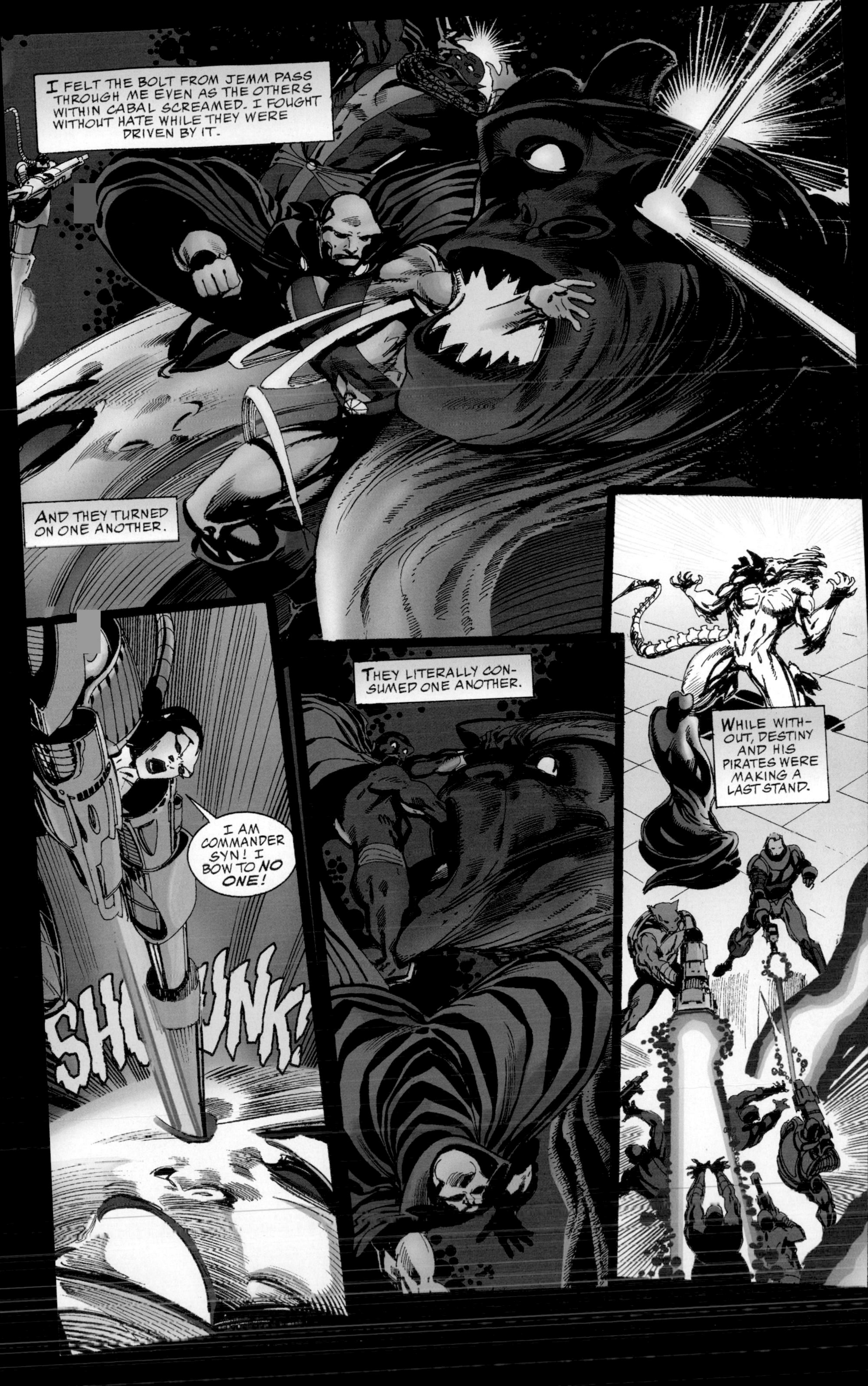
I FELT THE BOLT FROM JEMM PASS THROUGH ME EVEN AS THE OTHERS WITHIN CABAL SCREAMED. I FOUGHT WITHOUT HATE WHILE THEY WERE DRIVEN BY IT.
AND THEY TURNED ON ONE ANOTHER.
I AM COMMANDER SYN! I BOW TO NO ONE!
SHUNK!
THEY LITERALLY CON-SUMED ONE ANOTHER.
WHILE WITH-OUT, DESTINY AND HIS PIRATES WERE MAKING A LAST STAND.

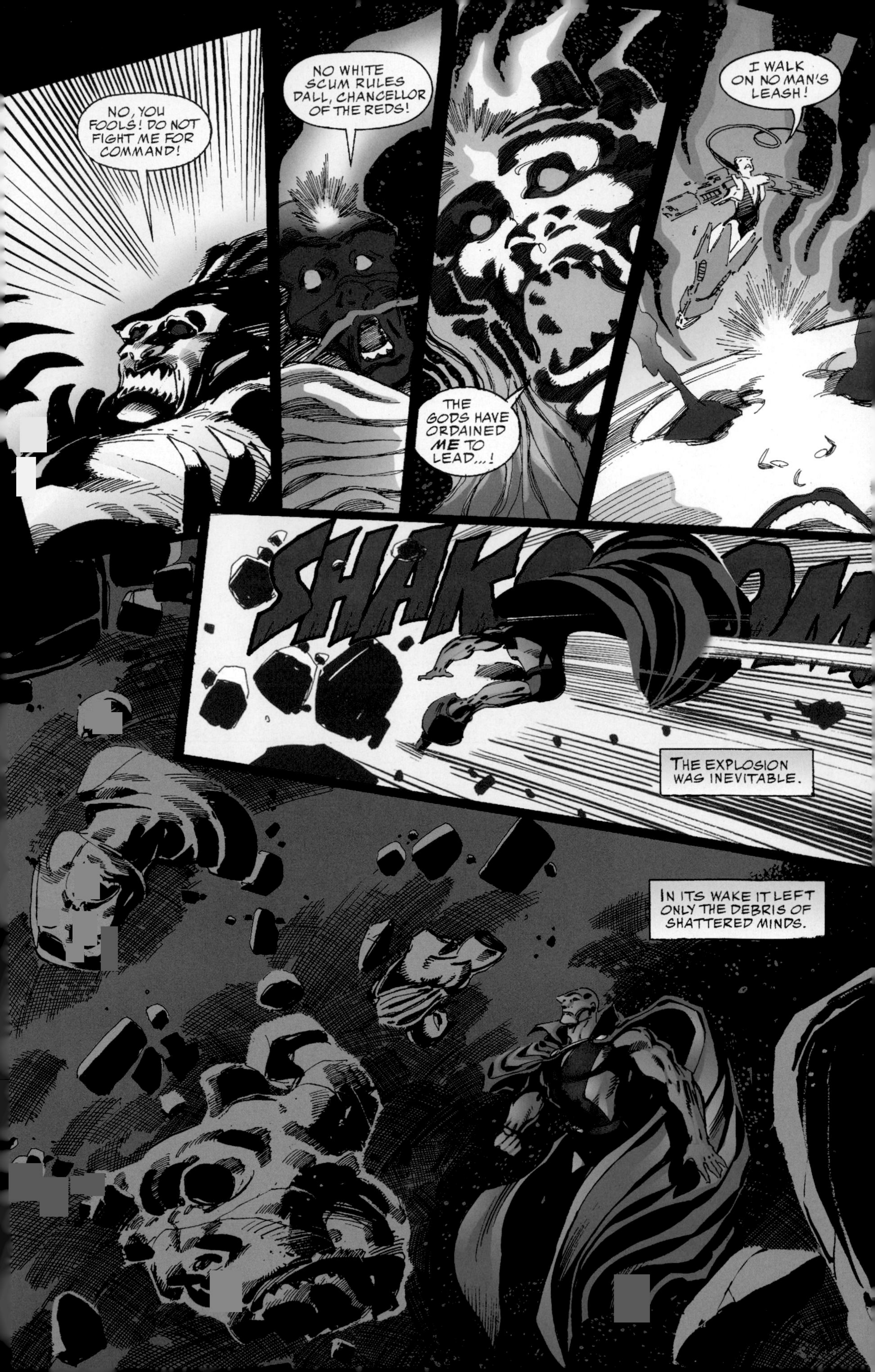
NO, YOU FOOLS! DO NOT FIGHT ME FOR COMMAND!
NO WHITE SCUM RULES DALL, CHANCELLOR OF THE REDS!
THE GODS HAVE ORDAINED ME TO LEAD...!
I WALK ON NO MAN'S LEASH!
SHAK
THE EXPLOSION WAS INEVITABLE.
IN ITS WAKE IT LEFT ONLY THE DEBRIS OF SHATTERED MINDS.

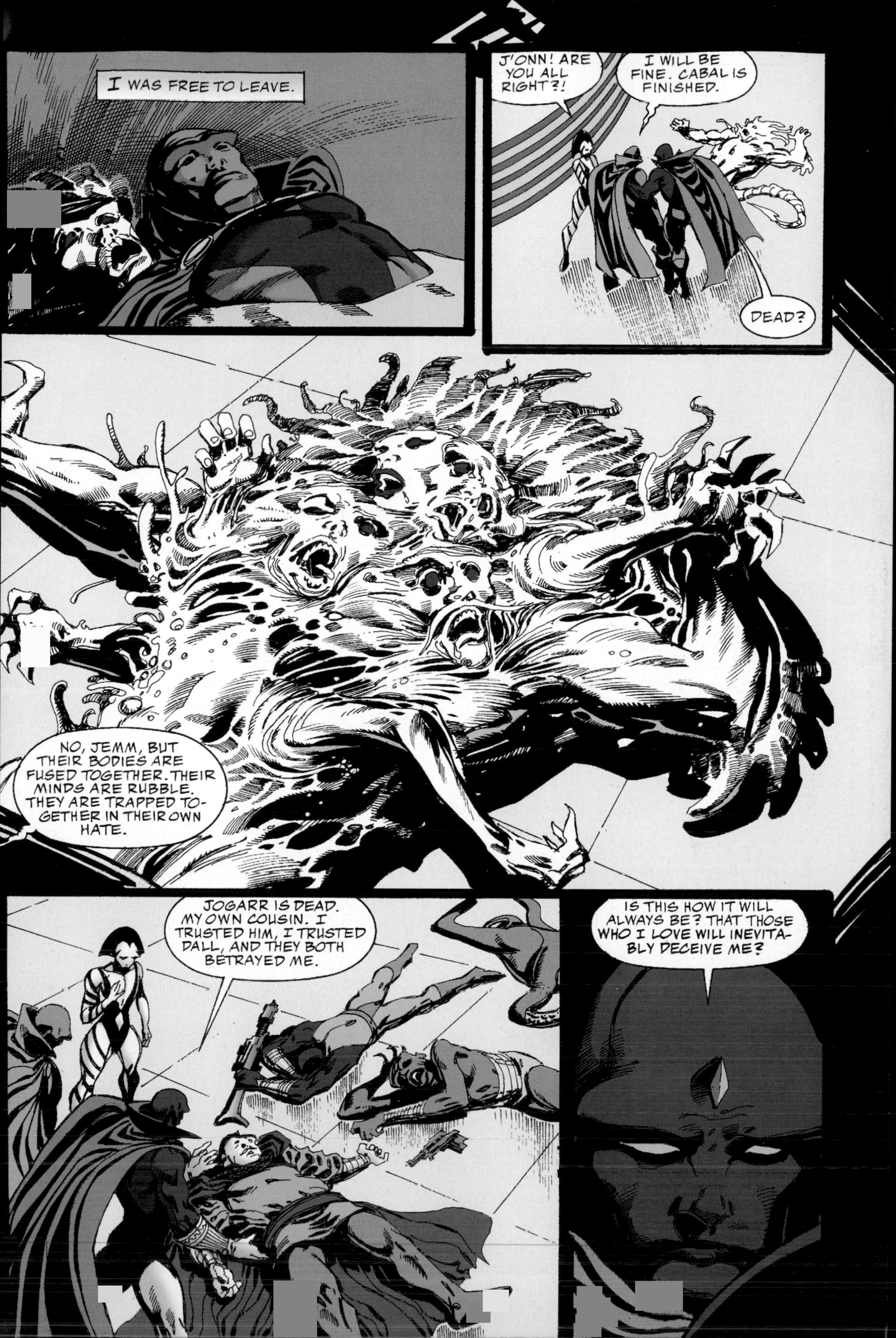

I WAS FREE TO LEAVE.
J'ONN! ARE YOU ALL RIGHT?!
I WILL BE FINE. CABAL IS FINISHED.
DEAD?
NO, JEMM, BUT THEIR BODIES ARE FUSED TOGETHER. THEIR MINDS ARE RUBBLE. THEY ARE TRAPPED TOGETHER IN THEIR OWN HATE.
JOGARR IS DEAD. MY OWN COUSIN. I TRUSTED HIM, I TRUSTED DALL, AND THEY BOTH BETRAYED ME.
IS THIS HOW IT WILL ALWAYS BE? THAT THOSE WHO I LOVE WILL INEVITABLY DECEIVE ME?

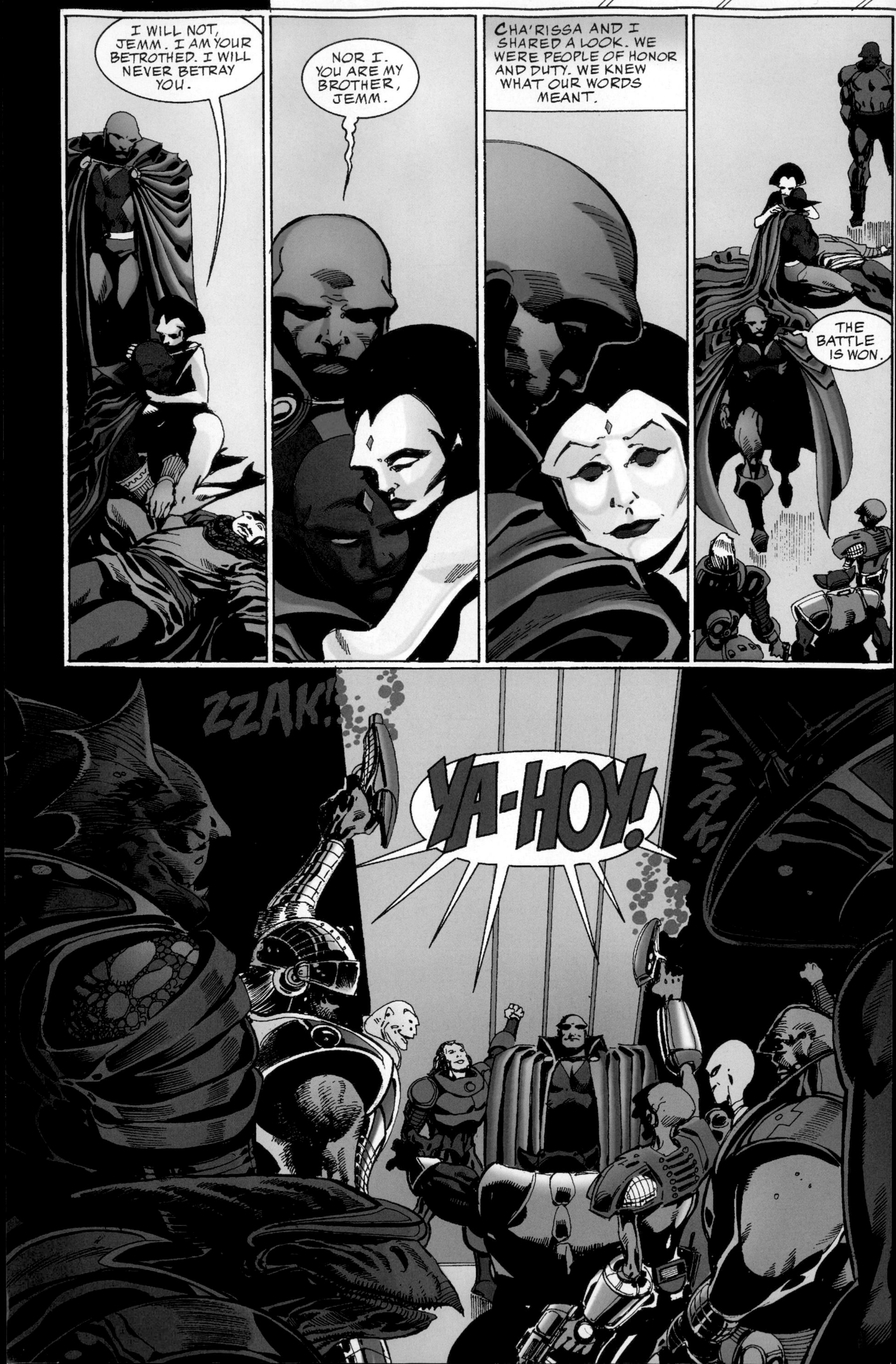
I WILL NOT, JEMM. I AM YOUR BETROTHED. I WILL NEVER BETRAY YOU.
NOR I. YOU ARE MY BROTHER, JEMM.
CHA'RISSA AND I SHARED A LOOK. WE WERE PEOPLE OF HONOR AND DUTY. WE KNEW WHAT OUR WORDS MEANT.
THE BATTLE IS WON.
ZZAK!
YA-HOY!
ZZAK!

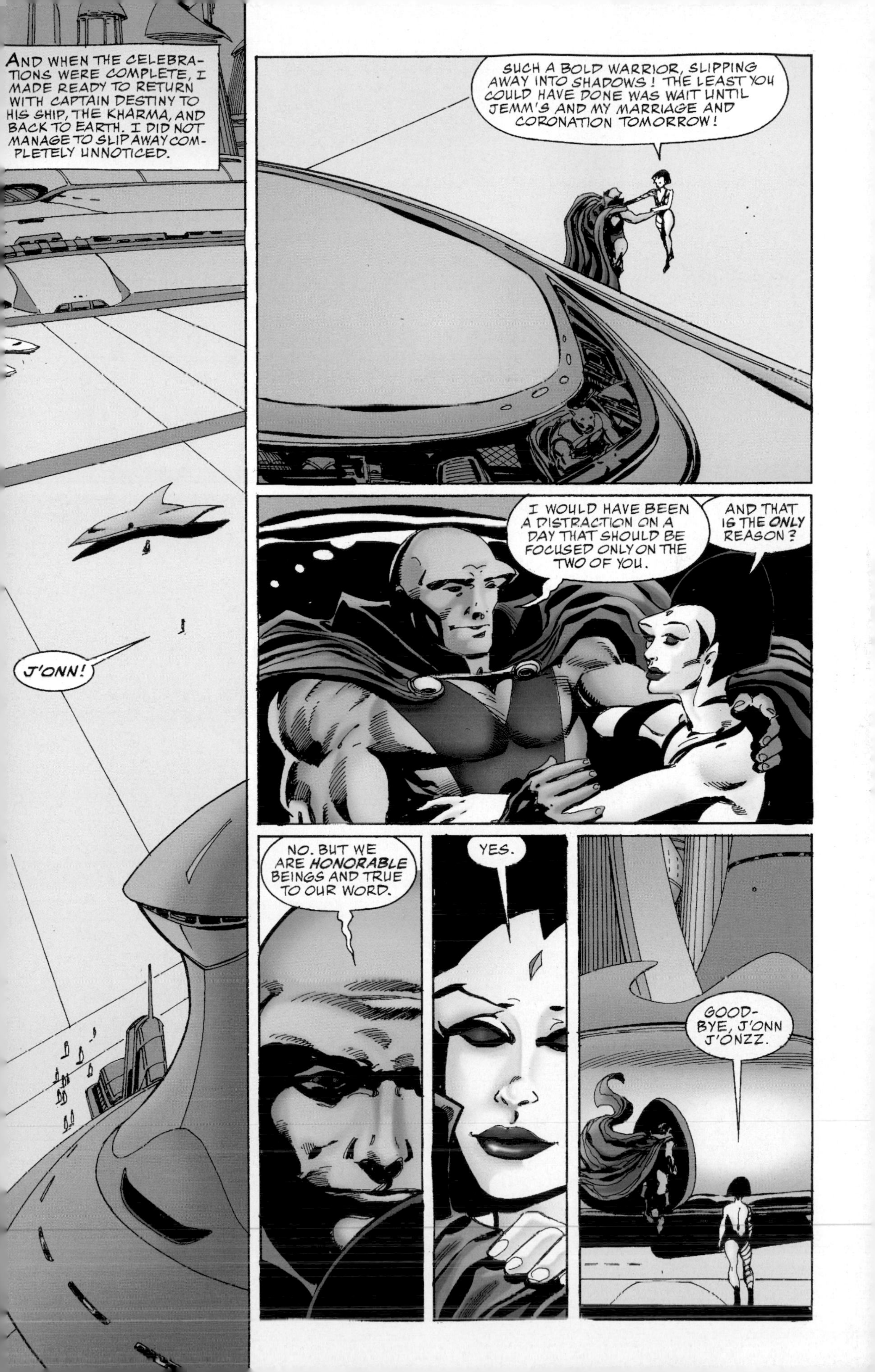

AND WHEN THE CELEBRATIONS WERE COMPLETE, I MADE READY TO RETURN WITH CAPTAIN DESTINY TO HIS SHIP, THE KHARMA, AND BACK TO EARTH. I DID NOT MANAGE TO SLIP AWAY COMPLETELY UNNOTICED.
J'ONN!
SUCH A BOLD WARRIOR, SLIPPING AWAY INTO SHADOWS! THE LEAST YOU COULD HAVE DONE WAS WAIT UNTIL JEMM'S AND MY MARRIAGE AND CORONATION TOMORROW!
I WOULD HAVE BEEN A DISTRACTION ON A DAY THAT SHOULD BE FOCUSED ONLY ON THE TWO OF YOU.
AND THAT IS THE ONLY REASON?
NO. BUT WE ARE HONORABLE BEINGS AND TRUE TO OUR WORD.
YES.
GOOD-BYE, J'ONN J'ONZZ.

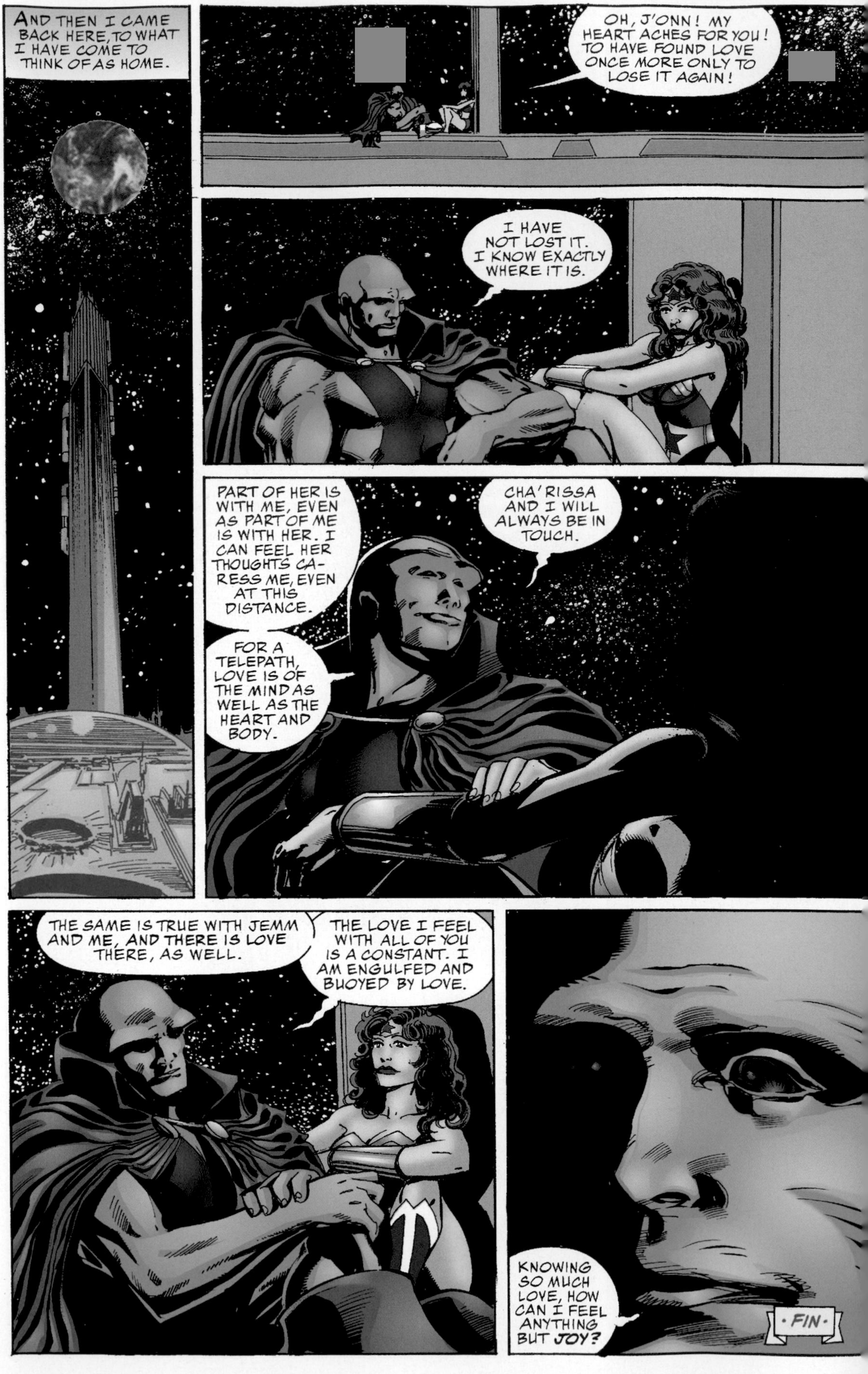
AND THEN I CAME BACK HERE, TO WHAT I HAVE COME TO THINK OF AS HOME.
OH, J'ONN! MY HEART ACHES FOR YOU! TO HAVE FOUND LOVE ONCE MORE ONLY TO LOSE IT AGAIN!
I HAVE NOT LOST IT. I KNOW EXACTLY WHERE IT IS.
CHA'RISSA AND I WILL ALWAYS BE IN TOUCH.
PART OF HER IS WITH ME, EVEN AS PART OF ME IS WITH HER. I CAN FEEL HER THOUGHTS CA-RESS ME, EVEN AT THIS DISTANCE.
FOR A TELEPATH, LOVE IS OF THE MIND AS WELL AS THE HEART AND BODY.
THE SAME IS TRUE WITH JEMM AND ME, AND THERE IS LOVE THERE, AS WELL.
THE LOVE I FEEL WITH ALL OF YOU IS A CONSTANT. I AM ENGULFED AND BUOYED BY LOVE.
KNOWING SO MUCH LOVE, HOW CAN I FEEL ANYTHING BUT JOY?
·FIN·

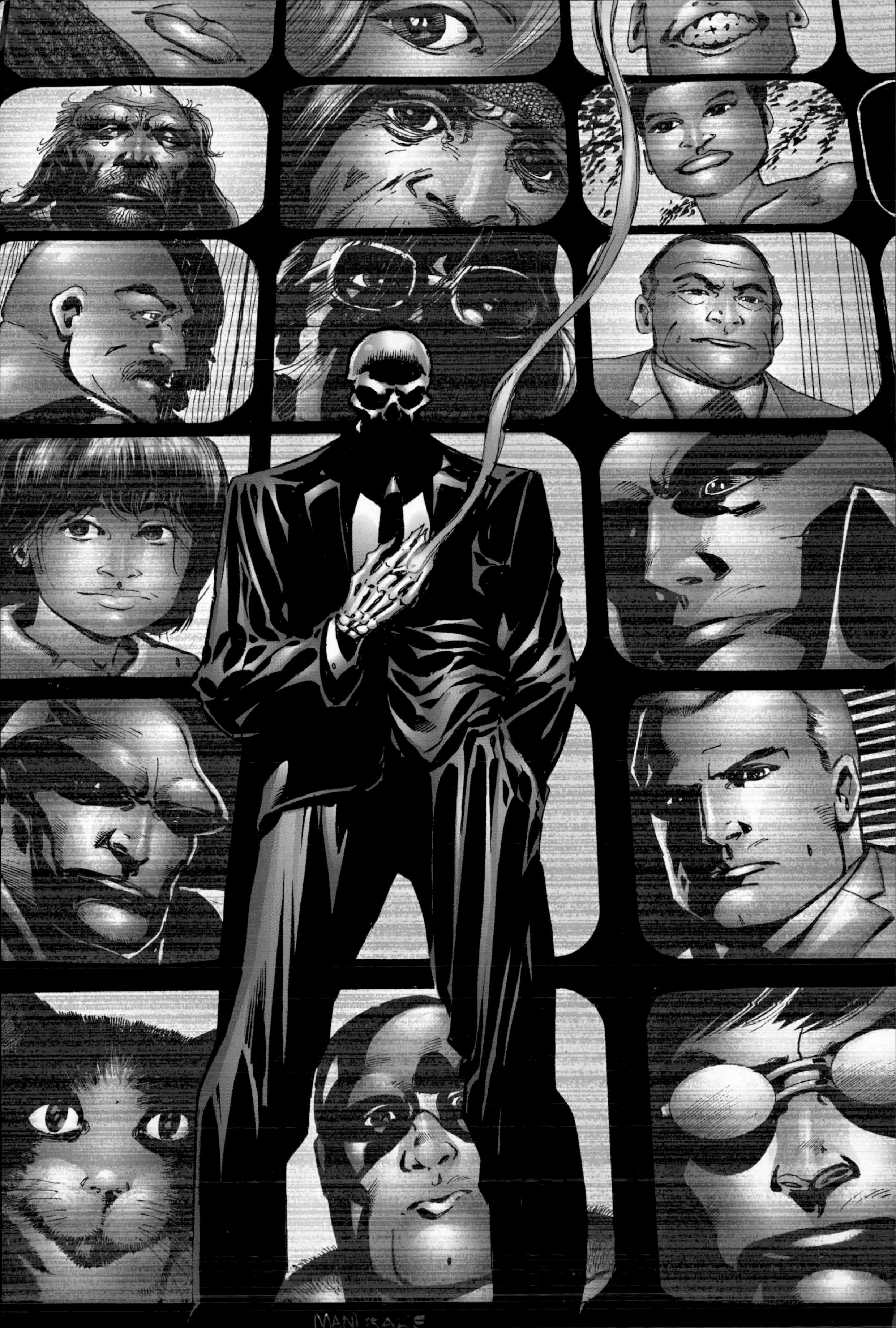

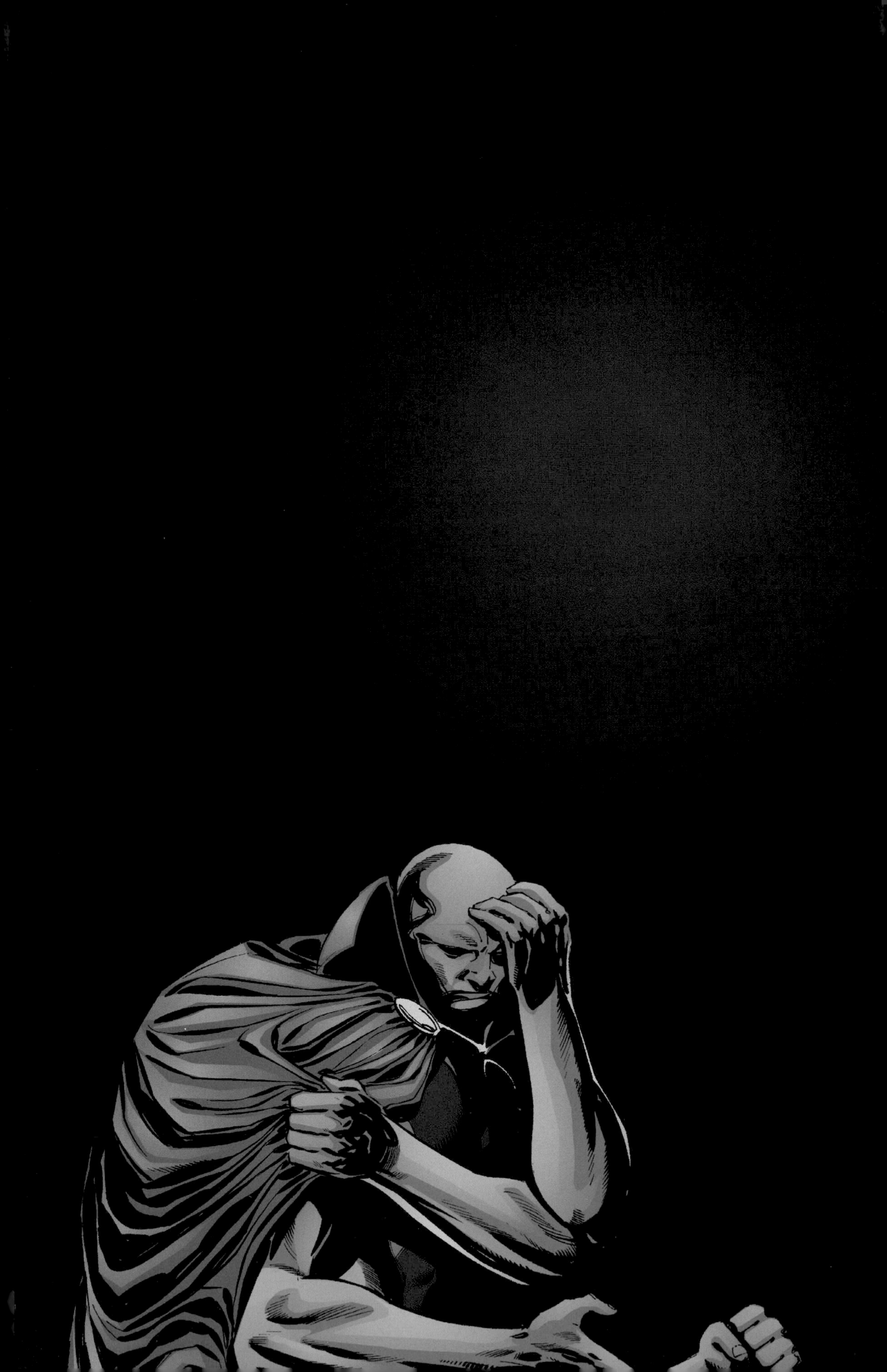

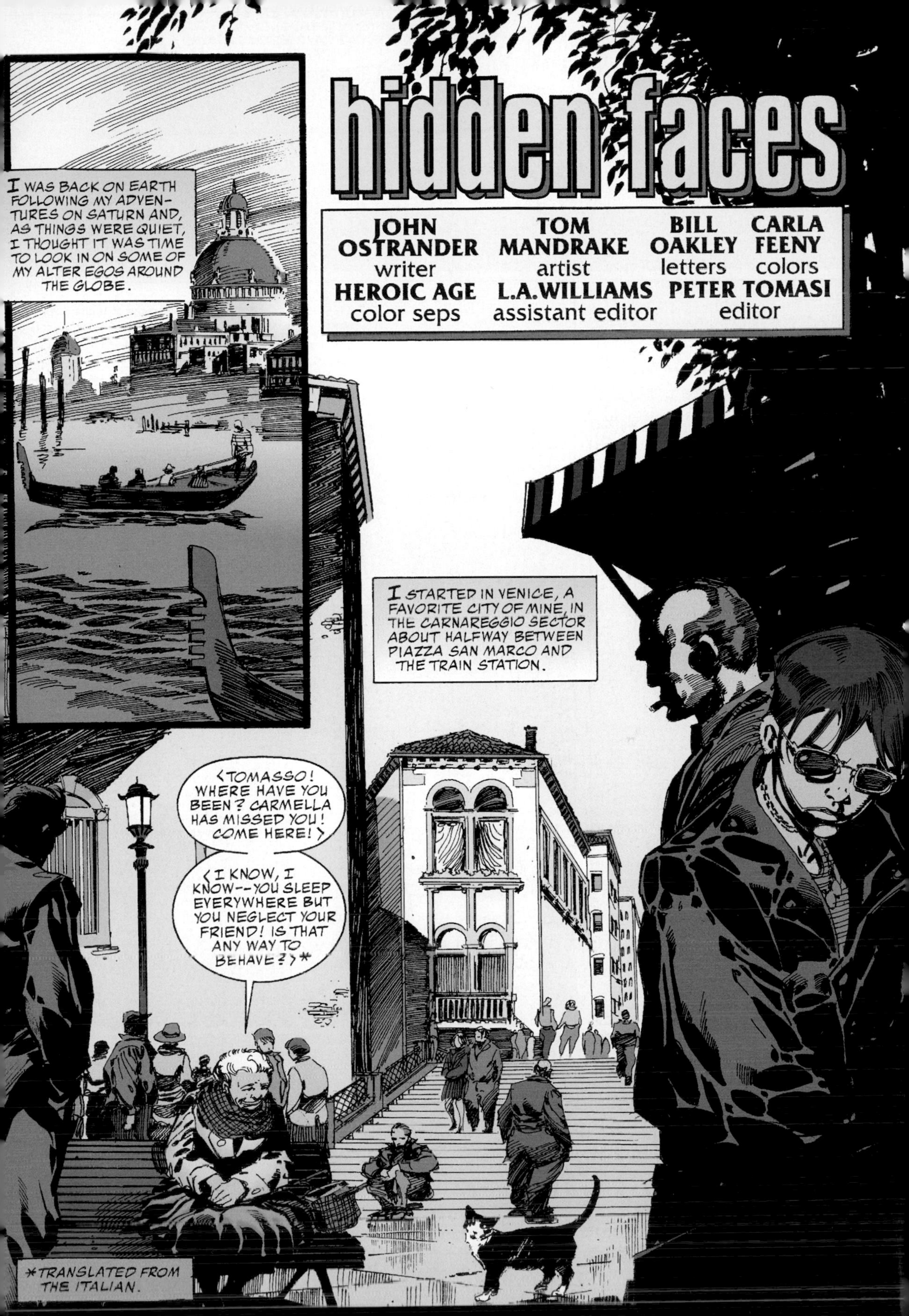

hidden faces
JOHN OSTRANDER writer
TOM MANDRAKE artist
BILL OAKLEY letters
CARLA FEENY colors
HEROIC AGE color seps
L.A.WILLIAMS assistant editor
PETER TOMASI editor
I WAS BACK ON EARTH FOLLOWING MY ADVENTURES ON SATURN AND, AS THINGS WERE QUIET, I THOUGHT IT WAS TIME TO LOOK IN ON SOME OF MY ALTER EGOS AROUND THE GLOBE.
I STARTED IN VENICE, A FAVORITE CITY OF MINE, IN THE CARNAREGGIO SECTOR ABOUT HALFWAY BETWEEN PIAZZA SAN MARCO AND THE TRAIN STATION.
<TOMASSO! WHERE HAVE YOU BEEN? CARMELLA HAS MISSED YOU! COME HERE!>
<I KNOW, I KNOW--YOU SLEEP EVERYWHERE BUT YOU NEGLECT YOUR FRIEND! IS THAT ANY WAY TO BEHAVE?>*
*TRANSLATED FROM THE ITALIAN.

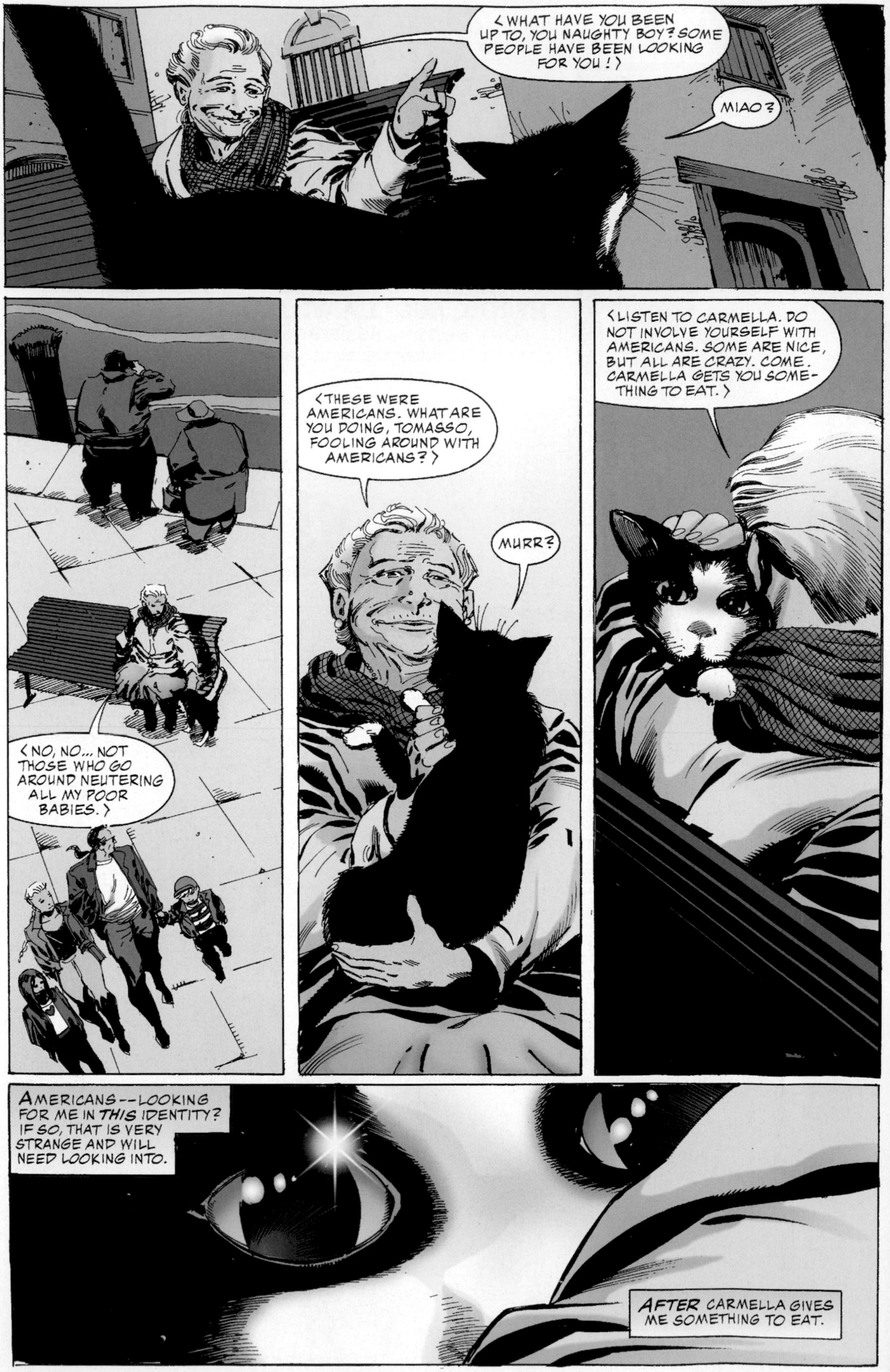
<WHAT HAVE YOU BEEN UP TO, YOU NAUGHTY BOY? SOME PEOPLE HAVE BEEN LOOKING FOR YOU!>
MIAO?
<NO, NO... NOT THOSE WHO GO AROUND NEUTERING ALL MY POOR BABIES.>
<THESE WERE AMERICANS. WHAT ARE YOU DOING, TOMASSO, FOOLING AROUND WITH AMERICANS?>
MURR?
<LISTEN TO CARMELLA. DO NOT INVOLVE YOURSELF WITH AMERICANS. SOME ARE NICE, BUT ALL ARE CRAZY. COME. CARMELLA GETS YOU SOMETHING TO EAT.>
AMERICANS--LOOKING FOR ME IN *THIS* IDENTITY? IF SO, THAT IS VERY STRANGE AND WILL NEED LOOKING INTO.
AFTER CARMELLA GIVES ME SOMETHING TO EAT.

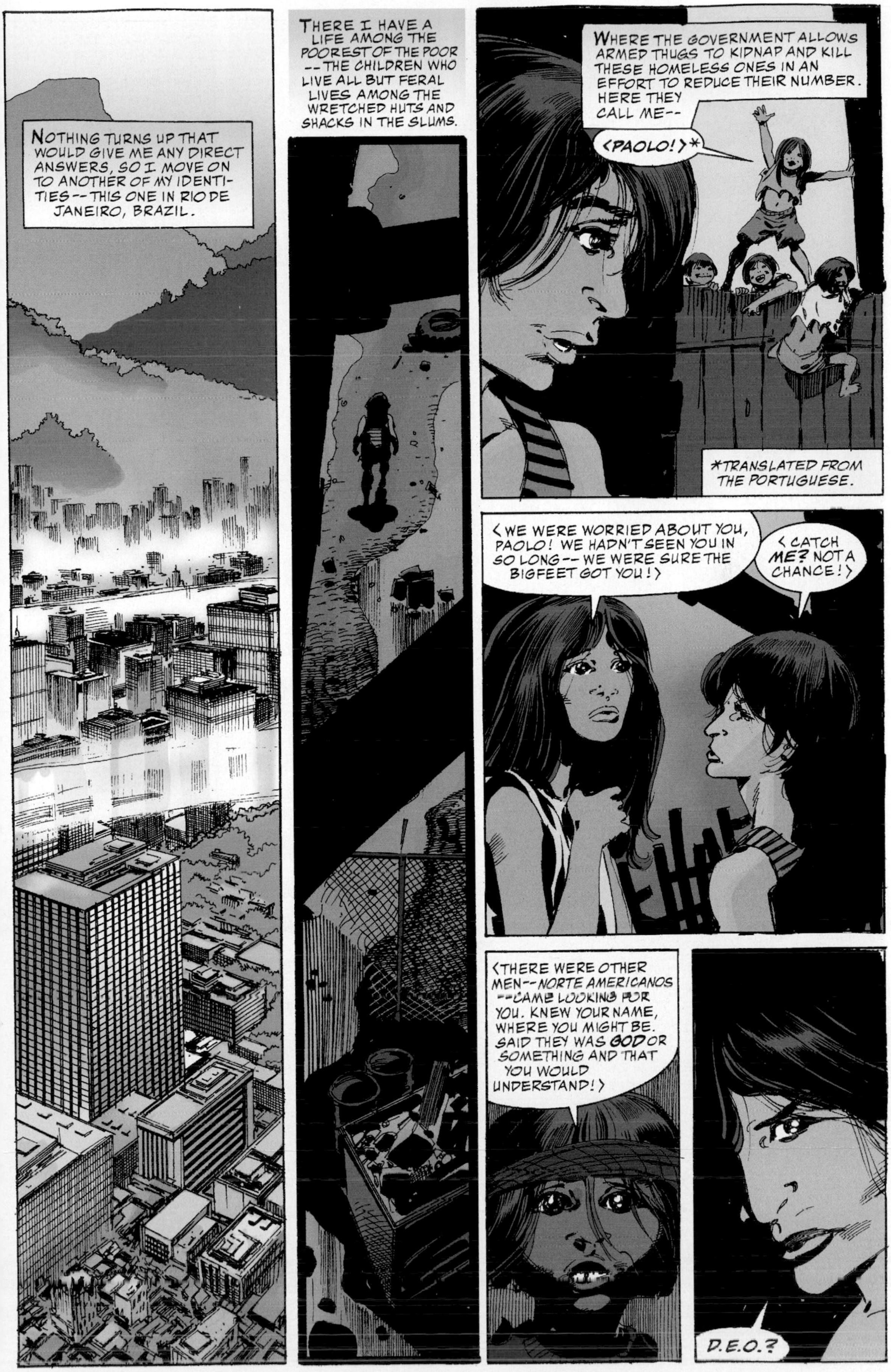
NOTHING TURNS UP THAT WOULD GIVE ME ANY DIRECT ANSWERS, SO I MOVE ON TO ANOTHER OF MY IDENTITIES--THIS ONE IN RIO DE JANEIRO, BRAZIL.
THERE I HAVE A LIFE AMONG THE POOREST OF THE POOR --THE CHILDREN WHO LIVE ALL BUT FERAL LIVES AMONG THE WRETCHED HUTS AND SHACKS IN THE SLUMS.
WHERE THE GOVERNMENT ALLOWS ARMED THUGS TO KIDNAP AND KILL THESE HOMELESS ONES IN AN EFFORT TO REDUCE THEIR NUMBER. HERE THEY CALL ME--
<PAOLO!>*
*TRANSLATED FROM THE PORTUGUESE.
<WE WERE WORRIED ABOUT YOU, PAOLO! WE HADN'T SEEN YOU IN SO LONG--WE WERE SURE THE BIGFEET GOT YOU!>
<CATCH ME? NOT A CHANCE!>
<THERE WERE OTHER MEN--NORTE AMERICANOS--CAME LOOKING FOR YOU. KNEW YOUR NAME, WHERE YOU MIGHT BE. SAID THEY WAS GOD OR SOMETHING AND THAT YOU WOULD UNDERSTAND!>
D.E.O.?

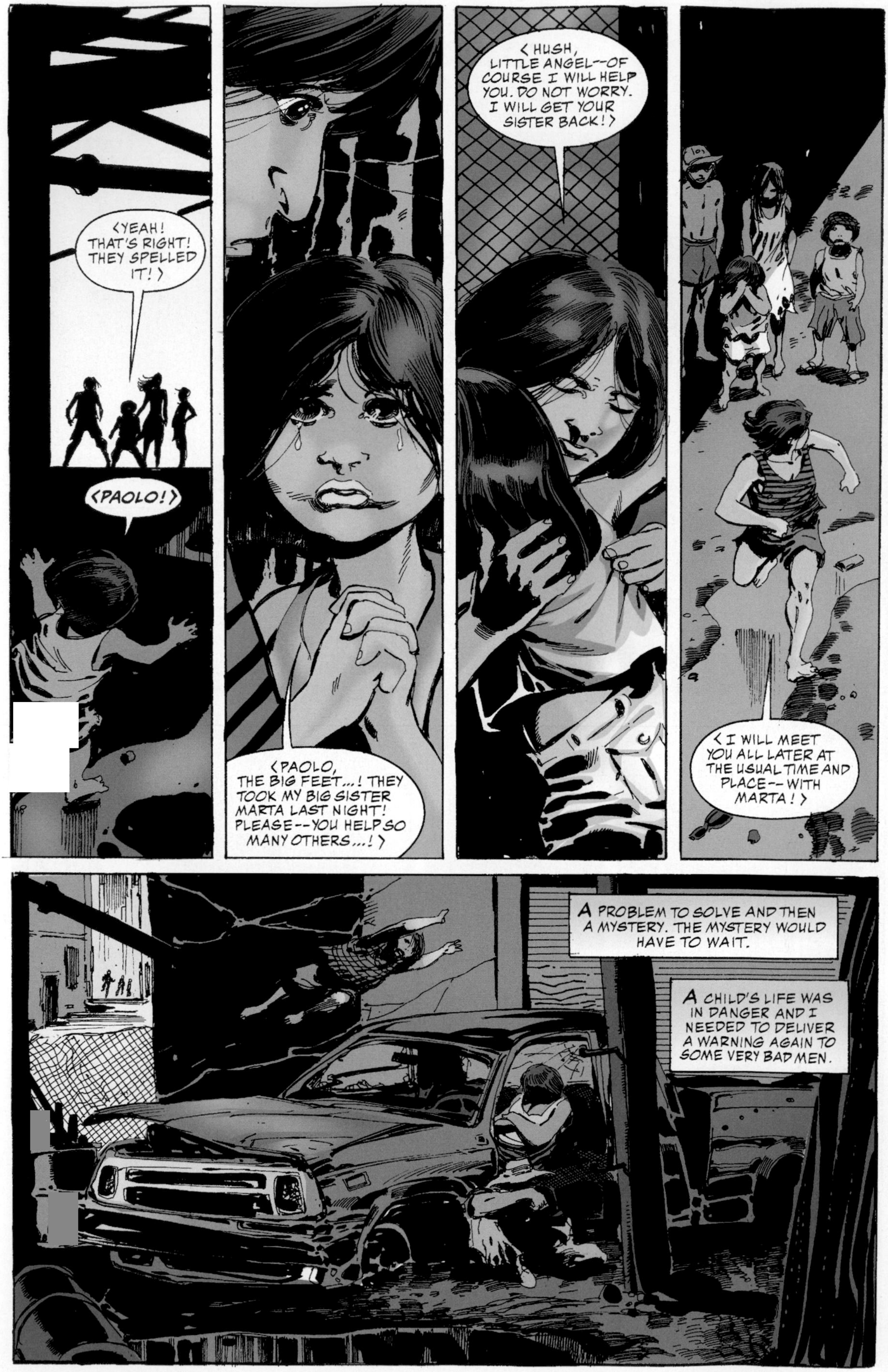

<YEAH! THAT'S RIGHT! THEY SPELLED IT!>
<PAOLO!>
<PAOLO, THE BIG FEET...! THEY TOOK MY BIG SISTER MARTA LAST NIGHT! PLEASE--YOU HELP SO MANY OTHERS...!>
<HUSH, LITTLE ANGEL--OF COURSE I WILL HELP YOU. DO NOT WORRY. I WILL GET YOUR SISTER BACK!>
<I WILL MEET YOU ALL LATER AT THE USUAL TIME AND PLACE--WITH MARTA!>
A PROBLEM TO SOLVE AND THEN A MYSTERY. THE MYSTERY WOULD HAVE TO WAIT.
A CHILD'S LIFE WAS IN DANGER AND I NEEDED TO DELIVER A WARNING AGAIN TO SOME VERY BAD MEN.

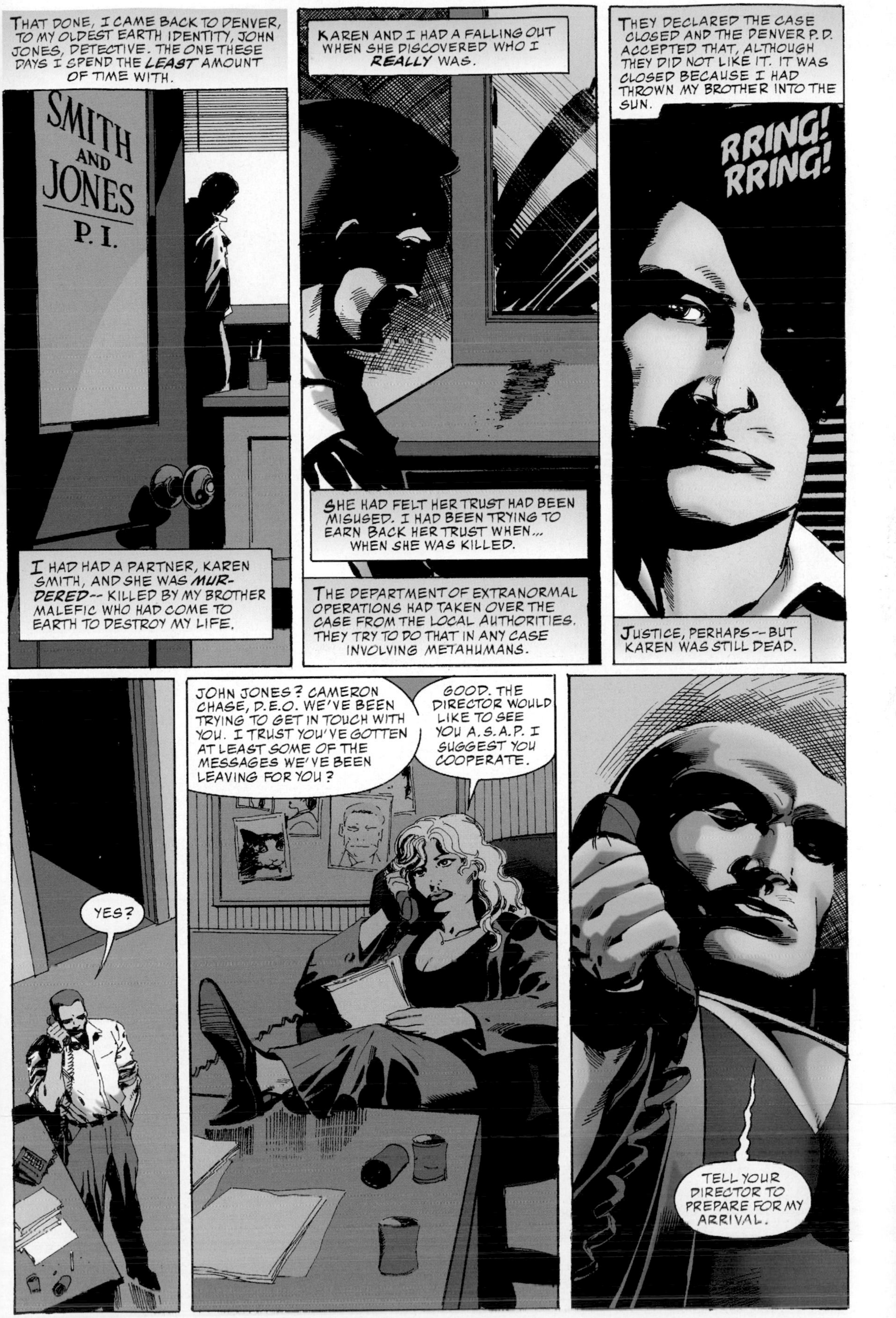
THAT DONE, I CAME BACK TO DENVER, TO MY OLDEST EARTH IDENTITY, JOHN JONES, DETECTIVE. THE ONE THESE DAYS I SPEND THE LEAST AMOUNT OF TIME WITH.
SMITH AND JONES P. I.
I HAD HAD A PARTNER, KAREN SMITH, AND SHE WAS MURDERED-- KILLED BY MY BROTHER MALEFIC WHO HAD COME TO EARTH TO DESTROY MY LIFE.
KAREN AND I HAD A FALLING OUT WHEN SHE DISCOVERED WHO I REALLY WAS.
SHE HAD FELT HER TRUST HAD BEEN MISUSED. I HAD BEEN TRYING TO EARN BACK HER TRUST WHEN... WHEN SHE WAS KILLED.
THE DEPARTMENT OF EXTRANORMAL OPERATIONS HAD TAKEN OVER THE CASE FROM THE LOCAL AUTHORITIES. THEY TRY TO DO THAT IN ANY CASE INVOLVING METAHUMANS.
THEY DECLARED THE CASE CLOSED AND THE DENVER P.D. ACCEPTED THAT, ALTHOUGH THEY DID NOT LIKE IT. IT WAS CLOSED BECAUSE I HAD THROWN MY BROTHER INTO THE SUN.
RRING! RRING!
JUSTICE, PERHAPS-- BUT KAREN WAS STILL DEAD.
YES?
JOHN JONES? CAMERON CHASE, D.E.O. WE'VE BEEN TRYING TO GET IN TOUCH WITH YOU. I TRUST YOU'VE GOTTEN AT LEAST SOME OF THE MESSAGES WE'VE BEEN LEAVING FOR YOU?
GOOD. THE DIRECTOR WOULD LIKE TO SEE YOU A.S.A.P. I SUGGEST YOU COOPERATE.
TELL YOUR DIRECTOR TO PREPARE FOR MY ARRIVAL.

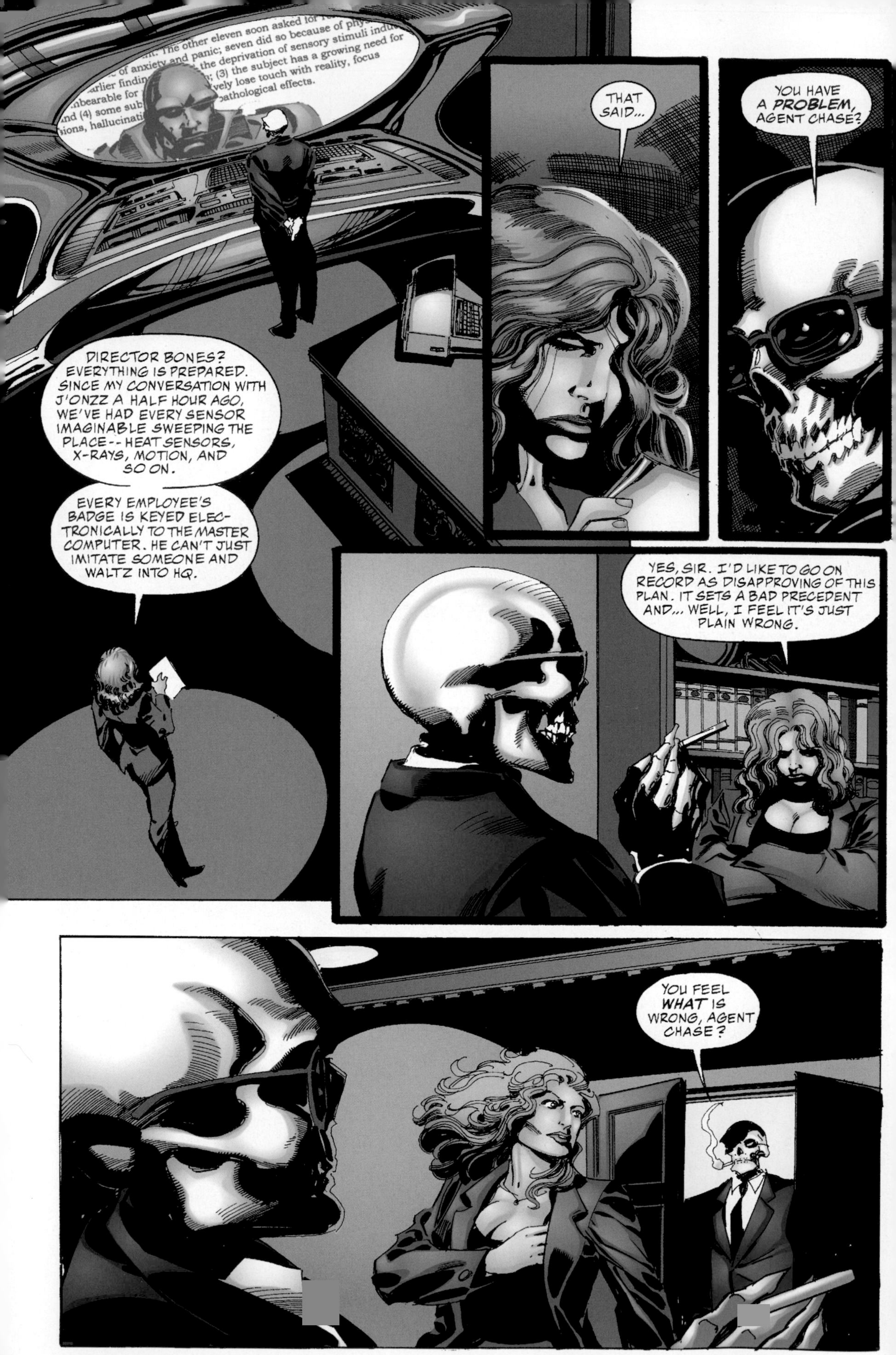
DIRECTOR BONES? EVERYTHING IS PREPARED. SINCE MY CONVERSATION WITH J'ONZZ A HALF HOUR AGO, WE'VE HAD EVERY SENSOR IMAGINABLE SWEEPING THE PLACE--HEAT SENSORS, X-RAYS, MOTION, AND SO ON.
EVERY EMPLOYEE'S BADGE IS KEYED ELEC-TRONICALLY TO THE MASTER COMPUTER. HE CAN'T JUST IMITATE SOMEONE AND WALTZ INTO HQ.
THAT SAID...
YOU HAVE A PROBLEM, AGENT CHASE?
YES, SIR. I'D LIKE TO GO ON RECORD AS DISAPPROVING OF THIS PLAN. IT SETS A BAD PRECEDENT AND... WELL, I FEEL IT'S JUST PLAIN WRONG.
YOU FEEL WHAT IS WRONG, AGENT CHASE?

FREEZE, J'ONZZ! I DON'T KNOW HOW YOU GOT PAST THE SENSORS...!

GOOD INSTINCTS. WRONG TARGET.

CHECK BEHIND YOU.

I ALSO APPLAUD YOUR INSTINCTS. YOUR MISGIVINGS ARE MOST INSTRUCTIVE.

I HAVE BEEN GOING OVER THE DIRECTOR'S FILES AND I CAN MAKE SOME PRETTY FAIR ASSUMPTIONS.

YOU WENT THROUGH MY OFFICE AND FOUND THE "PEACE OFFERING" I MEANT TO GIVE KAREN BEFORE SHE WAS KILLED. YOU HAVE CORRECTLY DEDUCED THEY ARE MY "ALTER EGOS."

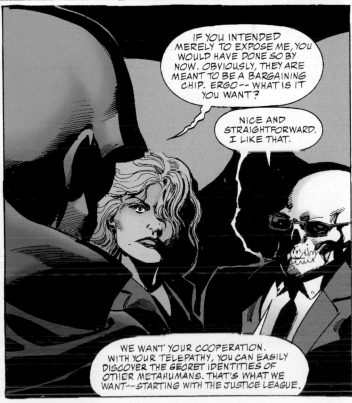

IF YOU INTENDED MERELY TO EXPOSE ME, YOU WOULD HAVE DONE SO BY NOW. OBVIOUSLY, THEY ARE MEANT TO BE A BARGAINING CHIP. ERGO-- WHAT IS IT YOU WANT?

NICE AND STRAIGHTFORWARD. I LIKE THAT.

WE WANT YOUR COOPERATION. WITH YOUR TELEPATHY, YOU CAN EASILY DISCOVER THE SECRET IDENTITIES OF OTHER METAHUMANS. THAT'S WHAT WE WANT--STARTING WITH THE JUSTICE LEAGUE.

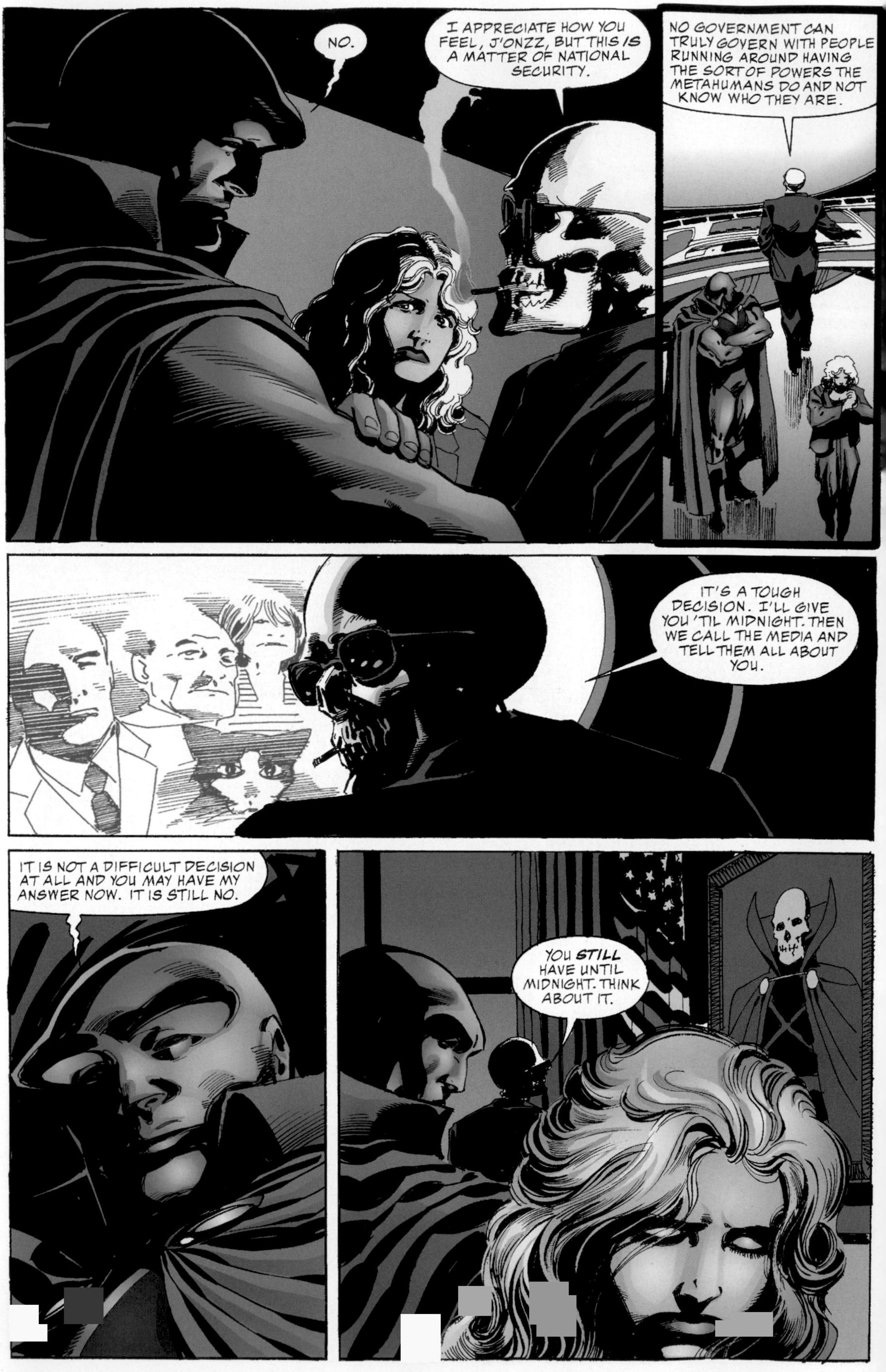
NO.
I APPRECIATE HOW YOU FEEL, J'ONZZ, BUT THIS IS A MATTER OF NATIONAL SECURITY.
NO GOVERNMENT CAN TRULY GOVERN WITH PEOPLE RUNNING AROUND HAVING THE SORT OF POWERS THE METAHUMANS DO AND NOT KNOW WHO THEY ARE.
IT'S A TOUGH DECISION. I'LL GIVE YOU 'TIL MIDNIGHT. THEN WE CALL THE MEDIA AND TELL THEM ALL ABOUT YOU.
IT IS NOT A DIFFICULT DECISION AT ALL AND YOU MAY HAVE MY ANSWER NOW. IT IS STILL NO.
YOU STILL HAVE UNTIL MIDNIGHT. THINK ABOUT IT.

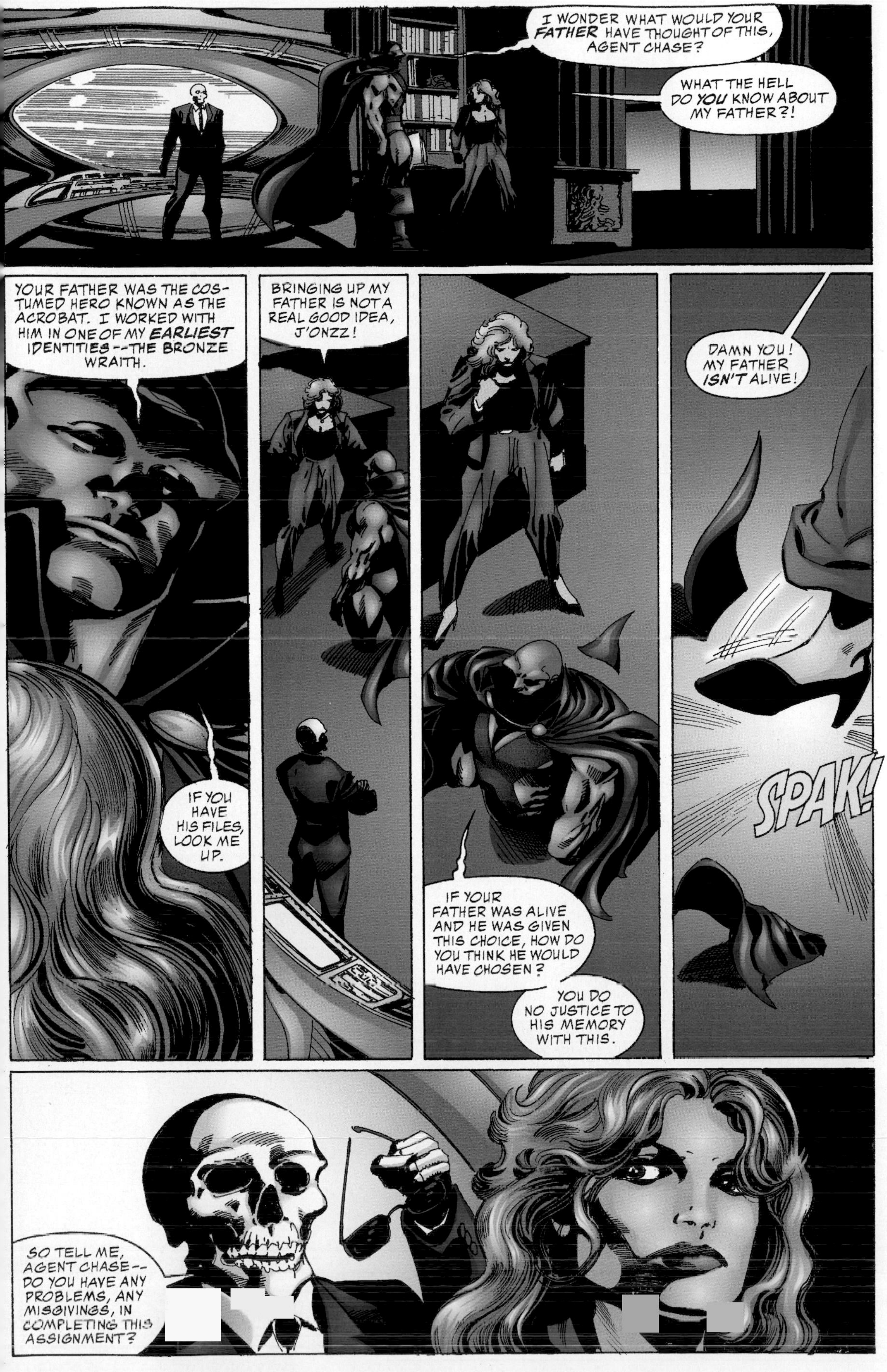
I WONDER WHAT WOULD YOUR FATHER HAVE THOUGHT OF THIS, AGENT CHASE?
WHAT THE HELL DO YOU KNOW ABOUT MY FATHER?!
YOUR FATHER WAS THE COSTUMED HERO KNOWN AS THE ACROBAT. I WORKED WITH HIM IN ONE OF MY EARLIEST IDENTITIES--THE BRONZE WRAITH.
IF YOU HAVE HIS FILES, LOOK ME UP.
BRINGING UP MY FATHER IS NOT A REAL GOOD IDEA, J'ONZZ!
IF YOUR FATHER WAS ALIVE AND HE WAS GIVEN THIS CHOICE, HOW DO YOU THINK HE WOULD HAVE CHOSEN?
YOU DO NO JUSTICE TO HIS MEMORY WITH THIS.
DAMN YOU! MY FATHER ISN'T ALIVE!
SPAK!
SO TELL ME, AGENT CHASE-- DO YOU HAVE ANY PROBLEMS, ANY MISGIVINGS, IN COMPLETING THIS ASSIGNMENT?

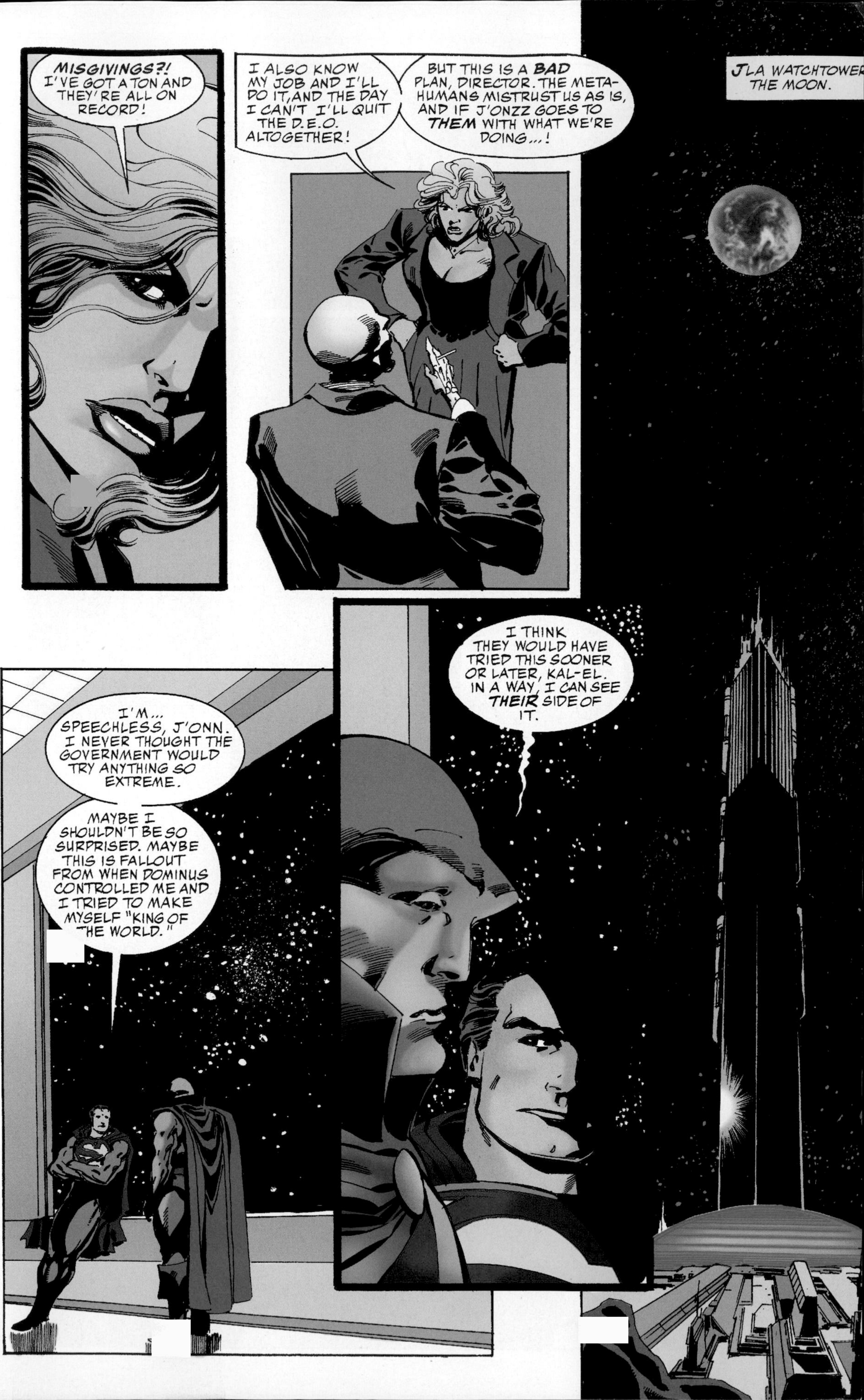
MISGIVINGS?! I'VE GOT A TON AND THEY'RE ALL ON RECORD!
I ALSO KNOW MY JOB AND I'LL DO IT, AND THE DAY I CAN'T I'LL QUIT THE D.E.O. ALTOGETHER!
BUT THIS IS A BAD PLAN, DIRECTOR. THE META-HUMANS MISTRUST US AS IS, AND IF J'ONZZ GOES TO THEM WITH WHAT WE'RE DOING...!
JLA WATCHTOWER THE MOON.
I'M... SPEECHLESS, J'ONN. I NEVER THOUGHT THE GOVERNMENT WOULD TRY ANYTHING SO EXTREME.
MAYBE I SHOULDN'T BE SO SURPRISED. MAYBE THIS IS FALLOUT FROM WHEN DOMINUS CONTROLLED ME AND I TRIED TO MAKE MYSELF "KING OF THE WORLD."
I THINK THEY WOULD HAVE TRIED THIS SOONER OR LATER, KAL-EL. IN A WAY, I CAN SEE THEIR SIDE OF IT.

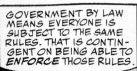

GOVERNMENT BY LAW MEANS EVERYONE IS SUBJECT TO THE SAME RULES. THAT IS CONTINGENT ON BEING ABLE TO *ENFORCE* THOSE RULES.

IF BEINGS SUCH AS WE DO NOT CHOOSE TO OBEY THE LAWS, HOW DO THEY ENFORCE THEM? AND IF THEY CANNOT, WHAT HAPPENS TO THE FORCE OF LAW?

YOU MAKE A... FRIGHTENINGLY FORCEFUL CASE FOR THE OTHER SIDE, J'ONN.

I TRAINED TO BE A PHILOSOPHER AS WELL AS A MANHUNTER. IT IS MY NATURE TO SEE AT LEAST TWO SIDES TO A QUESTION.

PERHAPS YOU COULD FIGHT FIRE WITH FIRE, J'ONN. PERHAPS YOU COULD USE YOUR TELEPATHY TO FIND OUT SOMETHING ABOUT THE D.E.O. THAT IT DOESN'T WANT KNOWN.

OR... MAYBE... CHANGE MR. BONES' MIND *FOR* HIM...?

THE THOUGHT HAS OCCURRED TO ME.

BUT THE FORMER WOULD MAKE ME AS WRONG MORALLY AS THE D.E.O. AND THE LATTER WOULD JUSTIFY THEIR FEARS OF ME.

I HAVE CHOSEN A PATH THAT I MAY WALK WITH HONOR.

NO MATTER THE COST, I WILL NOT STRAY FROM IT.

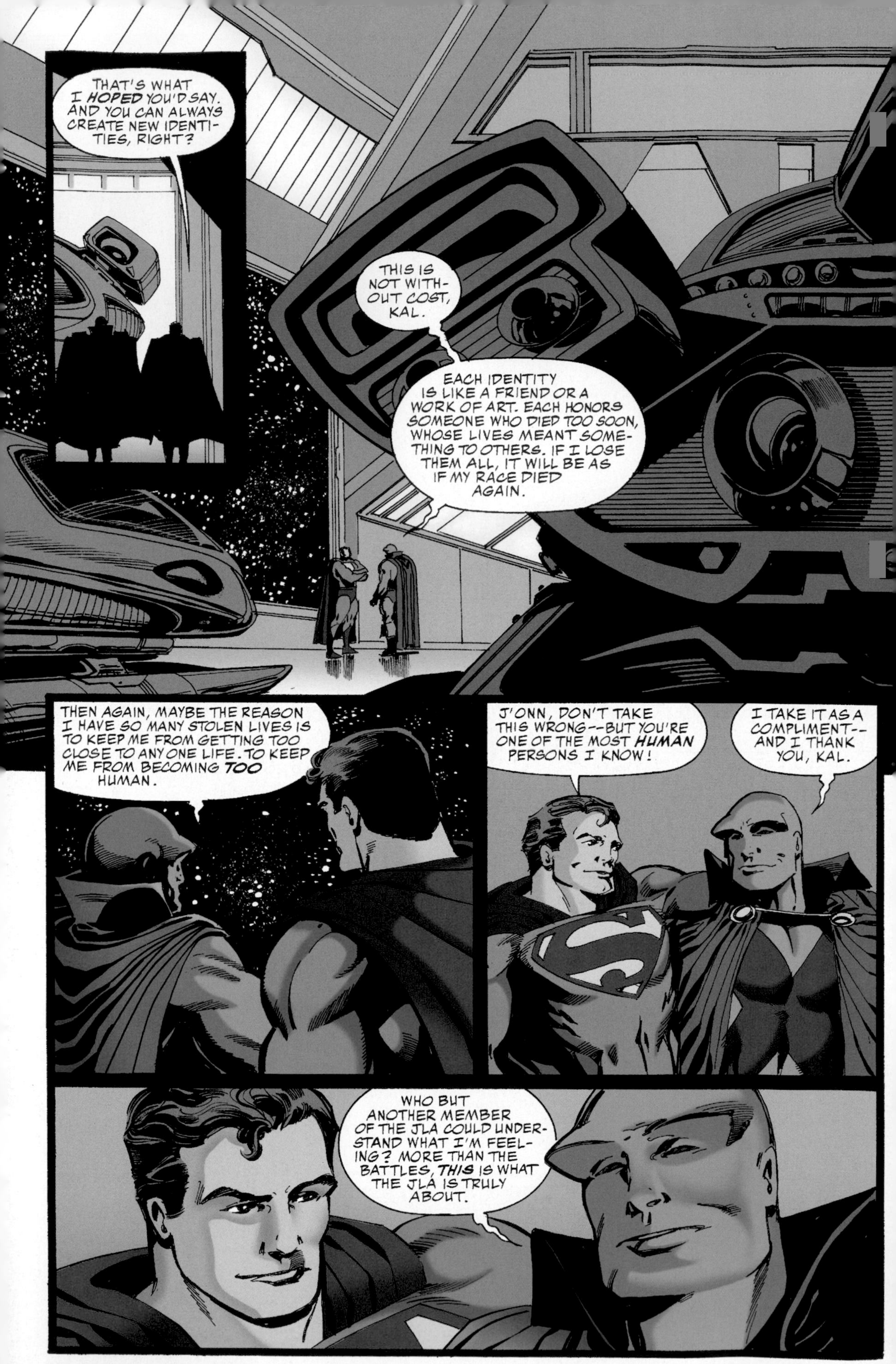
THAT'S WHAT I HOPED YOU'D SAY. AND YOU CAN ALWAYS CREATE NEW IDENTITIES, RIGHT?
THIS IS NOT WITHOUT COST, KAL.
EACH IDENTITY IS LIKE A FRIEND OR A WORK OF ART. EACH HONORS SOMEONE WHO DIED TOO SOON, WHOSE LIVES MEANT SOMETHING TO OTHERS. IF I LOSE THEM ALL, IT WILL BE AS IF MY RACE DIED AGAIN.
THEN AGAIN, MAYBE THE REASON I HAVE SO MANY STOLEN LIVES IS TO KEEP ME FROM GETTING TOO CLOSE TO ANY ONE LIFE. TO KEEP ME FROM BECOMING TOO HUMAN.
J'ONN, DON'T TAKE THIS WRONG--BUT YOU'RE ONE OF THE MOST HUMAN PERSONS I KNOW!
I TAKE IT AS A COMPLIMENT--AND I THANK YOU, KAL.
WHO BUT ANOTHER MEMBER OF THE JLA COULD UNDERSTAND WHAT I'M FEELING? MORE THAN THE BATTLES, THIS IS WHAT THE JLA IS TRULY ABOUT.

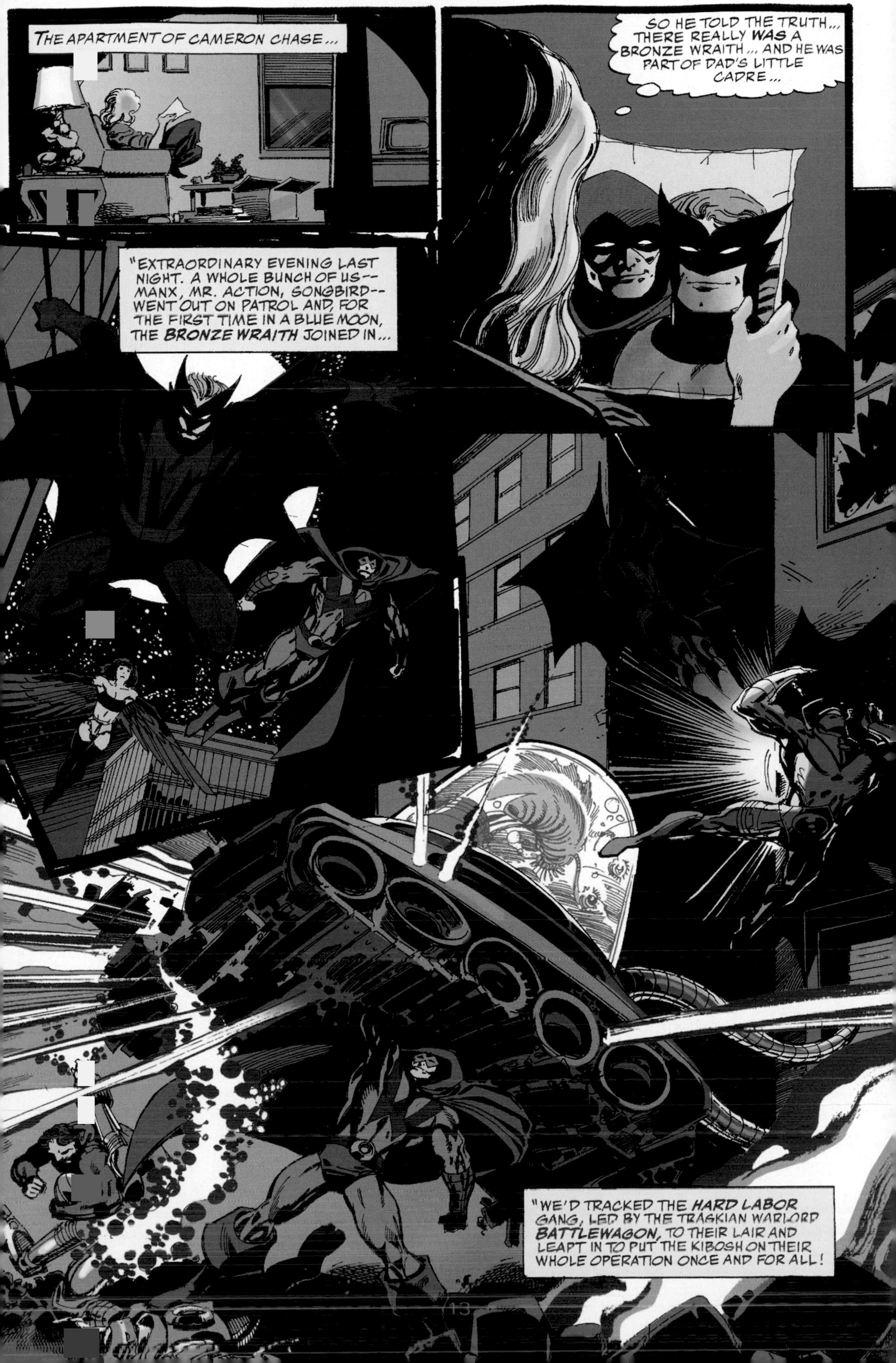
THE APARTMENT OF CAMERON CHASE...
SO HE TOLD THE TRUTH... THERE REALLY WAS A BRONZE WRAITH... AND HE WAS PART OF DAD'S LITTLE CADRE...
"EXTRAORDINARY EVENING LAST NIGHT. A WHOLE BUNCH OF US-- MANX, MR. ACTION, SONGBIRD-- WENT OUT ON PATROL AND, FOR THE FIRST TIME IN A BLUE MOON, THE BRONZE WRAITH JOINED IN...
"WE'D TRACKED THE HARD LABOR GANG, LED BY THE TRAGKIAN WARLORD BATTLEWAGON, TO THEIR LAIR AND LEAPT IN TO PUT THE KIBOSH ON THEIR WHOLE OPERATION ONCE AND FOR ALL!

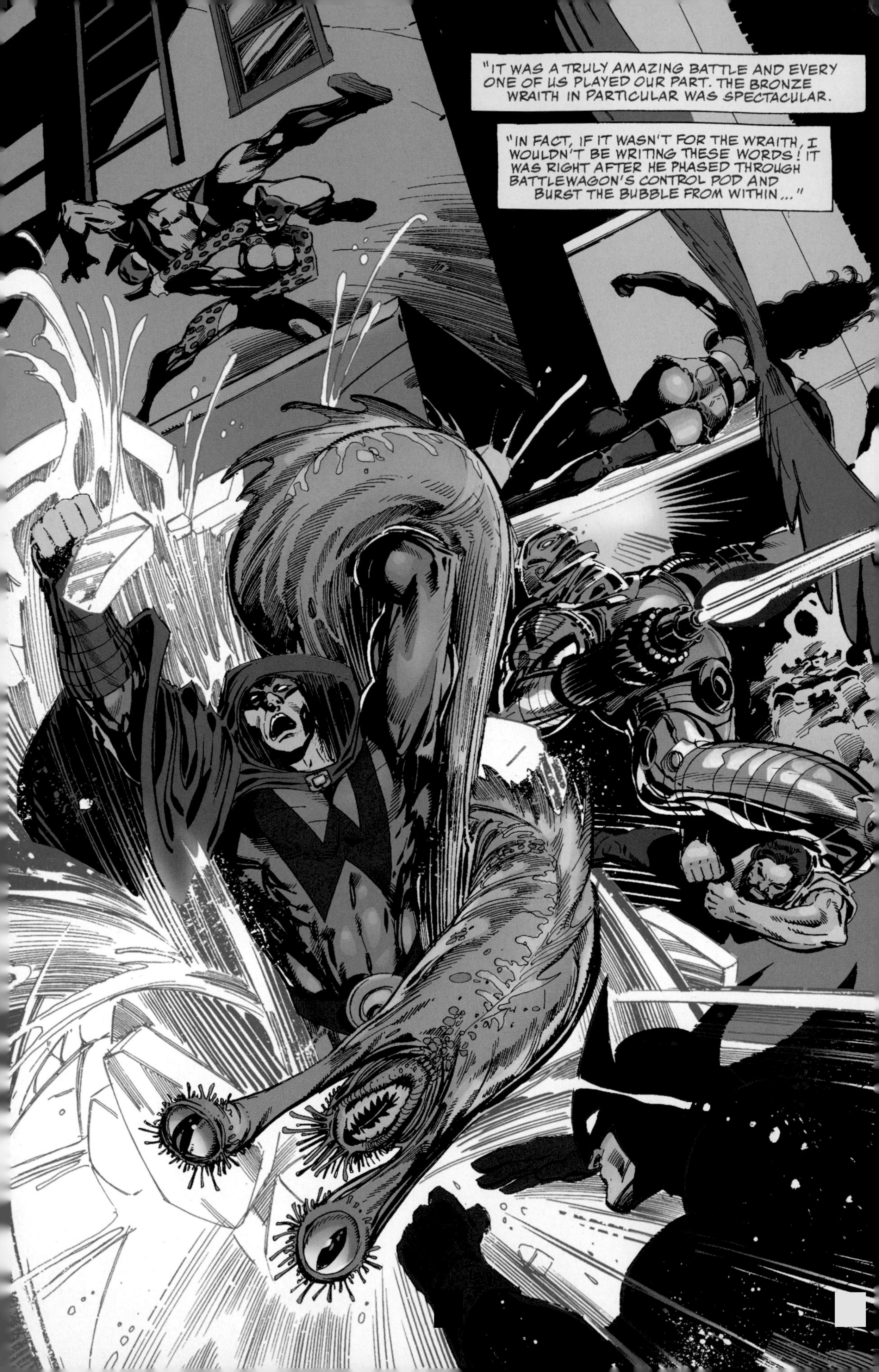
"IT WAS A TRULY AMAZING BATTLE AND EVERY ONE OF US PLAYED OUR PART. THE BRONZE WRAITH IN PARTICULAR WAS SPECTACULAR.
"IN FACT, IF IT WASN'T FOR THE WRAITH, I WOULDN'T BE WRITING THESE WORDS! IT WAS RIGHT AFTER HE PHASED THROUGH BATTLEWAGON'S CONTROL POD AND BURST THE BUBBLE FROM WITHIN..."

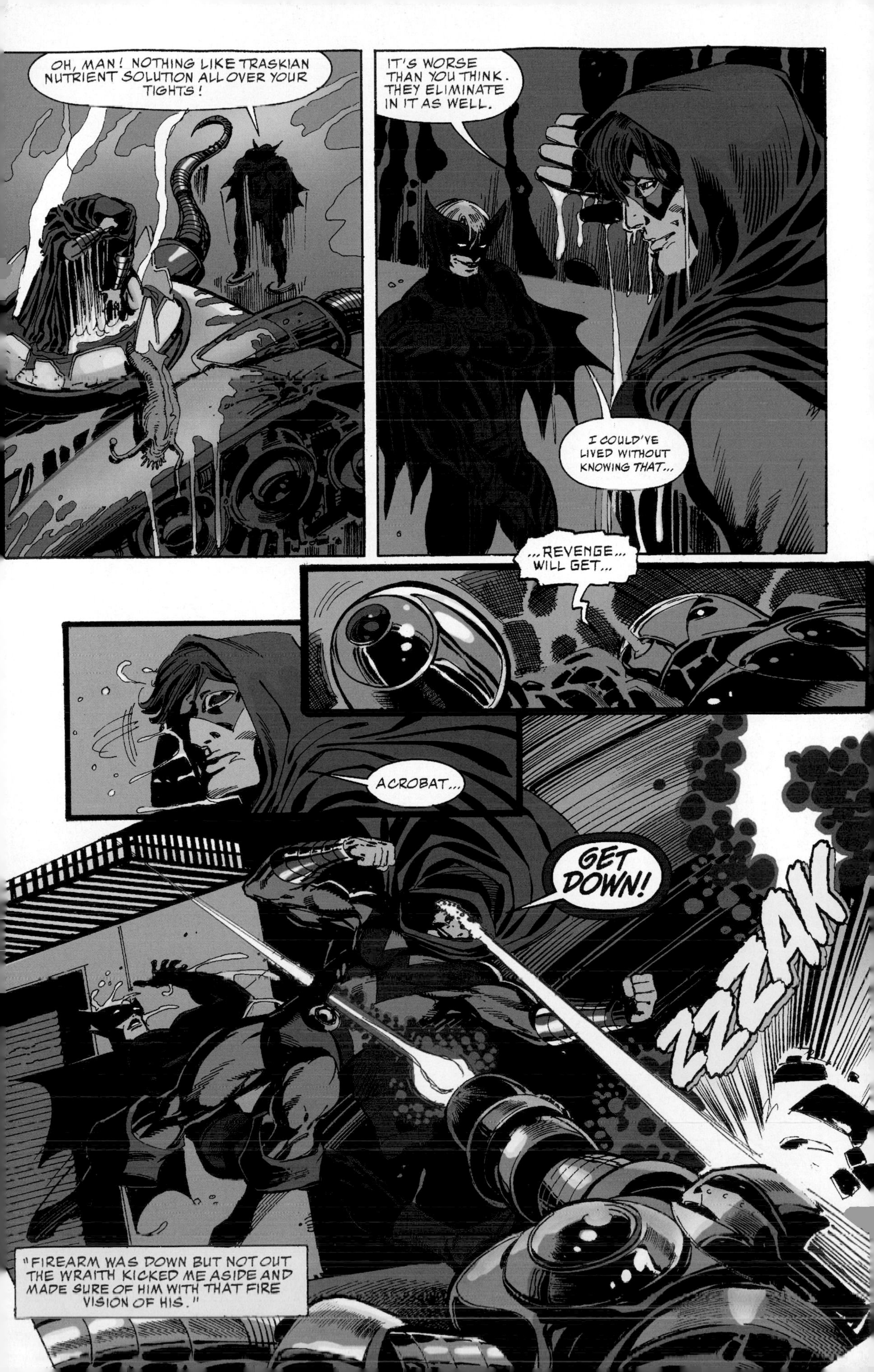

OH, MAN! NOTHING LIKE TRASKIAN NUTRIENT SOLUTION ALL OVER YOUR TIGHTS!
IT'S WORSE THAN YOU THINK. THEY ELIMINATE IN IT AS WELL.
I COULD'VE LIVED WITHOUT KNOWING THAT...
...REVENGE... WILL GET...
ACROBAT...
GET DOWN!
ZZZZAK
"FIREARM WAS DOWN BUT NOT OUT THE WRAITH KICKED ME ASIDE AND MADE SURE OF HIM WITH THAT FIRE VISION OF HIS."

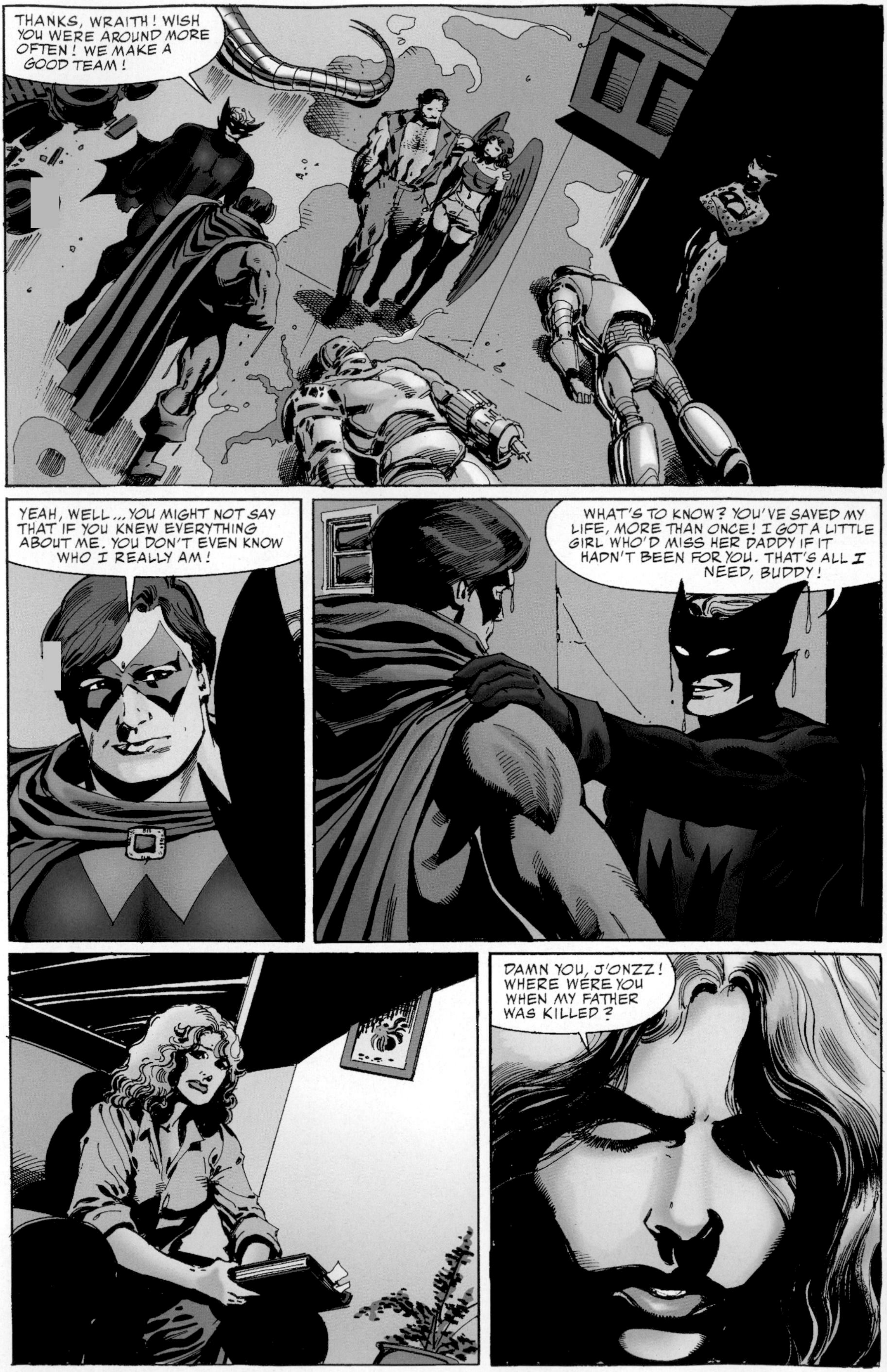
THANKS, WRAITH! WISH YOU WERE AROUND MORE OFTEN! WE MAKE A GOOD TEAM!
YEAH, WELL... YOU MIGHT NOT SAY THAT IF YOU KNEW EVERYTHING ABOUT ME. YOU DON'T EVEN KNOW WHO I REALLY AM!
WHAT'S TO KNOW? YOU'VE SAVED MY LIFE, MORE THAN ONCE! I GOT A LITTLE GIRL WHO'D MISS HER DADDY IF IT HADN'T BEEN FOR YOU. THAT'S ALL I NEED, BUDDY!
DAMN YOU, J'ONZZ! WHERE WERE YOU WHEN MY FATHER WAS KILLED?

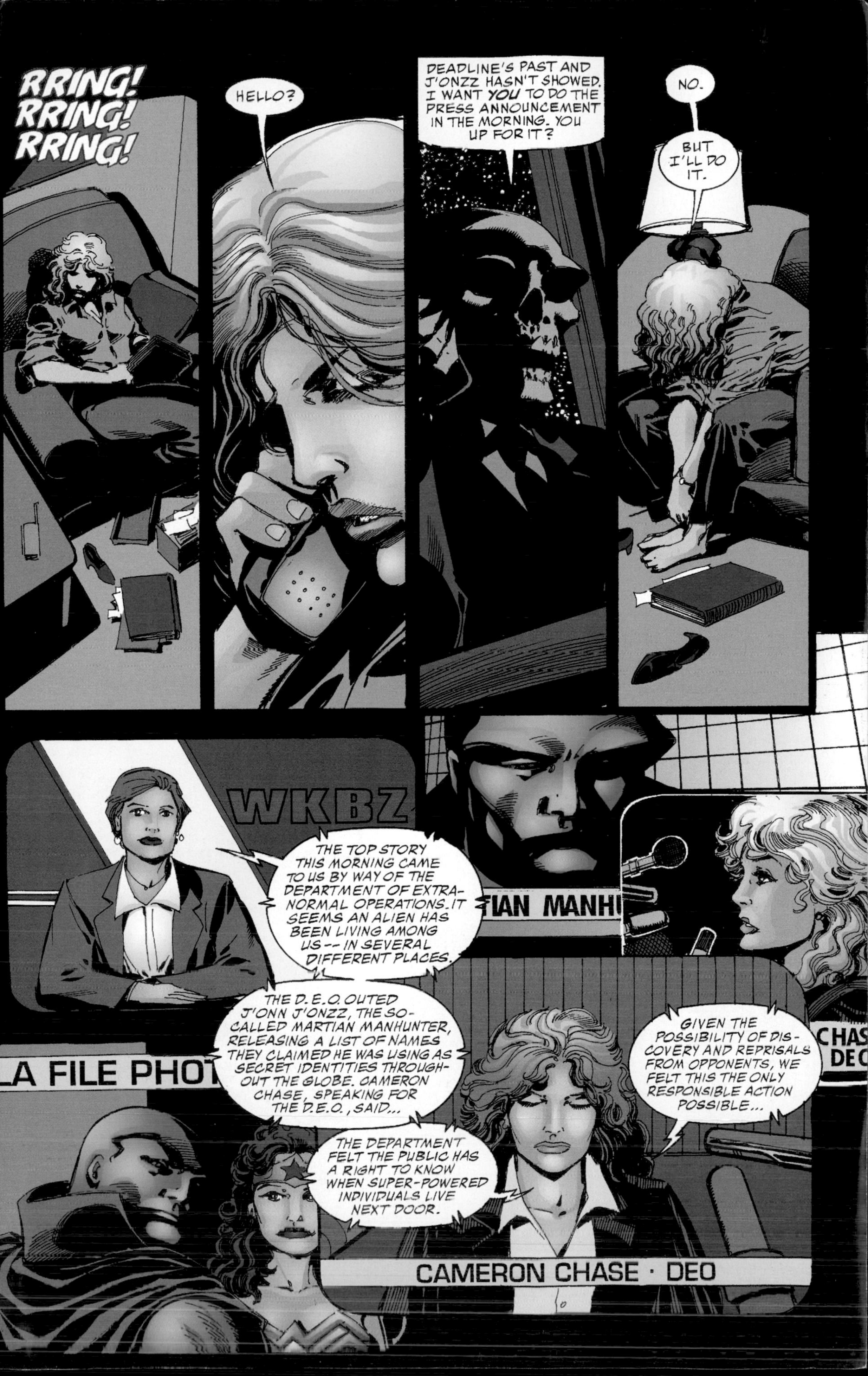
RRING! RRING! RRING!
HELLO?
DEADLINE'S PAST AND J'ONZZ HASN'T SHOWED. I WANT YOU TO DO THE PRESS ANNOUNCEMENT IN THE MORNING. YOU UP FOR IT?
NO.
BUT I'LL DO IT.
WKBZ
THE TOP STORY THIS MORNING CAME TO US BY WAY OF THE DEPARTMENT OF EXTRA-NORMAL OPERATIONS. IT SEEMS AN ALIEN HAS BEEN LIVING AMONG US -- IN SEVERAL DIFFERENT PLACES.
TIAN MANHU
THE D.E.O. OUTED J'ONN J'ONZZ, THE SO-CALLED MARTIAN MANHUNTER, RELEASING A LIST OF NAMES THEY CLAIMED HE WAS USING AS SECRET IDENTITIES THROUGHOUT THE GLOBE. CAMERON CHASE, SPEAKING FOR THE D.E.O., SAID...
LA FILE PHOT
GIVEN THE POSSIBILITY OF DISCOVERY AND REPRISALS FROM OPPONENTS, WE FELT THIS THE ONLY RESPONSIBLE ACTION POSSIBLE...
CHAS DEO
THE DEPARTMENT FELT THE PUBLIC HAS A RIGHT TO KNOW WHEN SUPER-POWERED INDIVIDUALS LIVE NEXT DOOR.
CAMERON CHASE · DEO

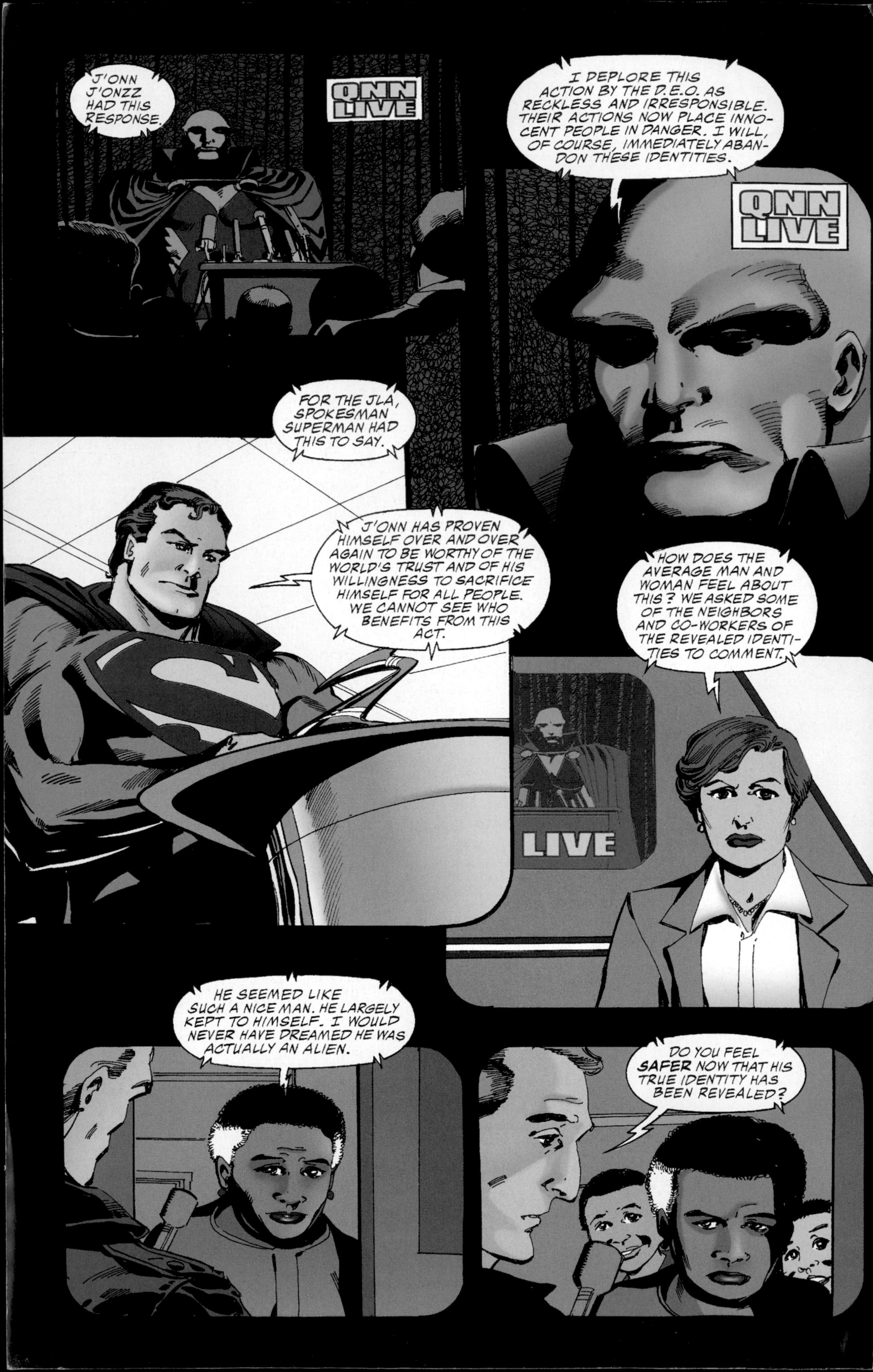
J'ONN J'ONZZ HAD THIS RESPONSE.
QNN LIVE
I DEPLORE THIS ACTION BY THE D.E.O. AS RECKLESS AND IRRESPONSIBLE. THEIR ACTIONS NOW PLACE INNOCENT PEOPLE IN DANGER. I WILL, OF COURSE, IMMEDIATELY ABANDON THESE IDENTITIES.
QNN LIVE
FOR THE JLA, SPOKESMAN SUPERMAN HAD THIS TO SAY.
J'ONN HAS PROVEN HIMSELF OVER AND OVER AGAIN TO BE WORTHY OF THE WORLD'S TRUST AND OF HIS WILLINGNESS TO SACRIFICE HIMSELF FOR ALL PEOPLE. WE CANNOT SEE WHO BENEFITS FROM THIS ACT.
HOW DOES THE AVERAGE MAN AND WOMAN FEEL ABOUT THIS? WE ASKED SOME OF THE NEIGHBORS AND CO-WORKERS OF THE REVEALED IDENTITIES TO COMMENT.
LIVE
HE SEEMED LIKE SUCH A NICE MAN. HE LARGELY KEPT TO HIMSELF. I WOULD NEVER HAVE DREAMED HE WAS ACTUALLY AN ALIEN.
DO YOU FEEL SAFER NOW THAT HIS TRUE IDENTITY HAS BEEN REVEALED?

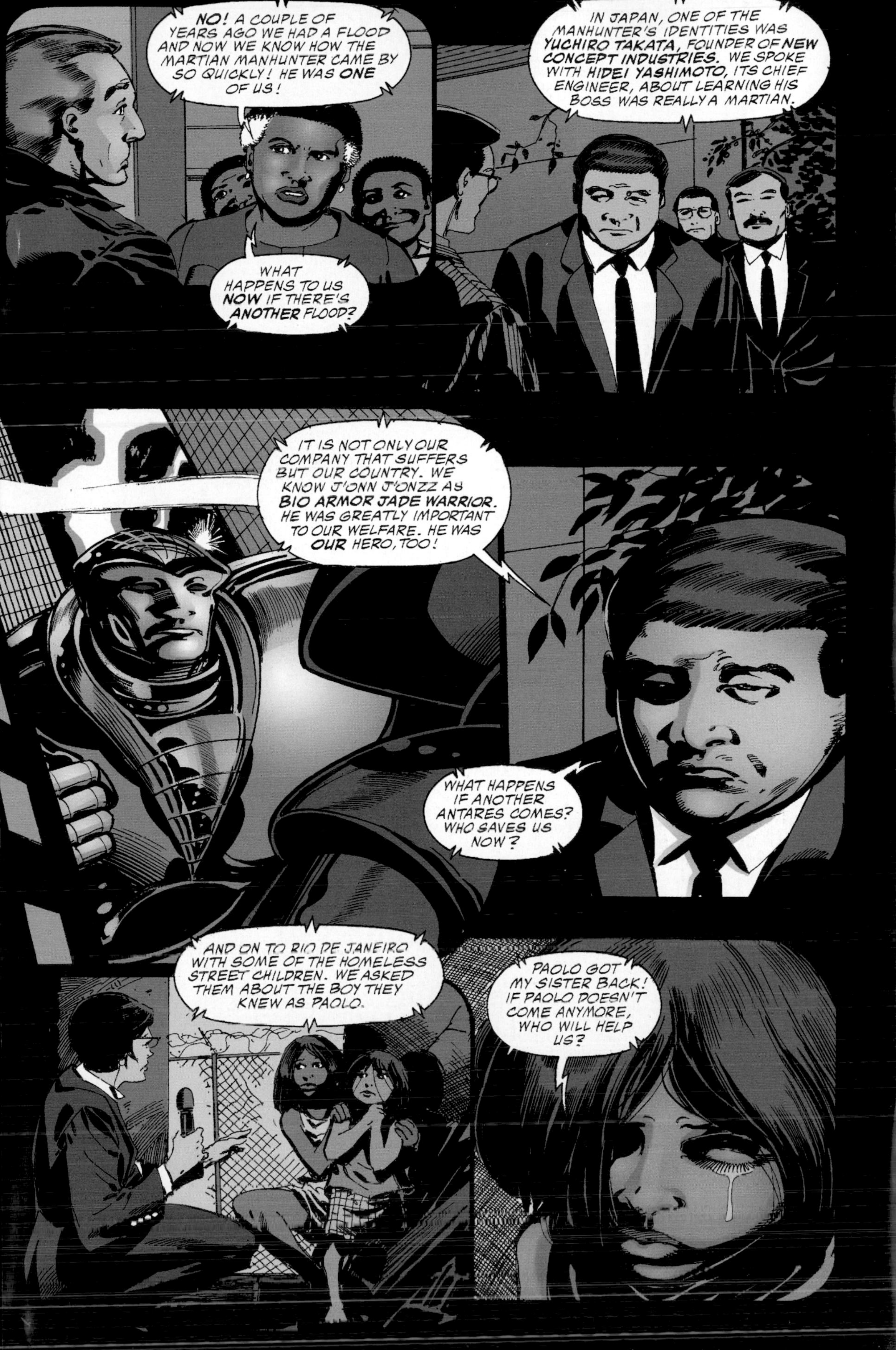
NO! A COUPLE OF YEARS AGO WE HAD A FLOOD AND NOW WE KNOW HOW THE MARTIAN MANHUNTER CAME BY SO QUICKLY! HE WAS ONE OF US!
WHAT HAPPENS TO US NOW IF THERE'S ANOTHER FLOOD?
IN JAPAN, ONE OF THE MANHUNTER'S IDENTITIES WAS YUCHIRO TAKATA, FOUNDER OF NEW CONCEPT INDUSTRIES. WE SPOKE WITH HIDEI YASHIMOTO, ITS CHIEF ENGINEER, ABOUT LEARNING HIS BOSS WAS REALLY A MARTIAN.
IT IS NOT ONLY OUR COMPANY THAT SUFFERS BUT OUR COUNTRY. WE KNOW J'ONN J'ONZZ AS BIO ARMOR JADE WARRIOR. HE WAS GREATLY IMPORTANT TO OUR WELFARE. HE WAS OUR HERO, TOO!
WHAT HAPPENS IF ANOTHER ANTARES COMES? WHO SAVES US NOW?
AND ON TO RIO DE JANEIRO WITH SOME OF THE HOMELESS STREET CHILDREN. WE ASKED THEM ABOUT THE BOY THEY KNEW AS PAOLO.
PAOLO GOT MY SISTER BACK! IF PAOLO DOESN'T COME ANYMORE, WHO WILL HELP US?

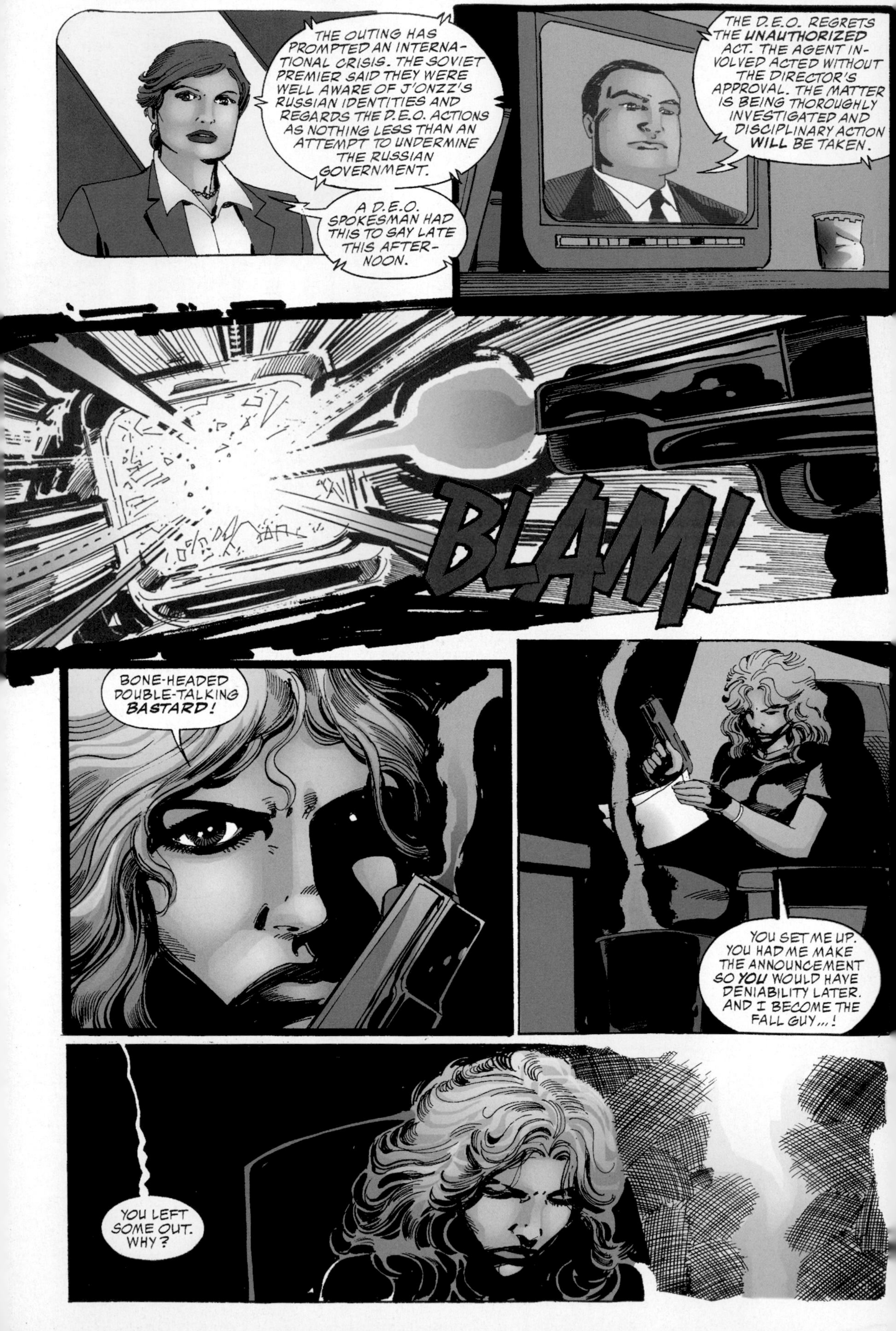
THE OUTING HAS PROMPTED AN INTERNATIONAL CRISIS. THE SOVIET PREMIER SAID THEY WERE WELL AWARE OF J'ONZZ'S RUSSIAN IDENTITIES AND REGARDS THE D.E.O. ACTIONS AS NOTHING LESS THAN AN ATTEMPT TO UNDERMINE THE RUSSIAN GOVERNMENT.
A D.E.O. SPOKESMAN HAD THIS TO SAY LATE THIS AFTERNOON.
THE D.E.O. REGRETS THE UNAUTHORIZED ACT. THE AGENT INVOLVED ACTED WITHOUT THE DIRECTOR'S APPROVAL. THE MATTER IS BEING THOROUGHLY INVESTIGATED AND DISCIPLINARY ACTION WILL BE TAKEN.
BLAM!
BONE-HEADED DOUBLE-TALKING BASTARD!
YOU SET ME UP. YOU HAD ME MAKE THE ANNOUNCEMENT SO YOU WOULD HAVE DENIABILITY LATER. AND I BECOME THE FALL GUY...!
YOU LEFT SOME OUT. WHY?

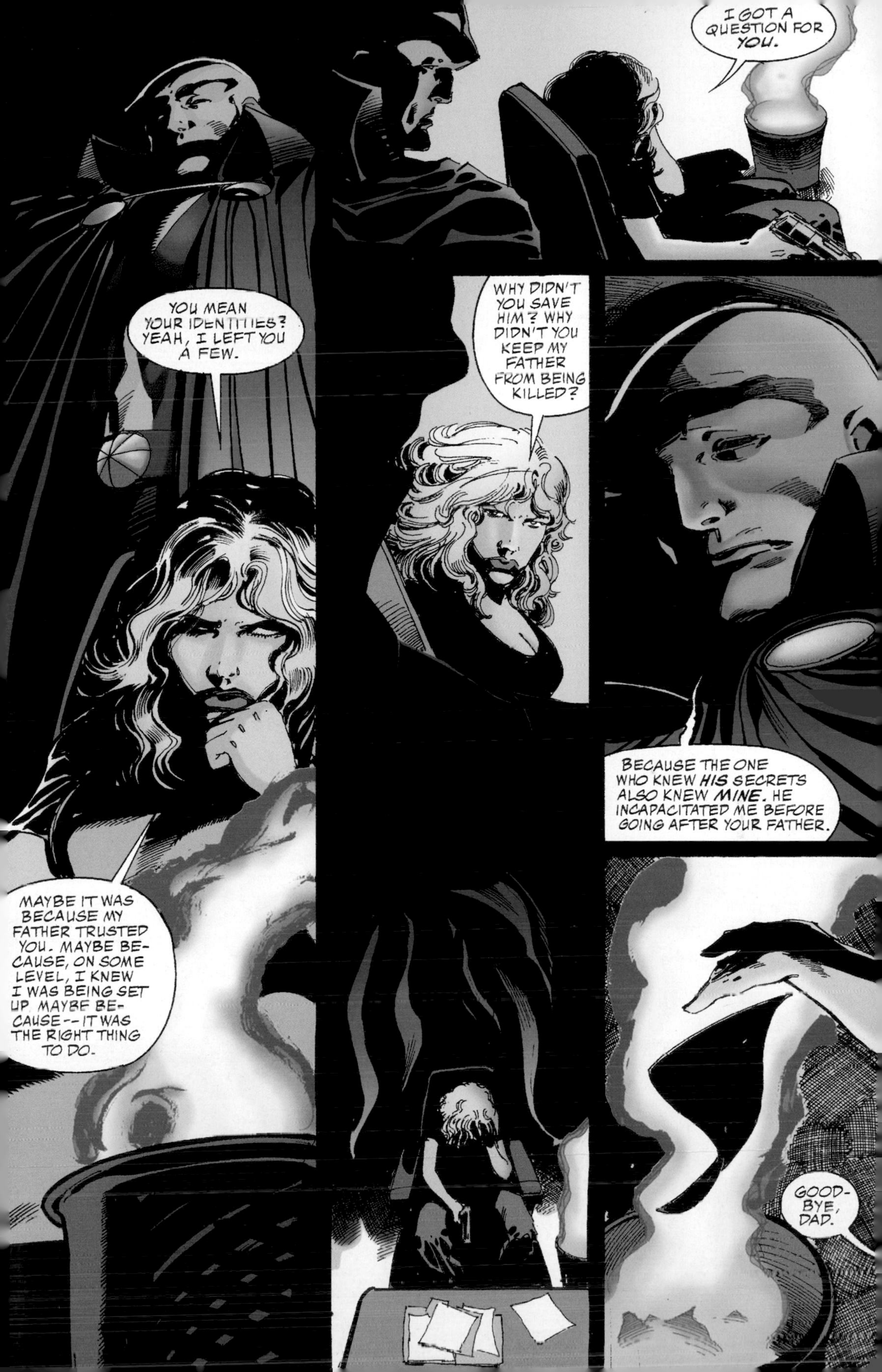
I GOT A QUESTION FOR YOU.
YOU MEAN YOUR IDENTITIES? YEAH, I LEFT YOU A FEW.
WHY DIDN'T YOU SAVE HIM? WHY DIDN'T YOU KEEP MY FATHER FROM BEING KILLED?
BECAUSE THE ONE WHO KNEW HIS SECRETS ALSO KNEW MINE. HE INCAPACITATED ME BEFORE GOING AFTER YOUR FATHER.
MAYBE IT WAS BECAUSE MY FATHER TRUSTED YOU. MAYBE BE- CAUSE, ON SOME LEVEL, I KNEW I WAS BEING SET UP. MAYBE BE- CAUSE-- IT WAS THE RIGHT THING TO DO.
GOOD- BYE, DAD.

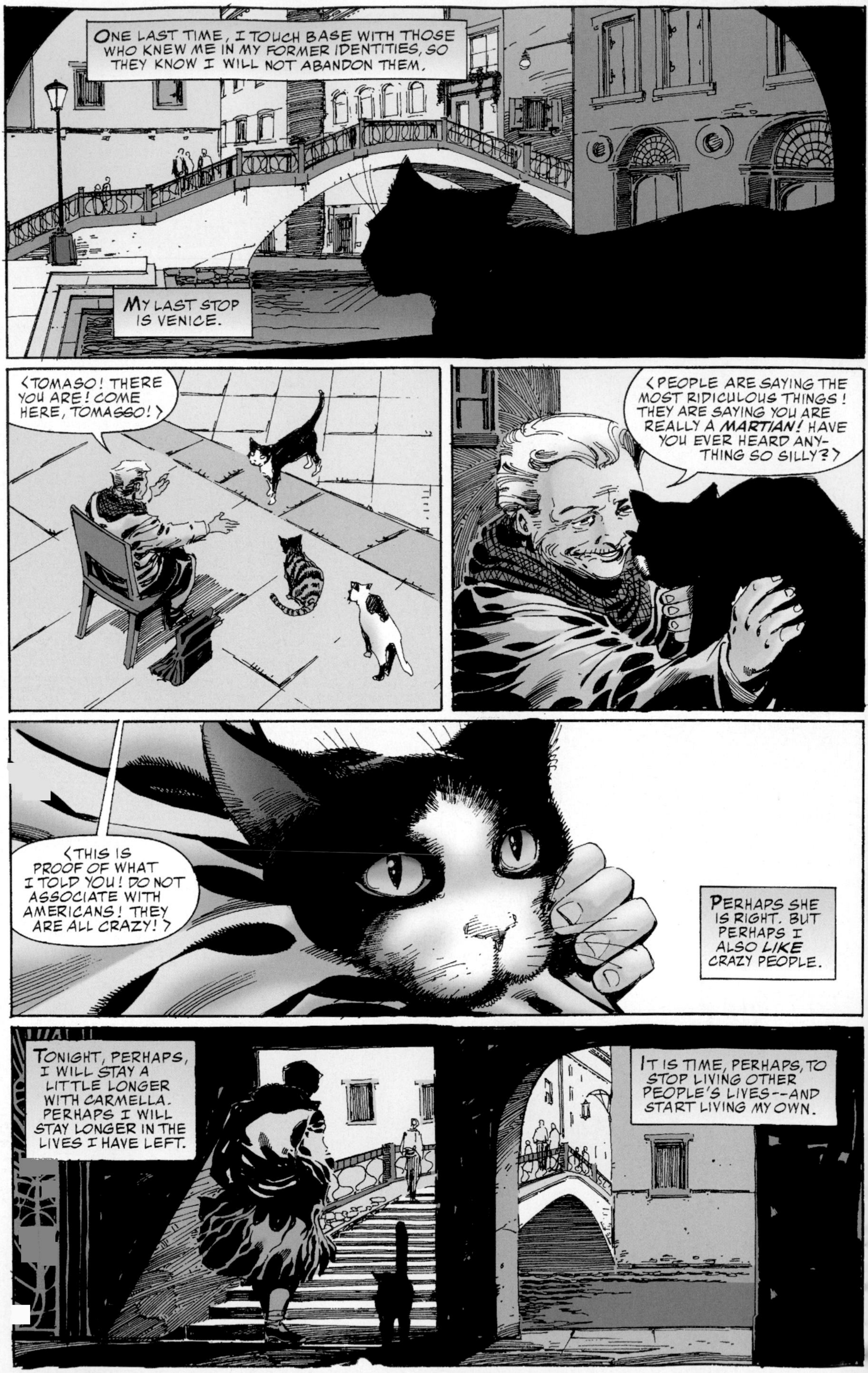
ONE LAST TIME, I TOUCH BASE WITH THOSE WHO KNEW ME IN MY FORMER IDENTITIES, SO THEY KNOW I WILL NOT ABANDON THEM.
MY LAST STOP IS VENICE.
<TOMASO! THERE YOU ARE! COME HERE, TOMASSO!>
<PEOPLE ARE SAYING THE MOST RIDICULOUS THINGS! THEY ARE SAYING YOU ARE REALLY A MARTIAN! HAVE YOU EVER HEARD ANYTHING SO SILLY?>
<THIS IS PROOF OF WHAT I TOLD YOU! DO NOT ASSOCIATE WITH AMERICANS! THEY ARE ALL CRAZY!>
PERHAPS SHE IS RIGHT. BUT PERHAPS I ALSO LIKE CRAZY PEOPLE.
TONIGHT, PERHAPS, I WILL STAY A LITTLE LONGER WITH CARMELLA. PERHAPS I WILL STAY LONGER IN THE LIVES I HAVE LEFT.
IT IS TIME, PERHAPS, TO STOP LIVING OTHER PEOPLE'S LIVES--AND START LIVING MY OWN.

"[A] comic legend." —ROLLING STONE

"[Grant Morrison is] comics' high shaman."
—WASHINGTON POST

"[Grant Morrison] is probably my favorite
writer. That guy has more ideas in his pinky
than most people do in a lifetime."
—Gerard Way from MY CHEMICAL ROMANCE

FROM THE WRITER OF ALL-STAR SUPERMAN AND BATMAN & ROBIN
GRANT MORRISON
with HOWARD PORTER

JLA VOL. 2

with HOWARD PORTER

JLA VOL. 3

with HOWARD PORTER

JLA VOL. 4

with HOWARD PORTER,
MARK WAID, and MARK
PAJARILLO

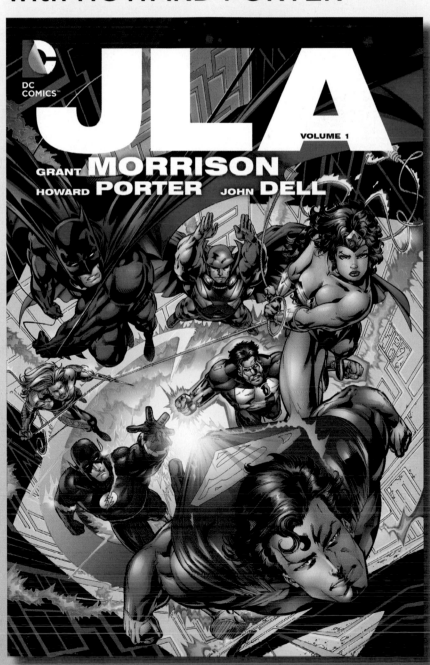

DC COMICS™

GRANT MORRISON
with FRANK QUITELY

FINAL CRISIS

with J.G. JONES, CARLOS PACHECO & DOUG MAHNKE

BATMAN: ARKHAM ASYLUM

with DAVE McKEAN

SEVEN SOLDIERS OF VICTORY VOLS. 1 & 2

with J.H. WILLIAMS III & VARIOUS ARTISTS

ALL ★ STAR SUPERMAN

GRANT MORRISON
FRANK QUITELY

JAMIE GRANT

DC COMICS™

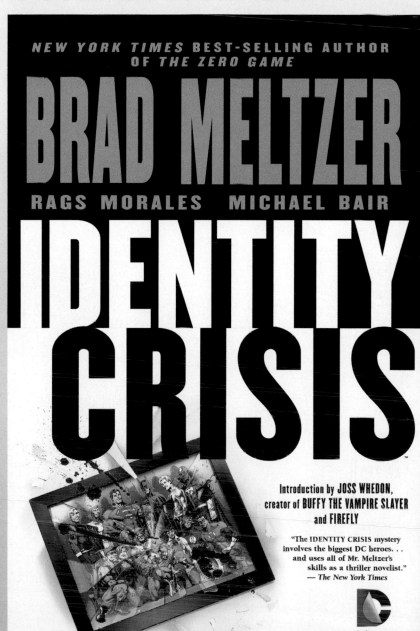

DC COMICS™

FROM THE *NEW YORK TIMES* #1 BEST-SELLING WRITER OF *BATMAN* & *ALL-STAR SUPERMAN*

GRANT MORRISON

with J.G. JONES, CARLOS PACHECO and DOUG MAHNKE

FINAL CRISIS: LEGION OF 3 WORLDS

FINAL CRISIS: ROGUES' REVENGE

FINAL CRISIS: REVELATIONS